The Prediction of Achievement and Creativity

THE PREDICTION
OF ACHIEVEMENT
AND CREATIVITY

RAYMOND B. CATTELL

Research Professor in Psychology, University of Illinois

and

H. J. BUTCHER

Professor of Higher Education, University of Manchester

The Bobbs-Merrill Company, Inc.
PUBLISHERS   *Indianapolis / New York*

PREFACE

The level of achievement and creativity reached by any human being represents more than his degree of self-expression. It is a measure of his potential in helping others. That the will to serve means to others only as much as the individual's effectiveness is obvious in a factory engineer, a doctor, a plumber, a pilot, an artist, or a gardener. It requires a sharper perception and a more liberal interpretation of achievement and capacity to realize that the same is true of, say, the mother in the home and blind Milton when he "stands and waits"—or even the income tax collector! In the criminal, achievement may be the measure of his capacity to damage, rather than help, society. But, for a healthy society, and for most individuals, achievement, though it may be motivated partly by competitiveness, remains a measure of the individual's capacity to serve and to give. The standard of living of a country is, in the end, not dependent on visible natural resources, or on monetary tricks of the economist, but is a function of the level of attainment and creativity prevailing among its citizens. There can, therefore, be few more important concerns than the theme we study here, namely, the understanding of the roots of achievement and creativity, defined in a comprehensive sense.

If we are to do better in raising the level of achievement of our citizens than previous ages have done, it is not enough merely to increase the expenditures and the years spent on education. We need rather to gain a more basic understanding of the whole process of attaining skills and creativity. Regardless of whether advances in learning theory lead us to teaching machines or other devices, an interaction will always remain between the teaching methods and the personality and motivation of the individual. The aim of this book is to advance our systematic understanding of the manner in which differences in personality, motivation, and ability lead to differences in achievement and creativity.

To this point, we may have seemed to imply a concentration on the school; yet we do not intend to restrict our discussion to examination-passing, but to keep in sight the wider meaning of attainment already stated—in occupations, in social life, in inner development, and in artistic and scientific creation, as well as in school attainment. Let us realistically admit, however, that despite this intention, and because by far the greater part of research has

v

been done by dedicated educational psychologists, the magnifying glass will focus most on achievement in school and university. In other areas, bare patches are inevitable: there, research knowledge is terribly thin, and our best service can be done by indicating research objectives, methods, and principles of analysis.

Because of this concentration on attainment through formal learning, the main reader for whom this book is shaped is the educational psychologist and administrator, the teacher, and the student in education. Even if it could deal adequately with all varieties of attainment, it would still be the educator —in the wider sense—who would be its reader, for the conversion of potential into actual attainment is his professional task. But this definition will include industrial and military educators, the artist among his apprentices, the parent with his children, and those concerned with moral and social leadership. We have tried not to forget that we are dealing with principles and findings that need to be expressed for this wider audience.

Some psychologists claim that learning theory and personality theory have already advanced more in educational practice in the last fifty years than had occurred in the preceding two or three millennia. Others think the fundamentals are unchanged. As far as new grasp of causes of individual differences in achievement is concerned, the chief wave of insight in those fifty years has come from applications of intelligence and other ability tests. This wave reached its boundaries perhaps a decade ago, and alert practitioners have been looking since then for basic science to send out new impulses to carry us further. Our belief is that the new impetus is coming from certain fundamental advances in the study of personality and motivation.

In themselves, these are as fascinating for the psychologist as were the pioneer steps of Spearman, Binet, Thurstone, and Terman in abilities, and our references will lead the reader who has time to the sources. Applications of the study of personality and motivation, however, promise to be at least as important, in regard to insight and effective control in respect to differences in attainment, as all that came from the gains in the first half of this century from the scientific analysis of abilities. To the second half of the century belongs the cultivation of the educational applications of the present rapid advancement of knowledge of personality and motivation measurement.

No analyst of achievement must ever forget that there are two sides to the coin: that represented by learning theory and that by personality theory (or individual-difference study). The former has to do with the teaching methods that can be applied to everyone, and that in the next fifty years may well raise everyone's standards of performance. The latter has to do with the reaction of individuals, according to their different capacities and interests, to the learning practices presented. Doubtless, in time, someone will present an adequate treatise on both—and their interactions—but here we have taken the scientific—albeit piecemeal—approach of considering the teaching practices to be held constant while we examine the individual differences that result from differences of personality, motivation, and ability. We have asked "How do we predict and understand achievement granted the educational and cultural milieu in which we now stand?"

As the main authors for such a work, it seemed best to unite a research specialist in the field of personality and motivation analysis—Professor Raymond B. Cattell of the University of Illinois—and an active member of the younger, quantitatively oriented educational psychologists—Professor H. J. Butcher of the University of Manchester. Incidentally, this gives us also the benefit of a perspective across two national cultures and educational systems, to eliminate any crudities of localism. The book has also had the benefit, in Chapter 13, of Dr. Herbert W. Eber, who has extensive experience in looking clinically at failures in occupations, and remedying them through rehabilitation services, and Drs. William W. Ronan and Erich Prien, specialists in evaluating occupational achievement.

This team of writers is keenly aware that it should be larger, to aim at something more encyclopedic than the present brief introductory text, and they are even more sharply aware of the gaps in the material needed for the systematic view attempted. Because of what seems, to the eager researcher, a series of quite unnecessary lags by practitioners in bringing advances in basic personality and motivation theory to bear, by measurement, in practical prediction problems, much is tantalizingly missing that could complete the theoretical circle. (For example, until the recent work by Miller and others, at the University of London, and Graffam in Pennsylvania, no university had applied primary personality factor measures systematically over years of observation, in relation to examination and research achievement—and even these results are too recent to have been published.)

Any excursion systematically covering the real issues and possibilities in this field consequently has to skate over very thin ice in several places; in other areas, it finds more repeated research than is really necessary. Consequently, on some matters, we can offer the practitioner formulas reliable to as many decimal places as the user generally applies with π, whereas on others, the counselor must be statistically alert to the fact that he is being guided by an inspired guess from perhaps two brief samples. What we are counting on is that the scanty pioneer investigations we have described, and the lessons learned from them, will stimulate substantial workers, with greater resources in educational research, to extend and finish the job thoroughly.

It should be perfectly obvious to the reader that our purpose has not been the all-too-familiar one of making a catalogue of personality and motivation tests, attempting merely to describe to a teacher all the published tests he may use. Such blind catalogues already abound. We are concerned fundamentally with pure research and theory on personality, motivation, and ability structure, based on experimental and correlational methods. The tests that emerge in response to the need to measure such structures are a secondary consideration. It happens that they are also few and largely the outcome of efforts in a small number of laboratories. Take away the scientifically, carefully constructed instruments of a dozen investigators—of whom Cattell, Comrey, Eber, Eysenck, Guilford, Horn, Hundleby, Meredith, Nesselroade, Porter, Schaie, Thurstone, Warburton, and Zimmerman may be taken as representative—and one is left in the catalogues with nothing but a crowded shop window of *ad hoc* scales. These are unrelated to any systematic and extensive experimental work on structure and development. We have spared the reader this window display and confined ourselves to measures based strictly on factor-analytic research on structure, because we are convinced—despite the publishers' exuberance—that the future lies with structured measurement. This is not narrowness: it is scientific rigor, and an appreciation of the fact that a broad expanse of effective application—here, a technology of achievement prediction and guidance—often needs to be approached through a "straight and narrow" channel.

How far this book can be effective (outside its use by the mature educational psychologist and teacher) as a textbook for the student in this area of psychology and education remains to be seen. If it presents any difficulties in this respect, they will not arise through any lack of dovetailing into the general scientific background of psychology. They may arise, on the other hand, from its being less pragmatic and "cookbook-ish" than many texts from which many counselors have hitherto been offered a rather stale nourishment. Unquestionably, for the typical student in education, for whom psychology can be only one of many necessary disciplines, this book will need a teacher, able to handle and compensate for those defects of the text and the field that we feel we cannot at present overcome.

Our greatest hope, however, is that its pages will open up to a sufficient number of educational psychologists a view of areas in which research is most urgently needed. Before us may lie social developments—truly coordinated test installations, and public understanding of values and technical goals. Professional developments may be near that will make possible a far more comprehensive, potent, and sympathetic handling of the achievement problems of the individual. These are now within our grasp if educational psychologists will work out the implications, thoroughly and in detail, of recent substantial advances in personality and motivation theory for the fostering of achievement and creativity.

RAYMOND B. CATTELL

Exeter, 1966

CONTENTS

Chapter **1**   **The Community's Task in the Fulfillment of the Individual**

1. THE GREAT AND INCREASING RESPONSIBILITY OF EDUCATORS   1
2. AIMS AND ASSUMPTIONS IN EDUCATIONAL GUIDANCE AND
   SELECTION   2
3. THE POTENTIALITIES OF APPLIED PSYCHOLOGY   6
4. RECENT AND RELEVANT TRENDS IN PSYCHOLOGY   8
5. PLAN OF THE BOOK   10
SUMMARY   11

Chapter **2**   **The Nature of Abilities**

1. INTRODUCTION   13
2. TECHNIQUES FOR THE ANALYSIS OF ABILITIES   14
3. PREVIOUS THEORIES OF THE STRUCTURE OF ABILITIES   15
4. HEREDITARY AND CULTURAL DETERMINANTS OF ABILITY   17
5. THE THEORY OF FLUID AND CRYSTALLIZED GENERAL ABILITY   18
6. THE RELATION OF CRYSTALLIZED INTELLIGENCE TO GENERAL
   LEVEL OF ATTAINMENT   21
7. THE DEVELOPMENT OF PERCEPTUAL AND CULTURE FAIR
   INTELLIGENCE TESTS   22
8. SOME FURTHER CHARACTERISTICS OF CULTURE FAIR TESTS   25
9. INDICATED REFORMS IN THE USE OF INTELLIGENCE TESTS
   IN SCHOOLS   27
SUMMARY   30

Chapter **3**   **The Relation of Abilities to Scholastic Achievement**

1. INTRODUCTION   31
2. PREDICTION FROM TWO KINDS OF ABILITY FACTOR   32
3. PREDICTION FROM PRIMARY ABILITY FACTORS   33
4. OTHER ABILITY FACTORS   39

5. THE PREDICTION OF ACHIEVEMENT FROM GENERAL INTELLIGENCE   41
6. THE RELATION OF ABILITIES TO ACHIEVEMENT AT UNIVERSITY
   LEVEL   43
SUMMARY   51

Chapter 4   **Measuring the Main Dimensions of Personality**

1. THREE APPROACHES TO THE STUDY OF HUMAN PERSONALITY   53
2. SOME MEANS OF ISOLATING THE PRINCIPAL PERSONALITY FACTORS   55
3. A TYPICAL PERSONALITY FACTOR   58
4. PERSONALITY FACTORS IN CHILDREN   61
5. OBJECTIVE TESTS OF PERSONALITY   63
6. THE PRACTICAL VALUE OF FACTORED PERSONALITY TESTS   65
7. THE USEFULNESS OF PERSONALITY MEASURES TO THE TEACHER   67
8. THE RELATION OF PERSONALITY TRAITS TO MOTIVATION   69
SUMMARY   69

Chapter 5   **Concepts and Measures of Motivation and Interest**

1. COMPLETING THE PERSONALITY PICTURE WITH DYNAMIC AND
   UNIQUE TRAITS   71
2. WHAT COMMON DYNAMIC STRUCTURES EXIST?   73
3. THE STRUCTURING OF ATTITUDES INTO COMMON AND
   UNIQUE TRAITS   74
4. THE SUBSIDIATION OF ATTITUDES AND THE DYNAMIC LATTICE   76
5. THE PRINCIPAL ERGS AND THE ATTITUDES THAT DEFINE THEM   78
6. THE NATURE OF SENTIMENTS, INCLUDING THE SELF-SENTIMENT   81
7. OBJECTIVE ATTITUDE MEASUREMENT AND MOTIVATIONAL
   COMPONENTS   84
8. THE DYNAMIC CALCULUS   86
SUMMARY   87

Chapter 6   **Principles for Evaluating Validity and Consistency
   in Psychological Tests**

1. MODERN REVISIONS OF PSYCHOMETRIC CONCEPTS   89
2. THE CONCEPTS OF VALIDITY   92
3. THE CONCEPT AND MEASUREMENT OF CONSISTENCY   98
4. TEST HOMOGENEITY AND FACTOR HOMOGENEITY   103
5. THE VARIETIES OF RELIABILITY COEFFICIENTS AND INDICES   108

6. TRANSFERABILITY   115
SUMMARY   117

Chapter **7**   **Scaling, Standardization, and Other Properties
Required in Psychological Tests**

1. INDICES OF UNIVERSALITY, DURABILITY, EFFICIENCY, AND UTILITY   119
2. THE RELATION BETWEEN VALIDITY AND RELIABILITY   123
3. THE RELATION OF HOMOGENEITY TO VALIDITY   125
4. CONDITIONS AND PRINCIPLES OF EQUAL-INTERVAL AND
   ABSOLUTE SCALING   129
5. PRINCIPLES OF TEST STANDARDIZATION: THE REFERENCE GROUP   134
6. TEST STANDARDIZATION. MODIFICATIONS FOR AGE, SEX,
   IPSATIZATION OF SCORES, AND FOR DIFFERENT FORMS OF A TEST   138
7. THE NUMERICAL EXPRESSION OF A STANDARDIZED SCORE   141
SUMMARY   143

Chapter **8**   **The Planning and Design of a Research
into the Prediction of School Achievement**

1. SOME GENERAL REQUIREMENTS OF RESEARCH   145
2. THE PROBLEM OF SAMPLING   146
3. REPLICATION OF THE EXPERIMENT   148
4. STANDARDIZATION OF TESTING CONDITIONS   149
5. ADEQUACY OF THE ANALYSIS OF RESULTS   150
6. PLANNING A PARTICULAR RESEARCH INTO THE PREDICTION
   OF ACHIEVEMENT   152
7. DESCRIPTION OF THE TESTS AND OTHER PSYCHOLOGICAL
   MEASURES USED   154
SUMMARY   159

Chapter **9**   **The Prediction of School Achievement from
Measures of Ability and the Structure of Abilities in
High School Students**

1. PRINCIPLES OF MULTIPLE PREDICTION   161
2. THE CONSISTENCY OF THE MEASURES OF ABILITY   162
3. PREDICTION OF THE MAIN CRITERIA   163
4. THE PREDICTION OF THE STANFORD SUBTESTS   170
5. "FORWARD" AND "BACKWARD" PREDICTION   173
6. THE FACTORIAL STRUCTURE OF ABILITIES   174
SUMMARY   178

Chapter **10   The Prediction of Achievement from Personality Factors**

1. PREVIOUS STUDIES OF PERSONALITY AND ACHIEVEMENT   181
2. PERSONALITY FACTORS MEASURED IN THE RESEARCH   183
3. SCORES OF THE ILLINOIS CHILDREN ON THE PERSONALITY FACTORS   184
4. THE PREDICTION OF SCHOOL ACHIEVEMENT FROM THE FOURTEEN HSPQ FACTORS   186
5. COMPARISON OF THE PREDICTIVE POWER OF ABILITY AND PERSONALITY MEASURES   191
6. PREDICTION OF ACHIEVEMENT IN THE RURAL SAMPLE   195
7. EVALUATION OF THESE RESULTS   196
SUMMARY   198

Chapter **11   The Observed Structure of Children's Interests**

1. SUMMARY OF PREVIOUS FINDINGS   201
2. THE DEVELOPMENT OF THE IPAT MOTIVATION BATTERIES   204
3. PREVIOUS KNOWLEDGE OF ERG AND SENTIMENT FACTORS   208
4. THE STRUCTURE OF CHILDREN'S ATTITUDES AS FOUND IN THE ILLINOIS SURVEYS   209
5. THE PREDICTION OF ACHIEVEMENT FROM INTERESTS AND ATTITUDES   214
SUMMARY   215

Chapter **12   The Associations of Environmental Factors and Achievement**

1. THE EFFECT OF CULTURAL DIFFERENCES ON THE PREDICTION OF ACHIEVEMENT   217
2. CROSS-CULTURAL RESEARCH ON MOTIVATION FOR ACHIEVEMENT   219
3. EDUCATIONAL ACHIEVEMENT IN PARTICULAR RACIAL AND REGIONAL GROUPS   225
4. THE CORRELATIONS OF ECONOMIC LEVEL AND SOCIAL CLASS   228
5. THE CORRELATIONS OF SCHOOL, NEIGHBORHOOD, FACILITIES, AND ATMOSPHERE   230
SUMMARY   234

Chapter **13** **The Prediction of Achievement in a Wider Context**

Authored jointly by Herbert W. Eber, William W. Ronan, Eric P. Prien, Raymond B. Cattell, and H. J. Butcher.

1. BEYOND THE SCHOOL: ACHIEVEMENT IN OCCUPATION, FAMILY, AND SOCIETY   237
2. TIME AND ACHIEVEMENT   241
3. CONSIDERATIONS OF CRITERION RELIABILITIES   245
4. THE DIMENSIONS OF ACHIEVEMENT   251
5. THE PREDICTIVE UTILITY OF VARIOUS TYPES OF DATA   257
SUMMARY   266

Chapter **14** **Originality and Creativity in School and Society**

1. CREATIVITY AND ITS ROLE IN SOCIETY   267
2. SOME PREVIOUS RESEARCH ON CREATIVITY   269
3. GENERAL ASSOCIATIONS OF CREATIVITY AND PSEUDOCREATIVITY   271
4. THE RELATION OF COGNITIVE ABILITIES TO CREATIVITY   273
5. THE ROOTS OF CREATIVITY IN PERSONALITY STUDIED BIOGRAPHICALLY   276
SUMMARY   279

Chapter **15** **The Prediction, Selection, and Cultivation of Creativity**

1. THE GENERAL PROBLEMS IN FOSTERING CREATIVITY   281
2. FOR WHAT WORKING CONDITIONS ARE WE SELECTING CREATIVE INDIVIDUALS?   283
3. DEFINING THE CREATIVITY CRITERION   285
4. CREATIVITY PREDICTION BY PSYCHOLOGICAL TESTS AIMED AT A "CREATIVE TYPE"   289
5. CREATIVITY PREDICTION BY REGRESSION ON A CRITERION OF EFFECTIVENESS WITHIN A RESEARCH GROUP   295
6. THE BROADER CONTEXT OF THE PREDICTIVE PROBLEM   298
7. APPLICATIONS IN EDUCATION   301
8. "TRAINING FOR CREATIVITY"   303
SUMMARY   305

Chapter **16** **The Organization of Practical Psychological Procedures for Predicting Achievement, Creativity, and Adjustment**

1. INTEGRATING TECHNICAL, SOCIAL, AND MORAL ASPECTS OF ORGANIZED PSYCHOLOGICAL SERVICES   307

2. THE CENTRALIZATION OF PSYCHOLOGICAL TESTING INFORMATION
   AND SERVICES IN THE SCHOOL SYSTEM   312
3. PERSONNEL AND PLANNING OF SCHOOL PSYCHOLOGICAL
   TESTING PROGRAMS   314
4. THE REQUIREMENTS IN AN EFFECTIVE SCHOOL TESTING PROGRAM   319
5. THE CHOICE OF TESTS TO MAXIMIZE SCIENTIFIC INFORMATION   323
6. SOME CONSIDERATIONS OF PRACTICAL EFFECTIVENESS WITH
   DERIVED SCORES AND COMPUTER AIDS   329
7. PROPOSED TESTING INSTALLATION PLAN FOR SCHOOL SYSTEMS   336
8. THE PROCESSES OF DECISION IN EVALUATION AND COUNSELING   344
SUMMARY   350

Table of References   355
Appendix   373
Index of Names   376
Index   381

Chapter One

THE COMMUNITY'S TASK IN THE
FULFILLMENT OF THE INDIVIDUAL

Section 1 **The Great and Increasing Responsibility of Educators**

From the unsocialized infant, wryly but accurately described by Shake-speare as "mewling and puking in the nurse's arms," to the mature adult in our complex society, the gap in development is immense. This gap, infinitely wider than in simpler societies, is widening even more every year as the full effect of scientific and technological developments on society begins to be felt; the rate of change itself is accelerating. Yet, somehow, this gap has to be bridged by our educational processes; the very existence and survival of our society depend on the capacity of educators to respond to this continually increasing challenge.

A sound evaluation of past educational experience is certainly needed, but the real hope for the future of education lies in new developments and a new approach. The challenge can only be met by an unprecedented advance in understanding of the behavioral sciences, especially of psychology, and by a skillful and widespread application of new discoveries. In a world where the physical sciences have made such strides, we can surely no longer afford to continue the relative past neglect of the social sciences. It has become almost a truism that, in the age of the hydrogen bomb and of space travel, our current practices and ways of thinking about educational psychology in the broadest sense have lagged dangerously and that the future of human civilization may depend upon our efforts to catch up. The massive application of research to basic education and psychology recently inaugurated by the United States Department of Health, Education and Welfare, of which the present book is one of the first fruits, is perhaps an indication of society's awakening conscience concerning the necessary basic research and revaluation of methods.

A century of development in our schools and universities has admittedly brought much progress, even if it has not been all that intelligent men and women had hoped. Aims and methods have shifted, indeed, but not always in the direction or at the tempo required.

The most notable change in the American outlook on education began soon after the turn of the century, largely under the influence of John Dewey. It consisted of a healthy reaction against the narrow, pedagogic, and over-formal curriculum and teaching methods then almost universal. Dewey's disciple, William Kilpatrick, has referred to the traditional viewpoint as the Alexandrian conception of education and remarked that it tended to reduce man to intellect alone, and intellect largely to mere memory. Against this, Dewey and his followers stood for a more child-centered education: for learning by doing, for treating the school and the class as dynamic social groups, for greater flexibility in curriculum and method, for less "discipline" and greater opportunity for creation and self-expression, and for the application of modern psychological findings (particularly those in the area of child development) to everyday educational practice.

Many of these revolutionary suggestions have now become traditional and established in their turn, and children's all-around development has undoubtedly benefited. But in many schools, and even in the whole field of American education, too many educators, we would suggest, were too zealous. For many enlightened teachers and intelligent laymen, the pendulum has swung back again. They have begun to realize that the reaction against intellect and discipline has often gone too far and that the traditional view of education, *if supplemented by modern psychological knowledge,* has more to recommend it than its wilder denigrators have admitted. Lately, the "child-centered" view has been tempered, in response to demands by such groups as the Council for Basic Education that "frills" be dropped in favor of fundamentals.

In Britain the "child-centered revolution," as it has been called, has been much milder and slower than in the United States and has met with heavier opposition. There has, therefore, been less need for a counterrevolution. The net result appears to be a closer approach in attitudes to education between the two countries than has been apparent for some decades. Certainly, in the United States, we have the advantage of greater material resources and probably of a more dynamic and optimistic approach to difficulties; but the same basic problem exists in both countries and, in spite of minor cultural differences, is likely to need and to receive a basically similar treatment.

Section 2   Aims and Assumptions in Educational Guidance and Selection

The most important question to be answered, by the philosopher of education and the educational administrator alike, is that implied by the title of this chapter. How can the potentialities of the individual be most fully realized from his own point of view and from that of society? In particular, since in Western societies the basic minimum of instruction and a rough approximation to equality of general educational opportunity are already assured, how can the higher creative potentialities, whether scientific, technical, or artistic, of young people, be most reliably identified and given adequate opportunity for development? This is the implicit theme of our whole book. Although in many parts a plunge into technical and methodological detail will be necessary, the techniques and methods should be seen as instruments to this main end. During the last ten years psychologists have shown increasing interest in the subject of creativity, which has grown beyond mere fashion. Our Chapters 14 and 15 discuss the results of this research in some detail, but many other chapters touch more or less directly on the same theme.

Setting aside, for the most part, economic, historical, and other aspects, we have concentrated upon the psychological influences. Believing, as scientific psychologists, that the best way to bring about the desired results in any area depends upon first discovering, through systematic observation and reliable measurement, the basic laws and regularities that function in the area, we have limited our topic still further to the effects of the individual's own abilities, personality, and interests upon his achievement and creativity. In much of this book, but not exclusively or in principle, we have also restricted the topic to achievement in school. In principle, we have thought it desirable to deal with psychological theories and methods of research relating to achievement anywhere and at any age and have interpreted the word widely, without confining ourselves to the discussion of purely intellectual or scholastic achievement. But because available research data are much more systematic and comprehensive concerning school achievement, and because the first positive steps can be taken in our schools, we are writing primarily for the educator. Indeed, our main aim is to show how much the psychology of individual differences can contribute to educational practice, taking for granted certain broadly conceived educational goals.

On the social side, we assume that, consistent with the economic resources[1] of the community, education is pledged to aim at a maximum development

[1] In comparative studies of sixty-nine countries (Cattell, 1949) it has been shown that the following variables are systematically related:

High expenditure per head on education,
High expenditure per head on luxuries and travel,
Low tuberculosis and other diseases of malnutrition,
Low general death rate (high longevity).

The existence of this relationship suggests either that high educational expenditure makes for such use of resources as keeps a nation rich, or that education is a luxury expenditure. There are good reasons for accepting the former view. However, it must be true in principle that there is an optimum plowing back of wealth into education (probably seldom reached!) that maximizes the community's real wealth. This optimum point would provide an objective definition of what we mean by giving maximum educational attention to every child "consistent with the economic resources of the community."

of the potentialities of every child. This does not mean any such misconception of democracy as would put every child with machine-like uniformity through identical schools, courses, and processes of learning. On the contrary, a scientifically and ethically informed treatment requires a wide range of opportunities, delicately and flexibly adjusted both to the flowering talent of the individual child and to the areas in which society shows its most acute needs.

Even though the practice has not always been as good as a wide application of psychological principles could make it, the essentials of "adjusted education" are already accepted traditions in most European and American schools. Special educational classes and schools, for example, have long been provided for the backward; and classes grouped by ability, progressing at different rates in different areas of the curriculum, have often catered to differential rates of development in the individual child. And as the resources of society have permitted upper stories to be built upon the main educational edifice, in the form of more prolonged education in technical colleges and universities for those capable of profiting by them, scholarship- and fellowship-selection procedures have become increasingly important.

These developments have not occurred without strife, some of which has arisen from a kind of struggle for survival among competing educational philosophies, some merely from lack of thought or organization, some from sheer human selfishness or envy. We shall assume that it is to the good of the community, and a matter of justice for the individual, that educational opportunity should not depend upon accidents of parental status or location, but be based on the best possible estimate of the capacity of the child to benefit by whatever privileges he receives and to return services to the community by his enhanced talents. Because this is a severe and ambitious ideal, it will not escape criticism.

The history of "eleven-plus" selection in Britain, which attempted to allocate children to different types of secondary school according to their needs and aptitudes, provides an excellent illustration of an attempt to revitalize an existing educational system by a greater equalization of educational opportunity. It also illustrates the opposition such reforms are likely to arouse and the irrelevant terms in which such opposition is frequently expressed. This whole selection procedure, which is further discussed in Chapter 3, was certainly open to reasonable criticism at several levels. First, the provision of grammar-school education varied widely in different parts of England and Wales, with the result that a child might easily be eligible for a grammar school in one locality but not in an adjoining one, on the basis of the same test performance. Second, although machinery existed, in principle, for the transfer of "late developers" from one type of secondary school to another, this machinery worked in practice rather haphazardly, its efficiency again varying from area to area. Third, the selection procedure undoubtedly often produced an undesirable "backwash" effect on both primary schools (or many of them) and on parents, in that misdirected and often irrelevant effort was devoted toward "getting the child through the eleven-plus." But the criticism that was felt most strongly and voiced most loudly was rarely along any of these lines. Although the "tripartite" selection was obsolescent in its methods of psychological examination, lacking much which we here argue to be necessary, and not wholeheartedly developing the necessary machinery for constant adaptations and revision of the direction given to individuals, it was upset really by more primitive objections than these. Godfrey Thomson, Cyril Burt, and others who laid its foundations were greatly concerned alike for social justice and technical effectiveness; but in the years which followed, these ideals seem to have lost their impetus.

Much of the more general criticism comes from a deep suspicion of all "social engineering" or planning, some again from plain resentment at anyone being classed as more able than anyone else. Many people would like life to proceed without the raising of any awkward questions about merit at all, as when the replacement of patronage by competitive examination as a basis for entrance to the British Civil Service caused considerable indignation in the nineteenth century.

> They talk of some strict testing of us—Pish!
> He's a Good Fellow and 'twill all be well.[2]

Nevertheless, in the selection of those who can best contribute in various ways to our society and its culture, the onus of proof is admittedly on those who wish to replace a plutocracy or an oligarchy by a meritocracy. They must demonstrate that the method of selecting merit that they propose is better than any other available method. Indeed, even before that, they have to prove that any system of selection by merit is better for the community than no selection at all, i.e., than laissez-faire, although the defense of a system of lawful, deliberate selection for merit should perhaps be unnecessary after the bloody centuries of our history. Whether it be in Imperial Rome or Nazi Germany, in a pirate's band or an underworld gang, the catch-as-catch-can style of promotion rewards ability and service to the community less than it rewards a red tooth and claw.

But this kind of jungle is always liable to develop unless the leaders selected by merit are as resourceful and determined as those who thrust themselves forward in times of chaos—and, at the same time, more moral and more intelligent. Without this insistence on a broader definition of merit, it is easy to fall into a stereotype of thinking, for example, that the present American Civil Service examinations, or the ancient Chinese selection of government officials by examination in literature, are what we are describing when we talk of "selection by merit." Admittedly, this is bound to be a

2 Edward Fitzgerald, "Rubaiyat of Omar Khayyam," LXIV.

continuous, longitudinal process. No method of selection will ever be error-free, and people will always be fired or promoted according to a long record of performance. But in this context we are primarily concerned with what are in principle the best methods of selection for merit in the sense of future promise.

So much for our fundamental assumption that some planning and selection are necessary, but that these can never be perfect. A second important assumption is that those responsible for such planning should take the longest possible view. We should not accept, for example, the notion that selection for a certain type of schooling aims at producing perfect correlation between selection indices and success *in that type of school.* The school in this sense is not life, but a preparation for life. The more important and fundamental aim should be to produce a high degree of correspondence between the selection indices for the given type of education and success in the range of careers for which that type of education prepares. Without this explicit realization, it is possible for even the best of present-day schools to become virtual training centers for teachers or, even more narrowly, for those who want to live the academic life.

Section 3   **The Potentialities of Applied Psychology**

When one speaks of educational diagnosis, selection, or prediction, the man in the street tends to think of the traditional examination. But although examinations have various uses, they are far from being the only available instrument. As every teacher and professor knows, good examination-passers are not necessarily the most intelligent, promising, worthy, or productive students. Part of the difficulty lies, too, in the fact that a school examination has many other purposes than that of selecting by merit. School examinations have always had several functions, such as:

1. Determining the status of the student in *actual present* achievement, skills, knowledge, personality, and character development;
2. By inference, determining how well the student is applying himself, relative to his resources;
3. By inference, determining how well the *teacher is teaching,* relative to his and the school's resources;
4. Acting, therefore, as a guide and *an incentive,* in the process of learning and teaching—as a spur, in fact, to both student and teacher;
5. Ensuring that a prescribed curriculum is being given the required attention, particularly in basic subjects and in primary education;
6. Selecting, on the basis of past performance, individuals who are considered promising, for assignment to an appropriate educational class in the future.

In psychological selection, we are concerned almost exclusively with the sixth function, though, as stated, we are also concerned with more than school achievement alone; whether the testing has any teaching value, or incentive, is as irrelevant to such prognostic purposes as whether a blood test contributes directly to health. Many misleading conclusions and three-fourths of the heated disputes about psychological testing have arisen from ignorance or neglect of these considerations.

Moreover, and this is a main theme of our book, the discussion of selection as if it were for merit in some single direction needs explicit correction. Many of the most highly developed tests and examinations in our schools today are devoted to "scholarship selection" or "university entrance," and at a later stage to "occupational qualification," in all of which there is a prescribed type of excellence. In selection for most "scholarships," in fact, the excellence sought is a purely intellectual one. But these narrow uses should not blind us to the principle that the psychologist is a servant of education, holding out means of selection that can serve the most profound or subtle philosophies of education. To some extent, these possibilities have been obscured by mistrust arising in the past between philosophers and teachers of the humanities, on the one hand, and scientists and, in particular, scientific psychologists, on the other. The former group has been contemptuous on occasion of the crudities of a young science, and the latter has reacted against the traditional domination of philosophy (in some universities, psychologists still form a subdepartment within a department of philosophy) and the entrenched "scholarly" prestige of older subjects.

But there are signs that the rapidly growing potentialities of properly applied psychological methods are coming to be appreciated at their full value. It is striking, for instance, that both the British Civil Service and the British armed forces, two supposedly conservative and traditionally minded institutions in a conservative country, have quickly and effectively adopted modern methods of psychological selection and allocation in times of real need and pressure.

For not only has psychological research led to widely used and relatively objective tests of scholastic ability, which have supplemented and partly replaced the traditional examination papers. The psychologist can also help in selection for engineering or medicine, can isolate the traits that indicate success with people rather than with ideas, can begin to analyze the components of musical and artistic talent, and, in general, can apply the analytic method that has been so successful in the study of primary abilities to a host of complex aptitudes and situations.

More fundamentally, the psychologist can, in principle, devise means of measurement and selection wherever the philosopher can define and describe a criterion of the good life or of the good citizen. Obviously, in practice, this will frequently tax the ingenuity of even the most able research workers.

The task is thus to be widely conceived, and part of our purpose here is to make an up-to-date study of the principles and technical procedures required for the prediction of achievement, together with some examples of how such procedures have already been effectively used, and some suggestions as to how they may fruitfully be extended. In concentrating on what modern psychology can do to ensure the guidance, selection, and proper recognition of individuals according to their diverse talents, one must constantly keep in mind the remaining half of the kingdom of educational psychology. To supplement the study of the *individual personality and its development,* we recognize also a broad area of psychological research on the learning process and its efficiency, covered by learning theory and the theories of information and communication. At the present time, this research on the learning process is contributing powerfully to teaching methods, to perceptual aids, and even to "teaching machines." It must be kept in mind as an adjacent field of research that interacts with our own, because generalizations about learning are always relative to style of teaching and to other aspects of a school system, and because the particular pattern of abilities required for success will tend to alter with the angle from which a subject is attacked and with the methods of instruction employed.

While our topic of the prediction of achievement is thus not as wide as educational psychology, but constitutes only one-half of that kingdom, conclusions that are technically sound and practicable can be reached only by keeping the whole area in perspective. Prediction is a tool of educational guidance; as such, it depends on the educational system and the values implicit in educational goals. We have also recognized, casting our net more widely than in some similar studies, that achievement should comprise achievement in school subjects, in the development of personality and character, and also achievement in later life as a citizen, which includes far more than occupational success. Psychological experiments and data do not yet exist, and may not exist for a generation, that would permit us to give technical help on these wider aspects. Yet our aim has been so to formulate and attack the problem that the extensions beyond academic achievement in the narrower sense can find a place in these formulations. Our methodological framework includes prediction equally of cognitive and emotional achievement, and it suggests instruments for studying both, although currently achieved research results remain mainly in the realm of scholastic achievement and creativity.

Section 4   Recent and Relevant Trends in Psychology

In this connection, we hope to distinguish our attempt from much that has hitherto been written on psychological measurement and educational prediction. First, we have added personality and interest measurement to the ordinary examination and ability measurement, but, more important perhaps, we have aimed to use psychological understanding and insight as well as actuarial, statistical prediction. The addition of personality and interest measures of a sort to educational guidance is not in itself entirely new and has generally *not* converted an actuarial approach to a clinical, or even to a satisfactory, approach. By the term "actuarial," in this context, we mean the use of statistics as an accountant might use them, so that as good a prediction could be made from this point of view by an accountant using the measures and following the rules of calculation as by a psychologist who knows to what the figures refer.

The opposite extreme to this actuarial approach is the traditional attitude of the clinician, who has always (with few outstanding exceptions) been prone to distrust statistical analysis and to take an excessively narrow view of the potentialities of the experimental method in psychology. A brief summary of this kind is always liable to oversimplify, but the vast majority of clinical psychologists undoubtedly, in our view, cling conservatively to outmoded techniques and to scientifically unverified (and often implausible) theories of personality, which they claim to supplement by clinical intuition and by close day-to-day observation of a few markedly unusual individuals. This is by no means to decry the value of clinical observation and insight. It does, however, give a one-sided picture, unless supplemented by experiment and statistical analysis, particularly when, as often, it remains tied to speculative and quasi-scientific theories.

By contrast, we prefer where possible to use measures of personality that have been derived from a long process of empirical observation and analysis, and that aim to assess the dimensions of personality that have been found to emerge in repeated inquiries over a wide range of age, social class, and nationality.

The development of objective personality theory in the last decade has been considerable. The kind of personality and motivation measurement employed here is organically integrated with that development. We are proposing, therefore, an approach in which a growing body of psychological understanding of personality and motivation structure is used to interpret educational measurement and to add something beyond actuarial prediction. This approach is newer and more promising than the purely clinical approach. It deals with empirically demonstrable personality and interest structures, with tests that are constructed from the beginning to measure such meaningful structure, and with psychological theories that avoid metaphysical speculation by being based on replicable analysis.

The general public knows little of new developments in the study of personality, motivation, and "depth" psychology, commonly believing that psychoanalysis provides the latest scientific understanding of human nature.

But, behind the facade of speculative psychology, there is steadily growing up, as yet accessible only to research groups, a body of knowledge of a different kind, rooted in measurement and complex calculation, and able to demonstrate its effectiveness to a degree that psychoanalysis has never achieved.

Section 5   Plan of the Book

We hope to show the relevance of some of this new knowledge to educational and to general achievement, and some understanding of these developments will be necessary to the reader. Although the professional psychologist will follow the arguments more easily, a large part of the book is also aimed at teachers. We hope that they will not find the technicalities too repugnant and that they may be encouraged to delve into some of the numerous research reports mentioned. We have tried to "sugar the pill" by frequent summaries of the main points.

Our plan of presentation, therefore, calls for an introduction to advances in quantitative psychology: first, in the field of abilities; second, with regard to the nature of personality factors; and third, in studies of interest measurement and motivation. This introduction occupies Chapters 2 through 5, after which follow two chapters on the technical requirements of psychological tests. The subject matter of these two chapters is, necessarily, rather technical and specialized, and some readers may be inclined to continue straight on to the later chapters and content themselves with studying the summaries of the main conclusions. But we would suggest that anyone with a serious interest in test construction and in questions of test homogeneity, reliability, validity, and so forth, should study Chapters 6 and 7 carefully. The current theory in this area, as expounded in many of the most widely read textbooks, is by no means entirely watertight or logically satisfactory. Many of our suggestions are original and even unorthodox; some, we venture to believe, are improvements on the usual criteria of good psychological tests.

In Chapters 8 through 11, an account is given of an actual survey carried out with urban and rural junior-high-school students, in which a wide variety of tests was administered, including measures of ability, personality, and motivation.

Finally, in the remaining chapters, we consider these findings, together with related findings in the areas of scholastic achievement and later achievement, and attempt to integrate them into a set of conclusions about the prediction of achievement in general. Because one author is American and the other British, we hope to have achieved a relatively "culture-free" attitude, which may enable many of these conclusions to be valid for the educational systems of both countries.

SUMMARY *of Chapter One*

1. Everyone concerned with education has in many ways a more difficult task at the present time than ever before. Development from infancy to an adult state in which the individual can make full use of all his capacities in a complex, technological society places a rapidly increasing burden on the educational system of Western democratic countries.

2. Changes in educational methods during the last half-century have been largely the result of increased psychological knowledge, particularly of child development. But there is a rapidly growing body of knowledge, some of which will be described in this book, that has not yet become familiar to educators. Many of these new findings are highly relevant to the problem stated immediately above.

3. Educational guidance and selection have in the past depended very heavily on measures of intellectual performance. But in recent years promising advances have been made in the study of personality and motivation, and particularly of factors affecting creativity. Knowledge in these areas is sufficiently advanced to be important to educators. Future policies of guidance and selection will probably give as much weight to these factors as to intellectual ones.

4. The prediction of achievement has in the past been too narrowly conceived. Apart from misunderstanding about the uses of examinations, the criteria have often been too exclusively academic. An important function of applied psychology in the future will be to devise means of assessing achievement and potentiality for achievement in the broadest sense, in life as well as in school. Many of the tools are already available.

5. The plan of the book is briefly outlined. It is designed to report a number of relevant psychological findings in the areas of ability, personality, and motivation; to recommend some new criteria for effective tests in these areas; to describe a survey of Illinois school students that related these measures to school achievement; and to review briefly what is known about the prediction of achievement in life as well as in school.

Chapter Two

THE NATURE OF ABILITIES

Section **1** **Introduction**

When the achievement of a boy or girl at school is discussed, the first question one tends to ask is "How intelligent is he or she?" But even in some areas of school achievement, such as behavior record or athletic performance, the answer to this question will not take one very far; one needs to consider both special aptitudes and traits of personality and motivation. When discussing an individual's achievement in life after school, one is as likely to turn first to qualities of personality and character as to intelligence, and this difference in emphasis is probably justified. Nevertheless, we can say here and now that general ability is the most important predictor of school achievement in our own studies. We would like to introduce a proper balance, however, by reminding the educator, who commonly stops with ability measurements, that a considerable improvement even in the prediction of scholastic achievement can, in principle and sometimes in practice, be obtained by adding motivation and personality measures; in later achievement, these probably become equally important with abilities.

Many educational psychologists believe that the field of ability testing has marked time for the last twenty-five years. That is, although there have been some slight improvements in method, there has been no radical advance, or fundamental change in theory. In this book, however, we are concerned not only with introducing motivation and personality measurements into prediction, but with showing that certain radical advances are possible in ability measurements, too. These are debatable issues, and it is therefore necessary that the teacher try to get a real grasp of the fundamental theoretical points involved.

Our account of the measurement of abilities will begin with a very brief introductory sketch of the methods of analysis used, and of some important historical stages, but will then proceed, in the main part of this chapter, to a formulation that is rather different from, and, we would suggest, in some ways an improvement on, the conventional account.

Section 2   Techniques for the Analysis of Abilities

Many, probably most, readers of this book will be familiar with the concept of *correlation*, which has been quite fundamental to the development of educational psychology, and particularly to the study of abilities, but a brief account may be useful.

All organized knowledge depends upon a study of the relationship between variables. In the physical sciences, the relevant variables can very often be manipulated in controlled experiments, and their relations can be directly studied in terms of cause and effect. The social and behavioral sciences are generally in a less fortunate position, because it is less possible to rely on controlled experiment with human beings, and there is greater need to supplement experiment with statistical analysis. The statistic called a *correlation coefficient* is simply an index of the relation between two variables, expressed in such a form that a perfect positive relation will yield a correlation coefficient of $+1.0$; a perfect negative relation, a coefficient of -1.0; and complete independence of the two variables, a value of zero. In practice, of course, most obtained correlations are of intermediate value, such as $+0.51$ or -0.25. Thus a test of numerical ability might correlate with a test of verbal ability $+0.40$, and this would indicate that the tests were neither completely independent, nor were they measuring exactly the same thing. If the tests could be accepted as sound, reliable measures of verbal ability and numerical ability, one could then say that these two kinds of ability to some degree overlapped or were positively correlated.

This point leads us straight to the second technique, that of *factor analysis*. It was very soon discovered, after the introduction of correlation as a tool of research, that measures of ability, whether in the form of standardized tests, examination results, or teachers' ratings, showed a strong general tendency to correlate positively with each other. This immediately suggested some more fundamental, underlying influence, which entered into each of the measures of ability and affected them in varying degrees. An analogy here might be that if one studied a group of children, and found them to be heavier, taller, and less prone to illness than their predecessors of a generation earlier, one might form the hypothesis that these changes were evidence of change in one underlying variable, say of an improvement in nutrition. Rather similarly, the preponderance of positive correlations between a wide variety of measures, each of which appeared to represent some aspect or other of ability, suggested that each was affected by an underlying, more fundamental variable of general intelligence; and statistical methods were devised to obtain measures of this general factor.

The techniques of factor analysis that thus evolved rapidly became highly complicated, particularly when it was found: (1) that explanation in terms of only one general factor was inadequate; and (2) that numerous alternative sets of factors could be obtained mathematically. It then proved necessary to decide which method of analysis into underlying factors of ability was the most satisfactory from the point of view both of scientific economy and of psychological sense.

The results of factor analysis are shown in tables of factor loadings. Each test in the analysis will have a loading between +1.0 and −1.0 on each of the factors that is found. A high positive loading on a factor of general intelligence will mean, for example, that that particular test is a good positive measure of general intelligence. Thus in table XXVIII on page 176, the best measure (other things being equal) of the first factor, interpreted as fluid general intelligence, is the IPAT (Institute for Personality and Ability Testing) Culture Fair classification subtest. Similarly, the measure most representative of Factor 4, interpreted as anxiety, is the High School Personality Questionnaire (HSPQ) subtest of timidity.

Section 3   Previous Theories of the Structure of Abilities

A very brief recapitulation of the theories of leading psychologists about the structure of abilities is as follows. About the turn of the century, Spearman in Britain came to the conclusions we have outlined in the last section: first, that all measurements of ability tend to be positively correlated; and second, that these positive correlations could be largely accounted for by a single general factor, which he called *g*. Simultaneously, Binet in France, probably without knowledge of Spearman's theoretical position, developed the first practical tests of general intelligence. For some twenty or thirty years, it was generally accepted that this one general factor accounted fairly satisfactorily for all the multifarious manifestations of human ability; insofar as general intelligence tests and measurements of IQ are still widely used and discussed, this probably remains the viewpoint of the educated layman.

In the 1920's and 1930's, however, psychologists became increasingly aware that Spearman's theory of one general intelligence factor, although a considerable advance on anything that had preceded it, was inadequate to explain all the facts. At this point, techniques in the United States and Britain diverged. There was agreement in both countries that important factors were left over when the general factor had been extracted, but the

American approach to this situation was more radical. In Britain, psychologists such as Burt and El Koussy, during the 1930's, established the existence of important group factors over and above, and independent of, Spearman's general factor, such as factors of spatial and numerical ability. Thurstone, in the United States, made the radical innovation of apparently doing away with the general factor altogether by extracting a number of separate factors, which were themselves correlated, but which could be shown to be determinate and worthy of recognition as genuinely distinct factors by the criterion of simple structure. Although it is not possible to explain here the technicalities of simple structure, the principle is of cardinal importance as giving a determinate criterion among an infinite number of possible structures. For a full account, the interested reader is referred to Thurstone (1947)[1] or, for an account that is probably more easily intelligible to the nonmathematician, to Cattell (1952a).

The important fact is that Thurstone thus established a set of between six and a dozen primary abilities, which he interpreted as verbal fluency, numerical ability, spatial ability, memorizing ability, inductive reasoning, and so forth. The factor of general intelligence appeared at first sight to have been superseded by this new analysis. It was soon realized, however, that because Thurstone's primary abilities were positively correlated, they could themselves be subjected to further analysis as though they were tests, and a second-order factor of general ability could be extracted from them. The two theories, thus, do not oppose, but complement, one another; and it is sometimes more convenient to measure one general, and sometimes several primary factors.

It is in some ways surprising, and probably indicative of the need for more and better-directed research, that there is no complete, agreed explanation of what the relationship of *g* to the primary abilities really means. One possibility, perhaps the most likely, would be that there exists in every individual an inborn general ability, which, by practice and experience, becomes directed in different degrees to different areas. For example, an individual who has a lot of practice in numerical calculation is likely to project his intelligence in this direction and to score more highly on the factor of numerical ability.

The second-order factor was shown to be larger in children than in adults, and it was assumed that this meant that in the course of aging the primary abilities become more distinct and independent. But a quite different explanation is possible, and is made below under the theory of fluid and crystallized ability; namely, that the uniformity of the school environment accounts for this higher correlation, and that it has something to do with the nature of

[1] This form of reference directs the reader to the Table of References at the back of the book, where titles and other details of works referred to will be found.

the common experiential environment, rather than with aging or development as such.

While the experimental and statistical analyses of ability were proceeding in this way, the ancient debates on the nature of intelligence continued. There were, in the first two decades of the twentieth century, almost as many definitions of intelligence as there were people. Indeed, some psychologists had come to the barren conclusion that "intelligence is what intelligence tests measure," although anyone is free to make up any kind of test and *call* it an "intelligence test." The analysis by Spearman had the great scientific advantage that, to a considerable degree, it tied down the pattern of abilities that could be considered general ability or intelligence, so that agreement became possible. Unfortunately, it did not mean that the interpretation of this general ability was complete, although some of the early definitions, such as "capacity to acquire capacity," "adaptability to new situations," and "rate of learning," certainly fitted well the tests that were found experimentally to be highly loaded in the *g* factor.

Spearman made a profound analysis of what was involved in the best intelligence tests as defined by their *g* saturations, and he came to the conclusion that *g* or general intelligence is "the capacity to educe relations and correlates." The limit of a person's intelligence thus depends upon the degree of complication in the relations that he can perceive, regardless of what fundamentals the relation deals with. This would explain, for example, the rather high loading of mathematics in general intelligence, because success in mathematics is considerably concerned with perceiving complicated relations as such.

Section 4 Hereditary and Cultural Determinants of Ability

The study of twins, identical and fraternal, and of unrelated children reared together pointed quite early to the conclusion that there is a considerable hereditary determination of the *g* factor. Burt; Newman, Freeman, and Holzinger (1937); and others, who carried out the most substantial researches in this area, arrived at results that suggested very strongly that 80 per cent of the variance in intelligence-test performance was due to heredity and 20 per cent to environmental differences. More recently, there has been renewed controversy on this topic, with the sociological school of educational writers attempting to minimize the effects of heredity on measured intelligence (Burt, 1955; Burt and Howard, 1956; Floud, Halsey, and Martin, 1957; Maddox, 1957; Warburton, 1958). In the light of this more recent evidence, the findings of the earlier researches, which indicated a preponderant influence for heredity, appear unshaken. One should keep in mind, however, that the environmental variance is not only that due to intellectual stimulation. Various diseases, such as encephalitis, may cause brain damage, so that if we say that 20 or 30 per cent of the variation in performance in intelligence tests among forty-year-old individuals is caused by environmental differences, some of this, perhaps half of it, must be ascribed to influences other than differences in education. Even so, it is of course clear that environment has an important influence, and a great deal of recent research has tried to pin down the effects of environment on the child's maturation.

Particularly relevant work is that of Piaget, who has suggested that a growing child reaches levels of generalization at certain relatively fixed stages of maturity, that these stages always follow a certain order, and that each stage opens up a whole new style of problem-solving. Such an idea or style of solving problems we may call an "instrument" or "aid." If an aid comes into existence a year or two earlier in one child than another, it may mean a difference in problem-solving capacity over a fairly wide range of performances, which, because earlier learning is more potent than later, results in his scoring better on an intelligence test through the rest of his school life. This is, though less spectacular, perhaps rather analogous to the effects of imprinting that have been shown in experiments with animals, but not too convincingly yet in human intellectual development. Admittedly, the aids (by which we shall henceforth refer to the main point of the Piaget school of psychology) have not been so adequately confirmed statistically as they have been persuasively described on the basis of a few closely observed cases, though work in that direction is increasing (Lunzer, 1960). Nevertheless, the theory put forward below takes due notice of the role of aids, while leaving as a task for later research an assessment of their quantitative significance.

Section 5   **The Theory of Fluid and Crystallized General Ability**

Cattell (1940) has put forward a theory that there is not a single *g* but two, and that these should be called "fluid" and "crystallized" general ability. The idea has been further developed, and has also been put forward independently by Hebb (1949), Newland (1963), and others, under slightly different names. Newland, for example, talks of "process and product," and Ferguson (1954) speaks of ability and learning set. We shall now describe this theory in some detail.

It has been increasingly realized that what is generally called "intelligence" in our culture does not account for all cognitive performance. Guilford has been prominent in making this point, and we shall return to it in our discussion of creativity (Chapter 14). But even in the narrower area of intelligence, our theory suggests that there is more than one general ability. On this theory, the main variation between individuals is accounted for by two second-order general factors, which are highly cooperative (Cattell, 1952a), in the sense that they both load positively most of the primary ability factors, while having largely zero loadings outside the intelligence field. Being cooperative, they have been difficult to separate; thus most previous analyses of ability have been satisfied to recognize their joint resultant as one factor. This one factor has been made the basis of IQ measurement and called general intelligence.

The special properties distinguishing these two hypothesized factors, which may be called fluid and crystallized general ability, g_f and g_c, are as follows:

1. Crystallized ability (whence its name) loads more highly those cognitive performances in which certain initial intelligent judgments have become crystallized as habits. That is to say, fluid general ability, which is in many ways the more fundamental of the two, has at some time been applied in this field, and the individual, by memorizing former responses, is enabled to make further new judgments. Success on Thurstone's verbal and numerical tests, or achievement in geography or history, might be examples of such products. Fluid general ability, on the other hand, shows more in tests requiring adaptations to entirely new situations, where crystallized skills are of no advantage because they do not apply to the particular data.

2. Before biological maturity (fourteen to eighteen years), individual differences between g_f and g_c will mainly reflect differences in cultural opportunity and interest. Among adults, however, these discrepancies will also reflect differences in age, because the gap between g_c and g_f will tend to increase with experience, which raises g_c, whereas it has frequently been shown (e.g., Vernon, 1960) that with increasing age some decay of g_f occurs.

3. Similarly, fluid and crystallized abilities will produce different patterns when plotted against age for the general population, because g_f tends to reach an early maximum at between twelve and fifteen years, where g_c increases to eighteen and beyond, depending on the general length of the learning period for persons in the given subculture. Thereafter, where g_f will decline increasingly from about twenty to old age, g_c will show a lesser and a later drop, if any. Of course, in all these comments on g_c, it must be understood that we are not talking about some single crystallized ability, but about the average performance across a broad array of crystallized abilities, the selection of which to measure g_c has to be defined by the common cultural experience.

4. The standard deviation of the IQ calculated "classically" for mental ages will be about twelve to sixteen points for g_c and twenty-four to twenty-five points for g_f. The latter will be more constant and biologically determined, whereas the former will depend upon conditions in the culture. For example, classroom systems that slow the bright and press the dull will

reduce the variation in g_c at any age level, and, therefore, the g_c standard deviation of IQ, when annual increment is constant.[2]

5. The relative effect of heredity and of environment will differ for the two general intelligence factors. In the case of fluid general ability, g_f, probably the only effect from environment will be that upon the physiological powers themselves, such as is due to encephalitis, brain injury, or some defect of brain metabolism or growth environmentally determined. In a culture with good medical services, this is relatively small. On the other hand, the environmentally determined variation in g_c may be considerable. If the educational system is highly uniform, it may not be so, but where there is any considerable variation of cultural opportunity, the environmental contribution will tend to be large. Presumably, the values found so far are an average of the values for g_c and g_f, so that the proportionate determination of intelligence by heredity and environment, respectively, might be 90/10 for g_f, and 70/30 for g_c. Some work on perceptual culture-fair intelligence tests, as described later, does show a higher hereditary determination of success at these than of success at traditional tests.

6. Day-to-day, or month-to-month, fluctuation, that is to say reversible changes, in intelligence level, should occur in g_f only with variations in general physiological efficiency. In the case of crystallized ability, these variations might perhaps be less, and although not unconnected with physiological variation, might show more relation to recent practice and to changes of interest.

7. The effect of local brain damage will be a general lowering of g_f, no matter where the damage occurs. But the effect on the g_c score may well occur only through consequent changes in localized ability, as in aphasia. If, therefore, intelligence is then estimated by a test or tests that do *not* involve the particular area concerned, no significant fall will necessarily be detected. The effect of general brain damage, e.g., atherosclerotic and arteriosclerotic, will be similar in both, but possibly more pronounced in g_f.

8. Where people compete in the same areas of learning, but have varying opportunities of acquiring skills in these areas because of educational and social selection, the contribution of the g_c factor will be large in relation to

[2] Traditional intelligence tests, i.e., those that are now most firmly established in the field, and that involve some verbal ability and scholastic knowledge, are mixtures of g_c and g_f. The standard deviation from such tests will be a function as follows:

$$\sigma\text{IQ} = k \sqrt{\frac{\sigma^2_{f(p)} + \sigma^2_{c(p)} + 2r_{cf(p)}\sigma_{c(p)}\,\sigma_{f(p)}}{\sigma^2_{f(a)} + \sigma^2_{c(a)} + 2r_{cf(a)}\sigma_{c(a)}\,\sigma_{f(a)}}}$$

where "p" subscripts mean across people at one age, and "a" subscripts mean across age (years) the latter being taken as variance of the means when people are averaged across an agreed number of yearly age groups. As σ_{fp} and σ_{fa} can be assumed to be biologically given, the IQ sigma on a traditional, culture-contaminated intelligence test will in general become smaller (over school years only), whereas schools produce a large age increment in scholarship where opportunity is not highly adapted to native ability differences, i.e., when $r_{cf(p)}$ is small.

that of g_f. Such conditions do prevail in regard to school subjects throughout school life. In adult life, skills in school subjects will continue to correlate (by "correlation of remnants"), but a more valid measure of g_c will be made through a wider range of performances.

9. The rate of learning in any particular area will be a function, as far as cognitive components are concerned, of g_f, g_c, and the level of the specific ability factor in that area. Insofar as g_c and the specific factor are concerned, we are saying that learning begets learning capacity. This is one reason why we do not adopt Newland's suggestion that these be called, respectively, process and product. In other words, there is a continuous chain of learning, and the process itself will usually be a product of earlier processes. Even so, the effect of g_c as a general factor should in most situations be somewhat smaller than that of g_f, because the variation not accounted for by g_f is likely to be attributable not only to g_c, but also to a number of limited group or specific factors, associated with what we have called aids above.

Section 6 The Relation of Crystallized Intelligence to General Level of Attainment

Some of the above propositions have been stated in provisional or subjunctive form, because the research necessary to establish them is incomplete. We suggest, indeed, that with the reorientation of the theory of abilities that we have outlined, a stimulus is given to a great deal of necessary research. For the nonstatistical reader, the whole relationship may perhaps be caught in the simile of a coral-reef growth. There, the form of the coral rock represents at the same time the influences of a living organism and the history of past development. So here, in the individual, the form of abilities at a given moment is a function of a living capacity, namely, g_f, that has also acted in the past in the acquisition of skills. The extent to which the skills will be correlated will be a function both of the extent to which they are dependent upon the single g_f ability, and of the extent to which they have received the same length of training and the same opportunities to improve. Any intellectual performance, considered simply as such, may therefore be considered to depend on a combination of the two general factors described, plus a specific ability peculiar to the particular task. In real life, it will also depend to some extent on personality and motivation factors, which we shall consider in detail in subsequent chapters.

From what we have said, it can be seen that the crystallized general ability factor represents a set of performances that tend to be higher *simultaneously* in one person than another in a given culture, partly because of the way in which subjects are taught in that culture, and partly because of the common action of g_f and of some minor factors. The parts of this organization of abilities are not functionally connected at a given moment but have, so to speak, the unity of a historical ruin. Although vocabulary skill and numerical skill are correlated in adults, if some influence interfered momentarily with the level of vocabulary skill, it would not necessarily produce any effect on the level of numerical skill. We can speak of crystallized general ability only to the extent that the culture has taught these things together, but it is nevertheless a useful concept; for, among all members of this culture, we have the advantage of being able to predict performance in particular fields to an appreciable extent from one single measure, namely, that of crystallized general ability. Like all historical ruins, however, it is likely to suffer specific changes. For example, the crystallized general ability resulting from individual learning during the 1920's might not have the same form as that found among persons learning in the 1960's in the same culture. Furthermore, in adult life, there will be differential forgetting, so that a man who continues, say, as a lawyer's clerk, may retain his verbal skills at a good level, whereas, as various researches have shown, people employed in jobs that demand less verbal skill will tend to suffer greater loss of vocabulary discrimination. The result is that the crystallized general ability factor is likely to become of less general use, in the sense that it contributes less to the variance of particular performances, as people get older, or when people of different ages are grouped together. This is well known to take place, though the reasons for it have not previously been very clear.

At this point a reader may ask, "But is not this crystallized general ability factor merely *general school attainment,* or, in adults, the general experience of life which comes with age?" The answer is that there *may* turn out to be a general factor of purely school achievement, or of general effectiveness in virtue of life experience, but this should appear as something quite distinct from crystallized or fluid ability. For in any general factor that might appear as a result only of common experience and common interest, rote memory would play as large a role as fluid intelligence. The degree of attainment in g_c is that part of attainment, and that only, which comes from the application of fluid general ability to learning. It should thus show itself to be loaded only in judgmental skills of the highest complexity, and not in all that has been learned in school through much repetition and memorizing. Remembering the names of all the battles in English history, or of all the U.S. Presidents, might correlate with general scholastic attainment, much less so with g_c.

Section 7   The Development of Perceptual and Culture Fair Intelligence Tests

So far the tests that have been found to be most purely loaded on the fluid general ability factor are of what is called the *perceptual* kind. It was found fairly early in the development of mental testing that, as Spearman had theorized, intelligence can be tested through highly complex relationships in simple, perceptual material, without using culturally imbedded material. Indeed, this perceptual material should avoid pictorial presentations and anything that would depend upon cultural knowledge. The presented material may be just shapes (since even geometrical material may be cultural), or shades of gray, and so on. It must be material in which, in a sense, everyone can be said to have reached the stage of "overlearned" understanding. In searching for possible material that would be thus overlearned and universal, Raymond B. Cattell, senior author of this volume, in early work published with colleagues between 1937 and 1940, pointed out that parts of the human body, celestial events, and even a few facts that have to do, say, with the properties of running water, are sufficiently universal and overlearned in their properties to be used in culture-fair intelligence tests even though they are not merely perceptual. Out of such material, more and more complex relations can be built up, as illustrated in the examples in Figure 1, which involve quite complex eduction of relations and correlates, and which prove to be highly saturated with the general ability factor. It will be noted that there is a convergence in research of the idea of fluid general ability and of the Culture Fair Intelligence Test, although the latter was originally developed more for social reasons and for research in anthropology where a test was required that could be used in many countries. However, the objectives of the Culture Fair Test turn out to be essentially the same as those of devising a measure for the fluid general ability factor.

A brief note on the history of Culture Fair Intelligence Tests is therefore appropriate at this point. Research on the similarities and differences between intelligence tests based on perceptual material and those of the more traditional kind involving culturally determined material was begun by a group of workers at the University of London in the late 1920's. Subsequently, a number of perceptual tests for practical use appeared, such as those of Pintner, Porteus, and Raven. The subject was taken up systematically again in the late 1930's by Cattell, Sarason, and others, who experimented both with the perceptual material and with "overlearned" or generally familiar material, such as parts of the body and geographically common features of the environment. In this work, it was shown that an immigrant group in the United States tested on traditional tests, such as the Binet and the American College Entrance Examination, along with the Culture Fair Test and the Grace Arthur Performance Test, improved on a second testing only on the Binet and the ACE. Thus both the perceptual tests and the performance tests were shown quite early to have some advantages over the traditional, verbal type of test in that they were less susceptible to cultural influences. Furthermore, when factor analyses were carried out, it was found that the general ability factor was poorly measured by the performance tests, but fairly well measured both by the perceptual ability tests and by the traditional type of intelligence test. Thus the conclusion was reached that the perceptual test

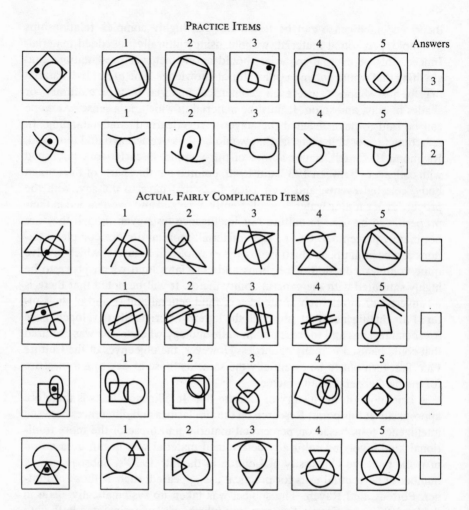

FIGURE **1.** *Examples of items from the new "topology" subtest in the IPAT Cattell Culture Fair Intelligence Test*

is the only general type that is at the same time reasonably culture free and also a good measure of intelligence.

The work just summarized should, however, be distinguished from some other research, superficially rather similar, but carried out with quite a different aim. We have already mentioned some controversy between educational psychologists and educational sociologists on the relative contributions to intelligence of heredity and environment. To most psychologists, sociologists often appear to indulge in special pleading in attempting to show both that intelligence is virtually unaffected by hereditary factors and that differences in intelligence between social classes are illusory. Perceptual tests of intelligence were developed by Davis, Tyler, and Eells in Chicago, that appear to have had this latter aim specifically in view, probably at the cost of failing to be good measures of the general intelligence factor.

Section 8   Some Further Characteristics of Culture Fair Tests

To return to the development of Cattell's Culture Fair tests, it was found that a subtest of the type designated as "topology" was highly saturated with general ability. A combination of this subtest with three others (series, classifications, and matrices) was therefore used in Scales 1, 2, and 3, each of which is constructed in two alternative forms. As pointed out above, it is safer and more representative to base a perceptual intelligence test on such a combination of subtests than on some single type of test, such as the matrices or the classifications.

A rather wide application of these Culture Fair or Culture Free tests, which were standardized in Britain, America, France, Italy, and Japan, and used also in the Congo, in Formosa, and in a number of preliterate cultures, brought out some interesting facts. It was found, as had been predicted, that gross changes of culture might be associated with negligible differences in intelligence as measured by these tests. For example, the mean and the standard deviation as found by Rodd for Chinese in Formosa, was almost exactly the same as the corresponding figures for American children of the same age in American high schools. Also, it was verified that the curve of increase of intelligence as judged by culture-fair tests flattens out much earlier than for traditional tests and coincides much more closely with the biological-maturation curve of the central nervous system. This is one of many respects that suggest that the culture-fair type of test is measuring what we have defined above on theoretical grounds as fluid general ability. That the traditional intelligence test is measuring a good deal of achievement in the sense of crystallized general ability is shown by the variations in the flattening-out period from subculture to subculture, according to the age at which formal instruction in schools ceases.

Around 1935 Finch pointed out that when traditional intelligence tests were reapplied to children in the same geographical area after a long period of time, the norms became inapplicable, because the mean score of children of the same age rises, or at least rose through the 1920's and 1930's. This shift of norms was confirmed on a large scale in Tuddenham's analysis of performance on the Army intelligence tests applied to American recruits in the two World Wars. Different methods of selection of recruits in the two wars may have accounted for some of this improvement but are hardly likely to explain a rise of about half a standard deviation. Thomson's careful work with Scottish children, using Binet and Moray House tests, showed the same kind of change, though to a lesser degree (perhaps because Scottish education has always been good, and so was not so likely to rise in this particular period). The general conclusion from these diverse experiments would seem to be that, in the first half of this century, the increasing efficiency of state schools, and the longer periods of time at school that increasing prosperity allowed, resulted in higher educational standards, which were reflected in those intelligence tests that did not completely separate intelligence, in the sense of g_f, from attainment and concrete, crystallized intelligence, in the sense of g_c. A check on this was made in 1949 by Cattell, who made a complete cross-sectional testing of 3,000 ten-year-old children in the city of Leicester and compared it with a similar complete cross-sectional test made by him in 1935 with the same Culture Fair test. The result was quite clear—the null hypothesis was not disproved in this case, and no significant change could be discovered.

These findings have implications that have not yet been thoroughly assimilated by intelligence testers or educational theorists. They show, in the first place, that despite the huge investments of time and money in very large samples of children in standardizing such tests as the Binet, or the WISC, the resulting norms tend to change almost as soon as the tests are published, and are thus less useful and consistent than norms on a culture-fair test, even when the last-mentioned are based on decidedly smaller numbers.

So far we have talked mainly about changes in test score up to the age of adolescence, but we should glance also at what happens thereafter. It has long been known, through the work of Lorge, Thorndike, Miles, H. E. Jones, and others, that the typical life curve in intelligence-test performance, providing the tests are to some degree speeded, is one of decline after the age of about twenty-five, which persists and accelerates up to old age. Admittedly, this decline has generally been inferred from cross-sectional rather than from longitudinal studies, but its existence is supported by converging lines of evidence and has been documented more fully in recent years by Rattner at Indianapolis. On the other hand, providing tests are administered as what Thorndike called a "power test," that is to say without any time limit, this decline in performance resulting from age occurs very much less markedly. The results obtained with culture-fair intelligence tests show the same kind of decline, though it is very likely that further research will find certain systematic differences, corresponding to the theoretically expected differences between g_c and g_f.

Section 9 **Indicated Reforms in the Use of Intelligence Tests in Schools**

We shall discuss the vital question of the validity of tests in some detail in Chapter 6, but in our present account of ability tests, and in particular of Cattell's Culture Fair tests, it is necessary to outline one or two important principles. Too often in the past, a new test has been "validated" by simple correlation with an existing test, such as the Binet or the Wechsler. It would appear much sounder to validate an intelligence test against a determinate factor, obtained by the best possible factor analysis of a large number of ability variables, together with sufficient other variables included in the analysis to provide a good hyperplane. When this is done, the validity of the Culture Fair, fluid ability measures is quite as high as that of traditional intelligence tests. Indeed, if, instead of taking a single general ability factor, we recognize the two distinct general ability factors, and decide that g_f is what we want, then it is actually a better measure of intelligence. Also, one must not forget that the types of crystallized ability that enter into the crystallized general ability factor are relatively more influenced by historical accident. They will be different in one country from another, different at one period from another, and different in the same group of people at different ages. The reason for the last difference is clear if one considers that eleven-year-old children share training in common reading, writing, and arithmetic, but in forty-year-old people, such as, say, a group of businessmen, fluid general ability will have become invested in quite a different set of specialties. In this postschool group, therefore, g_f is a much more meaningful concept than g_c and one that future research may well show to account far better than any collection of acquired judgmental skills for the most important individual differences in ability.

The distinction we have drawn between two kinds of general intelligence factor leads to another principle of validation. This is that to correlate an intelligence test with measures of school achievement may be indirect evidence of the validity of a test of crystallized ability but is much less relevant to the validity of a test of fluid ability. For there is no sharp line that can be drawn between scholastic, and indeed many varied kinds of, attainment, and what we have called crystallized general intelligence. This being true, we should expect a traditional intelligence test administered to children in a particular year to correlate better with school achievement measured in the following year than would a culture-fair test measuring g_f, for the criterion that we are out to predict is already being partly measured in the test that sets out to predict it. But this slightly higher value in the correlation within a few months should not blind us to three considerations: (1) in predictions five to ten years hence, the culture-fair test is likely to do much better; (2) the traditional test may be systematically unfair to individuals who do not happen to have had training in the particular skills in the preceding years relative to those who have such advantage; and (3) we obtain less psychological insight into what is happening in individual cases. Indeed, we are running in circles, by merely predicting what we already know! When one studies the individual child, the important thing is the difference between his intelligence, g_f, and his school-attainment level. We want to know how well individual children are performing in relation to their full capacity. And if we select them for scholarship purposes, we should be more concerned with their performance five years hence than with their performance at the present moment or six months hence. Furthermore, to predict even so far ahead will still leave us open to the justified criticism of the man in the street that achievement in life consists of much more than mere scholastic success. A good deal of the discrepancy noticed by observers between performance in school intelligence tests and success in later life need not be accounted for by personality factors, but may be due to inadequate measurement in the ability field itself. The fluid general ability factor is likely, according to the theory put forward, to be well correlated with a man's shrewdness in judging people, his capacity to acquire new judgmental skills in a new occupation, his business sense, his political wisdom, and so forth. The test of crystallized intelligence, on the other hand, puts more emphasis on verbal and numerical skills as they are taught in school. If all children are equally exposed to, and equally interested in, literature and numerical skills, tests of attainment in these subjects will be pretty good measures of g_f. Because this "if" is a very big one, we shall know better what we are doing in selecting children for scholarships that affect their opportunities in the years ahead, if we use a culture-fair test instead of the culture-bound one. Although we have thus argued that a test of intelligence is likely to be of use in long-term prediction very much to the extent that it is free from cultural contamination, it must be admitted that there is plenty of scope for further research, both on the relative freedom from such contamination of various tests and on their long-term predictive power.

Another effect of measuring intelligence in the crystallized form is that one gets an appreciable sex difference, the girls being higher in each age group, as occurs, for example, in the Henmon-Nelson, the Detroit-Alpha, and other traditional tests. It is probably the greater conscientiousness and application of girls in school that results in their scoring slightly higher on knowledge and performance in these tests, whereas on the Culture Fair Test no significant difference exists between boys and girls.

We have stressed a number of advantages to be obtained by using an intelligence test that is free as far as possible from cultural influences. But scores on such a test will not be uninfluenced by practice. Although the Culture Fair tests are designed to be as free as possible of effects from the wider cultural background, they are no different from other intelligence tests in their susceptibility to what Thouless first called "test sophistication." For this reason, any intelligence test, if repeated at short intervals, will tend to show some appreciable change between the first and second, a slighter change between the second and third, and a negligible change between the third and fourth administrations. Of course, even the first change will not occur if the children have been subjected within a year to intelligence tests that required a similar kind of orientation to time and place. In talking about an adequate measurement, we would normally speak of one in which all the subjects had equal exposure to practice, and in which the test is at least half an hour long. Furthermore, although intelligence does not vary as much from day to day as people might think from their subjective experiences, yet it would be desirable to have A, B, and even C forms of the test administered some days apart and to take the mean score as the estimate of the individual's intelligence.

A special problem that arises in the usual process of changing from raw scores to standard scores resides in the much greater variance obtained in a single age group by culture-fair, g_f, measures compared with those from traditional intelligence tests. In the latter, the standard deviation of the IQ has typically stood at fifteen to sixteen points, occasionally creeping up to seventeen in tests that have become, accidentally rather than through systematic planning, somewhat more free of cultural elements. On the other hand, the standard deviation of IQ on the Culture Fair Test is about twenty-four points or twenty-five points of IQ, i.e., about 50 per cent larger. The reason for this resides in the equation already given in the footnote on page 20. The standard deviation of the IQ depends essentially on a comparison of within-age variance in performance with between-age variance in performance. If one were to take the whole range of school children, including all age groups, there should be a very high correlation between school attainment and g_f increase. Within any age group, however, this is imperfect, and it tends to be made still more imperfect by the school philosophy of allowing the bright to mark time while pulling the dull along at what is to them a more rapid rate. The result is that the traditional intelligence test does not give such a big discrimination between individuals as does the fluid general ability measure. However, so large a proportion of teachers and school psychologists are accustomed to thinking in terms of an IQ deviation of fifteen, and such a large revision of practice would be necessary to change this, that the Handbook of Culture Fair Intelligence tests usually transforms the classical IQ with its twenty-four-point range, *to a standard score IQ,* which gives a fifteen-to-sixteen-point standard deviation and a normal distribution. This is a mere convenience of the transformation to standard scores.

The upshot of this discussion for practical purposes is that in many circumstances we should probably use two measures of general intelligence, one consisting of a culture-fair test to calculate g_f, and one of a traditional test to calculate g_c. Additionally, in any wide problem of achievement prediction, as in vocational guidance, we should measure some separate primary abilities, such as verbal ability, spatial ability, numerical ability, inductive ability, and manual dexterity; in this connection, useful tests are provided in French's kit for fifteen factors available from the Educational Testing Service, Princeton, New Jersey, or Dr. J. King's primary aptitude battery, available through Industrial Psychology, Inc., or the new special ability battery developed by Hughes for IPAT. The question of how these primary abilities and the general ability factor should be combined in predictions is better taken up after further chapters have developed the general theoretical position.

SUMMARY *of Chapter Two*

1. Abilities form the most important group of predictors of school achievement, but even in this context, personality and motivation must not be forgotten. In achievement after school, the last two are probably of equal importance with abilities.

2. Historically, one general ability factor was the first to be isolated. Subsequently, in the United States, an analysis into correlated primary abilities has often been preferred. These two ways of analyzing ability are complementary, not contradictory. The analysis into primary abilities can be carried further, and a more precisely determined factor of general ability can be extracted as a second stage.

3. A theory of *two* general factors is put forward, one of fluid, one of crystallized, general ability. Some empirical evidence is given to show that these, though easily confused, can be distinguished.

4. Fluid general intelligence is of more fundamental importance. Crystallized general intelligence develops from former applications of fluid intelligence, but it is to be distinguished from attainment, because attainment depends not only on the applications of general intelligence but also of rote memory and routine skills.

5. A number of hypotheses and predictions are described that arise from this theory of two kinds of general intelligence. Some of these have already been verified, and others suggest a fruitful field of further research.

6. It is suggested that the traditional type of intelligence test measures a mixture of the two general intelligence factors, and that, of presently existing tests, the type that comes nearest to measuring fluid intelligence accurately is the perceptual and relatively culture-free type of test.

7. The culture-fair type of test, besides its theoretical advantages, will have practical advantages: (a) norms will remain more constant; and (b) the test will, if the writers' hypotheses are confirmed, give more reliable long-term prediction of achievement (though possibly less accurate prediction in the short run).

Chapter Three

THE RELATION OF ABILITIES TO
SCHOLASTIC ACHIEVEMENT

Section 1 **Introduction**

In our account of the nature of abilities in Chapter 2, we have laid considerable stress on the theory of *two* general intelligence factors and on the consequent distinction between fluid and crystallized general intelligence. We have also suggested that Cattell's Culture Fair Intelligence Tests come nearer than most other tests to measuring fluid general intelligence. A corollary of this view is that the traditional type of intelligence test, which tends to measure crystallized intelligence or at least a mixture of the two, may often have higher validity in predicting concrete measures of attainment, because it comes nearer to being an actual measure of attainment itself. But this apparent superiority is offset by lower construct validity, and probably by lower concrete validity in the long run.

But it must be admitted that much of what we have urged on these lines is still to some degree theoretical and urgently requires further research to substantiate or disprove it fully. Therefore, to avoid overstressing our own theoretical position, and because most of the findings reported in the literature are derived from tests that are, in varying degrees, culture contaminated, our survey of the relation between abilities and scholastic achievement will attempt to provide a brief bird's-eye view of the whole field. This field is a vast one, and whole books have been written on separate aspects of it. The best we can hope to do in the space at our disposal is to describe a representative sample of the more important researches. In Chapter 9, we shall return to this subject and describe some empirical findings of our own, in which both a Culture Fair Test and Thurstone's tests of primary abilities were used to predict school achievement.

31

Section 2   **Prediction from Two Kinds of Ability Factors**

As described in the last chapter, the type of prediction from ability factors will be affected by whether one uses primary or second-order factors. The present chapter will survey results obtained by both British and American psychologists; the former until recently have followed the "unrotated first component" definition of general intelligence of Burt and Vernon, but the notion of a second fluid ability is now more widely accepted.

Much of the early pioneering work in isolating the constituent factors in ability was done by British psychologists, such as Spearman, Burt, and Thomson. In recent years, close attention has been paid in Britain to the problem of prediction in connection with the system of secondary education in that country, in which children are often segregated into two or three types of secondary school at the age of eleven or twelve. A great deal of the recent British research to be surveyed in this chapter was done with reference to this selection process. American research, by contrast, has ranged over a wider field, and, in general, larger samples and more efficient machine methods of analysis have been available.

British factorists, following Spearman and Burt, have generally preferred to concentrate their attention on a massive factor of general intelligence (or *g*), which, as we have pointed out, is in effect a *second-order* factor, if the American system of factoring is followed. American researchers have paid more attention to isolating *primary* factors of ability, themselves not entirely independent but to some degree correlated, and then, more recently, to determining the second-order factor or factors from these primaries. This latter approach has the advantage of providing factors that are relatively invariant from one study and one sample to another, if the invariance of simple structure be accepted. On the other hand, the use of one massive factor, as in British work, has produced good results in practice and is much more justifiable in the sphere of abilities, than, say, in personality or motivation research, where it would be quite inadequate.

As the careful reader of Chapter 2 will be aware, the existing research on prediction from ability measures, as yet available for our survey in this chapter, has often been conceived in older, and sometimes illusory terms. First, one must recognize that when a single general ability factor has been taken out of a pool of tests, it has commonly had nothing but a tradition of sound "commonsense" test choice to prevent its "wobbling" in meaning, as a first component mathematically must, with the particular choice of tests. This problem does not arise when one goes through previously fixed primaries. Secondly, the verbal-educational and spatial-practical-mechanical factors which then follow as additional components, orthogonal with the first, (in the orthogonal approaches, as by Guilford or Humphreys in America, and Vernon in Britain, and called v:ed and k by the last) should on no account be compared with the concepts of crystallized and fluid ability. A superficial resemblance exists, but the difference is fundamental. Thirdly, provided one works with two general second-order ability factors, there is no contradiction or antithesis between working with a battery for general abilities, or one for six to a dozen primaries. It is purely a matter of time and convenience, since one can calculate the two second orders from the primaries. However, when testing is carefully done, there is or should be some gain in total prediction from using the extra variance in, say, eight to ten primarily ability measures. McNemar and Vernon are able to quote research which gives negligible extra prediction from the extra time taken to test primaries, instead of using the general crystallized ability factors, but this depends on what one is out to predict. Neither primaries nor second orders are the "more fundamental": they are different ways of cutting the same pie.

Although, in accordance with recent research advances, we should prefer to discuss results in terms of fluid and crystallized general abilities and primaries, one might have to wait a decade for such results to become available. The results of the last decade must largely be discussed in the terms on which they were designed.

The present chapter will deal with achievement prediction strictly in the sense of the relation of scholastic achievement to ability factors. The prediction of achievement in a wider sense will be discussed in Chapter 13.

Section 3 **Prediction from Primary Ability Factors**

In this section, we shall describe and compare a few of the best known multifactorial tests of abilities and discuss their relation to school achievement.

Some of the most thorough work on primary mental abilities in the United States was done by the late Professor L. L. Thurstone, and five of the principal correlated factors are embodied in the Primary Mental Abilities battery that emerged from this research.

These consist of V (verbal-meaning), R (reasoning), S (space), N (number), and W (word fluency). The power of prediction of school achievement of these factors is summarized as follows in the test manual (PMA 11–17, 3rd ed., May 1958, p. 1):

> The V (verbal meaning) test and R (reasoning) test have proven to be the best predictors of high-school work. These two scores have consistently shown satisfactory reliabilities, and have proven to yield substantial correlation with teacher grades, standard measures of educational development, and several tests of "general intelligence."

The S (space) test and N (number) test have shown useful, although lower, validities in terms of high-school success. Also, the reported reliabilities for these tests have been found to run a little lower than was originally estimated, although they are sufficiently high for identification of students who are remarkably strong or weak in these expressions of mental ability.

The W (word fluency) test has not to date produced positive evidence of predictive value in research dealing with scholastic and vocational predictions. The word-fluency score does, however, continue to show good differential power—that is, it provides evidence of mental functioning beyond that provided by the other four scores.

Evidence is also provided of the relation between PMA factors and measures of achievement, such as the Iowa Tests of Educational Development, grade-point averages in high school, and teachers' ratings of progress in vocational high schools.

As reported by Schneider (1956), who gave both the PMA and the Iowa tests (ITED) to 600 tenth-graders, the main relations were as follows: The Iowa tests are eight in number, ranging from "social studies background" and "correctness in writing" to "quantitative thinking" and "reading-natural sciences." The correlations between PMA factors and ITED subtests range between +0.13 and +0.73. There is thus a considerable range of variation in predictive power, but what is most noticeable in these results is that there is comparatively little such range within each factor. In other words, one factor, such as V, predicts *all* the eight diverse achievement tests at a high level, the lowest correlation being +0.42; a second factor, such as R, predicts them all moderately well; a third, such as S, predicts none of them conspicuously well (highest $r = +0.29$). The same trend is also clearly visible in the results quoted from Shinn (1956), although the correlations are generally somewhat lower, and in this case multiple correlations of the five factors are also reported; here again, there is a remarkable uniformity in the extent to which the eight apparently contrasting achievement subtests can be predicted, with none of the eight coefficients of multiple correlation (R's) diverging appreciably from +0.60. Out of the Iowa tests there has now developed the SCAT (see Anastasi, 1961) around which research results on achievement prediction are accumulating; but the essential findings are similar to those just discussed.

Though this research is not reported in the test manual, rather different results were obtained by Wolking (1955), who found that for eleventh-grade students certain subjects were predicted better by all the factors and also by the Differential Aptitude Tests. These subjects were science, geometry, and algebra. It is possible, however, that the grades in these courses were more reliable or more objectively determined, and that this accounted for their greater predictability.

When grade-point averages are used as the criterion, i.e., as representative of achievement, as in a study by the Thurstones on 348 ninth-grade students in the Chicago area, the verbal and reasoning factors again emerge as clearly the most efficient predictors, both with correlations around the +0.50 mark.

Another research is quoted in which the measures of achievement were ratings of progress in subjects such as electric wiring and woodworking in vocational high schools in New York City. Multiple correlations of all five primary factors against the ratings were between +0.17 and +0.38, and it is suggested that the lowness of these figures is probably due to the unreliability of the ratings.

Finally, a study by Wellman (1957) showed that the addition of the PMA to the Otis quick-scoring mental ability test significantly improved prediction of grade averages of Iowa eleventh- and twelfth-grade students. It is not stated, though, whether the inverse would also have been true, and whether the Otis test would significantly have increased prediction beyond the degree obtained by using the PMA alone.

The researches so far described are mainly quoted from the manual of the PMA test, and the descriptions give a fair idea of the predictive efficiency of the test in terms of school achievement. But school achievement, as assessed by ratings and achievement tests, is in itself an intermediate goal, a measure of potentiality rather than of success in life; it will be necessary also to take a long-term view. As Anastasi (1954, p. 459) puts it, "Like any other type of test, achievement tests should be regarded as tools, not goals. Moreover, it must be remembered that they provide only partial information, and need to be supplemented by other observations."

An attempt to trace the predictive power of the PMA a little further was made by Schmidt and Rothney (1954), who tried to relate tenth-grade students' vocational preferences to their differential scores on the PMA.

These researches using the PMA five-factor test have been discussed in some detail as typical of many other investigations. In very rough terms, correlations between ability and achievement from a single measure seem typically to be in the range of +0.3 to +0.6; multiple correlations, which predict an achievement measure from the best weighted composite of ability measures, generally appear to vary between +0.4 and +0.7.

Most of the researches quoted deal with "simultaneous prediction" and were obtained with samples of tenth- or eleventh-grade students. But figures that are not much different have been obtained for the correlation between ability and achievement in first- to fourth-grade children (Barnes, 1955). The predictions would be lowered to some degree, if a long period of time, i.e., several years, passed between administration of the ability measures and the measure of achievement, but not so greatly as one might suppose. In this approximate long-term stability lies the great strength of ability measures, in contrast to many other types of psychological measure.

To summarize the advantages and disadvantages of the PMA tests, these have first and foremost in their favor that they were developed from Thurstone's classical research into ability factors. Second, they are available in forms suitable for ages from seven right up to adulthood. Third, they are well-established tests, and considerable information is available about their reliability and validity. It was for these reasons that the PMA battery was used, along with other measures of ability, in the research by the authors that will be described in later chapters.

It should be pointed out, however, that the PMA tests have their critics, and many psychologists would prefer the Differential Aptitude Tests (DAT) as a multifactor measure of abilities. Nunnally (1959), for instance, criticizes the PMA battery on the grounds that some of the tests are too heavily speeded and that they do not take into account the latest knowledge about the factorial analysis of abilities; he appears to think more highly of the DAT. This battery, however, is suitable for eighth grade and beyond, and the Illinois research to be reported was with seventh-grade students.

The authors of the DAT battery were influenced only partly by factor-analytic findings. They speak of a "compromise between the desire to measure 'pure' mental abilities that arise from factor analysis and the practical necessities continually encountered by personnel and guidance workers through the years." The first five tests appear to be relatively good measures of independent ability factors. The DAT contains the following subtests:

1. Verbal reasoning
2. Numerical ability
3. Abstract reasoning
4. Spatial relations
5. Mechanical reasoning
6. Clerical speed and accuracy
7. Spelling
8. Sentences

It has the advantage over the PMA of having been constructed more directly as a predictor of achievement in school and in subsequent career, but as Nunnally (1959, p. 187) points out, it is doubtful whether the tests would be so successful in a wider range of testing situations. However, a great deal of information about norms and validity in terms of correlations with school grades and similar criteria is summarized in the test manual of the DAT (Bennett, Seashore, and Wesman, 1952), which is of great interest and has been highly praised as a model test manual.

Another difference between the PMA and the DAT is that the DAT is oriented toward "power" rather than "speed"; most of the students for whom it is designed finish the tests within the fairly generous time limits allowed, the only exception among the eight tests being that of clerical speed and accuracy.

The DAT battery has, however, been criticized as a predictive instrument on the grounds that the intercorrelations between the eight subtests tend to run rather high, in some cases over +0.6; for this reason, one would expect multiple correlations from all eight tests not to exceed the correlations from individual tests so strikingly as if the subtests were comparatively independent.

Some of the correlations between scores on the DAT tests, as given in the manual and extracted by Nunnally (1959) are shown in Table I.

TABLE **I**

Median correlations of differential aptitude test scores with school grades

TEST	English	Mathe- matics	Science	Social Studies, History	Lan- guages	Typing	Shorthand
Verbal reasoning	.50	.39	.54	.50	.30	.19	.44
Numerical ability	.48	.50	.51	.48	.42	.32	.27
Abstract reasoning	.36	.35	.44	.35	.25	.27	.24
Space relations	.27	.32	.36	.26	.15	.16	.16
Mechanical reasoning	.24	.22	.38	.24	.17	.14	.14
Clerical speed and accuracy	.24	.19	.26	.26	.23	.26	.14
Spelling	.44	.29	.36	.36	.31	.26	.55
Sentences	.52	.36	.48	.46	.40	.30	.49

Reproduced by permission of McGraw-Hill Book Company.

One can see from Table I that results obtained with the DAT are comparable in several ways with those from the PMA, which we have already summarized. With the PMA, the verbal-meaning and reasoning tests were in general the best predictors of high-school work; and when we come to discuss our own research in later chapters, we shall see that this in general proved true in the Illinois survey also, particularly with regard to the verbal-meaning (V) factor.

With the DAT, the verbal-reasoning test gives the highest prediction of school grades in science (see Table I) and social studies and history. A slightly higher correlation with school grades in English is obtained from the "sentences" test, as is not surprising, because this test involves knowledge of grammar and punctuation. The numerical ability test is the best predictor of high grades in mathematics, but also of high grades in languages! One must remember, however, that these correlations do not greatly differ, and that many of the differences should certainly be ascribed to sampling error.

Furthermore, the rather high correlations between the tests in the DAT battery will tend to obscure the differential pattern of prediction.

As with other tests of ability, the general pattern of Table I shows that the more scholastic subjects, such as English and mathematics, are the more predictable, because they are more directly dependent on general intelligence as measured by objective tests. Subjects such as typing and shorthand are relatively more dependent on quite narrow specific abilities, and consequently less predictable by a general-purpose test, although it is possible that some of the difference in predictability may be accounted for by less reliable grading in the less scholastic subjects. All the tests of abilities we have discussed so far have in this sense the limitations of their advantages, in that as good measures of fundamental and primary abilities they are less good measures of specific skills. Specific skills are more predictable from some of the more specific factors to be discussed in a later section.

A third multifactorial measure of abilities that is widely used in the United States is the General Aptitude Test Battery (GATB). At this point, the reader may ask why we continue to talk of tests that bear the title of *aptitude* tests as though they were tests of *abilities,* when these terms are often thought of as pointing an important distinction. A clue to the best answer has already been given in quoting the authors of the DAT as attempting a compromise between the measurement of pure abilities as determined by factor analysis and the measurement of aptitudes as indicators, e.g., of vocational leanings and suitability. The distinction is made much clearer if we follow Michael's (1960) description of abilities, aptitudes, and achievement as lying on a continuum that consists of the amount of specific learning involved. Tests of abilities in theory discount specific learning as far as is practically possible— and this is still truer of culture-fair intelligence tests, as described in the previous chapter—whereas tests of achievement or attainment frankly aim also to measure specific learning in a particular field.

Tests of aptitude will in theory occupy an intermediate position, but in practice they tend to overlap a great deal, as we have seen, with tests of abilities.

The GATB, whose distribution is limited to state employment agencies, consists of fifteen tests. Scores are derived from these tests, which are stated to measure ten factors—general intelligence (G), verbal aptitude (V), numerical aptitude (N), spatial aptitude (S), form perception (P), clerical perception (Q), aiming (A), motor speed (T), finger dexterity (F), manual dexterity (M). It is described here principally for the sake of completeness, and because extensive data have been compiled on the relation of these factors to vocational achievement. However, as Thorndike and Hagen (1955), from whose account this description is largely taken, point out, it is unfortunate that these data are still restricted and not generally available to school counselors.

Section 4 **Other Ability Factors**

Although there is little doubt that the ability factors we have described are those known to have the closest relation to school achievement in general, a great number of others have at one time or another been reported in the psychological literature, perhaps as many as a hundred.

The critic of factor analysis often points to this multiplicity of factors as evidence of the disagreement among psychologists or of the fallibility of the method, but such a conclusion is premature. There are two or three considerations that enable one to see the situation in better perspective. First, as stated earlier, one *can* find factors that are more specific than the primary factors of ability if one selects a number of tests that are comparatively similar. To find primary factors, one needs to sample the whole area of abilities; if, instead, one assembles—for example—a number of tests of spatial ability, the spatial factor will be split into several less inclusive factors, each of which represents a probably interpretable aspect or facet of spatial ability, and to which it is possible to give a name. For many purposes, and particularly from the point of view of pure research, this may be well worth doing. But the issue is rather one of strategy in research than of pure methodology. It seems more useful in the present state of psychology as a science to establish the broad lines and the primary factors, both on the general grounds that this is the most logical approach, and because the primary factors will enable us to make predictions in a wide variety of situations and with a practically negotiable number of factor scores.

It is probable, however, that the future development of the psychology of abilities and cognitive processes will include a study of some "subprimary" or semispecific factors, even though these may not have the wide predictive powers of the primaries. The most promising work along these lines has been done by Guilford and his associates, who have generally been concerned with factors that are more specific than the commonly accepted primaries. For example, he distinguishes a number of different factors of fluency and of flexibility, which he fits into a rather elaborate hypothetical structure representing the components of intellectual ability. Guilford's original overall conception of this structure is shown in Figure 2.

The elaborateness of the scheme is shown by a consideration of the factors that Guilford (1957) believes to be involved even in the "divergent" subcategory of productive thinking, as shown in Table II. More recently, the scheme has been further developed. Five kinds of operation (of which divergent production is one), six kinds of product (including, e.g., units, classes, relations) and four kinds of content are distinguished. In this scheme, Table II would be expanded into 24 cells, and for 16 of these, factors and

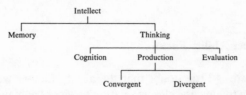

FIGURE **2.** *Guilford's (1957) classification of cognitive processes, particularly as related to artistic creation**

*Note that convergent and divergent are versions of Spearman's noegenetic and anoegenetic, restricted to thinking processes.

available tests are described in the latest report (Guilford and Hoepfner, 1966).

Guilford's research has the merit of linking the classical study of primary abilities with the newer field of research into creativity, which we shall consider in detail in Chapter 14. It is possible that some of his factors, although at a more specific level than has seemed practical to the majority of psychologists, will assume great importance in the prediction of creative achievement. At present, however, most of these factors lack concrete or direct validation of the kind we have discussed in connection with primary abilities.

A second reason for the multiplication of factors is similar. Many of the factors reported in the literature as factors of ability should perhaps be described as factors of aptitude or achievement and, like the semispecific factors that result from splitting the primaries, will have less relevance to scholastic achievement *in general*. For example, there is a considerable literature, well summarized by Vernon (1950), on the factors that determine aesthetic, or

TABLE **II**

A table of the productive-thinking factors of the divergent-thinking type

TYPE OF RESULT PRODUCED	TYPE OF CONTENT		
	Figural	*Structural*	*Conceptual*
Words		Word fluency	Associational fluency
Ideas			Ideational fluency
Expressions			Expressional fluency
Shifts	Flexibility of closure	Adaptive flexibility	Spontaneous flexibility
Novel responses			Originality
Details	Elaboration		Elaboration

musical, or physical attainment. Work in these areas is advancing rapidly, and is clearly of great importance, but has still hardly reached the stage of general acceptance.

A third consideration that has tended to give the impression of a multiplicity of competing factors in different researches is the existence of "formal" or "nonsubstantive" factors, such as difficulty, speed, or instrument factors. We mention this class of factors here only for the sake of completeness. We do not suggest that they are all of the same degree of artificiality, but much methodological work remains to be done on clarifying their status and conditions of appearance. Chapter 11 will consider some of these problems in more detail, in connection with the structure of interests. In some respects *convergent* and *divergent* have been dangerously oversimplifying stereotypes. For example, divergent is a logical category which may cut across several natural categories of fluency which are functionally diverse and different in nature.

Section 5   The Prediction of Achievement from General Intelligence

Although research continues to some degree in the United States on the relation between general intelligence and scholastic achievement, the great bulk of work in recent years has been concentrated on prediction from primary factors, as described in an earlier section of this chapter. Consequently, the present section will deal almost entirely with results of research in Britain.

Many of the studies carried out in Britain on the prediction of school achievement have had as their primary aim the improvement of the method of selection at the age of eleven-plus. The most authoritative summary of these researches and of the psychological basis of selection for different types of education in Britain is in the report prepared by a committee of the British Psychological Society and edited by Vernon (1957). The following description of results will be largely based on that report.

Maintained secondary schools, i.e., public schools in the American sense, have until recently been of three types—grammar, technical, and modern. The grammar schools provide the most academic type of education, intended in general for the most intelligent children, because it is almost essential to attend this type of maintained school if the student aims to go on to a university. Secondary technical schools provide a more vocational kind of education, with some emphasis on applied science. And children without either a markedly high scholastic aptitude or a marked leaning to the kind of subjects dealt with in the technical school are assigned to a secondary modern school.

It was the intention of the 1944 Educational Act that these three types of school enjoy "parity of esteem," but this appears to have been an unrealistic expectation. Because, in general, the grammar school leads to jobs and professions with greater prestige and greater earning power, and because places in grammar and technical schools are competed for, with the unsuccessful candidates being assigned to secondary modern schools, the principle of selection tends inevitably to produce a hierarchy of esteem rather than a tripartite system of equal status. In the last few years the system has been changing quite rapidly, and it seems probable that comprehensive, non-selective secondary schools will soon be in the majority.

Be this as it may, the following up of the results of selection has provided a great deal of important evidence about the relation of abilities to school attainment. There has been no prescribed technique of selection at eleven-plus laid down by the central Ministry of Education, and each local education authority in Britain is free to employ its own method of selection or, indeed, to abandon the whole principle of three separate types of school. A fairly standard procedure has evolved, however, which has been adopted by a majority of the local authorities. This procedure has usually employed as measures of selection an intelligence test, standardized tests of attainment in English and arithmetic, and an estimate from the children's primary school as to their suitability for a particular type of secondary education. The predictive power of these measures against a scholastic criterion several years later has been extensively studied. Most commonly, the criterion selected has been performance in the General Certificate of Education examination (GCE), which is taken by grammar-school students (and by a few students at technical and modern schools) at the age of about sixteen. Some of the studies quoted refer to the old "School Certificate" examination, the precursor of the present General Certificate of Education. As is pointed out in the BPS report, this criterion of achievement, although most commonly adopted, is by no means ideal in several respects. First, it is narrowly limited to scholastic achievement, as distinct from all other achievement. Second, it may tend to underestimate the full extent of correlation between abilities and achievement, because of the differential effect of different schools and because of the quite lengthy period of time between the selection tests at eleven-plus and the GCE performance at about sixteen. On the other hand, research has shown that prediction over four or five years is not greatly lower than over one or two years unless special factors, such as differences between schools, are taken into account. Third, very little is known about the reliability of the GCE examination. Fourth, because the follow-up procedure is limited to a selected group, the correlation between selection tests and criterion is artificially lowered, and a correction needs to be applied (known technically as "correction for selection") to obtain the true relationship that would have obtained if it had been possible to follow up with the same criterion both the grammar-school pupils and the other groups.

Considering, first, the general size of the relationship between the objective tests used in the selection process and later school performance, we found that a typical correlation coefficient (uncorrected for selection) is of the order of +0.4 or +0.5. Corrected for selection, this generally increases to +0.7 or +0.8, and even higher correlations have been obtained with suitable combinations of predictors and criteria. Such a statement is naturally approximate, because performance in certain GCE subjects such as Art is much less predictable from the selection tests than performance in, say, English or History, as we shall see later.

If one compares the predictive power of the three objective tests used in eleven-plus selection, the most general conclusion points to the superiority of the intelligence test. This is not necessarily true in each individual study, but it is strongly supported by an overall view of all the relevant research. Typical findings quoted in the BPS report are those of Peel and Rutter (1951) and of Emmett and Wilmut (1952). Peel and Rutter found the intelligence test to be the most efficient predictor of success in GCE both for arts and science subjects. The English test was the second best for arts subjects and the arithmetic test second best for science subjects. According to the report (Vernon, 1957, p. 73):

> In order to achieve the maximum prediction of a criterion composed of equally weighted marks in English Language, English Literature, French and Mathematics, the three entry subjects, Intelligence, English and Arithmetic, had to be weighted respectively 1, .87 and .27.

Rather similar results were reported by Emmett and Wilmut. The two-part Table III, reproduced from the BPS report, shows both the zero-order and multiple correlation coefficients (and regression weights) for the three selection tests and a number of examination subjects. The smaller number of school courses in the second half of the table is presumably due to the small numbers of students examined in the subjects that are omitted.

It can be seen from Table III that Emmett and Wilmut's findings confirm in most respects those of Peel and Rutter already mentioned. With few exceptions, the intelligence test proved the best predictor, whether one considers the correlations in the upper part of the table or the regression weights in the lower part. The most conspicuous exceptions are English Literature and French, for which the English test was the most predictive. There were no subjects for which the arithmetic test gave the highest prediction; even for the mathematics paper, which one certainly might have supposed to be most efficiently predicted by the test of arithmetic attainment at eleven-plus, the superiority of the intelligence test as a predictor is clearly shown.

Section 6   **The Relation of Abilities to Achievement at University Level**

The problems of selection for university places and of the prediction of university success are rather different from the corresponding problems with a younger age-group, for several reasons. The criteria of scholastic success are different, almost in kind and not simply in level of difficulty. Although this difference may in some ways be narrowing, there are still certain requirements for success as a university graduate that go beyond those for success in high school.

TABLE **III**

Extract from Emmett and Wilmut's (1952) Tables IV and V
   Correlation, uncorrected for selection, of 11+ Tests
   with different school certificate subjects

SCHOOL CERTIFICATE SUBJECT	N	CORRELATIONS WITH		
		IQ	E.Q.*	A.Q.**
English Language	153	.505	.498	.204
English Literature	153	.296	.298	.266
History	153	.383	.336	.328
French	153	.451	.463	.359
Mathematics	153	.514	.299	.429
Physics	96	.401	.224	.319
Chemistry	105	.386	.254	.366
Latin	81	.443	.388	.396
Geography	139	.285	.101	.071
Biology	67	.124	.038	.046
Art	66	−.020	.115	−.048

* E.Q. = English quotient.
** A.Q. = Arithmetic quotient.

Regression weights for maximum prediction

CRITERION	Intelligence	English	Arithmetic	R
English Language	.504	.432	−.171	.772
English Literature	.164	.261	.222	.620
History	.324	.153	.251	.701
French	.236	.380	.200	.785
Mathematics	.745	−.289	.330	.790
Physics	.694	−.289	.220	.638
Chemistry	.492	−.167	.340	.660

One of the obvious differences between achievement at school and at a university is the university student's greater need to work with little guidance, and to form habits of work and study and independent thinking. This is particularly emphasized in European universities, where it is broadly true that greater individual initiative is demanded, but there are also signs of a swing in this direction in the United States. It is doubtful, however, whether quite as much can ever be demanded from American students, because of the much greater opportunities for university education in this country, and the consequent lower *average* level of undergraduate ability. European universities gain by limiting themselves to the production of an educational elite, but the universities' gain is the nation's loss; and in some European countries, a desperate attempt at university expansion is aiming at narrowing the startling gap in percentage of the population that attends a university. The recent position in Britain was cogently summarized in a detailed survey by Furneaux (1961):

> If our educational system could be modified so that the 50% of children showing the greatest promise at 11 were able to attempt courses leading to their taking at least five G.C.E. papers at O-level, and if those capable children who now leave grammar schools without attempting A-level papers could be persuaded to attempt advanced work, then nearly 7 per cent of all boys and over 4 per cent of all girls could eventually reach the stage of applying for admission to a university.
>
> The proportion of boys who would then be entering universities would be about 1.8 times as large as in 1955, whereas for girls the proportion could be increased approximately 2.8 times.

The gap between the United States and Britain both in the availability of university places and in attitudes toward the function of a university, is still wide, though perceptibly narrowing, and necessitates some separate discussion of selection and prediction problems in the two countries.

Common to both, however, is a recognition that tests of abilities alone are probably not the best instrument for the prediction of scholastic success at this level. The acquisition of mental skills is cumulative, and by the time students are old enough to enter a university, previous attainments and special aptitudes are beginning to assume a more important role than pure abilities. This conclusion is suggested by a large number of studies, and particularly by a careful and thorough survey made by Sanders (1961), who compares British, American, and Australian methods of university selection. Even at the university-selection level, abilities have not become anything other than *relatively* less important, and hardly even that. But crystallized ability, as described in the last chapter, is beginning to assume greater importance in relation to fluid ability. To put the same point in another way, the statement that achievement becomes more important at this age as a predictor of further achievement is not to deny the continuing importance of abilities, because achievement can never be entirely isolated from abilities, although as we have tried to indicate in Chapter 2, abilities *can* be very largely isolated from achievement.

The amount of literature about students' psychological qualities and behavior is vast—so much so that the science of psychology has sometimes been accused of being concerned only with the psychology of university freshmen and sophomores. We are therefore limited in this section to a very brief statement of general principles and a few references to typical findings.

Two of the most widely used test batteries at the university-entrance stage in the United States have been the American Council on Education's Psychological Examination (ACE) and the College Entrance Examination Board's Scholastic Aptitude Test (SAT), which was originally developed by Carl Brigham. The former has now been discontinued, but a great deal of information on the norms and predictive power of these tests, and of such achievement batteries as SCAT at the school level, and of the ACT at university entrance, is available.

The ACE was originally constructed by L. L. and T. G. Thurstone in 1924, at the Council's request, and consisted of six subtests, yielding two main scores, a "Q" (Quantitative) and "L" (Linguistic), or, if necessary, a combined "gross score." The SAT is superficially similar, giving "V" (Verbal) and "M" (Mathematical) scores, but it is generally used in conjunction with a selection of the College Board's achievement tests in specific subjects such as French, chemistry, or social studies. All these achievement tests are objectively scored multiple-choice tests, with the exception of General Composition and parts of the English Composition test.

Dyer and King (1955) give some information about the relative predictive power of SAT-V, SAT-M, and high-school record, together with the multiple correlation against average freshmen grade provided by all three measures.

These data are given separately for a number of colleges, but we have compressed their table by taking the median value of the correlation coefficients in each column. The resulting figures are shown in Table IV.

TABLE **IV**

Median correlations between Various Predictors and average freshman grades

	SAT-V	SAT-M	High-school Record	R
Boys in Liberal Arts	.48	.36	.50	.57
Girls in Liberal Arts	.45	.32	.46	.58
Boys and Girls in Engineering	.42	.52	.44	.68

Dyer and King also provide a comparison of the SAT and the ACE in their power of predicting college freshman marks. The median correlations based on seventeen groups of students who took both the SAT and the ACE prior to entering college are shown in Table V.

TABLE **V**

SAT-V (*Verbal*)	SAT-M (*Mathematical*)	ACE-L (*Linguistic*)	ACE-Q (*Qualitative*)
.49	.37	.44	.28

In interpreting these figures, one should take into account that eleven of the seventeen groups were liberal-arts students, so that one would expect the verbal and linguistic scores, respectively, to give higher correlations with scholastic success than the mathematical and quantitative. It is noticeable that each of the SAT scores gives better prediction than the roughly corresponding ACE score, although high-school record can be seen from Table IV to be better than either of the SAT scores, except as a predictor of success in engineering. In general, the College Board achievement tests correlate to a similar degree (i.e., similar to the figures quoted for the SAT) with freshman performance in the corresponding subjects. Thus the median correlation of the College Board achievement test in English with freshman performance in English, based on ten different college groups in 1951 (Dyer and King, 1955) was +0.42.

The quoted results appear to be fairly typical of those reported in a number of similar researches with the tests most commonly used on entrance to American universities (e.g., Garrett, 1949; Chauncey, 1952).

The information available from Britain about the predictive power of various measures against university success is much more scanty. The position in 1952 was surveyed by Warburton (1952), on whose account the following paragraphs are largely based.

As was true at the high-school level, the emphasis is rather on selection than prediction, and this has become a more urgent problem because of the increasing competition for places in British universities. Although the number of places available roughly doubled between 1939 and 1949 from about 50,000 to about 100,000 and has been increasing rapidly again in the period 1963–1966, the demand has increased even faster, and the scholastic standard required for entry has been raised. This now involves as an absolute minimum requirement the passing of the General Certificate of Education at advanced level in two or three subjects.

Selection is based on performance in this examination (and on the GCE at "ordinary" level), together with a report from the schools, and in some cases an interview by members of the university staff. Correlations between performance in "A" level GCE or in the HSC examination and university examinations have been found to run fairly high, usually between +0.3 and +0.5 for individual subjects such as English or geography when university performance is measured by final degree class, and rather higher with freshman performance. Approximately similar results have been found, *mutatis mutandis,* in Scotland and Northern Ireland (Sutherland, 1948; Gould and McComisky, 1958; Petch, 1961).

Little use has been made of objective tests in university selection, partly because of conservatism, partly because of skepticism about the relation between existing tests and creative, independent thinking. Warburton quotes F. C. Bartlett, a former professor of psychology at Cambridge, as being particularly skeptical in this respect. The general situation, however, is one of rapid transition in attitude to selection, corresponding to a rather frantic and belated expansion. The viewpoint of many university selectors is probably similar to that of Dale (1954), who writes:

> When we approach the question of selection the matter becomes more complex, . . . The causes of the complexity are many and varied. Not the least of these is the kaleidoscopic change which has taken place in British education in the last few years. The large increase in the numbers clamouring for admission, the revolutionary changes in the examination system, the sudden widening of scholarship provision, are each quite violent in their impact upon the problem of selection. When to these ingredients are added serious inequalities of standard between examination boards, marked anomalies in the minimum standard fixed by various local authorities for the award of scholarships, known unreliability of marking especially in literary subjects at both Advanced Certificate and University levels, suspected unreliability of performance in mathematical subjects, and the temerity with which the interview may be used by those who are unaware of its dangers, the resultant syllabub is indeed dark and turbid. Nor is its darkness relieved in the slightest by the addition of what is after all its chief constituent. Human nature is an element elusive and volatile, in behaviour unpredictable. Ability, both general and special, can be measured, but the emotions which control the use of ability are in no wise so stable or measurable. Nor can the selectors guarantee good health to the candidate, his parents and siblings, persuade his sweet-heart to remain true, or provide a happy atmosphere in the home—the lack of any of which may cause forecasts to go awry. Even the genius of a Shaw may remain unmotivated, the tenacity and talent of a Winston S. Churchill lack a sufficient objective; and lesser mortals falter likewise. . . .

However, what little evidence is available suggests that tests of ability by themselves are not very effective in predicting student grades in British universities (Himmelweit, 1949; Warburton, 1952), partly, no doubt, because of the highly selected nature of the population. Opinion in Britain appears to be moving more in the direction of a compromise between complete reliance on examination results and commitment to objective tests as an instrument of student selection. Skepticism and opposition to the latter are still powerful, but educators are also becoming more conscious of the unfavorable "backwash" effect in terms of overspecialization produced by exclusive reliance on "A" level GCE results. Considerable interest has been shown in recent years in the general paper (Oliver, 1955), which has now been adopted by the joint examination board of five Northern universities as a GCE "subject." This paper incorporates tests of abilities, and is to a large degree objectively scored, but it also includes essay-type questions designed to assess general knowledge and the power of independent, creative thinking. The paper has been standardized so as not to favor arts candidates at the expense of scientists, and there is some evidence that it is an effective instrument in predicting achievement at British universities.

Since the first draft of this section was written, very rapid changes and advances have taken place in Britain. The publication of the Robbins Committee report greatly stimulated the study of higher education, several research units and research posts have been established for this purpose, and there is an active and productive Society for Research in Higher Education. Similarly, the ten or a dozen examination boards that administer the GCE have now mostly established their own research units, which are in some cases busily concerned with developing objectively marked tests and examinations for possible use as alternatives to or supplements of traditional types of paper.

In the more experimental atmosphere of American education, the problem is probably open to a wider range of social solutions, and this has implications for the design of test installations. For example, it is true that traditional, crystallized ability, g_c, intelligence tests correlate more highly, by the university ages, with further attainment, and that scholastic attainment tests predict later university achievement even better. This conclusion in Britain, however, is based on the persistence of a very arbitrary and unquestioned pedagogic tradition of what constitutes "culture." In the American university, intellectual exercise may range from Greek to computer science, from farm tractor design to modern poetry, and from geography to the logistics of department stores. The strictly scholastic judgmental skills which, because of the form of the high school curriculum, appear as a "general ability," located factor analytically as g_c, can scarcely hope to show transference over so wide a field. The contamination of the g_f in the traditional intelligence test with a substantial variance from such skills, therefore, ceases to be an asset and one would clearly expect that culture-fair intelligence tests, more saturated in g_f, would yield predictive correlations both higher and less biased systematically than would result from the "intelligence" tests now prevalent.

One does not, however, have to step outside the walls of Oxbridge in order to appreciate this truth. Even within predominantly classical curriculum institutions, there is, as Dale says, "skepticism about (the) relation between existing tests and creative, independent thinking." Although, as is stressed in the chapter on creativity, the fluid general ability measure does not itself contain the whole productive machinery of imagination, it at least does not contain the *obstacles* to imagination present in the habits of crystallized intelligence. Furthermore, it must not be forgotten that selection for the university should not be based on success *at* the university, but *after* it, and as yet we have no evidence that the correlation of the latter is satisfactory with traditional intelligence tests and unsatisfactory with culture-fair tests. (We *do* have evidence, from preliminary comparisons of the two tests in the high ability level members of the *Mensa Society*, that among adults, in middle life, the agreement of the two tests is only moderate.) In the last resort, however, the argument for using measures of fluid instead of crystallized general ability —even if the achievement to be predicted lies in the narrow scholastic grooves in which the latter gives a closer immediate prediction—is that tests are used for *analysis,* and for *understanding* how achievement is reached. The objection to a patent medicine or "the mixture as before" is not that it is ineffective—it is often most potent—but that the practitioner cannot regulate the components to see how each operates. So here, it is important to know how much of the prediction is due to fluid intelligence, how much to existing scholastic attainment, how much to the persistence of good study habits, and so on to the personality and motivation components studied in Chapters 4, 5, and 10 below.

Let us face the fact that the ripe experience and educational research evidence which we have been able to quote in this chapter are necessarily based —as happens with sad frequency in modern life—on already partly obsolete instruments. Educators and liberal intellectuals are even more prone than the military figures at whom they smile, to plan today's campaigns with yesterday's weapons. No one knows just what the relative powers and points of maximum effectiveness of fluid and crystallized intelligence tests are, or what the primary abilities, when more fully explored and properly measured, can help us to understand in this and that specialized educational or occupational achievement. The results of a first skirmish of new measures with old educational problems show that culture-fair test correlations center on 0.45 with (same year) school achievement, whereas traditional crystallized ability tests center on 0.60.

On the other hand, the culture-fair test: (a) predicts achievement in Chinese as well as achievement in English, (b) correlates closer to 0.2 with social status of the child (a probably more true value) than nearer to 0.4, as with a traditional test, (c) has higher saturation with the pure general ability factor—.79 as against .56—in the recent analysis by McArthur.

The applied research now urgently needed should spring from conceptions more recent and more precise (though still not final) than those which gave the harvest on which we have had to report. Those conceptions are of two general intelligence factors, plus certain other broad factors which Horn (1965) has revealed as vizualization, speed, and fluency, and which, though widespread in action in the cognitive field, are *not* appropriately called intelligence. These five or so "general" (better "broad," since *no* factor is general) factors are derived from some 15 primary abilities.

These inquiries can probably be extended in number from adding Guilford's creativity tests, when the correlations among the latter have been re-examined to recognize the natural oblique factor meanings, in place of the orthogonal, subjective abstractions which have so far been made out of them. Granted that there are some twenty or more primary abilities, the psychologist can either predictively use the measures of them as they stand or take out the broad factors—at least the fluid and crystallized intelligence factors—and use the latter plus the specifics which remain over, separately measured, in his predictive scheme. The latter seems likely to us to be the system most congenial to the future work of psychologists, concerned as it will be with wider regions of educational, occupational, and clinical counselling than is the more pedestrian practice of today. With on-line harnessing of computers to all kinds of local decisions, there will be no difficulty in handling this more comprehensive and realistic coverage of the student's abilities.

SUMMARY *of Chapter Three*

1. Although we have proposed a distinction between, and a separate measurement of, fluid and crystallized general intelligence, most of the available studies of the relation between abilities and achievement are based on tests that confound these two aspects of intelligence. But for this very reason, traditional measures of ability will tend to correlate at least as highly as "culture-free" tests with most concrete measures of achievement.

2. Numerous studies are available of the predictability of achievement both by (a) primary mental abilities (correlated, relatively narrow, factors); and (b) tests of general intelligence. Some of the more important studies of these two types are discussed and evaluated.

3. Of the primary mental abilities, the factors, such as V (verbal meaning), that are the better predictors of school achievement generally tend to predict almost all forms of achievement better. Those which are less predictive, such as W (word fluency), are again relatively ineffective against almost all criteria.

4. Experience from studies of selection for secondary schools in Britain strongly suggests that a test of general intelligence, given at age eleven, is more effective in predicting school attainment than tests in English or arithmetic.

5. Predicting success in university courses raises a new set of problems. There is good evidence that ability at this stage is beginning to become less important in relation to attainment.

Chapter Four

MEASURING THE MAIN DIMENSIONS
OF PERSONALITY

Section 1 **Three Approaches to the Study of Human Personality**

The study of human personality is at present in an interesting stage of transition. There are three major approaches that have helped in our understanding of personality. The first comprises the literary insights of imaginative writers, who had built up a large, but unsystematized, body of intuitive knowledge before psychology appeared as a science in the late nineteenth century. This approach has more recently been absorbed into the psychology of personality and is represented by such distinguished psychologists as Gordon Allport and Gardner Murphy in America, and L. Klages in Germany. The second approach, which began around 1880, is a purely experimental attack, originating particularly in the laboratories of Wundt in Germany, and of J. McK. Cattell in America. Third, the clinical approach, with a long history in medicine, made great strides in the late nineteenth century in the work of Kraepelin and of Bleuler and, a little later, in that of Freud, Adler, Jung, and their followers. This clinical approach, which attained its finest flowering in the work of Freud, has been scientific in intent and values, but much less so in method, depending almost entirely on unaided observation, without the benefits of controlled experiment or statistical analysis.

As Meehl (1954) has convincingly shown, the diagnoses of psychiatrists are considerably more prone to error, as judged by the overwhelming majority of comparative studies, than even a mechanical and actuarial type of prediction from test scores and relatively objective measures. Similarly, no convincing reply has been offered by clinical psychologists or psychiatrists to Eysenck's provocative criticism that the recovery rate of neurotics is virtually constant whether they are treated by commonly accepted therapeutic methods or go untreated.

This is not to say, however, that clinical theories and clinically based concepts are worthless. There is considerable experimental and statistical evidence that they frequently result from remarkable insight and correspond to scientifically demonstrated psychological processes. Our point here is that it is necessary to distinguish insight from fantasy by rigorous empirical methods.

For some decades, the experimental attack made relatively little progress, and to this day, as far as the man in the street is concerned, the psychology of personality is thought of as based mainly upon psychoanalysis. In the last twenty years, however, the experimental approach has made very solid progress and is now in process of superseding, both in theory and in practice, the systems that arise from psychoanalysis and similar approaches. It is able to do this because a branch of research that may best be designated multivariate experimental psychology has broken away from the traditional experimental psychology. The failure of the latter to make any progress in the field of personality comparable with the progress of clinical studies in the early part of the twentieth century lay mainly in its simple experimental method, borrowed from the physical sciences. The researcher using this method looks at two variables at a time, comparing a change in one with certain induced changes in the other; the method presupposes that the experimenter can control in a manipulative sense the data with which he is dealing. Human nature, for better or worse, is by no means easy to manipulate in any important respect, so that the psychologists who adopted this approach found themselves increasingly thrown back upon investigations of emotionally unimportant matters, such as those concerned with perception and with the special senses. They also tended to retreat into the study of animals, and especially of rats, because it is possible to subject rats to a variety of experimental situations that may not be imposed upon human beings.

What was needed was a method that could, while still using exact methods of measurement and computation, deal with whole patterns of behavior, instead of with single variables. For, in studying personality, single reactions rarely interest us; we look for total response patterns, such as those we call traits and types of temperament, and, second, for types of growth and change. Fortunately, there also existed in experimental psychology a tradition, derived largely from Galton and Spearman, that simultaneously investigated many variables in patterns, especially by the methods of correlation and of factor analysis. These methods have long been used in the study of abilities, and, as we have seen in the preceding chapters, factor analyses have indicated the existence of eight to ten primary abilities, all interrelating and combining to form two second-order factors of general ability.

Around 1930 it occurred to a number of investigators, notably to Burt and R. B. Cattell in Britain, and to Guilford in America, to investigate personality by similar methods, in order to see whether the unitary patterns that the clinician talked about could be demonstrated by measurement and calculation. The results came in relatively slowly in the first decade; but between 1940 and 1960, a number of systematic interlocking studies developed, notably by Cattell and his associates in America, and by Eysenck and his associates in London. The latter concentrated somewhat more on the needs of clinical psychologists, choosing their variables for study with particular relation to neurotic and psychotic phenomena. The former worked with the notion of deliberately sampling the total behavior of human beings, developing for this purpose the concept of the personality sphere. Although research of this kind in the personality field started twenty years later than similar research into abilities, it is probably true that a larger number of well-established and replicated factors of personality have been discovered than of abilities.

Section 2 Some Means of Isolating the Principal Personality Factors

The main problem in the study of human personality is to measure the factors, influences, and sources of variation that are most significant. By this, we mean common traits occurring in the normal personality in our culture, which are important for developmental reasons, and which can be understood in terms of general psychological theory. If one simply chooses any psychological quality, as defined from an armchair, it is quite unlikely to possess these properties. The strategy of research in this area has therefore been to sample the total personality sphere and thus gradually to distill, so to speak, from an enormous variety of variables the major dimensions of personality that crop up repeatedly in different researches and situations. Factor analysis, like any other scientific method, can only find out the relationships between those variables that it is given to examine, and the researcher can only find the important structures when a sufficiently broad range of material has been analyzed. Thus we have adopted the concept of the total personality sphere, which has been derived in the last resort from the dictionary, where some 3,000 to 4,000 terms exist describing specific kinds of personality and of corresponding behavior. A gradual distillation of these terms, and the successive correlation and factor analysis of the still numerous remaining specific traits, rated upon normal individuals, have resulted in the location of some twelve to twenty distinct dimensions of source traits.

In this work the experimental observations have been of three kinds:

1. Observation, by actual records, such as time sampling counts, or behavior ratings, of personality manifestations in everyday life. These might consist, for example, of occupational performances or automobile accidents. These we call *L-data* or Life Record Data.

2. Self-evaluative or questionnaire data, in which the individual introspects and replies as in a consulting room. Such self-report we call *Q-data*.

3. Objective test data, or *T-data,* in which the person is asked to respond in some miniature situation, and his actual behavior, but not what he says about himself, is measured.

Some of the dimensions discovered in these three media turn out to be those that had already been recognized by the clinician in similar situations. Thus what Cattell has called Factor A, of which a full account is given in Section 3 of this chapter, corresponds to the broad temperamental dimension between schizothymia at one pole and cyclothymia at the other as described by Kretschmer, which has some resemblance to the distinction between manic-depressive psychosis and schizophrenia in the psychotic sphere. Other dimensions to be described include one that ranges between ego strength and ego weakness; the dimension ranging from superego strength to superego weakness; the general intelligence dimension; the dimension of surgency versus desurgency, which is an important component in extraversion; and so on. A list of these primary factors is contained in Table VI.

TABLE **VI**

List of Personality Traits measured by the 16 PF test

Trait designation by letter	TITLE OF TRAIT
A	Affectothymia versus Sizothymia
B	General Intelligence versus Mental Defect
C	Emotional Stability or Ego Strength versus Dissatisfied Emotionality
E	Dominance or Ascendance versus Submission
F	Surgency versus Desurgency ("Enthusiasm" versus "Melancholy")
G	Superego Strength versus Lack of Internal Standards
H	("Adventurous" versus "Timid"). Technical name: Parmia versus Threctia
I	Protected Emotional Sensitivity versus Tough Maturity. Technical name: Permsia versus Harria
L	Protension versus Alaxia ("Suspecting" versus "Accepting")
M	Autia (Autistic Temperament) versus Practical Concernedness
N	Sophistication versus Rough Simplicity (or "Shrewdness" versus "Naiveté")
O	Guilt-Proneness versus Confident Adequacy ("Insecure" versus "Confident")
Q_1	Radicalism versus Conservatism
Q_2	Self-Sufficiency versus Lack of Resolution
Q_3	Strong Self-Sentiment versus Weak Self-Sentiment
Q_4	High Ergic Tension versus Low Ergic Tension

In addition to this confirmation and clarification of patterns already hypothesized by clinical psychology, the factor-analytic approach has also discovered
new unitary traits that had not previously been recognized, such as one that
has been named the I-Factor, or Premsia-Harria, and is described briefly in
Table VI. This can roughly be described as a factor of tender-mindedness
versus tough-mindedness, and its closest anticipation in earlier theory can
be found in the writings of William James. Another factor that gives a new
slant to earlier theory is the O-Factor, which is clearly interpretable as
proneness to guilt, and which appears to be different from the factor of
superego strength. The discovery of two such separate factors throws new
light on the psychoanalytic concepts of guilt and superego action. It must
be stressed at this point, however, that in general we see the two poles of
each personality dimension as ethically neutral, and it would be a superficial judgment that would assign a "good" and a "bad" direction to each
factor.

Encouraged by this evidence of consistent structure in the rating or L-data
field, psychologists proceeded next to factor-analyze questionnaire responses.
Here they deliberately chose a wider array of items than had been used in
questionnaires before 1945. Cattell and Saunders first performed this factorization of what might be called the personality sphere seen as a mental
interior—that is to say in questionnaire, introspective responses—and found
some twenty dimensions. The sixteen of these twenty that recurred most consistently and that made the largest contribution to variation in behavior, were
included in the Sixteen Personality Factor Questionnaire (16 PF), as shown
in Table VI. The dimensions found are almost identical in meaning with
those found in ratings. The predictive value of these factors measured by the
16 PF test has been shown in a variety of situations, such as occupational
differences and requirements, the prediction of leadership in small groups,
the identification of neurotic individuals, the ascertainment of differences in
profile between different psychoneurotic syndromes, the recognition of delinquent and psychopathic tendencies, and many others.

Some evidence indicates that about five or six further major personality
factors exist in the questionnaire field over and above those measured by the
16 PF questionnaire. Also, a great deal of work remains to be done on determining more precisely the nature and correlates of the sixteen factors measured. Meanwhile, however, they seem to provide much of the prediction
needed in practical situations.

The Sixteen Personality Factor Questionnaire has been translated into
French, Italian, German, Spanish, Portugese, Polish, Hindi, Swedish, and
Japanese. Independent factor analyses have been carried out in three countries, showing that essentially the same factors exist in these cultures as in
the American and British cultures; and the same seems to be tolerably certain
for Australia and some other countries in which the tests have been used.

Certain minor modifications have been found, however; for example, the factor of superego strength takes on rather more authoritarian and external characteristics in the Italian culture than in the American, and in one or two countries the dominance factor, E, seems to vary according to the different ways in which dominance is acceptable. The fact that these dimensions reappear in cultures as remote from each other as those of the United States and Japan does seem to suggest, however, that we are dealing with rather basic dimensions of personality, practically characteristic of human nature wherever it appears. This is not to deny that certain dimensions, at present not in the questionnaires, may be found that will be unique to particular cultures, but these are more likely to appear in the field of roles than in that of basic personality factors.

Section 3 A Typical Personality Factor

Within the scope of this chapter, we can only hope to arouse the reader's interest in this whole fascinating and very rapidly developing field of research and cannot describe all the primary personality factors in detail. But we should like to avoid the impression that little is known about the nature and correlates of these factors. We therefore give, in the next few paragraphs —as an example of the state of knowledge and depth of research findings— an abridged account of the nature and role of one factor. This is Factor A of the 16 PF and HSPQ tests, named Affectothymia-versus-sizothymia, and already briefly described earlier in this chapter. For a fuller discussion of this factor, see Cattell (1957).

The Mean Factor Pattern

A+ *Positively loaded*	A— *Negatively loaded*
Easygoing	vs. Obstructive, cantankerous
Adaptable (in habits)	vs. Inflexible, "rigid"
Warmhearted, attentive to people	vs. Cool, indifferent
Frank, placid	vs. Close-mouthed, secretive, anxious
Emotional, expressive	vs. Reserved
Trustful, credulous	vs. Suspicious, "canny"
Impulsive, generous	vs. Close, cautious
Cooperative, self-effacing	vs. Hostile, egotistical
Subject to personal emotional appeals	vs. Impersonal
Humorous	vs. Dry impassive

Other Lesser Indicated Variables

Other variables on the lower or middle range of significance in certain studies—always listed here consistently in relation to the left-hand, cyclothymic pole, as positive—are: submissive (Bryant), emotionally mature (vs. demanding, impatient), mild, emotionally stable, well-adjusted sexually, skilled in appropriateness of emotional expression, has insight into himself, expresses marked overt interest in the opposite sex (Kelly), friendly, enthusiastic, affectionate, sympathetic, soft-hearted, tends to enjoy "good things of life," tactful, calm, not attention-getting, placid (vs. worrying, anxious, emotional), responsible (vs. frivolous), persevering (vs. fickle), trustworthy in large issues, popular, kind on principle, showing "evenness of temper back of drive."

Variables found expressing the negative (right) side are: prone to jealousy, grasping, stubborn, more intellectual and interested in ideas, tenacious (but, in children "flitting from task to task"), seclusive, not popular, possibly has homosexual tendency, destructive, pouting and sulking (infants), of uncertain conscience, given to attacking others, and domineering. In connection with the last, it should be pointed out that some studies have found difficulty in separating this factor from the dominance factor and that there is evidence of a second-order factor connecting them. Physiological associations of large P.G.R. deflection [change in psycho-galvanic reflex] and good recovery, for sizothymes, are indicated by Koch.

Associated Criterion Variables

There is evidence of substantial hereditary determination of this factor, i.e., it is a temperamental tendency. The kind of occupational performance associated with it is overwhelmingly that of success in "dealing with people" for cyclothymes, and "dealing with things or ideas" for schizothymes. In the area of clinical criteria, the distinction is equally clear and still more important, for in that area the commonly reported association is proneness to manic-depressive disorders for cyclothymes and proneness to schizophrenic breakdown for A— individuals.

The tendency to such occupational choices as "manager" or "salesman" in the A+ person and "forester" or "physicist" in the A— has to be inferred from correlations of L-data Factor A with Q-data Factor A. But there is also direct evidence, notably in Kelly and Fiske, of substantial correlations of A+ with nine criterion evaluations, including "good in individual psychotherapy," "good professional interpersonal relations," "good at group therapy," "well placed in clinical psychology," "good as an administrator," "good as a supervisor"; and some personal relations also had a correlation of 0.37 with A, though its larger correlations was with G below. On the other hand, as might be expected, success with abstraction (intelligence being equal) is greater for schizothymes, and correlations about 0.3 and 0.4 have been obtained between A— rating score and academic examination success (Bryant). Academics generally, and outstanding researchers in particular, are significantly more schizothyme than the general population.

Clinical Semi-Interpretive Observations

Both Jung and Kretschmer have made sensitive clinical analyses resulting in description of a normal continuum very like the present one, though we have shown that the former was describing a composite cluster rather than a source trait. On the other hand, Kretschmer's detailed descriptions, despite clinical rather than statistical means, describe the present pattern with great fidelity.

Some psychologists have criticized our retention of the term "cyclothymia-schizothymia" for this major factor, and have suggested such terms as "socially adjusted" versus "socially hostile." No label, of course, would go uncriticized. However, it should be realized that we initially adopted the term "cyclothymia-schizothymia" from a belief in the desirability of historical continuity and research interaction whenever the newer and the older methods can sincerely be brought together. Here the new method produces, with amazing correctness of detail and emphasis, the pattern described by many clinicians, and perhaps with greatest clinical art by Kretschmer. In fact, no research should proceed further without trying to link whatever can be contributed now from both of these methods.

Modification of Pattern in Special Groups

As one might expect, this pattern is efficacious enough to show itself in groups of different age, sex, and degree of normality. There is no discernible, significant difference in the pattern for men and women. On the other hand, there are indications—resting, unfortunately, only on three adequate studies—that the pattern is somewhat different and less emphatic in children before adolescence. (Does adolescence, as suggested by the high incidence of schizophrenia, emphasize, extend, and bring out new features in this dimension?) The study on eleven-year-old children gave a distinct emphasis on jealousy and selfishness in the A— pattern; but the seven-year-old pattern in Coan's studies, respectively with parent ratings and teacher ratings, while still giving more emphasis on jealousy than does the adult pattern, was more true to type, as follows (combined parent and teacher items):

Expressive, frank	vs.	Secretive, reserved
Cheerful in disposition	vs.	Solemn, serious
Rarely complains	vs.	Hard to satisfy
Free of jealousy	vs.	Jealous of other children
Adaptable	vs.	Rigid sulks and pouts
Imaginative	vs.	Practical and concrete
Fewer temper tantrums	vs.	Frequent tantrums
Cries less than average	vs.	Cries a lot
Generally does what adults ask	vs.	Resists adult requests and commands

Both the multiple-variance analysis results recently obtained on normals, and such studies as those of Kretschmer and Kallman on abnormals, leave little doubt that there is a substantial hereditary component in this factor.

On the other hand, there have been many naive, value-confused interpretations of A+ as "adjustment" and A— as "social maladjustment." So frequent a mode of interpretation in the general literature calls for some comment here. It is true that a purely environmental explanation in terms of "adjustment" is initially possible, insofar as psychological meaning is concerned, though only a superficial observer would want to call it simply "adjustment." Actually, most of the traits of A— would fit the concept of "general frustration level," for the combination of hostility with withdrawal completes the possibilities of reactions to generally frustrating situations. Yet these may arise less from actual frustration than from a tenacity of temperament which experiences more setbacks to its higher demands.

Section 4   **Personality Factors in Children**

The next question that presents itself is one that is especially relevant to the main topic of this book. "Do the same personality dimensions appear both in children and in adults?" Beloff, Coan, Porter, Howarth, and a number of other investigators have continued the factor analyses at the twelve-year-old level, at the eight-year-old level, and at the four- and five-year-old levels. From the studies made in the range from twelve through sixteen years of age, a questionnaire has emerged that has been called the High School Personality Questionnaire, or HSPQ. Theorists have, in general, favored the view that personality structure might be expected to be simpler with younger children, and the probability that fewer personality factors would be evident. This hardly seems to be true, for some fourteen to fifteen factors have been found at the high-school level and almost the same number in the younger age groups. For example, in addition to the Affectothymia-Sizothymia, general intelligence, ego strength, and superego strength factors mentioned above in the adult 16 PF structure, we find the dominance factor, E; the surgency-desurgency factor, F; the parmia-threctia factor, H; the premsia-harria factor, I; and two or three others present in the HSPQ range, just as they are in the 16 PF. Factors L, M, and N, which are fairly important with adults, seem to be of relatively small importance in differentiating children, as also does the Factor Q_1 of radicalism-conservatism.

On the other hand, to compensate partially for the disappearance of these four dimensions of the 16 PF, there appear in the childhood range two new factors, namely, D, excitability, and J, a factor apparently connected with conflict and with the development of the superego, which contributes substantially to the variance of behavior in children. The Excitability factor, D, is not entirely absent from adults, but it does not seem so important in differentiating their behavior as it does with children. Thus, in a sense these differences are relative, in that it becomes desirable in the interest of economy to drop a certain factor at a certain age when it begins to contribute too little to the total behavior, though in fact these same factors are probably present in some small degree at most ages.

Further exploration of the age range from eight through twelve, from six through eight years, and of younger children still does show a successive tendency for factors to drop out at the earlier ages.

Other questionnaires constructed on the same principle as the HSPQ are available for these age ranges. Exploration in the four-to-five-year range is incomplete, however, and no questionnaire has been made available, except to research groups, and then only on some six or seven factors. The main difficulty in working with questionnaire measures of personality with younger children is that one seems to need more items per factor in order to get the same degree of reliability as with adults, because children appear to be less reliable in their responses. Unfortunately, this need for more items per factor clashes with the need to cut down the length of the total questionnaire with children, in order to get proper attention and freedom from fatigue. Of course, in the Early School Personality Questionnaire (six-eight years) and the Pre-School Personality Questionnaire (four-five years) the questions are asked by the teacher or psychologist. The child checks a picture list in the first test, and the examiner himself checks off on the list of the preschool child. But even so, it seems that one should arrange for several more sessions and shorter sessions in personality testing with a child than is necessary with adults. Consequently, far more research has actually been done with questionnaires for adults, which can be administered conveniently in about an hour, than with those for young children, where one must plan for a series of sessions.

Two other interesting and important topics are allied to this question of the developing factor structure at different ages. First, how do measurements on the separate factors develop or wane with increasing age? Second, what are the relative contributions of heredity and environment to the various personality factors? These questions are fully dealt with by Cattell (1957). Suffice it say here that some extensive studies of heredity on personality factors have already been made, and it is clear, for example, that the A and H factors, which enter into extraversion, are strongly determined by hereditary influences, whereas F and certain other factors that also enter into the extraversion concept are strongly determined by environment. Accordingly, one might expect school and social situation to affect some components in extraversion much more than others, and it is important to know what these components are. One can, in fact, reasonably turn to physiological, temperamental theories to account for those dimensions such as A, H, and O that have a heavy hereditary component, and to explanation in terms of learning theory to account for those such as F, J, and Q_3 that appear to be far more environmentally determined. It is to be hoped that the next decade will see a rapid growth of scientific information in this respect. Already we have quite good information about the average age curves on various factors; for example, that level of surgency drops steadily after the adolescent period, and that anxiety, notably in Q_4 or ergic tension, reaches a maximum in the adolescent period. When this information is more fully organized and supplemented, it will enable our predictions from personality tests to be much more than statistical predictions, for they will be informed by our knowledge of the way in which particular factors will normally be expected to develop with time and social situation.

Section 5   Objective Tests of Personality

The questionnaire approach has been valuable and is fairly reliable in the research situation with cooperative subjects. It must be obvious to anyone, however, that any questionnaire is liable to distortion, either from dishonesty or from lack of self-insight in the respondent, particularly when it is employed in an important situation where motivational distortion might be expected. The motivational distortion can sometimes be handled by special scales, as in Form C of the 16 PF, where one tries to discover how much distortion is being attempted, and to allow for it. But a much better way is to seek out questions that make it difficult for the subject to see how his answer is going to be evaluated. Some of the scales that have been developed in the Laboratory of Personality and Group Analysis, headed by R. B. Cattell, at Champaign, Illinois, have aimed at this kind of precaution. Nevertheless, because it has always seemed desirable to have a second string available, a great deal of research has been done on what are called objective personality tests.

By an objective personality test we mean a miniature situation, possibly involving laboratory apparatus, in which the subject cannot identify the particular aspects of behavior on which he is being assessed, or, if he can discern them, he cannot effectively influence the score. Among the older examples of tests of this kind are the well-known Rorschach inkblot test, the Downey "will-temperament" test, the Szondi test (in which photographs of diagnosed patients are presented to the respondent), the rigidity measures of Cattell and Stevenson, and the fluency measures of Spearman. A very large production of tests of this kind has gone on over the last fifteen years and, as a recent compendium (Cattell and Warburton, 1967) shows, there are now some 300 such tests, yielding over 600 performance variables. Some, which involve apparatus, have to be given in an individual test situation, but it has been possible to make the majority into group tests, which may sometimes require projectors and sound systems but which are often performed simply with pencil and paper. However, one must distinguish between the pencil and paper test that is simply a questionnaire, and the pencil and paper test that involves miniature situations of judgment, stress, memory, conflict, and so forth.

As with the questionnaires, factor analyses of these objective tests have been made after their administration to representative samples of normal people at different age levels, and it has been found that essentially the same personality factors persist through cross-sections of the population at different ages. Work of this kind has been carried out, for example, by Coan, Howarth, Damarin, and Gruen on children aged eleven, eight, and five years. Some twenty different factors are now known, and batteries for measuring them, both at adult and child levels, called the adult Objective-Analytic (O-A) battery and the children's O-A battery, have been made available. In order to avoid a prematurely definitive interpretation of these factors, they have been labeled U.I. 16 through U.I. 35. The meanings of many of these factors are, however, fairly clear. For example, U.I. 17 is a factor of general inhibition or timidity; that labeled U.I. 20 is similar to the superego concept; that labeled U.I. 24 is undoubtedly what we mean by general anxiety; and that labeled U.I. 23 is a central factor in neuroticism and apparently the same as Eysenck's "neuroticism" factor. The predictive value of these factors in various fields has also become clear, even though their full nature is not completely understood. For example, Cattell and Scheier (1961) have shown that six of these factors significantly distinguish neurotics from normals at the $P < .01$ level of probability and that a combination of measures on these factors will effectively separate a group of neurotics from a group of normals. There have also been nature-nurture studies on these factors by Blewett, Beloff, Stice, Kristy, and Cattell, as well as by Eysenck and Prell; and it is clear that some of them have a high hereditary and others a high environmental determination. What is not so clear as yet is the mode of translation from these objective test factors to those found in questionnaires, and the degree of correspondence between the two sets of dimensions. In some situations, it is evident that the questionnaire is, as it were, a more finely grained instrument and that it yields a set of related factors where the objective, analytic approach gives a single factor. For example, what comes out as a second-order factor of anxiety from questionnaire data emerges at the first-order level from the objective tests as U.I. 24, which is also a factor of general anxiety. One can thus choose to measure anxiety in one medium or the other according to the degree of cooperation of the subject, and other circumstances. But with some other factors, the correspondence between questionnaire factors and objective test factors is still a matter for researchers to work upon and debate.

In summary, therefore, one can obtain measurements on the main personality dimensions through any one of three media: first, through what we have called L-data, which are principally derived from individuals rating each other; second, from questionnaires that yield what we have called Q-data; and third, by means of controlled miniature situations, with tests of performance and behavior that we call the realm of T-data or of objective personality measurement. Each has its advantages and its disadvantages, but because rating is seriously distorted according to the character of the rater and his official relation to the ratee, the psychologist will generally be well advised to obtain his estimates of personality either through Q-data, as with the 16 PF, or through T-data, as with the O-A battery.

Our own researches therefore hinge partly on questionnaire measures of personality dimensions, and partly on objective test measures, though the former were used exclusively in the surveys to be reported in this book and will therefore play a much larger role in our conclusions. They are likely to be applied more often in schools than are the objective tests, which require specialized psychological skills for adequate administration.

Section 6 The Practical Value of Factored Personality Tests

Granted that we are dealing with major dimensions of personality, the question now arises of their relation to actual performance and behavioral response. In other words, having taken the individual to pieces by analytical methods, and having obtained his measurements on the main factors, how do we now put him together again in terms of the interaction of these traits? The simplest way to put the person together again is by adding his various traits in the proportion to which they normally contribute to success, or magnitude of response, in a given situation. As a hypothetical example, it is conceivable that success at tennis is partly determined by general intelligence, partly by emotional stability, and partly by a trait of general manual dexterity. We could therefore write an estimation or specification equation somewhat as follows:

$$T = .2g + .5M + .1C + .1G + .1F - .1Q_4$$

where T = tennis ability, g = general intelligence, M = manual dexterity, and C, G, etc. refer to the primary personality factors as listed in Table VI.

This particular equation supposes that intelligence is positively related to performance in tennis, but not nearly so much as is manual dexterity. It further supposes that other personality dimensions play relatively little role, so that the four additional factors listed above receive weights of only 0.1.

The values for these weights are of course found from the factor analysis itself, and by correlating measures of the separate factors with the criterion. It has been almost universally found that this simple model, in which the factors act additively to produce certain effects, works out pretty close to the best estimates, though of course it must be recognized that in some cases the relations might not be linear and that some interaction might take place between the factors. Until evidence of such interaction is demonstrated, however, we are justified in proceeding with the simplest kind of estimate, especially because it will facilitate calculations made by teachers and other users of the available measures.

Commonly, as indicated above, one would determine the correlations of the personality factor with a criterion one wished to predict by experimental means. Thus, for a particular sample of children, one would correlate the score on the personality factors with the score on the criterion, which latter might be achievement, leadership, delinquency, or neuroticism. Moreover, we know enough about these factors now, and about their relation to many of the criteria, to venture a prediction in many cases without a previous correlation by experimental means. For example, it would seem likely, in the light of research findings, that high G factor, i.e., superego strength, would contribute to better school performance among individuals with the same intelligence, in that they would apply themselves more conscientiously to school work in general. Similarly, in relation to leadership, there is a strong probability, both a priori and as a result of cumulative studies, that individuals of high surgency with all the opportunities for social distinction that this creates, will tend to be selected for leadership positions more frequently than desurgent individuals. Furthermore, our general psychological knowledge of the factors will help prediction, in that we can realize that the shyness shown by low score on the H factor, as distinct from that related to desurgency, is not likely to change much with time and circumstance, because it is largely constitutionally determined. On the other hand, we would expect the high-spiritedness of surgency to follow a typical curve toward greater soberness of behavior through the late adolescent period, because we know the characteristic trend of development for this factor.

Another aspect of personality measurement that perhaps needs a brief comment here is that personality can be assessed not only through the first-order factors, about which we have so far spoken, but also through what are called second-order factors, which are broader influences pervading a certain group of first-order factors, in just the same way as that in which we have described these two types of factors in discussing abilities. The main second-order personality factors that have been clearly and repeatedly demonstrated are the factors of extraversion-introversion and of anxiety-adjustment. Extraversion is a second-order factor that shows itself by a pattern of positive loadings on A, Affectothymia; F, surgency; H, parmia; as well as in negative loadings on L, protension; Q_2 self-sufficiency. Anxiety shows itself on loadings of C—, ego weakness; L, protension; O, guilt-proneness; Q_3 —, low self-sentiment strength; and Q_4, ergic-tension level. For certain purposes, one may want to ascertain the level of a child on the second-order factors, though a certain amount of precision is always lost by switching from first-order to second-order factors. Consequently, it is best to operate in the first-order realm, with the primary factors on the 16 PF or HSPQ, and to use the second-order factors only for special purposes.

A word of caution is also necessary in the interpretation of correlations and factor loadings. In all work concerned with the relation of personality factors to criteria, one must not forget that it is possible for a correlation to indicate causal action in either of the two possible directions. Thus, if one should find that people of poor academic performance are desurgent, the question would next have to be raised whether desurgency is a cause of low academic performance, or whether the disappointment and frustration occasioned by low academic performance is the cause of the person's desurgency. Questions of this kind can only be answered by specific experiments, in which one ascertains, through a time sequence, which comes first. So far, extremely little has been done in that direction, and studies throwing further light on the direction of causality, rather than on the mere fact of correlation, are urgently needed.

Section 7 **The Usefulness of Personality Measures to the Teacher**

Much of the discussion in this and the preceding chapters has been, in effect, an introduction to a comprehensive theory of individual differences in human functioning. The more practical applications will receive attention in the second half of this book. But before proceeding to administer even severer doses of theory in Chapters 5 through 7, let us sketch briefly a few of the practical and important uses to the teacher of an adequate measuring instrument for children's personality.

First, it can be of inestimable value to identify and screen out those children who, through home background or temperamental endowment, carry a heavier burden of anxiety than their fellow pupils, or who need help with emotional conflicts. Similarly, it is a perennial problem for teachers to be sure which are the racehorses and which the cart horses among their children— which need a very delicate controlling hand, and which will benefit from being driven fairly hard. These and countless other questions of differences in individual temperament are always with us, and generally have to be dealt with by intelligent sympathy, but often by what is little more than guesswork. We should be the last to claim that the administration of a personality questionnaire is a panacea. Intelligent laymen have rightly scoffed at some of the wilder attempts in this direction (Whyte, 1956). But, at the very lowest, it can give extremely useful pointers, particularly when one studies a profile of scores on the whole range of factors and notes the more outstanding peaks and troughs.

Second, an increasing body of knowledge is developing about the relation of "underachievement" and "overachievement" to temperamental factors. We shall discuss this more fully in Chapter 10, but suffice it to say here that the importance of such factors is not in dispute among educational psychologists. There is still some doubt and controversy about the exact circumstances in which, say, a given degree of anxiety is an asset or a liability in scholastic progress, but the general influences and their direction are becoming clear. These influences are well discussed and summarized by Warburton (1962a; 1962b).

Third, a knowledge of the adolescent's general pattern of personality and motivation can be of great service in all the problems of vocational guidance. Questionnaires and tests have, of course, been used for a long time in this connection, but, only too commonly, they have been highly specific to a job or group of jobs. Thus, unless the candidate did most of the important deciding for himself, they told him only whether he appeared suitable or not for a particular job, not for which out of the enormous range of jobs he was most suitable. Or alternatively, the more general questionnaires of this kind, such as those of Strong or Kuder, have tended to proceed by a blind empiricism, and what success they have achieved has been an actuarial kind without insight into the basic factors of personality. Our recommended approach by means of factored personality measures is much more promising in theory, and a great deal of knowledge has been built up about the types of personality profile that indicate likely success in a particular job. Detailed examples and a survey of present knowledge are provided by Cattell (1957, Chapter 17).

Finally, the teacher can continue research in this field. It is to be hoped that some readers of this account will be thinking of the innumerable questions that we have not touched on, and that at least a few will take the further step of attempting their own research. Although the teacher is usually at a disadvantage, compared with the trained psychologist, in knowledge of research design, experimental precautions, statistical methods, and so forth, he has the great advantage that he knows the children, often has contact with their parents, has seen the processes of development, and can throw a mass of light on all sorts of aspects that elude the statistical psychologist. There is, therefore, a strong case for groups of academic psychologists and teachers to pursue joint research projects. Something of the kind has been attempted in Manchester, England, and quite a wide range of research, principally into the relation of personality factors to school attainment, will be summarized in a book by Warburton, scheduled for publication in 1967 or 1968.

Section 8   **The Relation of Personality Traits to Motivation**

Finally, as a bridge to the next chapter, in which we discuss measures of motivation as distinct from personality traits, it will be useful to clarify our terminology. We have spoken of motivation measurements as something additional to general personality measurements, and although this may appeal to many readers there will be some who will ask, "Why is not motivation also an aspect of personality?" It is true that measurements of motivation are also measurements of personality in a broad sense of the term, but there are advantages in making a psychological distinction and in using "personality dimension" exclusively for those massive traits that are common to all humanity, and which are not concerned with the specific interests that motivate people in a particular culture. When we talk of motivation, we talk of something that is far more likely to be idiosyncratic to the individual or to the culture. As has been shown, the uniqueness of the individual in terms of personality is defined as a unique combination or pattern of measures on traits that are common to everybody in some degree. On the other hand, interests can be highly local in the sense that a child living on a Pacific island may have a strong interest in swimming and a correspondingly strong aversion from sharks, whereas such an interest is meaningless to a child in Indianapolis who has never been outside the boundaries of his home state. This is not to argue that interests and temperament are entirely independent, for we recognize that temperamental traits may often project themselves into interests, and particularly so when all the people concerned have an equal chance to acquire certain interests. The relation between personality and motivation traits is something to which we contribute information in later chapters of this book. Meanwhile, everybody recognizes that, in a general way, personality traits are one thing, and interest traits another, insofar as we often see instances of individuals with quite dissimilar interests, through their historical backgrounds, who, in terms of personality, are highly similar. Therefore, the present chapter has concerned itself with the general and primary dimensions of personality, and specific interest attainments and motivational variations will be discussed in the next and subsequent chapters.

SUMMARY *of Chapter Four*

1. The study of human personality has progressed along three rather separate lines: the literary, the clinical, and the experimental-statistical.

2. Although the educated layman is most familiar with clinical, and particularly with psychoanalytical, theories, the experimental-statistical work has progressed very rapidly in the last twenty years, and it can be claimed that many of the most important personality traits can be isolated and assessed in individuals.

3. Cattell and his associates have carried out extensive analyses aimed at covering the whole personality sphere in normal adults and children. These have been based on three kinds of data, L-data concerned with "real-life" situations, Q-data derived from introspective and questionnaire responses, and T-data from objective tests.

4. Between twenty and forty factors have been found, some corresponding to concepts already formulated by clinicians, some new.

5. One such factor of considerable importance, Factor A, has been described in detail in this chapter, in order to give some idea of the depth of research carried out.

6. Most of the factors found in adults have also been found in children, although some differences are described.

7. The possibility of reliably assessing individuals on basic personality factors is clearly of great importance to teachers and other people working in education. Possible uses are most diverse, but, in particular, the measurement of personality traits should be of considerable value in educational and vocational guidance and in the study of school attainment.

Chapter Five

CONCEPTS AND MEASURES OF
MOTIVATION AND INTEREST

Section 1 **Completing the Personality Picture with Dynamic and
Unique Traits**

Our brief introduction to the study of human personality by the methods
of experiment and factor analysis has left us with three main conclusions
about the structure of personality and its relation to clinical theories:

1. A number of clinical concepts have appeared as measurable factors.

2. At least as many entirely new concepts, mainly of temperamental nature, have also been developed.

3. The new dimensions are just as important as the old, when their predictive power in practical situations is compared. In other words, they receive at least as heavy a weight in the predictive formulas.

Although these results represent a considerable advance in the understanding and measurement of personality, and have numerous possible practical applications, neither the clinician nor the educational psychologist has
until recently made much use of them. This situation is partly due to their
unfamiliarity with scientific methods that have been developed in another
area, but also to a justified feeling that something of great psychological importance has still been left out. Missing from these general personality dimensions is what the educator thinks of as interest, attitude, and motivation,
and the clinician as dynamic psychology.

Although the experimental researcher claims to know what he does know
more reliably and exactly than either the clinician or the speculative theorist,
he does not claim to know what he has not investigated. And the experimenter must agree that until the last decade his understanding of motivational phenomena was very slim. Purely statistical evidence showed him
clearly that persons of exactly the same degree of intelligence, ego strength,
and schizothyme temperament might yet perform in very different ways in

71

the same situation, such as in writing a historical essay or in helping to run a club. The realm of specific interest, drive, motivation, and conflict seemed relatively untouched by mental measurement.

Considerable advances have been made in this direction, but a chasm has still persisted between clinical psychologists and psychometrists. In the last resort, the psychometrist is measuring *common traits,* that is, broad psychological qualities with which everyone is to *some* degree endowed, but the clinician (and also the common-sense observer or the literary biographer) is concerned with interest and motivation that often seem peculiar to the given person. The clinician may indeed be tempted to say that he is concerned—and that the psychometrist is not—with what makes the given individual "go." Yet this is the wrong distinction, for the measurement of common traits may be concerned with motivation, for example, with the strength of such common drives as sex or self-assertion. The real distinction is that the clinician and biographer are often concerned more with those particular motivational traits, such as a habit of collecting sixteenth-century daggers or an interest in people who have been in jail, that are relatively uncommon and that, if measurable, would not yield a normal distribution. These *unique traits* exist in all three modalities of measurement—cognitive, temperamental, and dynamic—but they assume relatively greater importance in the third, dynamic modality that we are now studying.

Admittedly, the third modality of individual differences, dealing with the tangle of motives, symptoms, conflicts, fixations, interests, and attitudes that we call dynamic traits, gives more scope to unique traits. It could easily lead the psychometrist on the wild-goose chase of trying to set up almost innumerable scales—on most of which most people would score zero. But the pleasures of studying the peculiarities and quirks of human nature must not blind us to one fact. In the motivational realm some massive common traits, such as strength of ambition, depth of attachment to a wife, level of gregariousness, or degree of devotion to a church can also be found that would appear to have both sufficient unity and sufficient range of application to justify attempts at measuring them. Similarly, in the clinical field, the therapist is compelled to proceed by undoing specific historical tangles and often to attempt cure by gradually working back to specific personal incidents, frequently of a traumatic nature. This approach, however, should not be allowed to obscure the equally important fact that his purpose, in one sense, is to change his patients' levels on *common* traits. His aim should be not merely to change the individual's attitude to a certain incident or incidents of his early childhood, but rather to use the re-evaluation of such incidents as a means of changing the main dimensions of the patient's personality, so that it will respond differently to all manner of situations yet to come. Indeed, whether or not the clinician sees his treatment in these terms, his real aim is to change scores on such broad common traits as ego strength, anxiety, superego strength, and so on.

We shall say more about unique traits later in this chapter; first, we must discuss what is known about the most important common traits of human motivation.

Section 2   What Common Dynamic Structures Exist?

Much has been written by philosophers of earlier centuries, also by Freud, Jung, Adler, Murray, and many eminent clinical psychologists, by Mc-Dougall, and by numerous systematists and ethologists arguing from biological observations in primates, about a supposed set of basic drives in man. The number, quite apart from the nature, of these drives varies from two or three (the libido, thanatos, and by implication, reactivity to threat), posited by Freud, to several dozen listed by Murray. Cattell (1947, 1950, 1957) has critically examined this field in a series of studies that the interested reader may pursue, but here we shall simply state the conclusion that good evidence is lacking in varying degrees for these varied enumerations, as also for the division into "primary" and "secondary" drives, for "drive reduction," and for many other fashionable concepts.

It is reasonable, however, on general biological evidence, to suppose that man is basically motivated by drives continuous with those of the mammals and especially of the primates, and that our complex cultural behavior is acquired as a more effective, although less direct, way of pursuing the satisfaction of hunger, sex, self-assertion, gregariousness, and so on. But only multivariate experimental methods are capable of properly checking and extending such a theory. What the work of the last ten years in this area of "dynamic calculus" has accomplished may be summarized as follows:

1. Research workers using factor analysis and similar methods have revealed the number and nature of what may be generically called *dynamic structure factors*. Our interests, attitudes, and motivational habits are *not* a formless, chaotic aggregate, but show a characteristic, discoverable "simple structure," in which certain major common traits repeatedly stand out, even among people of different ages and different cultural groups. It is as useful and meaningful to measure the individual strengths of these major common sources of motivation in the dynamic realm as it is to measure primary abilities or major dimensions of temperament in the cognitive and temperamental realms, respectively.

2. When the nature of these factors is examined, some of them appear to be drives. The attitudes grouped by these factors have the same emotional goal, although they are concerned with alternative means to this goal. These factors we have called *ergs,* to avoid the tangled misconceptions and semantic debates connected with such terms as "instinct" and "drive." The chief ergic structures so far found are: sex, fear (escape), parental protectiveness ("succorance"), curiosity (exploration), appeal, self-assertion, narcissism, gregariousness.

3. Other factors have been found that differ from the above in that their contributory attitudes have some cultural object common to them, such as a church, but that satisfy quite a variety of emotions. For example, in the unitary church sentiment these could be charity (protectiveness), appeal (need for help), gregariousness (social activities), and so on. These unitary structures are distinguished from ergs as *sentiments*. It is hypothesized that ergs are innate and common to all mankind, whereas the sentiment factors represent learned groupings of attitudes and would be expected to differ in number and nature from culture to culture, although this has not yet been proved. However, it should be pointed out that even though an erg be innate, the particular cultural investments of the erg, that is, the attitudes and courses of action that it groups together and through which it achieves its dynamic goal, will differ somewhat from culture to culture. At least they will do so in all but the consummatory activity, such as eating or avoiding pain. The ergs are thus to be regarded as sources of energy or reactivity, and the current strengths of energy in an individual at a given time will be represented by his various ergic-tension levels. The sentiments, on the other hand, reflect the social institutions of the culture by which the individual is influenced in his years of learning. We should expect to find in our society a sentiment for each of such areas as one's career, one's religion, one's home, and one's hobbies, and for many others. The measurement of the strength of a sentiment tells us how much interest the individual has invested in the given concrete or abstract object. Some uniqueness enters into these measurements—not all men, fortunately, can be measured with respect to their interest in one and the same wife—but it makes sense to talk of "strength of sentiment toward a wife" in comparing the life interests of many different men. Common dynamic traits are thus worthy of measurement.

Section 3   The Structuring of Attitudes into Common and Unique Traits

The actual elements measured, that is, the bricks out of which broader dynamic structures such as sentiments and ergs are built, are attitudes. But an attitude is not defined by dynamic psychologists in the same way as by pollsters and social-survey workers—as a check mark "for" or "against" a statement. We shall see in a moment that one does not depend on verbal self-evaluation in the newer methods, and also that one deals with *a course of action* rather than with an object or a statement. An attitude is a stimulus-response habit, in which the actual performance is dormant and potential at any given moment, but in which the strength is defined by the strength of action. The essential parts of an attitude may be defined by the paradigm:

"In these circumstances	I	want so much	to do this with that"
Stimulus		*Intensity*	*Response Course*
Situation	*Organism*	*of Attitude*	*of Action*

It is necessary to keep these parts in mind because the strength (intensity) of an attitude will depend upon the degree to which its potential course of action is allowed to satisfy itself and thus upon the level of provocation in the currently present stimulus situation.

We acquire our attitudes in such a way that they tend to lie in chains, separated by subgoals, the attainment of each of which is the provocation for the succeeding attitude, thus:

> I want to do well in my courses
> (as a precondition to my being able to reach:)
>
> SUBGOAL (*1*)   I want to become an engineer
> (as a precondition to my saving money to satisfy:)
>
> SUBGOAL (*2*)   I want to get married

When we look closely into the life of a given individual we find that these *subsidiated* chains, as it is convenient to call them, crisscross in a *dynamic lattice*; the attainment of one subgoal may actually provide the stimulus for a different set of attitudes to develop and intensify. For example, the intention of getting a balance in the bank can be the precondition of a wide variety of new attitudes and consequent actions. Eventually, however, the chain of "doing this in order that I may do that" ends in a state satisfying in itself, such as eating, drinking, finding company, or sexual consummation, which we call the ergic goal, defined by particular consummatory behavior. If we throw our preconceptions aside—as we should in so complex a field—the locating of the number and nature of these ergic goals should be a matter for experiment and statistical analysis. All the attitudes that subsidiate to a particular ergic goal should tend to vary together. For example, if wanting to watch a football game, or join a club, or go to the movies, or read a funny book, are all means of assuaging loneliness, then all four will increase (or tend on the average to increase) when the stimulus situation has aroused the need for gregarious activities or when the need for company has been starved. This tendency of groups of attitudes to vary together enables us, by the same techniques of correlation and factor analysis already described in earlier chapters, to explore the underlying structure. Factor analysis of attitude measures thus provides us with a means of deciding the number and nature of the ergs.

Usually we factor across groups of people, just as with abilities or general personality traits, intercorrelating perhaps sixty diverse attitudes for 300 people and finding the factor groups (patterns) among the attitudes. This sort of factoring, in which the scores of a considerable number of people are intercorrelated, is called R-technique; but we can, alternatively, take *one* person and measure the sixty attitudes upon him every day, for, say, 200 days. These series can be intercorrelated and factored, and this kind of analysis is called P-technique. A detailed account of the similarities and differences between these two varieties of factor analysis and of their respective uses is given by Cattell (1957). If our theory is correct that multivariate methods are capable of revealing the unitary drive (ergic) structures in man, then the same ergic factor patterns should appear by P-technique as by R-technique: as loneliness, for example, the essential source of the impulse toward gregariousness, rises and falls in the one individual, the set of attitudes that have proved to relieve loneliness will tend to rise and decline *together*. Thus, in theory, attitudes should be analyzable into the same structure of underlying factors, whether studied in one person or in a group of people.

This is exactly what has been found; the ergic patterns discovered by the two approaches are recognizably the same, including ergs of sex, protectiveness, fear, and so forth. However, the analysis of one individual's attitudes by P-technique, instead of giving the *average* pattern of the *common* trait, as in R-technique, gives the truly *unique* trait, which clinicians and personality theorists such as Gordon Allport have long wished to see psychometrists tackle. Thus, when we isolate by P-technique the factor of, say, gregariousness in one individual, we find grouped together not only the main attitudes, such as perhaps wanting to be in a football crowd, which many people share, but also whatever unique attitudes, symptoms, or behavior, such as perhaps going to the zoo, that the individual has acquired in his own particular experience of life.

In the last resort, and to gain complete psychological understanding, we ought to know these individual idiosyncratic expressions, but whether we can afford the leisured study to do so depends on purposes and on economics. The clinician, studying a case for a hundred hours and more, needs to do so; the educator, with time to measure a hundred children for two or three hours at most, must accept the approximations of dealing with common trait measurements.

Section 4   The Subsidiation of Attitudes and the Dynamic Lattice

We have already mentioned in the preceding section that attitudes tend to cluster in complicated chains, so that several may be directed to the same intermediate goal; that the attainment of this goal is often the starting point for a new set of attitudes directed to a further goal; and so on. Before we go on to examine the nature and pattern of the chief ergs and sentiments, let us consider in a little more detail the nature of these chains of attitudes.

Figure 3 shows in schematized form how a pattern of this kind, which we have called a dynamic lattice, may develop.

Thus Attitude c in Figure 3, "I want to arrange to marry Miss X," may have subsidiated to it, as a necessary condition, Attitude b, "I want to find means to make enough money to get married." This, in turn, may have sub-

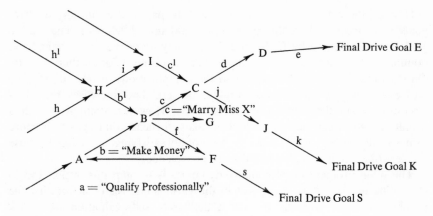

FIGURE **3.** *A hypothetical dynamic lattice*

sidiated to it Attitude a, "I want to work to get qualified through my professional examinations."

Thus all attitudes can be perceived to run in subsidiation chains (represented by such lines as "a, b, c, d, e" and "h, i, c^1, j, k" in Figure 3). Each attitude in the chain is linked to its successor by the verbal expression: ". . . in order that I may . . . ," corresponding to the creation of a fresh stimulus situation, through the action of the first attitude, which is perceived as appropriate for release of the response defined in the second. These subgoal-stimuli to the next course of action are represented by the capitals A, B, C, H, I, etc. Obviously, the development of the corresponding subgoal action courses, and of the subsidiation relation, arises because, in the complex frustrations of our culture, the person frequently finds that the initially sufficient course of action responding to Situation C, to gain Goal D, no longer suffices. He then has to learn first to create or bring about Situation C, as itself a necessary subgoal. The native who once pulled coconuts off trees must now first pay for land and tend his trees. And as a culture grows in security and complication, the individual has always to tack on an additional course of action, A, to create the state of affairs labeled B, and so back to still others.

Two or more attitude actions may frequently subsidiate to the same subgoal, e.g., two ways or more of making money, directed to Goal B. Conversely, some achievement of this goal can also, in turn, be a sufficient condition and stimulus for several new courses of action, ending at C, F, G, etc. Such a subsidiation of one action to several goals is, incidentally, what the psychoanalyst calls "overdetermination" of behavior. Thus the structure of human attitudes becomes more than a collection of attitude chains: it takes on the form of a lattice or grid. Moreover, as we examine it further, through clinical and general observation, we find that in this network there are feedbacks or retrofluxions, as from F to A in the figure.

Now all the courses of action, i.e., the "chains," end eventually in drive goals, if we accept a drive theory of human and animal behavior. These drive goals are represented by E, K, and S, and they mark the fixed, right-hand boundary of the lattice; beyond them there is no need for further activity. On the other hand, by education and the complications of our culture, the lattice is being extended constantly to the left. This increases the long-circuiting strain that the individual sustains. However, compared with a primitive and direct path to biological goals, it means that his life is more safe, socially acceptable, productive, and totally satisfying, especially because it is less likely to be cut short by disease or violence.

The main problem of personality dynamics is to map this lattice and to determine the strengths of interest in the various courses of action. To the psychologist who is ready to accept deliberate self-evaluations, the task appears easy. A subsidiation chain can be mapped, except where it goes "underground" in unconscious connections, by "free association" and the usual clinical interview, i.e., by asking, "Why are you interested in doing this?" Such a series of "'but why's" will lead continually to the right, from attitude to attitude, until it comes to a drive goal, e.g., "Because I eat," at which point further questioning or answering is purely philosophical. Needless to say, psychologists can no longer be scientifically content with these verbal makeshift methods, begotten of clinical urgency. Indeed, as insisted earlier, it is necessary to recognize that a minimum proof of dynamic connection is statistically established covariation, if possible on a basis of objective measurement.

Section 5 The Principal Ergs and the Attitudes That Define Them

Conceptually, in terms of understanding how measured interests will affect future performances, the distinction between ergs and sentiments is an important one. In considering ergic-tension levels, we are dealing with values that may fluctuate with provocation and habitual opportunities for satisfaction. A student away from home, for example, might stand at different levels of tension on appeal, escape, and gregariousness from those he generally experienced at home. By contrast, we should expect comparative constancy, except for the slow trends of learning, in scores on sentiment strengths, and we should expect to find other differences between ergs and sentiments. Consequently, it is best to discuss ergs and sentiments separately in this and the succeeding section, although in practice we cannot always be quite certain whether a particular factor should be classified as an erg or a sentiment.

The existence of a particular erg is shown by the appearance of a clear, determinate factor among attitude measurements (determinate by the criterion of simple structure), and the nature of the erg is inferred from the content of the salient attitudes that contribute most to the factor, or, in slightly more technical terms, those that have the highest factor loadings. For example, the erg of escape, with its accompanying emotion of fear, has been inferred from the pattern shown in Table VII, which has been found in three separate studies. It will be observed that all the attitudes, though differing widely in cultural content, share the goal of escape from threats of danger. At the same time, no attitude concerned with danger either appeared in another factor or failed to appear in this one.

TABLE **VII**

Factor loadings of attitudes on the erg of fear

I want my country to get more protection against the terror of the atom bomb	+.5
I want to see any formidable militaristic power that actively threatens us attacked and destroyed	+.5
I want to see the danger of death by accident and disease reduced	+.4
I want to see those responsible for inflation punished	+.4
I want never to be an insane patient in a mental hospital	+.4
I want to see a reduction of income tax for those in my bracket	+.3
I want to take out more insurance against illness	+.3
I want to become proficient in my career	+.3
I want my country to have power and influence in the world	+.3
I like to take part in political arguments	+.3

In Chapter 11 we shall be studying the application of the same techniques to children's motivation. In general, the same ergs and sentiments have been found, with only slight differences, comparable with the slight difference in the pattern of temperamental factors between adults and children, as already referred to in Chapter 4. But a larger body of research findings exists for adults, and most of our present illustrations of the pattern and nature of ergs and sentiments will be in terms of the findings with adults, where repeated experiment has made the main structure quite well established.

An erg of particular interest to educators is the exploratory drive, with its accompanying feeling of curiosity and its powerful contribution to almost all aspects of learning. Attitudes that have been shown to contribute to this factor are listed in Table VIII. This table suggests, and other research has tended to confirm, that there is quite a close connection between aesthetic appreciation and curiosity, closer perhaps than many theorists or philosophers in the field of aesthetics have previously suggested.

We have already listed briefly in Section 2 of this chapter the eight primary ergs that have been found repeatedly in studies of adult motivation, and space does not permit us to discuss in detail their full patterns and correlates. A short note follows on each of the six not already discussed, but the

TABLE **VIII**

Factor loadings of attitudes on the erg of exploration (curiosity)

I like to read books, newspapers, and magazines	+.5
I want to listen to music	+.5
I want to know more about science	+.4
I like to satisfy my curiosity about everything going on in my neighborhood	+.3
I want to see more paintings and sculpture	+.3
I want to learn more about mechanical and electrical gadgets	+.3
I like to see a good movie or play	+.3
I am not interested in being smartly dressed	+.3

interested reader is referred for a fuller description to Cattell (1957) and to Cattell and Baggaley (1958).

The Sex Erg. This factor has never failed to appear. The statistical approach has usually also confirmed the considerable importance of sexual motivation, in that this has frequently been the largest factor—or in slightly more technical terms, the one that contributed most to the total variance. Attitudes in favor of travel, drama, and music, as well as more explicitly sexual attitudes, contribute to this factor. So also do attitudes in favor of smoking and drinking, although these contribute more to the factor of narcissism.

The Erg of Gregariousness. This factor has been found repeatedly but has not always been so clearly marked or free from alternative interpretations as one might wish. Several of the attitudes that load the factor most highly are concerned with participation in sports and games. There is some evidence that the factor as found so far is closely associated with the cyclothymia-sizothymia dimension of temperament.

The Erg of Parental Protectiveness. This factor is wider than the title might suggest and includes a wide range of protective, succorant, and compassionate attitudes. It fits closely the pattern described by McDougall (1954). Interests in the drama have some loading on the factor, which may be a reflection of the ancient observation that the drama achieves a "catharsis" or purging of the emotions by arousing pity.

The Erg of Self-Assertion. This is a well-established factor, which has appeared in every analysis, but the attitudes defining it have shown some variability according to the sample of persons who have been studied. Thus among academics, for instance, the highest loadings have been concerned with prestige and salary, but among United States Air Force officer cadets, with personal appearance and social life.

The Erg of Narcissism (Narcissistic Sex or Inverted Superego). This factor has appeared in nearly every study, although no such pattern was initially hypothesized. The highest loadings are associated with a wish to smoke, drink, enjoy delicate food, and enjoy solitude. There is some evidence that this erg works in opposition to the sexual erg, and that the two may represent mutually exclusive expressions of the same libido.

The Erg of Appeal. This is the least well-established of the eight ergs we have discussed. In many studies (e.g., Cattell and Baggaley, 1958), the attitudes with highest loadings have been concerned with religious beliefs. It is possible, therefore, that this factor should receive an alternative interpretation and may, in fact, be better described as a sentiment toward religion.

These illustrations must suffice for the present. A fuller account of the nature of the factors and of the evidence for their interpretation is to be found in Cattell (1957). A recent survey of methodology and a summary of evidence about findings in this area is provided by John L. Horn (chapter 20 in Cattell, 1966b). We shall be returning to the subject in Chapter 11, where we discuss the analysis of ergs and sentiments in children.

It is worth pointing out, however, that the discovery and charting of these distinct "drives" in human beings may well lead to new and profitable research in the field of learning. Theorists of learning have been prone in the past to suppose that all "drive" acts in the same way. It may well be, however, that different ergs function in quite different ways in providing motivation for the learning process. Further research on these lines is urgently needed.

Section 6   The Nature of Sentiments, Including the Self-Sentiment

We have already suggested that the division of dynamic structures into ergs and sentiments depends at present on two facts: (1) that ergs are defined by attitudes with a common emotional goal but different cultural purposes, whereas sentiments are defined by attitudes to a common social or institutional object but with diverse emotional qualities of satisfaction; and (2) that the ergs correspond to patterns supposed to be constitutional from studies of mammalian and primate behavior.

Among the principal interest structures so far recognized as sentiments are those centered on career, on religion, on mechanical and hobby interests, and on sports and games. Three of these are shown, in Tables IX, X, and XI, though only the last is clear also in children, as one would expect. Indeed, one source of evidence for a structure being a sentiment rather than an erg is that it can be found at some ages, or in some cultural subgroups or roles, but not others. The attitudes that define sentiment to career in Table IX are those studied in a group of Air Force cadets (Cattell and Baggaley,

1958). The same sentiment has been found, defined by slightly different attitudes, in studies of other groups.

It has been noted both in earlier researches (e.g., Sweney, Radcliffe, and Cattell, 1960) and in those reported in Chapter 11 of this book, that sentiment structures have not been found so clearly in children as in adults. In the formative period of life, one would certainly expect that they would be less clearly established on a common plan and would be more transient and

TABLE **IX**

Factor loadings of attitudes on sentiment to profession (Air Force)*

I want to make my career in the Air Force	+.70
I like the excitement and adventure of combat flying	+.63
I want to get technical education such as the Air Force provides	+.58
I enjoy commanding men and taking the responsibility of a military leader	+.44
I do not want to take more time to enjoy rest and to sleep later in the mornings	−.41
I like being up in an airplane	+.41
I want to satisfy my sense of duty to my country by enlisting in its most important defense arm in threatening times	+.39
I want to become first rate at my Air Force job	+.36
I do not want to spend more time at home puttering around	−.36

* Here, as in other tables setting out factors, the signs of the loadings are given as they occur for all the positively directed ("I want") attitudes in the original list of variable. For the reader's convenience in reading the list of salients, the qualifying "not" is inserted whenever the loading has gone negative. The attitudes thus read consistently as they stand and need no change.

TABLE **X**

Factor loadings of attitudes on the sentiment of mechanical interests

I enjoy a good car or motorcycle for its own sake	+.51
I like to handle mechanical things—gadgets, engines, etc.	+.46
I enjoy buying and selling things and trying to make a profit in business deals	+.40
I do not want to have my parents' advice and heed their wishes in planning my affairs	−.31
I like to own a home and have things I can call my own	+.30
I like being way up in an airplane	+.29
I am not interested in my parents' never lacking the necessities of comfortable living	−.25
I want to know more about physical science—electricity, chemistry, engineering	+.20
I like to make things with my hands in wood, metal, or clay, to paint, etc.	+.15

TABLE **XI**

Factor loadings of attitudes on sentiment to sports and games

I like to watch and talk about athletic events	+.75
I like to take an active part in sports and athletics	+.63
I enjoy hunting and fishing trips	+.27
I do not like to make things with my hands in wood, metal, or clay, to paint, etc.	−.20
I like to get into a fight, particularly if my rights are involved	+.20
I like to spend (some of) my spare time playing cards with the fellows	+.16

less important than the ergs in sustaining activity. Even the sentiments to peer groups, parents, school, and nation are not so clearly established as one would expect them to be.

Both in adults and children, however, we encounter two clear-cut patterns, apparently sentiments, that are of the greatest psychological importance. The first is a pattern of attitudes centered on the self-concept (just as upon any external object) and concerned with the physical, social, and moral preservation of the self. The second corresponds fairly closely to the psychoanalytic concept of the superego. If space permitted, it would be extremely interesting to enlarge on these two concepts and on the relation between them. Briefly, however, the most promising present hypothesis is that the superego, with its strongly, unconsciously implanted "need to do right," is one of several needs to which the self-sentiment is often subsidiated. The attitudes of wishing to appear socially correct, of wanting to do one's duty, of practicing self-control, which are central features of the self-sentiment, are partly influenced by social approbation and partly by the demands of superego. There is thus an intricate and probably unique relation of the self-sentiment to other sentiments, in that it acts as an organizer of almost all of them.[1] The strength of the self-sentiment shows the extent to which the child has developed a concept of himself, against which he checks his actions, and it would therefore be expected to correlate with achievement, in the sense of civic achievement, and acceptance of community standards and responsibilities.

[1] It might be urged, and we should have considerable sympathy with this criticism, that the sentiments which we have identified as the self-sentiment and the superego are of such importance and play such an integrative role as to be on a different level from the other, relatively more specific, sentiments. The justification for classifying them as sentiment is that they have emerged empirically on the same level as the other sentiments. It is certainly true that although we have criticized the methodology and the scientific status of psychoanalytic theory, some of Freud's hypotheses in this area showed brilliant insight. Particularly relevant is his account of the integrative function of the ego and its difficult task in reconciling the claims of "three stern masters," i.e., the id, the superego, and external reality.

Section **7**   **Objective Attitude Measurement and Motivational Components**

These new developments in the measurement of interests, attitudes, and motivation, which have been called by Cattell the "dynamic calculus," differ in two ways from earlier practices and theories, as follows:

1. This "dynamic calculus" determines by objective experimental methods those aspects of the dynamic structure with which measurement can deal, as already discussed above.

2. It shifts the measurement of attitude and interest strength from verbal, self-evaluative techniques to objective techniques, by which we mean not only objectively scored, but unfakable, either because they are disguised or because they depend upon physiological responses.

In this section, we must interrupt our account of the structure of motivation to discuss some features of the appropriate measuring devices.

By taking some one attitude, as defined above, such as "In my present environment, I want to such an extent to play football every week," and attempting to assess this extent by a large number of different devices— questionnaires, various so-called projective techniques, changes in heart beat and electrical skin resistance when provocative things are said about football, measures of spontaneous visual attention and memory when pictures of football are displayed, and so forth—one can compare the effectiveness of these various kinds of test. One method of doing so would be to pool the scores of all of them and to correlate score on each in turn with this total score, to see how well any one device agrees with the verdict of all those measures that, by general consent of psychologists, have some claim to be called manifestations of motivation.

A more informative means of analysis, however, is to intercorrelate the different devices and to factor-analyze them, which enables us to discover whether they are all in fact measuring one kind or one single dimension of motivation strength, or whether one must indeed reckon with different dimensions.

The reader may be puzzled at this point about the manner in which the factors that emerge from such an analysis differ from the ergs and sentiments already referred to and about the meaning of the new factors. To recapitulate, ergs and sentiments are isolated by correlating a number of expressions of attitude, as described earlier in this chapter. Each attitude is normally measured by one test or device. These two kinds of factor emerge from the same type of analysis, at the same level, and are only distinguishable from each other by their interpretation.

Suppose, however, that one take a single attitude, measures it by quite a large number of different kinds of testing technique, correlates the resulting scores, and finally carries out a factor analysis. The factors that emerge, which we call motivational components, will, when rotated to simple structure, correspond to types or sources of motivation in general as abstracted from the particular expressions of attitude and motive. If, as has been found, similar factors occur, practically regardless of what attitude is being assessed by the multiplicity of devices, their generality and importance is thereby emphasized.

When this is done it has been found that there are some *seven* distinct factors, which we shall refer to as the *primary motivation components*. The first three of them strongly suggest the components that Freud considered entered into each symptom or attitude. One loads mainly wishful, unrealistic expressions of interest and could be called the id component, though at present we cautiously label it *alpha.* Another, *beta,* shows itself in such measures as information about the topic, quickness of intellectual association, and willingness to learn, and could be called the realized ego component. The third, *gamma,* component loads devices that suggest the attitude "I ought to be interested in this" and could well be the superego component. The fourth motivational component (*delta*) seems to be a common element of the physiological responses, and the fifth (*epsilon*), a component from unconscious complexes. The evidence about the last two, *zeta* and *eta,* is more provisional, but it appears that *zeta* may be described as a factor of urgency or impulsivity. The most recent research evidence about these motivational components is fully summarized and discussed by Cattell, Radcliffe, and Sweney (1963).

Therefore, experiments in the Illinois laboratory concerned with devices for measuring motivation have shown that effective measurement of the strength with which a person wishes to carry out the course of action defined by a given attitude theoretically involves the measurement of no fewer than seven components. For these seven motivational components presumably behave differently—one may be changed by argument, another is unconscious; one will change with physiological condition, another will not; one will respond to an appeal to the individual's "better self," another will not; and so on. Consequently, simply to sum them to give a *single* score for attitude or interest strength—as psychologists have done in the past—must lose much information.

Nevertheless, the price of full information, entailing the construction of small batteries of objective devices for each of the seven components, is forbidding to practitioners, especially because many of the devices need to be individually administered. Consequently, a search was made for a possible single second-order factor among these seven correlated primary motivational components. The researches of Radcliffe, Sweney, and others (see, for instance, Sweney and Cattell, 1961), show that both in children and adults there is not one but *two* main second-order factors (and others of small variance), and that these are clearly: (1) a second-order component, U, which consists of all unintegrated and generally unconscious sources of a given interest; and (2) a second-order component, I, which combines the integrated, conscious, components. For most practical work, including all the measurement of interests that we shall discuss in this book, it makes best sense to measure only these two second-order motivational components, or to add them with equal weight to produce a single factor score.

The Motivational Analysis Test (MAT) for adults (Cattell, Horn and Butcher, 1962; Cattell, Horn, Sweney, and Radcliffe, 1964) and the School Motivational Analysis Test (SMAT) (Sweney, Cattell, and Krug, 1967) employ two short batteries of objective tests for each attitude measurement, and these I (Integrated) and U (Unintegrated) components are added later into a single total interest score, although they can also be considered separately. The second battery of tests (SMAT) will be described in more detail in Chapters 8 and 11.

One of the most important aspects of these new batteries of tests is that a single score on an attitude will no longer be the result of a self-conscious statement of preference, as in questionnaire methods, but will represent the sum of several objective measures, each representing a different kind of motivational component or contribution to total attitude strength. If educational testers could afford the time for a thorough clinical analysis of each child, which is of course a wildly impractical aim, it might be worthwhile to study all seven motivation components. Meanwhile, the provision of a possible breakdown into integrated and unintegrated motivational sources for an interest provides a good compromise, although most users will continue to use a single total score.

Section **8**   **The Dynamic Calculus**

The strength of an attitude, defined as the intensity of interest in the corresponding course of action, can be represented in terms of the dynamic factors we have described, in the same way that the level of performance in a cognitive task is represented by the specification equation for primary abilities. The only differences are that in the latter case the factors are of two kinds, ergs and sentiments, and that one would expect them to fluctuate in the individual more than do abilities. The specification equation will be of the type shown in Formula 5.1 below, where the E's refer to ergs and M's to sentiments.

5.1

$$I_{ji} = s_{E1j}E_{1i} + s_{E2j}E_{2i} \ldots + s_{Enj}E_{ni} + s_{M1j}M_{1j} + s_{M2j}M_{2i} \ldots + s_{Mnj}M_{ni}$$

where I_{ji} equals the strength of interest in an attitude defined by the situation j, to which it is a response, e.g., strength of interest in geography in the way in which it is taught in a given school, for the individual *i*. The subscripts on the situational indices (s_n), obtained as factor loadings, define the situation *j* in which testing is done, and from which they are derived, and the dynamic structure factors to which they apply, $E_1 \ldots E_n \ldots M_1 \ldots M_n$. For example, if *j* is the situation of being asked to see a football match, then the largest *s*'s will be on the *E* that is the gregarious erg and the *M* that is sentiment to games.

A special development of the dynamic calculus is that in which the extent of cancellation of positive and negative loadings in Formula 5.1 is taken as an operational measure of conflict. This has worked very well in practice, and is potentially of considerable importance in clinical work, but for an account of this development, the reader must be referred to Cattell (1957).

Our general thesis has been that achievement is a function of the total personality, and that cognitive, temperamental, and dynamic traits must all be taken into account in the best possible prediction. Using P for general personality factors and D for dynamic factors, this could be stated:

5.2 $$\text{Achievement}, K = s_a A + s_p P + s_d D$$

That is to say, all the factors, in all three media, should ultimately enter into a single specification equation, and each of the three summative terms on the right of Formula 5.2 would include, if written in full, a set of terms such as were shown on the right of Formula 5.1.

SUMMARY *of Chapter Five*

1. Even when abilities and temperamental factors have been taken into account, a very large range of individual human behavior remains unaccounted for. This is the domain of interests, attitudes, and motivation, often described as dynamic psychology. Although unique personal characteristics are more typical in this field than in the fields of ability and temperament, there are still many broad common motivational traits that can be studied and measured.

2. These common factors have been found to fall into two types: (a) "ergs," or instinctive patterns comparable with drives observed in nonhuman higher mammals; and (b) sentiments, or aggregates of attitudes that focus on a common social institution.

3. The complicated network of interacting human interests and attitudes can be clarified by the concept of "subsidiation." Thus, in human society, interests and attitudes are frequently not directed to immediate "ergic" or instinctual satisfaction, but to an intermediate subgoal. The subgoal may then be the starting point for a new set of attitudes, which may crisscross in an intricate "dynamic lattice."

4. The ergs and sentiments can be operationally isolated and measured by the factor analysis of a wide range of attitudes. This measurement of attitudes is best done by disguised, relatively objective, and unfakable tests rather than by the traditional questionnaire method.

5. If one attitude is measured by a large number of these different techniques, and the resulting scores intercorrelated and factor-analyzed, factors can be found that represent different facets or strands of motivation and that can best be called motivational components.

6. Batteries of tests have been constructed that aim to measure the main sentiments and ergs, each by several techniques; the techniques have been chosen so that each represents an important motivational component. Such batteries are available for use with adults and children, respectively.

7. The prediction of achievement should take into account motivation as well as ability and personality, and the most complete specification equation will therefore contain loadings for ergs and sentiments as well as for abilities and personality factors.

Chapter Six

PRINCIPLES FOR EVALUATING
VALIDITY AND CONSISTENCY IN
PSYCHOLOGICAL TESTS

Section 1   Modern Revisions of Psychometric Concepts

It is a sound general maxim in scientific work that measurement should conform to structure. As in the physiological and anatomical field, so in psychology; measurement should be related to function, and the multiplication of psychological scales to fit the dictionary or the predilections of a particular investigator has little value. Test practice is today in rapid transition from a "pragmatic" to a "functional" basis. For this reason, our account in the earlier chapters has been mainly concerned with defining basic concepts and with outlining some of the most important findings about the general structure of abilities and of personality and motivation, upon which modern tests are based.

Before we use tests, however, whether of ability or personality, we must understand the evaluative principles to be applied to psychological tests in general and the criteria by which their effectiveness should be assessed. We will have to refer constantly in what follows to reliability, homogeneity, efficiency, and to other properties of tests, and to principles of scaling and standardization. This chapter and Chapter 7 will therefore deal with these *psychometric parameters* of tests in general, as studies in that subscience of psychology that we call psychometrics.

Psychometrics has some of the abstract qualities of mathematics, for it deals with concepts that have general application to all mental testing operations. Its technicalities are necessarily such that the reader who has little background in mathematics or statistics would probably be well advised to skip this chapter and Chapter 7 on a first reading of the book. One might think that for the teacher whose training has included no psychometrics we could sketch the simpler ideas in such a way that the rest of the scientific treatment would be comprehensible. Unfortunately, it is difficult to provide a half-way treatment in this field, because the concepts are either technically precise or they are misleading. Consequently, we must beg the reader, even if he skips these two chapters at first reading, to study them sufficiently before he forms his final judgments on the findings as a whole.

At present, the difficulties of the student of psychometrics are unnecessarily increased, because the natural complexities of the subject are compounded by muddled nomenclatures and by misplaced emphases arising from a too narrow approach. Here, as with certain other topics, such as intelligence measurement, research is rapidly altering the picture to which mental testers have been accustomed for the past thirty years. The prevalent narrowness of outlook has been due largely to the fact that psychometry in the 1930's and 1940's rested largely in the hands of specialized educational psychologists, who were concerned with achievement measures and with ability tests. As research broadened to include personality and motivation measurement, concepts derived from the cognitive field alone proved to be inadequate and biased, and the psychometric principles and systems of nomenclature that had become prematurely specialized could no longer be said to apply to this newer and broader field.

For example, probably three-quarters of the writers of standard psychometric textbooks tend to assume that any score on a test must result from adding up responses to a series of discrete, atomistic "items." But in the general field of psychological measurement, and particularly in personality assessment, there are many response possibilities other than a series of items. So important is it to distinguish between the rather rigid scaling procedures that have grown up in the cognitive field and the wider range of techniques developed for the study of personality and motivation, that Cattell (1957) has suggested that the term "itemetrics" be used for the division of psychometrics that operates with this particular model of an ultimate set of equal particles. Other characteristics that are inveterate in the itemetric division of psychometrics will become evident as we proceed. Although, in the present book, most of our personality measurements are analyzable into items, personality measurement in general may use such diverse types of response as change of electrical skin resistance in ohms, the time taken to complete a finger maze, the number of times a person falsely reacts to sound when he is concentrating on reacting to a light stimulus, the pattern of response when a person tries to copy a picture, and many others. In fact, personality measurement deals a good deal with *patterns* and *styles* of behavior, beginning with ratio and difference scores, such as the percentage of ideas remembered by a subject when another person agrees with him (compared with the number remembered when the other person disagrees), and extending to complex mathematical functions of scores in what we have defined as structured or patterned tests. Moreover, even when our present tests use items, we put quite a different emphasis on such test properties as homogeneity and validity from the emphasis that has been characteristic in the itemetric school.

It may be worthwhile to pause a moment to consider one particular instance of this difference of emphasis. Many psychologists (and particularly educational psychologists, such as Cronbach, Loevinger, Kuder, and others) have put a strong emphasis upon homogeneity as a desirable characteristic of a test. We will define homogeneity more precisely in a little while, but for the present we can describe it as the degree of similarity of the different items in a test with regard to what they measure. The teacher has been taught to regard homogeneity as invariably desirable and to value reliability, another form of test consistency, very highly, although this high valuation may be at the expense of validity. This tendency to undervalue validity is understandable when one reflects that validity has come cheaply in educational measurement, because one can usually tell that a test is valid simply by reference to a content area. If it is to test geography, it must contain geographical items, and a naïve dependence on "face validity" is practicable. On the other hand, in personality and motivation measurement, the question of validity is typically much more complex. The result has often been that the study of reliability and homogeneity has been carried to extraordinary lengths of pedantic elaboration, whereas the validity issue has been treated quite naïvely. When carried over uncritically to the personality field this tradition results in dicta[1] that lead teachers to prefer measuring something of virtually no importance or validity with a textbook reliability of +0.95, to measuring an important general psychological concept with a reliability of +0.60.

Furthermore, the discovery of remarkable paradoxes can always be ensured by starting off with sufficiently narrow, artificial, or erroneous initial definitions. One result has been an untidy proliferation of labels and beliefs among psychometrists, as satirized by Cureton. So much so, in fact, that a committee was set up by the American Psychological Association some fifteen years ago to bring order by fiat and to stabilize the recommended nomenclature and meanings, but the compromises agreed upon by a committee are often rather unsatisfactory. Only the broadening of the whole subject in the last fifteen years, notably by: (1) more highly developed measurement of personality and motivation; (2) the use of information and decision theory (Cronbach and Gleser, 1957); and (3) regard for the basic analysis of sources of variance in the covariation chart, or Basic Data Rela-

---

[1] Even Cronbach (1960) complains that the relatively low reliability of an early version of the 16 PF scales makes the test "doubtful" for drawing conclusions about individuals. This ignores a wider principle involved in the validity-reliability relationship, which is best put in terms of information theory and which we describe in Chapter 7 below. Contingently and briefly, we may state it here, however, and claim that more predictive value is achieved, *relative to most criteria,* by expending a given amount of testing time in measuring *several independent factors* with moderate reliability, rather than one or two with scrupulously high reliability. The 16 PF measures sixteen distinct and important dimensions, with reliabilities of +0.6 to +0.8, in the time (35 minutes approximately) commonly consumed by many psychologists in getting information on only a single dimension, such as intelligence (Factor B in the 16 PF).

tion Matrix (Cattell, 1952b), could have brought us to more acceptable concepts and terms. It follows that the framework of concepts adopted here is often a radical departure from the recommendations of the above-mentioned and should be considered in the light of first principles as a possible advance from current psychometric practice.

Section 2   The Concepts of Validity

Traditionally, in examining any test, one begins by asking how reliable it is and then proceeds to ask if it is also valid. But if a test has no validity, and no utility (see Chapter 7), one need not waste time studying its reliability! A still more compelling reason for studying validity first—which is what we propose to do—is that reliability is kept in its proper perspective if we consider it primarily as a modifier of validity. Similarly, in buying some mechanical instrument, we may wish to know whether it is lasting and dependable, whether it will rust, for example, or fall to pieces on a second use; yet one's primary concern is whether the tool will do the job one has in mind.

Validity, in the generic sense, is the ability of a test to predict some behavioral measure other than itself. However, there are three distinct major parameters to the type of prediction made. These three parameters, dichotomized, can yield eight kinds of validity coefficient. Let us first define the three parameters.

The first is the "degree of abstraction" parameter: the dimension from conceptual to concrete (or particular) validity. Psychological theory and basic research are generally most concerned with whether a test properly represents a certain personality concept or construct, whereas applied research is more frequently interested in the capacity to predict a quite particular concrete performance, such as skill at a specified job or the recovery rate under a particular kind of therapy. Applied psychologists with a practical turn of mind may even assert that they are not interested in anything beyond a concrete validity—and when one considers the vague, verbal constructs that theorists often discuss, one can sympathize with this viewpoint. But an undue emphasis on concrete-particular validity has two unfortunate consequences. First, it shelves the fundamental scientific necessity of *understanding* validity and of understanding *why* the correlation exists. Any immediate, exclusive concern with the relation between test and external criterion is apt to end in mere actuarialism, which neither advances nor uses psychological science. Second, an exaggerated concern with the concrete aspect of validity fails to take into account that, in considering the total utility and worth of a test, we are usually concerned with many validities, with a host of varied practical situations in which the test may predict, rather than with just one. Indeed, a great deal of thinking about this subject has been perverted by the habit of talking about the *validity,* rather than about the *validities,* of a test, and for this reason the evaluation of the concrete validity of a test may become an endless undertaking and dispute. (Of course, a test might also have several conceptual validities, but it is at least possible, and often occurs, that test design is aimed at only *one* concept validity.)

To consider the opposite pole of this dimension, that is, *conceptual validity,* we have preferred not to follow the APA committee in speaking of "construct validity," because an empirical construct, in logic and epistemology, is only one particular form of a concept. The psychologist is often interested in validity for other kinds of concepts, such as are logically deducible from general postulates; and concept validity therefore appears a more accurate term. Similarly, while on semantic matters, let us point out the desirability of avoiding a distinction between "internal" and "external" validity as a basic parameter. Concepts may be of external denotation, in rather the same way as particular percepts may be considered as external to the perceiving person. Moreover, the notion of "internal validity" tends, for reasons to be mentioned, to become confused with homogeneity. As far as the test is concerned, any concept, such as "intelligence" or "anxiety," that can also be measured by another test, is just as external as a concrete criterion of "acceptance by the rest of the team" or "degree of recovery under tranquilizer *X.*"

The concept against which a test measure is validated must, of course, be tied down in a set of operations, if any figure for validity is to be experimentally obtained. Early work on intelligence tests, for example, before the introduction of factor analysis by Spearman, and much more recent attempts to validate tests of psychoanalytic concepts, failed to face the need for any statement of the concept in operational terms. The many technical ways of tying down a concept operationally reduce essentially to four:

1. Defining it as a uniquely rotated factor (normally by the criterion of simple structure), in other words, as a source trait or state dimension and pattern. This is the main definition of the validity of personality and motivation tests in this volume.

2. Defining it as a *surface* trait or correlation cluster, that is, as an apparent entity or syndrome that has not been submitted to sufficient or sufficiently determinate analysis to ensure that it represents a causative influence. As pointed out elsewhere (Cattell, 1957), this is rarely satisfactory. Except by introducing arbitrary values, unique determination of a surface trait, as with any sort of natural entity, is impossible. Consequently, this approach finishes up frequently as nothing more than concrete-particular validity.

3. Defining the criterion by a type, or to be more precise, by a dimension distinguishing one type from another. For example, the criterion might be that which is capable of discriminating the neurotic person, the psychotic,

the delinquent, the mental defective, and so forth. This approach has always been popular among applied psychologists, for it seems to ensure that the validity will have immediate relevance to problems of selection and diagnosis, but in relation to systematic psychological concepts it is not very satisfactory. In the first place, it requires that we have an objective methodology for locating types. "Common sense" apparently tells us what a neurotic or a delinquent is—until two psychologists disagree. Tsujioka (1965) has systematically set out concepts and formulas for locating types; but it must be recognized that, just as with surface traits, some arbitrary decisions must be made. This principle of adopting as a criterion the maximum discrimination between two named types of person is exemplified in Eysenck's (1950) ingenious method of "criterion analysis," which might be more accurately described as "criterion rotation," but one must remember that two types will *not* (except on the millionth chance) differ only on one pure factor, but on several. Type validity has a place—a small place—in applied validity considerations. But it should not be confused with validity in terms of an objectively determined concept, and if one bears in mind the superior range and relative universality of such concepts, the difference between the particular and often local types is a poor substitute.

4. Finally, we may define a concept by a set of logical conditions, operating on other assumptions. If the latter are real, we may have concepts like those in Euclidean geometry, which fit reality; alternatively, we may start with arbitrary assumptions and have a "non-Euclidean psychology," internally consistent, but not designed to refer to real people. If the former is followed, the concepts will generally arise from conditions and abstractions that any individual psychologist cares to lay down in relation to real constructs of the kind reached in 1, 2, and 3 above. For example, he may say that the test is designed to test degree of "socialization," this trait being defined perhaps as that which will be found to be low in delinquents, high in neurotics, average in normals. Or again, he may choose logically to define "degree of conflict" as the algebraic sum divided by the arithmetic sum of quantitative projections of attitude vectors upon an ergic coordinate factor, as proposed by Cattell (1957) and Williams (1959).

Definitions of criteria by methods 1 and 4 are the most fundamental and probably the most satisfactory. However, it should be noted that the definition by a set of logical conditions does not absolve one, in the end, from the methodological necessity of proving that what one is talking about is a functionally unitary entity. One must follow 4 by 1. In fact, the satisfactory use of logical conditions as a means of attaining concept validity theoretically does, and in practice has, required the use of factor analysis in the great majority of instances. All this discussion of the abstract pole of the abstract-concrete dimension of validity should point up the fact that the abstract end, though fundamentally more valuable in pure, and in the long run in applied, science, requires methodological sophistication for its proper use.

The second parameter is the "degree of naturalness" parameter, from naturally occurring to artificial criteria of validity. Any validity referent, whether concrete or conceptual in the sense of our first parameter, can arise either from naturally existing cultural or psychological data *in situ,* or from some behavior artificially arranged by the psychologist, as in the laboratory. Psychological science is a part of culture, but it is a special part, and what it sets up as a controlled laboratory performance cannot be called "natural." For example, in validating intelligence tests, some psychologists have put more emphasis on predicting "success in the life situation," whereas others have turned to agreement with the Binet or with other established tests. Obviously, the latter course involves a great risk of developing a small and vicious circle of professional subjectivity. Indeed, for some test users early in this generation, there grew up a kind of apostolic succession, in which the validity of an intelligence test was assessed by its agreement with a revered older example. This kind of validity is more appropriate to religion than to science! But we do not wish to press this point too hard, or to suggest that all "artificial" criteria are damnable, or all "natural" ones adequate. To validate test *X* by its degree of correspondence with some well-known and highly standardized test *Y* may offer greater precision than reference to *some* cultural-natural behavior. Indeed, in conceptual definition, "artificial validation" is often quite useful and legitimate.

The third parameter is the "degree of directness" parameter; from direct to circumstantial validity. What we are defining here as "direct validation" is quite familiar, for it consists of that direct correlation of the test with the criterion that for most people constitutes all validation. On the other hand, the process of indirect validation, which has received less attention, involves more subtle procedures and a fuller examination of the meaning of "identity." In the simplest sense, the validity of test x, as a measure of concept X, seems sufficiently evaluated by the goodness of its correlations with X. But logically it depends also upon its *not* correlating with what is not-X. This point is somewhat analogous to the logical principle underlying the criterion of simple structure, where, as we have already described, the "irrelevant" variables indirectly yield precious information, just as Sherlock Holmes drew important inferences from the dog that *did not* bark during the night! It is similarly important that the test x, to be valid in terms of the concept X, should fail to correlate with those variables that are independent of X, and in the same general degree. Operationally, therefore, one must obtain a measure of agreement, between the whole profile of correlations, of X with $a, b, c, \ldots n$ and of x with $a, b, c \ldots n$. Statistically, the best procedure is to use the Fisher z transformations of the columns of r's and to use r_p instead of r in evaluating the agreement of these two columns. That the direct validity coefficient for a particular scale may be very consistent with the indirect validity coefficient was first shown in the case of the High School Personality Questionnaire (Cattell and Nuttall, 1967). The notion of a sound measure of circumstantial validity implies that the referents in the surroundings should be evenly and comprehensively sampled, and correlation with a whole series of other factors is therefore usually desirable. The upshot of this discussion is that as a general principle and practice in applied psychology, a more explicit attempt should be made to supplement and check *direct* validity measures with indirect, circumstantial estimates of validity.

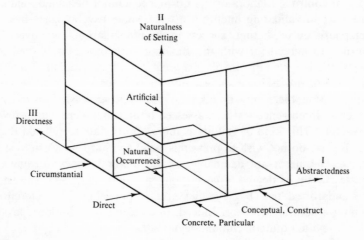

FIGURE **4.** *The three parameters of validity and the resulting eight varieties of validity coefficient*

By definition, the above three parameters of validity coefficients are independent, and can be combined in any way. They are illustrated graphically in Figure 4. For example, the distinction between direct and circumstantial validity can be applied equally to the conceptual or concrete, and to the natural or artificial criteria. However, this combination of the parameters in all possible ways may not yield the $2^3 = 8$ types of validity that seem theoretically possible, because some conjunctions, though theoretically possible, may not be practically realizable or useful. In principle, all eight are viable, though agreement on terms for them is lacking, but four are likely to be of salient practical importance, and we therefore tentatively suggest the following terminology and symbolism for these four:

1. $r_{v(pd)}$ = Particular, Direct Validity (or Direct-Concrete)
2. $r_{v(cd)}$ = Conceptual, Direct Validity
3. $r_{v(ci)}$ = Conceptual (or Indirect), Circumstantial Validity
4. $r_{v(pi)}$ = Particular, Circumstantial Validity

It is suggested that these be so described when the conceptual validities, 2 and 3, are derived from laboratory, artificial data and the particular validities from natural data, and that primes be attached to indicate the four corresponding, but less used, validities that are not given names here.

The relation of these three basic parameters, and of the eight resulting kinds of validity coefficient, to notions and names still in varying degrees of popular use will be self-evident and requires no illustration. Nevertheless, a few comments may be helpful on the place of such existing terms as *content* validity, *semantic* validity, *predictive* validity, *fiat* validity, and *face* validity. Perhaps the less psychology seriously entertains the last two, the better! Fiat validity is invoked when a psychologist arbitrarily tells us that a test, a key, or a personal coding of data measures some concept that he says it does. Copious examples spring to our minds, but the reader with any knowledge of psychological literature will be well able to supply his own. This kind of "validity" might be described as univariate operationalism carried to its ultimate logical emptiness. Face validity, properly satirized by some psychologists as "false validity" and "faith validity" is little better than fiat for most purposes. Probably the most justifiable resort to the concept of face validity in general psychology today is as an act of diplomacy, for example, when a psychologist has to make a test which, in addition to meeting technical standards, shall be convincing to company executives who, like most laymen, have strong convictions on technical psychological matters. And even this resort may only be justifiable if the test is concerned with psychological qualities of a fairly superficial nature, such as do not require disguised techniques of assessment.

There is obviously some need for content validity in assessing tests of attainment, where it is desirable that an examination in history should *not* contain questions on algebra, but even here it has some limitations as an ultimate criterion, for Edward Gibbon's, H. G. Wells's, and Henry Ford's ideas of the nature of history obviously differ enormously. When we turn to more general considerations and to fundamental psychological principles, content validity is at best secondary, and often, in the case of disguised, objective measures, actually undesirable.

Finally, among types of validity we may briefly mention the distinction drawn by the APA Committee between "concurrent" and "predictive" validity. This is a real distinction but *one which unfortunately confuses the property of the test with that of the trait.* Assuming that in science the term "predictive" has a general meaning that has lost its narrow, temporal connotation of "predicting the future" and refers to the prediction of a relationship, the correctness of which can be empirically checked by other means (e.g., when a test predicts the kind of early experiences a child has had), then one can accept the distinction between concurrent prediction and time-remote prediction. But overlooked in this notion is that the difference between an immediate, concurrent prediction and a future prediction has to do not only with the test but also with the behavior of the trait. For example, consider the questions, "Does the trait normally fluctuate from day to day?" "What is its curve of maturation?" "What influences of environment or physiology are likely to affect this trait between the present moment and the time to which the prediction refers?" Thus a test may be extraordinarily valid for a particular trait at a particular moment, but deficient in long-term prediction of this trait. This is not necessarily a lack of validity in the most appropriate sense of the word, because the test may be stable and the trait conspicuously liable to fluctuation. As the following pages attempt to show, this difference is much more clearly conceived and handled under the notion of *utility* than that of validity. As far as any evaluation of a *test* is concerned *all* validity can have meaning only as concurrent.

Section 3　　The Concept and Measurement of Consistency

The consistency of a test may be defined as the extent to which it continues to measure the same thing despite the changes that will always occur when a second measurement is made (either with the whole test again or with another part of it). An operational definition of "measuring the same thing" may be obtained by comparing the predictive power of the test and its correlation with other variables on the two occasions. Consistency is the most important property of a test after validity, from which it is conceptually independent. We shall consider three aspects of consistency, under the names of *reliability, homogeneity,* and *transferability.*

Changes on the second measurement may arise from uncontrollable variation in the conditions of testing and scoring, from a different selection of items in a second half or form of the test, or from differences in the sample of people to whom it is administered. Thus the concept of consistency is in some ways wider than the traditional one of reliability, but it also excludes some sources of variation that have usually been thought to affect reliability. For example, the usual test-retest coefficient of reliability, based on two administrations of a test with an interval of days, weeks, or months, includes as "error" not only chance variation, but true variation of people on a trait; this may be particularly misleading for some personality traits that of their very nature fluctuate rapidly. A test that produced a very high coefficient of test-retest "reliability" or stability in these circumstances would be insensitive, inconsistent, and invalid.

Let us examine, therefore, the possible sources of error that cause any consistency coefficient to fall short of unity. Obviously, not all of them really have to do with the test itself. Some do, such as ambiguities in the meaning of items, printing that is unclear in poor lighting, or scoring instructions that allow different examiners to assign discrepant scores. Other factors are uncontrollable because of circumstances of administration that are not peculiar to the test. The very notion of a rigid distinction between "true variance" and "error variance" can be misleading. Just as, in the physical world, "dirt" is only matter out of place, so, in psychological measurement, one man's error variance is another man's true variance, depending on the nature of the test and the purpose of the experiment.

Our object here is to systematize the discussion by integrating the whole analysis within the framework of the Basic Data Relation Matrix (Cattell, 1952b, 1957, 1966b). This, henceforth called the BDRM or Data Box, and in its earlier development called the covariation chart, is a set of Cartesian coordinates representing the conditions that may vary in any psychological measurement. Among these variables are the sample of people, of stimuli, of responses, of what we may call inmodulators (such as changing moods in the subjects), exmodulators (such as variable external circumstances), and of observers or scorers. If we consider the stimulus fixed, as it is in a test (except for the background stimuli, which are exmodulators), this leaves us four dimensions of variation, which may be represented as four coordinates. Experimental error and sampling error, which together make up the error concept, need to be systematically viewed within this framework. For example, in the method of factor analysis known as P-technique, correlations are calculated between two tests repeated over perhaps a hundred days. What to the traditional user of the reliability coefficient is "error"—the difference between one test administration and another—is here the real variance out of which psychological relations are mined.

Let us consider from a psychometric point of view the general experimental BDRM as shown in Figure 5, with five edges to a five-space parallelopiped. The coordinates or axes here are:

1. A series of different persons (examinees, subjects, patients, candidates). Axis I.
2. A series of different observers (scorers, in most test work). Axis II.
3. A series of different test items, in this case chosen to measure the same thing. Axis III.
4. Changes within the individual himself, because of varying stimuli and internal physiology, that we may call *inmodulators* and represented by Axis IV.
5. Changes in the ambient stimuli and conditions around the subject that we may call *exmodulators* and represented by Axis V.

It will be noted that what in "differential psychology" we call true or real variance runs only along Axis I (different persons), and Axis IV (inmodulators, states of the organism). Axes II, III, and V contain the variance that is commonly called error, occurring through uncontrolled conditions (exmodulators), differing observers (administrators, scorers), and differing items (✔ or parts of the same test).

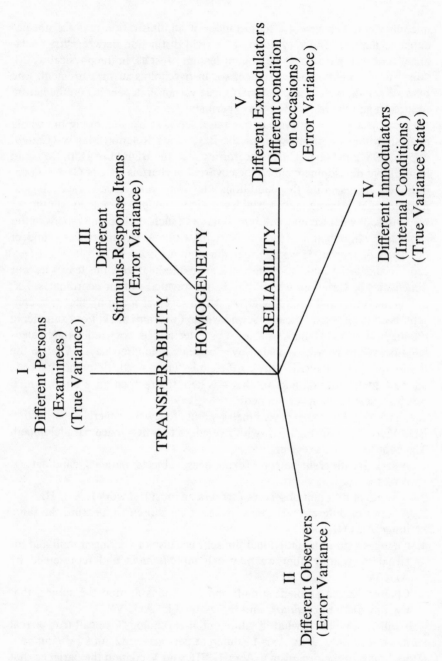

FIGURE **5.** *The three main forms of test consistency related to variance sources in the Basic Data Relation Matrix (BDRM)*

These axes can only be drawn in a kind of perspective in Figure 5, but it will be realized that this parallelopiped could be regarded as built up of slabs, each slab being a matrix bounded by two series of entities, e.g., a matrix of a series of people measured on one test over a series of occasions, a matrix of a series of people measured on one test (and also constant as to occasion modulation) by a series of different observers, and so on. These are the essential "score sheets," one of them the familiar list with school subjects at the heads of the columns, and students' names down the side. There are $^5C_2$, i.e., 10 such matrices possible, and, of course, they cut across each other orthogonally, but because inmodulator test variance has been ruled out, as comprising "function fluctuation" rather than error, there are only $^4C_2 = 6$ matrices concerned with types of error variance, namely:

1. Observer-Person matrix (test items and exmodulators fixed)
2. Exmodulator-Person matrix (test items and observers fixed)
3. Item-Person matrix (exmodulators and observers fixed)
4. Observer-Exmodulator matrix (test items and persons fixed)
5. Item-Observer matrix (exmodulators and persons fixed)
6. Item-Exmodulator matrix (persons and observers fixed).

Any one of these matrices could theoretically be examined in two ways— variance among rows or variance among columns. However, the variance among persons we call *true* variance, so one direction of analysis on 1, 2, and 3, must be excluded from error analysis, leaving 9, instead of 12, possible analyses.

It will now be evident that by this scheme one analyzes test consistency in a far broader context than is usual. For example, it includes the concept of reliability in terms of P-technique (No. 6), which would compare the A and B forms of a test on one person (or on an average of a group of people) across many occasions (two measures per occasion), as well as the reliabilities in the traditional R-technique. It also includes in No. 4 the examination of error among observers scoring the same items on the same occasion on the same people. This has sometimes been called interjudge reliability, and we shall evaluate it later in our discussion of the "conspection coefficient." The advantage of this comprehensiveness is that all sources of "error" are simultaneously considered and compared. However, in a brief exposition we must in some way limit discussion and illustration, that is, by considering from the 12 possible analyses only those 6 which hinge on properties of the test. These, it will be found, yield the concepts we have started with, under the titles of *homogeneity, reliability,* and *transferability* (each in two directions).

Generally speaking, the consistency of tests has been evaluated in the past by *correlating* two sets of scores. But a full analysis of the variation should take account of level as well as pattern, i.e., a change of means as well as a change of order of scores is a sign of low consistency. Thus any of the above matrices may be analyzed in terms of two parameters and by two methods: first, by analysis of variance that assesses the difference between means relative to the variance of each; and second, by agreement of pattern, i.e., correlation. It must also be explicitly stated that the above analysis should and does recognize, and allow for, the possibilities of interaction and covariance among the sources of variance that have been conceptually separated.

With this survey completed, let us now scrutinize more closely the three main forms of consistency-inconsistency. It will be noticed that in deriving these from the BDRM we have made a condensation in one respect and an extension in another. Two of the three axes that represent sources of error variance, namely, the error from different observers and that from different external conditions, have been thrown together to form the wider concept of "error from changing conditions," which constitutes *unreliability*. An extra source of variance, not cognate with the others, has meanwhile been brought into consideration in terms of changes of validity and consistency as one goes from one subcultural group to another. This last is really right outside the framework of the BDRM in Figure 5, from which only two of the following derive directly:

Homogeneity. Along Axis III the various items or subtests that purport to be measures of the same thing may not be entirely consistent. The degree to which *consistency as homogeneity* has been attained can be assessed by two correlations of the kind shown (in Figure 8) within each of the paired series: (1) over people, labeled AP (Across People) *homogeneity*, and (2) over modulating occasions, AO (Across Occasion) *homogeneity* (Matrices 3 and 6 above).

Reliability. Consistency over time, that is, between two successive administrations of the same test, may not be complete. The degree to which such reliability has been attained can be shown by two correlations of the kind shown within each of the paired series: (1) over people, labeled AP (Across People) *reliability,* and (2) over items, labeled AI (Across Item) *reliability* (within one person) (Matrices 2 and 6 above). It will be noted that these are placed at two points on the exmodulator axis, since the inmodulator deals with function fluctuation over time, though the question of how to distinguish true function fluctation from mere change of conditions must be left to fuller discussion elsewhere. We may also note that the original meaning of reliability was freedom from experimental error. The present definition, by which reliability is distinguished from homogeneity, restores this original meaning.

Transferability (or "Hardiness"). Tests will produce different results when given to different samples of people, but some tests will vary less than others in this respect. The degree to which such transferability has been attained in a test may be shown by two correlations of the kind shown in each of the paired series: (1) over items or parts of tests, labeled AI *transferability,* and (2) over occasions, labeled AO *transferability* (Matrices 2 and 3). It should be noted, too, that though the paired series in Figure 8 are shown as starting at two individual cases, they could also represent two *means* of groups. In the fullest sense, however, (see Cattell and Warburton, 1967) transferability estimates require two factor analyses, on the two cultural groups being compared, and a pattern similarity coefficient, r_p, calculated between the two series of weights for the given test, to get a quantitative transferability coefficient.

The nature, meaning, and statistical formulation of each of the above concepts will now be described in more detail, but in summary the main point to be made is that consistency, when logically analyzed, has three basic senses. We intend to reserve for these three aspects, respectively, the terms *reliability* for what has to do with consistency across *occasions* (exmodulating conditions); *homogeneity* for what has to do with consistency across *test parts and forms;* and *transferability* for what has to do with consistency across *samples and populations.*

Section 4 Test Homogeneity and Factor Homogeneity

Let us now turn from our analysis of the generic term "consistency" to a more detailed study of homogeneity, reliability, and transferability. In particular, we need to describe the possible operations for the measurement of these test parameters. It is helpful in this connection, as in our earlier treatment of validity, to keep in mind the ways in which a number of further concepts and coefficients—both subordinate and supraordinate, can be systematically derived from the basic ones, because some of these further deviations are of practical importance. In the first place, the source of variance along any one of the error axes can be restricted to some special condition; e.g., over items and tests parts, one can consider odd-even and other patterns, whereas over exmodulators one can separately consider administrators, scorers, conditions, and so forth. Second, one can consider certain combinations of the primary parameters, such as, for example, the validity multiplied by the reliability, or the homogeneity divided by the reliability, each of which gives a specialized and often important assessment of the test as a test. Third, one can take higher-order concepts and indices, such as the consistency of the validity, by forming supraordinate relations among a series of the primary parameters. Space prevents our handling these ideas systematically, but this perspective will help when occasional references are made below to important instances.

Turning first to the operational treatment of *homogeneity* as distinguished above, we recognize it as the extent to which two or more parts of a test measure the same thing. In terms of the Basic Data Relation Matrix, departure from perfect homogeneity is caused by the variance associated with the different elements along the stimulus-response axis, which will frequently consist of test items.

This brings us to two major subdivisions of the homogeneity concept, according to whether we are dealing with structured (pattern-scored) or unstructured (atomistic) tests. Let us speak of *unstructured test homogeneity* when, because of the particular and intentional structure of the test, some items will be differently evaluated from others. Proposals for unstructured test homogeneity coefficients began, historically, with the random "split-half correlation" and proceeded through the various "homogenized" Kuder-Richardson (1937) formulas to the logical conclusion of Cronbach's (1951) alpha coefficient. The essential feature of this last coefficient is that in spatial terms it indicates how densely the swarm of points constituted by the items drawn in factor space closed in upon the centroid of the swarm, as shown in Figure 6. Algebraically, this extent to which all items are compressed about the central point of the test, and are therefore homogeneous in what they measure, can be expressed by:

$$r = \left(\frac{n}{n-1} \right) \left(\frac{\sigma_t^2 - \Sigma pq}{\sigma_t^2} \right)$$

In this general Kuder-Richardson formula, p is the percentage passing any given item and σ_t^2 is the total test variance. Homogeneity can also be calculated as the mean split-half coefficient when all possible splits are taken, these being,

$$\frac{n!}{2 \frac{.n!}{2} \frac{.n!}{2}}$$

in number.

The concept of homogeneity has been developed recently by Cattell and Tsujioka (1964) into formulas for (1) the homogeneity in a test relative to the natural density of available items in the area and (2) the concept of homogeneity separately considered on (a) a *wanted* and (b) the *unwanted* factor(s) in a factor scale.

The Cronbach and Cattell-Tsujioka formulas provide the necessary treatment of homogeneity for an atomistic, unstructured test. But structured, pattern-scored tests are far more frequent in personality and motivation measurement. The homogeneity of these must be assessed in terms of their special structure, but an illustration can be given, from the region of cognitive achievement tests, of a simple form of patterned homogeneity coefficient. In a general school-achievement test covering, say, ten subjects, it would be no reflection on the test's homogeneity, if, say, the geography items do not correlate with arithmetic items. The same is true of any kind of structured test in which the structure is based on stratification. The splitting into two parts of any stratified test must be symmetrical with respect to these parts, and the appropriate coefficient is the *symmetrical-split* or *fishbone coefficient*, obtained thus:

$$
\begin{matrix}
a & a^1 \\
b & b^1 \\
\cdot & \cdot \\
\cdot & \cdot \\
n & n^1
\end{matrix}
\qquad {}^r(a + b \ldots + n)(a^1 + b^1 \ldots + n^1) = \text{``Fishbone''}
$$

$$\text{Reliability Coefficient.}$$

each part—*a* through *n*—being split according to one of the principles used above for unstructured tests.

Another even more common structured homogeneity coefficient is that between two equivalent forms of a test, in the *equivalence coefficient*. Usually, each form is constructed as a self-sufficient whole, such that the splitting of one form is not the same thing as the splitting of a total battery into pre-designed equivalent forms A and B. For example, one is quite likely to arrange balanced suppressor action to operate within each form as a unit, but not within fractional units. Later, a word will be said on the relation of homogeneity to suppressor action and the production of buffered scales. Here, it suffices to introduce the notion of suppression, which occurs when one has selected an item x for its good loading on the wanted factor, W, but when it has also an appreciable positive loading on the undesired factor, U. Then one proceeds to balance the unwanted loading by including an item y, which measures W positively and U negatively. This cancellation of loadings on unwanted factors, U_1, U_2, etc., is then carried as far as possible. However, any two random sets of equal numbers of items selected from Form A will not usually be properly buffered and will therefore not agree as well as the designed A with the designed B. The coefficient of equivalence is therefore properly applied only to the correlation between an entire Form A and an entire Form B, but not to subsamples of items. There are other structured homogeneity coefficients, notably as in objective motivation batteries, where measurement of a given erg (drive) can be both symmetrical across devices and weighted according to the factor contribution of the parts. Here, one can have homogeneity on device factors with or without homogeneity on dynamic structure factors.

The last examples commented upon above already begin to introduce the idea of *factor* homogeneity as something distinct from *test* homogeneity. To deal clearly with this, we must distinguish among the notions of a *unifactor scale*, a *factor-true scale*, and a *factor-homogeneous scale*. We define a *unifactor scale* as one in which the items have a single common mathematical factor that is not necessarily a psychologically meaningful factor. This definition amounts to the mathematical definition that the items produce a correlation matrix of rank one. Such a factor is likely to be psychologically composite, for it does not represent a factor rotated to a unique simple structure position, although of course, *one* factor cannot be rotated without at least another common factor with which to rotate it. A unifactor scale is thus of limited psychological value, its mathematical neatness being rather pointless if unaccompanied by psychological uniqueness. Expressed spatially, as in Figure 6, the unifactor test is a single vector, but its direction relative to psychologically meaningful factors may be unknown. The common factor among its items could in fact be a linear combination of two or more simple structure factors.

A *factor-true scale*, on the other hand, is a scale that has both the property of measuring only *one* common factor, and the additional property of measuring a factor that has been uniquely rotated, by the criterion of simple structure, to a more meaningful position, and thus represents a particular psychological source trait. However, this is true only of the final, total score, for if one pulls the test apart into items he may find several common factor dimensions represented that have been made to cancel out in the final score by the previously mentioned buffering or mutual suppressor action. In spatial terms, as shown in Figure 6, the items of a factor-true scale may scatter across several other common factors (in the flat diagram, naturally only *one* other factor can be represented), but the centroid vector of the test measures only one factor.

In a *factor-homogeneous scale* (whether unifactor or factor-true), however, an attempt has been made to bring all items to the same composition, namely, a loading *only* on the pure factor. In a common factor-homogeneous scale, the items will all fall on the wanted factor axis, as shown in Figure 6, but will have varying loadings on a specific factor.

Finally, a fourth concept, that of a *factor-pure scale*, can be introduced here as one that is not only factor-true, but one in which the items do not have the dispersal over unwanted factors. However, if we consider specifics also as unwanted factors, then a factor-pure scale is the limiting case of a factor-true scale in which all items cease to have projection on any other factor. This kind of scale, even if desirable, could be approached but never reached and thus need not concern us, though a formula for degree of approach to such a condition is a useful concept. A factor-pure scale is also, in a slightly different sense, a limiting case of the factor-homogeneous scale.

In using these concepts, psychologists need to keep in mind that although the dichotomy of common and specific factors is neat enough mathematically, yet psychologically, in nine cases out of ten, the distinction is relative, and specifics are common factors not as yet revealed as such. Thus what was a specific factor yesterday is apt to become a common factor today, and any differentiation of tests by this criterion is apt to be ephemeral.

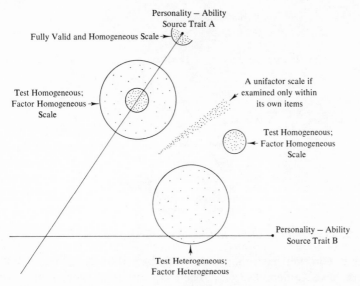

FIGURE **6.** *Varieties of homogeneity, illustrated in a two-space example*

Apart from certain issues concerning those special kinds of score that are ratios, differences, patterns, special combinations of speed measures, and so forth, the main issues of homogeneity measurement have been summarized above. A little more will be said about these special cases in a later section. We also defer to the next chapter the whole question of the relation of homogeneity to reliability, validity, and transferability. However, let us state two positions immediately: (1) high homogeneity of subtests in a personality-factor battery should not be considered a goal in itself and is undesirable beyond that which is necessary for maximum validity; (2) in tests scored by the summation of items, such as the usual cognitive tests, maximum homogeneity is undesirable, both for the reason just alluded to and because a good range of difficulty is impossible with maximized homogeneity.

The principal homogeneity coefficients and concepts resulting from the above discussion are set out in Figure 7.

Among the issues on which degree of homogeneity has special bearing are those of computing the homogeneity and validity of extended tests, as by the Spearman-Brown and Cattell-Radcliffe (1962) formulas. The difference of the C-R from the S-B formula is that the former is designed for factor-true tests and the latter only for homogeneous tests. In calculating from a known reliability coefficient what reliability a test *n* times as long would have, the S-B formula assumes that the new items will have exactly the same composition as the existing ones—and this may be a factorially very complex composition. The C-R extension formula, on the other hand, assumes that

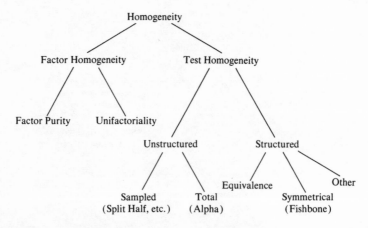

FIGURE **7.** *The relations of homogeneity coefficients*

each new item will have the same loading on the wanted factor but will otherwise have a different specific. There is a certain unreality in the assumption on which the S-B formula depends, whereas the extension of a factor-true scale, for which the C-R formula was designed, is in most ways a more important aim.

With the traditional issues handled, we should glance around more comprehensively at possibilities not commonly considered. It is important to bear in mind that in all treatment up to this point the item or test element has throughout been considered an *indivisible stimulus-response bond* unit. Consistently with this, item variation has been regarded as a *single* parameter of the BDRM. However, in the most comprehensive analysis, as stated in introducing the BDRM, separate stimulus and response variabilities are to be considered. In the last resort, therefore, the homogeneity theorems above can be applied separately to measurement elements differing in *stimulus* characteristics, on the one hand, or in *response* characters, on the other. Indeed, this division into test-stimulus homogeneity and test-response homogeneity has practical importance in some test construction, notably in the construction of motivation tests, but can merely be indicated here.

Section 5   The Varieties of Reliability Coefficients and Indices

Reliability has been defined above as consistency between occasions of testing. But we know that any measured variability between occasions arises from two sources: (1) *true function fluctuation*, that is, change of those psychological entities that the test sets out to measure, because of "inmodulators" of all kinds, (a) reversible, such as changes in moods of the subjects, and (b) relatively irreversible, as in maturation, deterioration, or learning;

(2) *error in the test score,* when the trait levels remain the same, but "error of measurement" still occurs because of "exmodulator" influences.

We should take steps to allow for the former, but we are concerned in *test evaluation* as such only with the latter. Furthermore, reliability is concerned with experimental error, but not with sampling error (except insofar as we want to know the sampling error of reliability coefficients and indices themselves), because the same persons are always involved in the retest.

Conventional treatments of reliability do not usually distinguish these separate sources of error, but it is essential to do so if steps are to be taken to evaluate them independently and to describe correctly the different possible kinds of reliability coefficient. Leaving aside function fluctuation, the second kind of variation described in this section's first paragraph can be split into corrigible, unordered error, traceable to differences in administrator, scorer, and conditions of administration; and incorrigible error, arising from the very fact that the subjects have taken the test once, twice, or more. Strictly, the latter belongs to change in the subject himself, but it is so closely bound up with the instrument as to require consideration in terms of reliability. But the most logical and exhaustive classification of these different types of measurement error is to be made in terms of the various sources of differences, such as differences of administrators, change of scorers, negligence of controllable conditions, variation in uncontrollable conditions, and so forth.

For the sake of precision, let us summarize all these symbolically in a single equation, as follows:

The total observed variance of a test may be written:

6.1

$$\sigma_t{}^2 = \sigma_w{}^2 + \sigma_{fw}{}^2 + \sigma_u{}^2 + \sigma_{fu}{}^2 + \sigma_{es}{}^2 + \sigma_{ea}{}^2 + \sigma_{ec}{}^2 + \sigma_{er}{}^2$$

plus covariances. For clearer writing and discussion, let us assume variance "to be written" and use only the distinguishing symbols. Then 6.1 becomes

6.2 $T = W + FW + U + FU + ES + EA + EC + ER$ plus covariances, where:

    W = variance among people on the factor we *want* to measure by this test.

  FW = variance within each person—function fluctuation—on this wanted trait. This function fluctuation or modulation over occasions will consist of both (a) FW' because of changing internal conditions, and (b) FW'' because of changing external stimulus conditions.

    U = variance on unwanted common factors and specifics (in the last resort we can ignore specifics).

  FU = function fluctuation on unwanted factors, similarly, the result of sources (a) FU' and (b) FU'' separately.

  ES = error because of scoring errors, divisible into that traceable (a) to different scorers, ES', which can be considerable, and (b) to errors by one scorer, ES'', which is usually smaller.

  EA = error because of failure to follow administrative instructions, (a) with different administrators, EA', and (b) with the same administrator, EA''.

EC = error because of changing conditions not defined in the conditions for administering the text, e.g., room temperature, lighting.

ER = error because of familiarity with the test from a previous administration, or more generally, test sophistication.

Usually the four last are lumped together as the error variance term, but some of the most useful things one needs to do with reliability coefficients require a differentiation of these sources. As in any consideration of modulators, one has to recognize that a changing condition, such as poor lighting, for example, may act directly upon the subject's perception and the meaning of the test, or it may produce function fluctuation in unwanted factors. In other words, experimental variation will affect reliability not only directly, but also indirectly through changing the validity. Thus we arrive at an important principle, that a test should not, if possible, alter the thing it is designed to measure, so that an achievement test should not produce actual changes in achievement, nor a test of anxiety introduce what might create anxiety. But one generally tends to be less careful about making sure that uncontrolled administrative conditions do not produce function fluctuation in the less central, unwanted factors that nevertheless contribute to a test score.

Now, corresponding to this list of sources of variance, one could distinguish as many concepts of reliability, and distinct names for reliability coefficients (as well, of course, as varieties of mean shift indices). To be exact, there can be as many as there are combinations, in sets of 1 to 8, of the above variance sources! ($^8C_7 + {}^8C_6 \ldots + {}^8C_1$, i.e., 240!) Obviously, we cannot consider all of them, and, in any case, most are only esoterically useful. Nor can we hope to set out in reasonable compass, except in principle and for the main values, the arrangement of testing operations by which they could be obtained.

For clarity, we may agree to call the coefficient from an *immediate* retesting the *dependability coefficient* (r_{rd}), and that after a week's lapse, or some such substantial period, the *stability coefficient* (r_{rs}). If the conditions of administration and scoring are the same in the two cases, the values of ES, EA, EC, and ER will be the same and the *differences* of these two coefficients will work out as follows (assuming unit variance for the test):

6.3	$r_{rd} = 1 - (ES + EA + EC + ER)$
6.4	$r_{rs} = 1 - (FW + FU) - (ES + EA + EC + ER)$
6.5	$1 - (r_{rd} - r_{rs}) = r_f = 1 - (FW + FU)$

where r_f (not a reliability coefficient, which will *always* be written r_r), is the *coefficient of function constancy,* a function of the amount of change in the actual factor traits.

It cannot, perhaps, be emphasized too often that the coefficient of function constancy (r_f) is *not* a parameter of a test, but is a characteristic of a trait or a combination of traits. Of course, such a coefficient is peculiar to a test to the extent that the particular test measures just that combination of traits, but quite other tests might measure the same main trait. Ultimately, therefore, it is strictly a characteristic of the trait and could best be computed by averaging across various kinds of tests of that trait. Since r_f accounts for a good deal of the departure from unity in the stability coefficient, this latter cannot be regarded as measuring only the reliability of the test. The stability coefficient is a hybrid product of test and trait characteristics. In our listing, the stability coefficient is therefore included with reliabilities, but as an outbred relative in the family of reliability measures, whereas—we would stress again—the *function constancy coefficient* is right outside the family and must never be considered to indicate the high or low consistency of a particular *test*.

Of the remaining possible reliabilities, perhaps the most important are:
The coefficient of conspection or *conspect reliability coefficient,*

6.6 $$r_{rc} = 1 - ES$$

which expresses the degree to which two different scorers obtain the same result from a test administered under identical conditions (or the same actual test answer sheet). The name comes from *con* ("with" or "together") and *spectare* ("to look at") meaning, thus, "the agreement of two different observers in judging the same response by the subject." Conceptually a very important coefficient, this is particularly valuable in bringing out the full extent of the difference between selective and inventive answer tests, and in assessing degrees of reliability among the latter. Educational tests will have a bimodal distribution on this measure, corresponding to the two main divisions of selective-answer and essay-type examinations.

The *coefficient of administrative reliability* represents the degree to which two different administrations agree, and is obtained by:

6.7 $$r_{ra} = 1 - EA$$

Variations of this formula will occur, according to whether the two administrations are by the same person or by different people.

In passing, it may also be pointed out that just as the introduction of tests that depend on recognition rather than recall, and upon the use of electronic-scanning machines, has, in all realms of mental testing, brought the conspection coefficient virtually to unity, so the use of automated administration may soon bring r_{ra}, the coefficient of administrative reliability, to unity. The administration of the 16 PF test, the Culture Fair Intelligence Test, and a number of personality tests has been automated with tape, headphones, and automatically timed page-turning devices for individual work, and with amplifying systems for group administration. The resulting dependability of timing, precision of wording, and avoidance of different vocal emphases have undoubtedly raised reliability coefficients of the r_{ra} type appreciably. Moreover, it would be possible to achieve this without losing the flexibility and rapport needed to respond to individual inquiries by subjects. For, if the testing agency is prepared to meet the initial expense, computers can in principle be programmed to respond to a sufficient range of possibilities, just as does the chess-playing computer.

The *coefficient of circumstance reliability* describes the extent to which the test is free of effect from changing circumstances or conditions *not* included in the controlled instruction situation representing the role of the administrator. It is obtained thus:

6.8 $$r_{re} = 1 - EC$$

It is also possible that automation—because the new test booths and amplifying systems control more of the subject's environment (lighting, temperature, interruptions) than the ordinary test administrator is normally able to control—will raise the coefficient of administrative reliability.

The *coefficient of presophistication or practice immunity* describes the extent to which further contact with a test fails to produce any change in score. It represents the extent to which people are already sophisticated with respect to procedures on that kind of test, as expressed in that particular test. As already stated, it is not strictly a characteristic of the test, but, like other reliability coefficients, a hybrid expressing the interaction of the test with the sample of people. It reveals any gain in sophistication and discloses whether the test is of a type for which sophistication matters.

6.9 $$r_{rp} = 1 - ER$$

Each of these coefficients is to be obtained computationally and experimentally, either by holding all conditions of variability constant except the one concerned, or, where this is not possible, subtracting one coefficient from another, e.g., as r_f is obtained above from r_{rs} and r_{rd}. The main coefficients are summarized in Table XII.

To recur to a point we have already briefly mentioned, it is very possible, and in some circumstances probable, that subjects, on being retested, will be placed in very much the same rank order, but will score on the average at a significantly higher level. Reliability, therefore, needs to be measured both by the appropriate reliability *coefficient* and by the corresponding mean shift reliability *index*. For, unless new norms are provided for the retest (as is done in the IPAT Culture Fair Scales), a serious source of unreliability lies in the differing level of score for everyone on a second administration. Unfortunately, practically nothing is known at present about the relationship between these two aspects of the test reliability parameter, or about its full consequences for test construction and use.

TABLE **XII**

The relations of the chief reliability coefficients—the r_r's

TRUE RELIABILITIES	Held constant
r_{rd} Dependability coefficient	Function fluctuation and all but uncontrollable administrative conditions
r_{rc} Conspection coefficient	Function fluctuation and all but scoring and scorers
r_{ra} Administrative reliability coefficient	Function fluctuation and all but variations possible within prescribed mode of administration
r_{re} Circumstance reliability coefficient	Function fluctuation and all but conditions beyond controlled and uncontrolled administration
r_{rp} Coefficient of presophistication	Function fluctuation and all that is due to encountering test a second time

Each of these has an R (across people) and a P (across occasions) form. By contrast to these TRUE RELIABILITIES we get a CONTAMINATED RELIABILITY in the r_{rs} Stability coefficient

REFERRING TO A TRAIT, NOT A TEST PARAMETER r_f Coefficient of function constancy (opposite in size to magnitude of function fluctuation) derived from r_{rs} and r_{rd}.

Before we go on to the third type of test consistency, that is, what we have called transferability, we should emphasize once more that the value of any reliability coefficient, as of any homogeneity coefficient, is a function not only of the test, but also of all the factors and circumstances that affect the measurement. One of these influences is the level and range of ability (if the test is an ability test) of the sample of people being tested, or in fact the level and range of the sample on whatever psychological quality the test is assessing. If comparison with another test is to be made in terms of reliability or homogeneity, these figures should be provided; and it is still better if reliability and homogeneity coefficients can be based on several samples differing in range and level, because there may be interaction effects of the test properties as such with these means and ranges in yielding the coefficients and indices by which we actually evaluate a test. For example, a small visual angle of some figures in the Culture Fair Intelligence Test, which teachers sometimes think will induce test unreliability, probably would do so in a group of visually handicapped individuals, or in lighting conditions far poorer than any permitted in a classroom, but normally the evidence indicates that these features do not contribute to variance. Nevertheless, there is no doubt that extreme variations in conditions of administration can have a marked effect on the reliability of any test. An account of the reliability of a test, therefore, always requires definition of the total setting, such as test manuals rarely give. It would not be impossible for Test A to have a greater reliability than B in setting X and a poorer one in setting Y. It is important to remember this before giving any weight to a difference of reliability between, say, $+0.80$ and $+0.95$ in two publishers' manuals.

A special point to be noted in this connection concerns the relative values to be expected for both homogeneity and reliability coefficients as they change from their R-technique (AP, across people) form to their P-technique (AO, across occasions) form, as defined above. The magnitude of the experimental error of measurement variance, because of administration, scoring, uncontrolled conditions, and so on, will tend to be the same in both, but the magnitude of the true variance will differ. In the R-technique, it will be variance because of individual differences (W and U), plus (if R-technique measures are made only once) function fluctuation (FW and FU), whereas in the P-technique[2] it will be only FW and FU, as shown in equations 6.10 and 6.11.

6.10   Variance analyzed in R-technique $= \sigma_w{}^2 + \sigma_u{}^2 + \sigma_{fw}{}^2 + \sigma_{fu}{}^2 + \sigma_e{}^2$

6.11   Variance analyzed in P-technique $= \sigma_{fw}{}^2 + \sigma_{fu}{}^2 + \sigma_e{}^2$

The variance traceable to individual differences is, for most traits, much larger than that caused by fluctuation. In other words, the alienation in R-technique is $\dfrac{\sigma_e{}^2}{\sigma_w{}^2 + \sigma_u{}^2 + \sigma_{fw}{}^2 + \sigma_{fu}{}^2}$, whereas in P-technique it is much larger, namely $\dfrac{\sigma_e{}^2}{\sigma_{fw}{}^2 + \sigma_{fu}{}^2}$. Consequently, reliability or homogeneity coefficients in P-technique will tend to run systematically lower than in the usual R-technique, and false judgments will be made about the reliability level of various tests if the critic does not keep these two universes in mind.[3]

A somewhat analogous situation exists in the case of personality and motivation tests, which usually should not be judged by the standards of

---

[2] There is always slight ambiguity in speaking of P-technique in the context of reliability and homogeneity, for, to determine reliability, the two measures *have* to be given consecutively, but consecutiveness (without immediacy, however) is also the characteristic of the whole series. The distinguishing point is that for reliability the readministration must be *immediate*. This is shown in Figure 8 by two very close lines running to the same test, whereas for homogeneity there are two test lines.

[3] Note in Figure 8 that in terms of possible series one would expect P-reliability to be where "internal reliability" is now written, whereas it appears as an extra couple of paired lines parallel to P-homogeneity. The reasons for this have been stated, but it may be noted that the "internal reliability" is the agreement of the order of the set of test parts when the test is readministered to one person (or scored as the mean of a whole group of persons). This tells us something about the reliability of the test—its consistency across occasions (conditions)—but it is not comparable to the other reliability coefficients. It is an AT (across test parts) coefficient, not an across-people or across-occasions (AP or AO) coefficient as reliability coefficients normally are.

reliability applied to traditional ability tests, if only because the latter are normally longer and simpler. Obviously, on the other hand, any particular test in any domain should be judged by the values current in its peers. Admittedly, the lower values current in personality and motivation tests are partly the consequences of a rough pioneer state, from which we shall no doubt emerge in due course. Some difference in evaluating excellence may always be necessary, insofar as the lower reliabilities are also probably partly inherent in the different, less tangible, and less simple qualities of personality and motivation traits.

So far we have spoken of reliability of *the whole test,* but it could be that in two equally reliable tests one is more reliable than the other in *that part which measures the wanted factor.* For example, suppose we have two personality tests, one of which is couched in language requiring much intelligence to understand it and the other is not; then, even if the intelligence factor is suppressed in terms of the factor validity of the tests by having the items on personality factor X balanced for intelligence, the reliability on the personality factor alone is likely to be reduced in the latter case. This is a very complex question, which can only be conceptually indicated and not operationally analyzed within the scope of our present discussion.

Finally, reliability, unlike homogeneity, is an unequivocally desirable characteristic in psychological tests, and the test constructor should always aim to maximize it. There is no simple, or even any logically necessary, relation between the homogeneity of a test and its reliability despite their confusion in several psychometric textbooks.

Section 6 **Transferability**

Transferability has been described in Section 3 of this chapter as an important third form of consistency. It is the tendency of a test to do the same thing and to retain its particular qualities—validity, reliability, and homogeneity—despite changes in samples or populations of people such as are caused by cultural or genetic differences.

Now, although the BDRM performs the function of reminding us that test consistency can be and should be examined in three directions—across (1) time and circumstance, (2) different parts of the test, and (3) different people—the actual coefficients and indices that can be used for assessing transferability are only partly on the same level as those for reliability and homogeneity, and the main formulas are actually of a "higher order." These higher-order coefficients answer the question of how constant or consistent are such first-order measures as validity, reliability, and homogeneity.

Insofar as some coefficients and indices of transferability can be calculated at the same level or order, they are shown in Figure 8, which summarizes

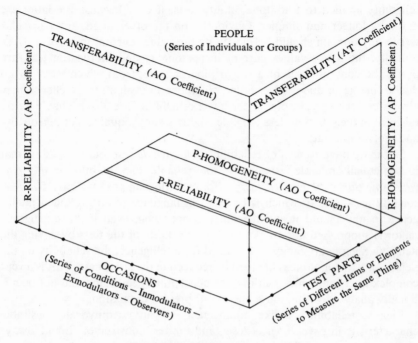

AO: The series correlated across occasions
AT: The series correlated across test parts
AP: The series correlated across people or groups of people

FIGURE **8.** *The three main types of consistency coefficients*

such transferability measures in relation to the reliability and homogeneity coefficients already discussed.

Here we recognize, as in the reliability coefficient, a firm form of transferability that is across test parts, in which the consistency of the test across two people of different cultures (or the means for two groups of different culture) is compared in terms of agreement in order of the test parts. The second transferability coefficient (AO) is derived from the total test score only, with no splitting into parts. The test is administered to two people or groups that are culturally different, and a correlation is obtained by testing on two or more occasions.

These measures, it is true, express some aspects of the consistency of a measure when it is used with different samples or populations. But, as has been indicated, the main sense of transferability is operationally realized only at a higher order, because we want to know how "hardy" and invariant the test is when tried across a whole series of subcultures; and the most important comparison of any two tests in this respect is concerned with the constancy of their validity and consistency coefficients. Higher-order derivatives are discussed more systematically in the next chapter, but for the sake of completeness, two indices are suggested here:

6.12   The coefficient of transferability, $C_t = \dfrac{1}{\sigma_{r_v}}$

where r_v is the concept validity coefficient, and

6.13   The index of transferability, $I_t = \dfrac{1}{\sigma_m}$

where m is the mean score on the test of a sample of defined size. (In 6.12, the validity coefficients should be converted from r's to Fisher z's before the standard deviation is calculated.) The sigma must be taken across a standard range of cultures.

Naturally, if tests are to be properly compared with respect to transferability or "hardiness" under changed conditions, it will be necessary, as suggested elsewhere (Cattell, 1957), to agree on a standard set of cultural subgroups to be tested. Two areas in which it is very often particularly useful and important to know about the hardiness of tests is with respect to (1) differences in age, and (2) educational and regional differences. Many tests, such as the WISC or the Miller Analogies, are obviously so tied to a rather narrow American verbal usage that we should not expect a high transferability coefficient even across the different regions and social classes of the United States, whereas the Culture Fair Intelligence Scales have been used, with absolutely no change of the test form, from Italy to China, with every evidence of constancy of their g saturation (coefficient of transferability) and of mean level on the regular standardization (index of transferability).

SUMMARY *of Chapter Six*

1. Test validity may be systematically analyzed according to the nature of the criterion. Criteria of validation may be (a) Concrete or Abstract, (b) Artificial or Natural, and (c) Direct or Circumstantial, yielding eight possible kinds of coefficient.

2. If one validates a test by the use of concrete, natural criteria, one must speak of *validities* rather than *validity,* for such criteria are innumerable. It makes better sense, therefore, commonly to put the emphasis on *concept validity,* or the soundness with which the test measures a psychologically well-known and stabilized source trait. Such a source trait will then have, in psychological textbooks, a large array of well-understood criterion predictabilities ("validities") or relevances. The test estimates the factor, and the factor is then used in psychologically informed predictions of various concrete criteria.

3. In aiming at concept validity, there are four main types of concept

from which we may choose: (a) factor, (b) cluster, (c) type, and (d) logical construct. But (b) and (c) are neither so determinate nor so useful as (a), and (d) may not emerge as a unitary criterion. Using, therefore, a factor criterion (a), one can aim at a *unifactor,* a *factor-true,* or a *factor-pure scale.* The first lacks simplicity of psychological meaning, and the last is virtually impossible to attain. Consequently, the best aim appears to be what we have called a factor-true scale (buffered by suppressor action among items with regard to unwanted factors). These definitions are expanded in the next chapter.

4. We have used *consistency* as a generic, inclusive term for three forms of test consistency—*homogeneity, reliability,* and *transferability.* These represent consistency across *test elements, occasions,* and *kinds of people,* respectively.

5. *Homogeneity* can be interpreted as a test homogeneity or factor homogeneity. If the former, distinct techniques are necessary for structured and unstructured tests. Maximum homogeneity is not normally something to aim at in test construction, because it will usually conflict with more important test requirements.

6. The concept of *reliability* has been systematically analyzed and split into several concepts, represented by their corresponding coefficients, notably the coefficients of *dependability, conspection, administrative reliability, circumstantial reliability,* and *presophistication.* A clear distinction should be drawn between the concept of reliability and that of function fluctuation, the latter being a property of a psychological trait and not of a test.

7. *Transferability,* or "hardiness," is defined as the extent to which a test retains its important properties, such as validity and consistency, when administered to groups of subjects differing in age, sex, cultural background, and so forth. It can be evaluated at two levels: On the first, it may be evaluated coordinately with reliability and homogeneity in the BDRM, as a coefficient between two kinds of people over (a) test parts, and (b) occasions. At a higher level, it may be evaluated as a coefficient inversely proportionate to the range or scatter of validity coefficients obtained with the various groups of people.

8. The inclusion of reliability, homogeneity, and transferability under consistency is part of a wider theoretical treatment of "error" within the framework of the BDRM, in which two sources of variation—persons and inmodulators (states)—are considered to deal with true variance, and three —observer-scorers differences, exmodulators (or circumstances and occasions), and test-elements—deal with variances commonly considered in psychometry as error. The BDRM thus permits a systematic and comprehensive analysis of relations among the various kinds of true and error variances, in which what is "true" from one aspect may, from other special aspects, be temporarily regarded as error.

Chapter Seven

SCALING, STANDARDIZATION, AND OTHER PROPERTIES REQUIRED IN PSYCHOLOGICAL TESTS

Section 1   Indices of Universality, Durability, Efficiency, and Utility

Psychometrics has been mainly concerned in the past with properties of tests such as reliability and validity, which can easily be reduced to formal precision, with the result that certain other concepts that are at least equally important have been almost entirely neglected. In the present chapter, we plan to discuss some of these neglected but important concepts, several of which have only more recently been expressed in formulas.

Some of these newer concepts will be derived from the more elementary properties of tests discussed in the last chapter. Again, therefore, the reader with no training in psychometrics might be well advised to skip the present chapter on the first reading or to combine the reading of this chapter with whatever reading or discussion of general psychometric textbooks is needed to make it fully comprehensible.

Higher-order relations have already been introduced in the last chapter, in connection with transferability, that is, the property of a test that makes it retain its validity and consistency across varying groups of people. We shall begin by looking at this quality a little more closely. It was first discussed some years ago by the present senior author under the title of "durability" or "hardiness." The latter terms, though they convey in common-sense language pretty clearly what is being sought, are perhaps not quite so apt in the theoretical framework of the BDRM as is the term *transferability*, which we adopted in Chapter 6 and shall henceforth use. A particularly important aspect of transferability is concerned with the extent to which a test retains its validity in different national cultures. For example, the senior author's Culture Fair Intelligence Test appears to maintain its validity across cultures (experiment has shown that the same identical form can be used in America, Italy, and Japan) better than, say, such commonly used intelligence tests as the WAIS, WISC, or the Binet. Transferability, in fact, is not to be conceived in the familiar statistical sense of "agreement across samples," defined in the classical way of samples from a parent population. Although "population" and "sample" are relative terms, transferability is more concerned with constancy across populations, that is, across groups systematically differing in such major respects as age, culture, or racial composition.

Another aspect of transferability, for which perhaps a separate name will eventually be needed, is that of transferability over time, or the constancy of the meaning of a test across decades or centuries. Here again, it may be claimed that, whereas most traditional tests show a marked and rapid shift in their norms, the Culture Fair Intelligence Tests have far greater constancy of standardization. Further, from the evidence of such studies as those of Tsujioka, Pichot and Rennes, and Vandenberg, the factor structure is also likely to remain more constant in factor analyzed tests. Intensive and extensive work has also been in progress for several years on the transferability of the personality tests that we described in Chapter 4, i.e., the Sixteen Personality Factor Questionnaire, and the High School Personality Questionnaire. These have been carefully translated and administered to French, Italian, Japanese, and other national groups and have been refactored to determine the extent to which the validity of the concepts is retained.

In the last chapter, a coefficient and index of transferability were formulated, but a closer examination of the concept suggests that several different coefficients are required to express transferability across age-groups, across periods of time, across national cultures, and possibly also across subcultures, social classes, and school systems. However, the prime distinction to be made is between the constancy of validity and the constancy of reliability. Accordingly, we would suggest that transferability retain the generic meaning, and that within this generic concept we distinguish a *coefficient of universality,* referring to validity, and a *coefficient of durability,* referring to reliability, as schematized in Figure 9.

FIGURE 9

TRANSFERABILITY	
Universality (Degree to which a test maintains *validity* in different samples and circumstances)	*Durability* (Degree to which a test maintains *reliability*)

Thus an age universality coefficient would be

7.1
$$C_{u_a} = \frac{1}{\sigma_{z_v}}$$

where z_v represents a Fisher transformation of the r_v's or validity coefficients obtained by applying the test at five ten-year age intervals, or at whatever ages a psychologists' committee might recommend for the sake of a standard procedure. It can be seen that this is but one example out of many, and that the same principle could equally well be applied to geographical areas, for example, as to age-groups.

A second higher-order concept of major importance in selecting a test is what we shall call its *efficiency*. No experienced psychologist selects his test mechanically by comparing the validities and reliabilites reported in manuals. Implicitly or explicitly, he takes into account the constancy over different groups that we have already treated under the heading of transferability, possibly by consulting some objective reference book, such as Buros' *Mental Measurements Yearbook,* to see how the reliabilities and validities behave over a wide array of populations. And his next question is likely to be "What is the length of the test?" In asking this question, he is implicitly considering the property of efficiency.

Although it is customary, as in the Spearman-Brown formula, to appraise the length of a test in terms of the number of items, a realistic evaluation of length must ultimately be expressed in units of testing *time.* For what the user of any test primarily needs is *so much effective decision-making per unit of time,* and this is the essential feature of what we propose to call test efficiency. Efficiency has been a dominant consideration in the construction of tests such as the 16 PF and the HSPQ, which at first glance suffer by comparison with some other tests in terms of reliability or even of validity. But it should be remembered that, even when both Forms A and B are used, about five or six minutes is given to each personality factor in the HSPQ, for example, and the efficiency is therefore at least as high as that of tests for which higher validity and reliability indices are quoted in their manuals.

In the estimation of efficiency, it is probably desirable and necessary, as with the other higher-order test properties, to use the term for the generic concept, but to distinguish separate indices for *validity efficiency* and *consistency efficiency,* thus:

7.2(a)
$$r_{v_s} = \frac{r_{v_0}}{\sqrt{\frac{t_o}{t_s}(1 - r_{r_0}) + r_{r_0}}}$$

7.2(b)
$$r_{r_s} = \frac{t_s r_{r_0}}{t_o + (t_s - t_o) r_{r_0}}$$

where r_{v_0} and r_{r_0} are the validities and reliabilities observed for the given test length; t_o is the time for the given test and t_s the standard time, say 30 minutes, to which all tests are brought for comparison.

Here r_{v_s} and r_{r_s} are the *standard validity and reliability* proposed by the senior author, obtained by changing length, either by the Spearman-Brown formula as above, or the Cattell-Radcliffe for factor-pure tests (Cattell and Radcliffe, 1962). If a committee of leading psychometrists would agree on the fixed time length at which tests should be compared, these formulae— 7.2(a) to be exact—would give us a useful index of standard efficiency. If we are interested in the potential value of a *type* of test, when made more reliable, the efficiency of that type would be expressed by dividing r_{v_g} by the root of r_{r_g}.

Yet a further concept of value in designing test installations is that of *economy,* which could be expressed as an index, by

7.3
$$I_e = \frac{r_{v_g}}{c}$$

where c is the cost of data gathered by the standard length test. Such a concept focusses our attention on the final sophistication of evaluating testing economy and efficiency in terms of the expense of the *psychologist's* time, as distinct from or in addition to the subject's time as considered above. In the future we shall see more automation of test administration, with increased accuracy as well as increased convenience. As we have previously mentioned, tests such as the 16 PF can already be given with headphones in individual testing or with loudspeaker and tape in group testing in such a way as to minimize the expensive and valuable time required of the trained psychologist. Notable differences among tests exist with regard to the objectivity and suitability for automation of their scoring procedures. Time saved for the psychologist, when he is spared the drudgery of laborious and inconvenient scoring, can be used for more detailed analysis and for more insightful interpretation of the results. It is, of course, difficult to express something as broad as the effectiveness we are now discussing in a single index, but a possible means of doing so might be in terms of cost, and to express the results of current clinical or school testing programs, with proper cost accounting, in terms of an economic efficiency index. This would represent the relative *gain in information* (taking into account the respective validities and consistencies) that could be obtained per unit of cost from various types of tests and programs.

A third important concept among the possible higher-order, derived coefficients is the *utility index.* This is a measure of the breadth of application of a test and aims to answer the question, "In how many predictive tasks will this test be useful?" Obviously, it will not be sufficient merely to make a simple count of the concrete, specific criteria against which the test has been validated. One has to consider also the more fundamental question of whether the criteria that it will predict are of psychological importance. For example, if Test X is a sound measure of Factor A, it enables the user to utilize all the psychological information and laws about the origins and effects of the trait defined by Factor A. It is therefore in respect of utility that the real gain of factored tests over narrow specific tests designed for one particular purpose is most clearly demonstrated. For example, in using, say, the HSPQ, one has measures that are psychologically and developmentally continuous from early childhood to adult life, with all the consequent research findings and correlates.

Therefore, although it would undoubtedly be much simpler and more convenient in the short run to assess the utility of a test by, say, counting the number of concrete criteria predicted with an r of $+0.70$ or higher, yet psychologists would do well to seek means of satisfactorily quantifying the more complex concept of scientific utility just discussed. Some further consequences of this concept of utility, which can be mentioned only briefly, are as follows:

(1) A test yielding scores on several factors in a given amount of testing time will have greater utility than one providing data on one factor only. This assumes, of course, that the factors are scored separately, because they will need to be combined with different weights for different criteria.

(2) Psychologists may find it useful regularly to calculate utilities separately for distinct fields, such as the clinical, industrial, and educational. For example, in the clinical area, the numerous predictions from a measure of the anxiety factor would give it a high utility index in that applied area, whereas a test of achievement in geography would have low utility. But in the school domain, their utility indices, used perhaps as an indication of their relative usefulness in a school-testing program, might turn out to be about equal.

Space prohibits our discussing further this fascinating problem of how best to quantify an index of scientific utility, but it is worth stressing again that its introduction might fulfill the valuable purpose of reminding test users *that psychometry is a part of psychology.*

Section 2 The Relation Between Validity and Reliability

Although in this chapter we are primarily concerned with the higher-order properties of tests, we cannot fully investigate these without first considering some of the relations between the simpler properties. Some of these relations, and particularly the relation of validity to reliability, are treated in the standard psychometric textbooks, such as that of Guilford (1965), and it is commonly said that validity cannot exceed the square root of the reliability coefficient. Although it would be possible to argue that even this fairly conservative statement is an oversimplification, let us accept it as generally applicable, and consider for a moment the well-known and closely related "correction for attenuation," which enables us to derive from the observed validity of a test an estimate of the potential or intrinsic validity by the well-known formula:

7.4

$$r_{vi} = \frac{r_{ro}}{\sqrt{r_{r_c} r_{r_t}}}$$

where r_{vi} and r_{ro} are the intrinsic and observed validities, and r_{r_c} and r_{r_t} are the criterion and test reliabilities. Application of this estimation formula has prevented many a wrong conclusion about the real worth or meaning of a test; the extent to which the low reliability of a short test may lower validity has often been underestimated, and so, in particular, has the unreliability of the criterion! Because criterion measures are often unrepeatable, and their reliability is usually unknown, it is easy to forget that both criterion **and test need to be corrected** for unreliability in the attenuation formula.

Sometimes, however, the correction to the criterion is not possible, even theoretically. When we take as the criterion the performance that Dick Smith made in "Grade Four" achievement tests in 1961, we are dealing with a performance that is unique, and for which no reliability *can* be calculated. Fortunately, or unfortunately, it is impossible to put Dick Smith through that year again to determine how consistent his performance would have been. How can we properly speak about a criterion of this kind as "performance in fourth grade" generally, referring to *any* school, when we cannot put the same children through fourth grade in a variety of different schools to obtain the average achievement under different conditions of teaching, physical environment, and so forth? Such examples remind us that though criterion scores, like test scores, have their various reliabilities, homogeneities, and other properties, we often have no satisfactory means of calculating them. It is important, therefore, to avoid enshrining the criterion, so to speak, as something beyond criticism, and thus regarding any failure of the test to predict the criterion as due to defects of the test. More often than not, indeed, it is probably the weakness of the criterion that accounts for a poor validity coefficient.

In considering conceptual validity, we are often in a much better position, because, as we have seen, the construct or concept against which a test is being validated is generally a factor. One advantage that is not always appreciated is that one can obtain correlations of tests with the pure factor even when one cannot produce a battery to designate the pure factor. This arises from the fact that the axis of a factor is defined by the hyperplane and need not have tests loading the factor very highly in order to define the direction of this axis very exactly. Consequently, by factoring a given test together with various indicators and measures of the factor in which one is interested, one can obtain a correlation of the test with the factor that does not require correction for the unreliability of the factor measurement as in Equation 7.4. Inevitably, some unreliability of a different kind, or rather an imperfect degree of validity, will crop up, because the simple structure can never be perfectly located. On the other hand, if one had used a battery to measure the factor, one would have needed to correct for the unreliability of the battery. Because the correction for unreliability is always an estimate, not an exact figure, there is an advantage in being able to come very near to the true validity without having to allow for the possibly cumulative unreliabilities of a whole battery of tests.

Of course, one may well ask what is the point of correcting a validity for the unreliability of the test, in an effort to get at the "true validity," when all one can use in practice is the actual, observed validity. The answer is that there may be ways of raising the reliability of a test in such a way that one can hope to approach the full, potential validity. Certainly, in the search for valid tests, one does not want to waste research time on embryonic tests that, even when corrected for unreliability, do not promise much validity. But if, on the other hand, one has started with a brief, rough test that happens to incorporate a really promising hypothesis in its construction, the correction for attenuation may clearly show that for all its unreliability the test could be made highly valid. In this event, one can follow up the lucky stroke, and develop that type of test with higher reliability as a means to highly valid measurement. At the beginning of Chapter 6, it will be remembered, we stated rather dogmatically that reliability has acquired excessive popular prestige in relation to validity, and that validity should always in fact take precedence in the construction and evaluation of psychological tests. The considerations described in the last few paragraphs clearly support this viewpoint.

Section 3 The Relation of Homogeneity to Validity

Several of the main points under this heading have already been covered in our treatment of homogeneity in Chapter 6, and a brief discussion will suffice. First and foremost, maximum homogeneity is not compatible with maximum validity.

The more obvious reasons for not aiming at maximum homogeneity when constructing a psychological test can be made plain without using mathematical formulas. Because it is more likely that any specific factor will be more peculiar to a given culture than will any common factor, a highly homogeneous test, in which all items virtually share one common factor, is likely to change more in meaning and validity from culture to culture. To speak of all items sharing a specific factor may sound like a contradiction in terms, but we shall return to this paradox later in this section. If the premise be accepted for the moment, it follows that homogeneity tends to be inversely related to universality and durability. It is also incompatible with a good range of item difficulties within a test of ability, and with the corresponding requirement in a test of personality. In a perfectly homogeneous test, with each item marked right or wrong, people will score either zero or *n, n* being the number of items. Because perfect homogeneity results in this crude kind of all-or-nothing discrimination, it becomes desirable when a graded discrimination is aimed at, to adjust the degree of homogeneity nicely to the range over which one wishes to discriminate, bearing in mind the various practical uses of the test. Thus Scale 2 of the Culture Fair Intelligence Test contains a pretty wide range of difficulty of items, because it is meant to discriminate over the whole range of normal young adult ability. On the other hand, Scale 3 is intended to give maximum discrimination among college students, so that it is finer in its distinctions at that level and less fine in its distinction at the lower ranges.

So far, our illustrations have been in terms of tests of ability, but additional arguments apply to personality tests. Most experienced constructors of items for personality tests have, often reluctantly, come to accept the fact that many of the most useful and satisfactory items are factorially complex. To obtain a good total score on the factor, we commonly have to arrange for suppressor action among such items. This means a test of low homogeneity. Conversely, when someone aims primarily at a test of high homogeneity, he is likely to achieve it by a collection of items that measure only some narrow attitude rather than a broad personality trait; the logical conclusion of achieving high homogeneity is a quite unacceptable and unpractical degree of specificity.

Thus, in the sphere of attitude measurement, the technique of obtaining unidimensional scales introduced by Guttman (Stouffer, 1950) is highly ingenious and logical, but one of the present authors can endorse from a fairly intensive practice of the technique (Oliver and Butcher, 1962) the generally accepted opinion among psychologists that any set of data that satisfies Guttman's stringent criteria of scalability is *too* homogeneous to be of much practical value. The satisfying logical neatness of the procedure is both its strength and its weakness, and one is reluctantly compelled to accept the force of Eysenck's criticism that the logical conclusion of aiming at this kind of homogeneity is to produce a scale in which the same question is rephrased a dozen different times.

Similarly, to use the more familiar language of factor analysis, and to resolve the paradox mentioned in the second paragraph of this section, the cultivation of maximum homogeneity almost inevitably involves the inflation of what should rank as a specific factor into an apparent common or general factor, as illustrated in Figure 10.

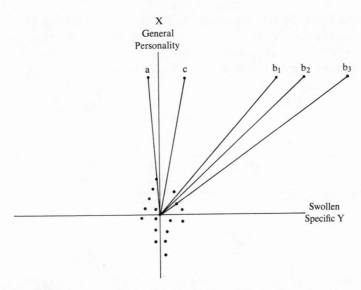

FIGURE **10.** *How a specific factor, in b, may wrongly appear to be a broad factor, through replication in b_1, b_2, and b_3*

Here, the additional shared variance upon what is really a specific factor (when seen in the context of personality factors in general) raises the correlation and homogeneity of items G_1 and G_2, but their projection on Personality Factor X remains unimproved. Moreover, though it has not yet been empirically demonstrated, it seems theoretically probable that this relatively specific variance that has thus been incorporated in the items will act not only as a contaminator, but also as a contaminator peculiarly likely to reduce the universality of the test, when being used across different cultural subgroups. By its very nature, a specific factor is more likely to be local to groups, as it is "local" to tests, than a general personality factor, which we have found usually to retain its validity in different cultural groups. Consequently, high homogeneity is probably to be avoided when seeking valid general personality scales and scales of high universality across subcultures.

When, instead of aiming primarily at homogeneity, we aim at high loading on the required factor and at mutual suppression among items on the unwanted factors, we have a situation that is shown in its simplest form in Figure 11. High validity, or even perfect validity in certain conditions, can exist when homogeneity has dropped to zero (or when the equivalence coefficient of A and B test forms is zero).

This point needs careful consideration. Figure 11 presents the essence of the argument in the simplest possible graphical form; the more general case is more easily illustrated algebraically, and we shall enlarge on it later in this chapter. In Figure 11 the test parts A and B could be items, or equivalent test forms, or any other test elements. Each correlates +0.71 with the wanted or criterion factor, W, that the test sets out to measure, whereas they correlate respectively +0.71 and −0.71 with the unwanted factor, U, which these elements therefore seek to remove from the test score by "suppression."

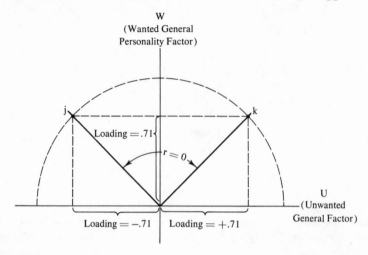

FIGURE **11.** *The possibility of perfect validity with zero homogeneity*

The simplifications made in this example for the sake of clarity are: (1) the test elements are only two in number; (2) they are perfectly reliable; and (3) they have no specific factor or further common-factor variance. It will be evident that in these circumstances they correlate zero and are orthogonal, giving the battery zero homogeneity, but that their sum is a pure measure of the required factor.

In the practical case, these three simplifying conditions will not apply, but the principle remains unchanged. With more than two elements, however, a mean homogeneity of zero can be maintained only if the loadings of the items on the factor fall below 0.71 with a new unwanted factor for each additional pair of items. This still yields a perfect validity and complete suppression of unwanted factors.

In the ordinary instance, where such symmetry of the unwanted factors is unlikely to occur, and where specific factors are involved, a perfect validity of the test in terms of the factor will no longer be obtainable. The unwanted common factors may be effectively suppressed, but the accumulation of specific factor variances will prevent a correlation of unity between factor and test. As Cattell and Tsujioka (1964) have shown in a more systematic analysis of this problem, the validity, r_{tf} (the correlation of the whole test with the wanted factor, w or f), becomes as follows:

$$7.5 \qquad r_{tf} = \frac{\Sigma_{i=1}\alpha_{iw}\sigma_i r_{iw}}{\sqrt{\Sigma\alpha_{iw}^2\sigma_i^2 + 2\displaystyle\sum_j^{n(n-i)/2} {}_i\alpha_{iw}\alpha_{jw}\sigma_i\sigma_j r_{ij}}}$$

where a_{iw} is the weight of the item i in estimating the wanted factor, σ_i the standard deviation of the item, and r_{ij} the correlation of any item with any other. There follows from this a necessary relation between the number of items and their mean loading on the wanted factor, if a perfect correlation is to be maintained, viz.:

$$7.6 \qquad \bar{r}_{iw} = \sqrt{\frac{1 + (n-1)\,\bar{r}_{ij}}{n}}$$

where n is the number of items, $\bar{r}_{ij}$ their mean intercorrelation and $\bar{r}_{iw}$ their mean correlation with the wanted factor.

Our main aim in this discussion of the relation between homogeneity and validity is to introduce a proper sense of perspective. Homogeneity is a desirable property of tests *up to a point,* but there is no simple linear relation between homogeneity and the more important test properties that we have attempted to outline. We do not wish to flog a dead horse, but equally we should not claim to be blazing a new trail. The more perceptive workers in the field of psychometrics have not only made a similar point, but have suggested a formula to regulate the optimum degree of test homogeneity. Humphreys, for example, has expressed this in a coefficient $r = \dfrac{r_{ic}}{r_{it}}$, where r_{ic} is the mean item correlation with the criterion, and r_{it} is the mean item correlation with the test.

Finally, for those readers who accept the general approach to problems of reliability and validity outlined in this and the preceding chapters, and who wish to probe a little deeper into recent developments, some important new formulas have been developed by Cattell and Tsujioka, and are presented in an appendix to this volume.

Section 4   Conditions and Principles of Equal-Interval and Absolute Scaling

Validity and consistency are admittedly the most important properties of a psychological test or battery, but a test may reliably measure the required concept and nothing else and yet not have scale units that are properly calibrated. The literature on the scaling of tests is very extensive, but once again our impression is that a large proportion of the published papers on the subject are excessively specific, and very often applicable only to, say, conventional opinion questionnaires of a very limited type.

By contrast, the four types of scale formulated by Stevens (1951) have won wide acceptance as useful categories and are well known to almost every psychologist. These consist, in ascending order of precision, of: (1) the nominal scale, in which numbers are used essentially as identifying labels, as numbers are affixed to the backs of football players (in other words, this type of "scale" really consists of a set of discrete categories); (2) the ordinal scale, in which the rank order conveys reliable information, but no such information is available about the relative size of differences between ranks; (3) the interval scale, in which such differences are meaningful and reliable, but no fixed, nonarbitrary zero point is available; (4) the ratio scale, in which all the properties of the interval scale obtain, with the additional advantage of a nonarbitrary zero point, and the consequent possibility of invariant ratios between measurements.

Admittedly, most psychological scales have to be classified as intermediate cases, falling, for example, between the categories of ordinal and interval scales. Coombs (1953) has attempted to amplify and refine this set of categories, but there is no doubt that Stevens' original four categories provide a useful starting point for discussion and classification.

As every psychometrist knows, psychology has made only sporadic advances from qualitative and ordinal to interval and ratio scales. Another major disappointment has been the failure to proceed from specific psychological measurement units to the *interactional* stage of definition (Cattell, 1957), in which units interact with, and are reducible to, the centimeter-gram-second units of the physical sciences.

Before plunging deeper into these questions, we must remind the reader of the differences between unstructured scales and structured tests. The former are composed of items similar in all properties, except in difficulty, when we are testing abilities, and, when we are assessing personality, in all respects except in the corresponding property that we shall call eccentricity. Structured tests are resolvable only into complex derivatives of separate responses. Thus unstructured scales consist of "atomistic" items, interchangeable in almost every respect, whereas structured tests have distinct parts, and scores may be, for example, ratios among the parts.

Personality and motivation tests, especially of the more recent objective kind here discussed, tend, far more frequently than ability and achievement tests, to be structured in such a way that the score is no simple or weighted sum applied by a uniform formula to all items. Consequently, such impressive elaborations of item-scaling procedures as those described by Thurstone and Chave (1929), Likert (1932), Gulliksen (1950), Guttman (1950), Torgerson (1952), Coombs (1953), Lord (1953), and others, which apply to unstructured tests, and which are now clearly and well summarized in several textbooks, are typically not very suitable for scaling the kinds of test with which personality and motivation measurement are increasingly concerned.

Let us start from the numerical values called raw scores, derived from our personality and motivation tests by whatever scoring rules have proved to give factor validity, and consider how these can be transformed to units that will have: a) equal-interval scaling properties; b) absolute scaling properties; and c) will form a ratio scale with a meaningful zero point.

With these aims, we shall consider in sequence three concepts, which differ in degree of sophistication: the assumption of a normal distribution; extremity-vector scaling; and relational simplex scaling.

The assumption of normal distribution is an old notion, at which seekers for equal-interval units have often clutched for lack of a better principle, and which is sometimes acceptable as a standby. It is applicable to an unstructured set of items or to a single score that may be derived in quite a complicated way, as in the structured type of test to which we have now extended our discussion. The assumption that equal-interval units have been found whenever a normal distribution of scores has been obtained is perhaps more defensible for single, factorially complex, variables than for factors. For the former, like any sum of many small variance contributions (each independent and random as to sign), are likely, in terms of de Moivre's theorem, to produce a normal distribution of scores when truly measured. Although a factor is estimated from variables, these are commonly both correlated and specially selected, so that the condition of random, uncorrelated, additive variances no longer applies. Furthermore, for scientific rather than statistical reasons, it would seem very unlikely that certain pure factors, such as one of the neuroticism factors, would be normally distributed in the general population. When normality *can* be reasonably assumed in the true, scaled scores, we can then accept as giving equal intervals that monotonic transformation of the raw scores which yields a normal distribution.

The *extremity-vector scaling principle* was described by Cattell (1957) and in its simplest form applies to a set of items or subtests. When yes-no items or other pass-fail elements in a scale are intercorrelated by the product-moment formula and then factored, elements of nearly equal difficulty will correlate, other things being equal, more highly than those of unequal difficulty. As the work of Demaree and Smith, Dingman, Wherry, and others has shown, factoring will yield "difficulty factors," distinct from the psychological content factors, that will load the most difficult items positively and the easiest negatively (or vice versa). Certain questions, however, still remain to be cleared up by further experiment, notably in regard to the rotational conditions necessary for the proper emergence of these factors.

In this connection, the notion of "difficulty," which is strictly peculiar to ability and achievement tests, has first to be generalized to measures of per-

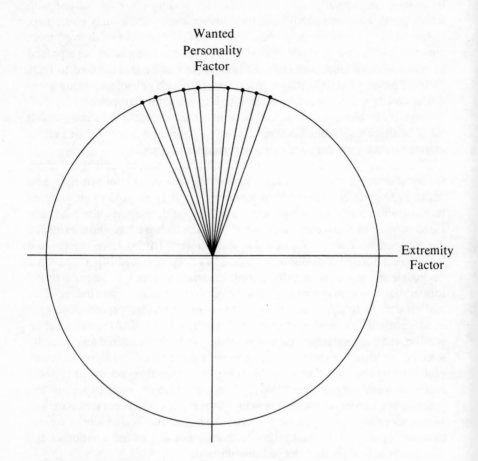

FIGURE **12.** *An extremity-vectored scale*

sonality, of motivation, and of individual differences in general; we then have the concept of "extremity" or "eccentricity" of response. With this extension, it is now proposed that the eccentricity scoring of a set of items be converted to a quantitative, equal-interval scale by using the factor loadings of the items on the eccentricity factor as the basic quantities. A properly scaled set of items, designed to give equal intervals, would then be selected from a larger set in order to arrange themselves as shown in Figure 12, in such a way that the increment of loading on the extremity factor from one element to the next is always the same. This we call an *extremity-vectored scale*, because the elements fall uniformly on the vector of the extremity factor.

In Figure 12 it is assumed for the sake of simplicity that the variance of each element is fully accounted for by the two factors, but in practice there would usually be other common or specific factors, so that the simple inverse relationship between content factor and difficulty factor loadings shown here would not constitute any special problem. Very little has yet been done (since the proposal of this design in 1957) to explore the ensuing properties of extremity-vectored scales; the underlying logic bears some similarity to the principle of "Guttman scales" (Stouffer, 1950), but the theory has the attraction of integrating scaling, the factor-trueness of scales, and the factor purity of items in the same frame of reference.

Probably the most satisfactory general basis for obtaining equal-unit intervals, and possibly ratio or absolute scales for personality, ability, and motivation batteries is that contained in the *relational simplex theory* (Cattell, 1962). It is applicable both to structured and to unstructured scales. The reader must be referrred to the paper cited for a full statement of assumptions and procedures, but a brief account can be given here. The theory has a special and a general form. The first states that a sample of psychological scales, in which experimental stretchings and contractions are being tried out, approaches nearest to the equal-interval condition over the whole sample of variables when the mean correlation among the scales reaches a maximum. As more detailed discussion will show, this is an extension of the notion of correction for attenuation, by which any departure from true scaling is considered an intrusion of error.

The general theory of relational simplex scaling goes further and states that the true scaling is achieved insofar as precision of prediction from one variable to another is achieved. This requires, of course, not only that we have correct scaling but also that we have the correct law connecting one variable and another, but the required precision certainly cannot be achieved without the former as well as the latter. The general theory may also go beyond the production of equal-interval scaling and embrace the detection of correct absolute zeros. For, when an incorrect zero is assumed for a scale, the true relationship of one variable with another will in general be underestimated. The relational simplex theory in either form derives its authority from the scientist's act of faith that Newton expressed as *"natura est simplex."* In other words, we adopt the simplest model among those that predict the empirical facts equally well.

Considering the above three principles of scaling, as well as the more traditional itemetric procedures mentioned, and with which the reader is probably familiar, it will at once be evident that no existing psychological scales of measurement can claim to have advanced very far toward the ideal of equal-interval and absolute scales. This could hardly be otherwise, because the discovery of the functionally unitary dimensions for which such scales need to be constructed has been so recent. Indeed, the factor vectors for such scales have still to be oriented with more accuracy, and the factor-true batteries have to be more efficiently constructed, before the transformations of such scales into ideal scales can be undertaken. These advances lie in the future, but when they are made, puzzling failures of theoretically anticipated relationships to materialize will probably be explained.

Section 5   Principles of Test Standardization: The Reference Group

Certain aspects of standardization are extremely important, but sheer size of the group of subjects beyond a moderate minimum is not one of them. Moreover, one should also bear in mind that important research can be done with tests that have not been standardized at all! If one's aim, for example, is to determine the correlations between some criterion, and say, intelligence or personality measures, this can be done just as readily with raw scores as with standard scores (assuming that equal-interval properties are possessed by neither or by both). Indeed, there is often an advantage in keeping to raw scores, because the standardization generally forces coarser grouping of scores, so that the correlations will tend to be underestimated. Also, additional clerical errors (which one must realistically admit to be inevitable) will tend to increase with each transformation of scores. On the other hand, one must admit that standardization may imply a step toward the scaling of scores in equal units, even if this aim is never fully achieved in practice. Indeed, the generally accepted division of psychological scales into four types—nominal, ordinal, interval, and ratio, which we have already mentioned—really needs refinement, because most actual scales are intermediate cases. But the simple transformation of raw scores into standard scores, in the sense of scores expressed in terms of the standard deviation of the group, although it does not normally result in truly equal units of measurement, produces some important advantages. Thus, when weights are to be applied to scores from different sources, as in a multiple correlation or a specification equation, there is the advantage that these weights can be applied without the additional correction for different standard deviations. Except in the conditions mentioned, therefore, which generally apply only to pure research, a good standardization has several desirable features that make its pursuit worthwhile.

Because certain quite unique problems arise in the standardization of motivation tests, their consideration is best deferred to the next section. However, in the total field of available factorized tests produced under the general direction of the present senior author, the three Culture Fair Intelligence Test scales, the series of personality questionnaires such as the 16 PF and HSPQ, and the motivation batteries are well standardized, but the Objective-Analytic Personality Batteries have still to be brought to an adequate standardization. The reason for deferring standardization of the last-named, even eight years after their initial appearance, is that they are still growing. One of the evils of a heavy investment in standardization, though it follows not as a necessary but only as an economic consequence, is that publishers tend to decide against desirable revisions of the test itself.

In factored tests, with which type we are mainly concerned here, one does not usually bother about any *separate* standardization of the component six to ten subtests, but only with that of the weighted sum of this collection of subtest scores, which constitutes the estimate of the factor. The weight of each subtest may be made unity, as commonly holds approximately, for convenience of scoring, just as when we add intelligence battery subtests of roughly equal range to get a single score. Very often, however, to make better use of our test information, we have to use a more complicated system of weighting. The convenience and simplicity of simply adding raw subtest scores as they stand has made this practice a widely adopted one in applied psychology, but the conditions of personality and motivation measurement usually demand more complex procedures. The simpler procedure is questionable on two grounds:

1. Since subtests are chosen to be approximately equal in their loadings on a particular factor, it may appear reasonable at first sight to disregard their slight differences in this respect and give them equal weight. But the possible grossly unequal standard deviations of the raw scores mean that, unless correction is made, they are in fact given very unequal weight in a variety of situations, and particularly in prediction.

2. With oblique factors, the weights to be given to tests in estimating a factor are often very different from the beta weights appropriate to the multiple correlation with the factor if it stood alone. For example, the factor estimation weights of variables can differ a good deal when the correlations with the factor differ little. The formulas for reaching oblique-factor weights proceeding from the first-obtained rotated reference vector structure matrix, V_{rs}, and the RV intercorrelation matrix, C_r, are given below.

In defense of the direct addition of raw scores, it is often pointed out that the correlation of the resulting sum with the more refined estimate is commonly so high (between $+0.75$ and $+0.95$), as not to "justify the extra work" of the latter. However, an r of $+0.8$ still means that only 64 per cent of the "true" variance is being handled by the "convenient" procedure, and it is doubtful whether convenience can justify throwing away as much of the available accuracy of estimate as this indicates. Probably, as computers become increasingly harnessed to the automation of test administration and scoring, it will be possible to introduce as a standard procedure the more precise weighting of subtests required to produce the most accurate factor estimate.

The actual weights for subtests to give the best estimate of a factor score in the oblique case are obtained by the following formula,

$$7.7 \qquad\qquad V_{fe} = R^{-1}V_{fs}$$

where R is the correlation matrix among the subtests, V_{fs} is the factor structure matrix, i.e., the correlations of the factors with the subtests, and V_{fe} is the required factor estimate or weighting matrix. V_{fs} is obtained thus:

$$7.8 \qquad\qquad V_{fs} = V_{rs}C_r^{-1}D$$

where C_r is the correlations among the reference vectors, and V_{rs} is the experimentally obtained simple structure among the reference vectors.

This weighting matrix V_{fe} is finally applied to each person's scores on the subtests as set out in the score matrix S_t, to obtain the factor score matrix S_f.

$$7.9 \qquad\qquad S_f = S_tV'_{fe}$$

After this illustration of the practical steps for the best possible derivation of the factor scores, we must remember that though the test scores in S_t are considered in standard scores, the scores in S_f, though centered on O, are not in standard scores. (They are short of unit variance to the extent that the squared multiple correlation is short of unity.) Parenthetically it should be pointed out, as Horn (1963) has done, that estimation of factors based on the reciprocal regression, as in the Dwyer extension principle, yield somewhat different values from those reached by this method.

With this view of factor scores, let us return to our main theme of score standardization. In all standardization, the main issues are essentially three:

1. What are the desirable procedures for obtaining a sample of that population which we designate as our *reference population?*

2. How can we best handle the required modifications of standardization with respect to *subclasses* of age, sex, educational group, etc.?

3. What *kinds of units* are most useful for expression of a standard score?

Obtaining the *reference population* is well handled in most statistical textbooks and needs little comment here, although we shall return to it in Chapter 8. Suffice it to say that the size of the sample is generally of less importance than the method of selection. A particularly important principle in selecting samples on which to standardize tests is that of stratification. For example, a careful weighting of subsamples of various occupational groups to produce a well-stratified sample of the population of England and Wales was made by Cattell in producing probably the first complete standardization of an adult intelligence scale (Verbal Scale III, 1933). It is surprising, after a further thirty years of intelligence test production, to find how rarely (about three times) adult intelligence tests have been standardized on a properly stratified sample. A systematic statement of procedures for stratified sampling has since been published by Cattell and Greene (1961), illustrating the standardization by this means of the 16 PF for adult American females. Therein women were sampled simultaneously with respect to: (1) the age distribution of adult women; (2) distribution by social class and education; (3) married and unmarried status; (4) geographical distribution. A sample of 880 cases appearing with proper frequency in the cells of such a cross-classification gives a better probability of obtaining a representative sample of American women, and consequently of fixing accurate norms, than does a vastly greater number gathered simply wherever they can be gathered.

A difficulty about the reference population that is seldom faced is that in some sense it needs to be sampled across time as well as across society. A special aspect of this is discussed below, but the main issue is that any test containing items subject to cultural influence produces scores that change from year to year as the culture changes. A proper treatment of norms really requires that changes in the culture that result in measurable changes in the distribution of test scores be determined at, say, five-year intervals, and that a yearly correction be calculated in anticipation and extrapolation of this trend for each year since the latest norms were established. In intelligence testing, we can avoid most of this particular source of error by using culture-fair tests. For, as pointed out in Chapter 2, the norms of traditional, culture-contaminated tests soar at a rapid rate with improving standards of education, shifting by about half a standard deviation in a generation, whereas those of culture-fair tests appear to show negligible change over about a fifteen-year interval.

It is not always realized that changes in measured IQ because of cultural drift may be large compared with variations resulting from sampling error. If one standardizes an intelligence test on a random sample of only 600 people (per year of age), the standard error of the mean will be well under one unit, or $\dfrac{15}{\sqrt{600}}$, whereas a test like the Wechsler or Binet, even standardized on 100,000 cases, can shift, through cultural drift, more than a whole point with each year that elapses. It would be better to restandardize a test every year or two (if it is not culture-fair) on 2,000 or 3,000 cases than on 100,000 every decade, because norms on a seriously culture-contaminated test tend in an important sense and to an appreciable degree to become obsolete from the moment the tables are printed.

Section 6   **Test Standardization. Modifications for Age, Sex, Ipsatization of Scores, and for Different Forms of a Test**

The second class of standardization problems listed in Section 5 presents us with a somewhat miscellaneous set of considerations.

Some abilities and most personality and motivation traits differ appreciably between the sexes, change systematically with age, and have different distributions in different educational, social, and regional groups. If we wish to know where the individual stands in relation to his own group, there are two main ways in which the necessary comparisons can be achieved:

1. We can work out regression "corrections" for sex, age, class, and so forth, before applying them to raw scores and consulting one single, *general* standardization table.

2. We can prepare separate standardization tables covering both the whole population and each subspecies within it.

The latter method, because it involves no correction calculations, seems to be more popular with test users and has been adopted for the 16 PF, the HSPQ, and other IPAT tests (though it is more troublesome and expensive to the test constructor and publisher). It does have one drawback for the user, namely, that with this *embarras de richesse* he has to distinguish between and sort through more tables and to make up his own mind more clearly about the choice of reference group for his purpose. For example, should the scores of a twenty-one-year-old woman student be looked up in norms for adult women, for women students, or for students (men and women combined)? The logic of choice is not always so easy as in this example. If, for example, comparisons of performance, selections for appointments, and so on, are to be made *within* student groups, then student norms are appropriate. But if the "competition" is in a wider realm, then a wider reference group must be taken. If, for example, a position is open equally to men and women of all subcultures and races, then it is not a question of, say, how intelligent the individual is in comparison with other women, but in comparison with the whole population.

It should be noted in this connection that some modes of scoring already have corrections built into them. For example, the IQ is corrected for age, yet for certain purposes the correction often needs to be taken out again, as when it is part of the aim of a research to assess *actual* mental capacity. Corrections for age are of greatest importance when predictions extend to remoter times. For example, Factor C (Ego Strength) in the 16 PF is known normally to increase with age. If Factor C were used in scholarship selection at eleven years of age in an attempt to predict performance in school for the next six or seven years and in different kinds of careers, then with children varying between ten and twelve years of age at the time of the examination a slightly more accurate prediction of say, the eighteen-year-old level on Factor C would be obtained by using standardized scores that incorporated a correction for age.

We have mentioned the importance of cultural changes and cultural "drift" in connection with the measurement of abilities, but there are two further points to be made about it. First, the normal correction for age actually incorporates both a true age correction and a correction for cultural changes, and these two should be strictly separated. Second, this applies at least as much to personality as to abilities. For instance, in the last fifty years, our culture has seen a decided diminution in incidence of conversion hysteria, an increase in psychosomatic illnesses, an increase in school-achievement standards, and a lesser incidence of manic-depressive psychoses. One can speculate that in terms of personality factors these may mean a cultural change, in the form of a fall in Factors A and F (see Chapter 4) and a rise in G and Q_3 (the superego components), and that these cultural changes will interact with and be confounded with other changes in personality factors among older people resulting from the actual process of aging. Whether or not these particular speculations are correct, there is no doubt that some cultural changes in personality factors must be taking place, about which no research yet exists to guide us. The first step toward the separation of age trend and cultural trend is to be made by: (1) testing people of different ages at a given time; and (2) retesting the same individuals over a time lapse, and then making the necessary comparisons. The need for an approach of this kind, the technical difficulties involved, and some designs for coping with them are summarized by Schaie (1965). Psychologists have still to make these and other longitudinal studies even of small samples.

A special and important problem in standardization concerns what has come to be known as *ipsative scoring*. It can best be illustrated in the field in which it is most useful, that of motivation measurement. (This discussion will continue our treatment of the measurement of motivation in Chapter 5 and anticipates further discussion in Chapter 11.) When an individual's degree of interest in a particular topic is assessed by the extent to which he remembers material relevant to that topic, it is necessary to make allowance for the general power of his memory. For example, if he has a very good memory generally, we shall overestimate his interest in, say, photography, if we score him literally by the amount he knows, compared with the knowledge held by some other person of generally poor memory. It is therefore necessary somehow to remove, or "partial out," the effect of good or bad memory in general; and the same principle will apply to other, similar ways in which to assess interests.

One possible answer to this problem, which was advocated by Cattell (1935) in an analysis of interest measurement, is to adopt deliberately what has been called the solipsistic assumption, namely, that *the total interest in the whole circle of the environment is the same for everyone.* This solipsistic theory of interests leads logically to the statistical procedure known as *ipsative scoring,* though not all ipsatizing operations derive from the theory. Suppose, for example, that we are making an attempt to sample the total field of interests of a group of people, and assemble one hundred separate tests, each representing a different interest, and each assessing the strength of interest by degree of GSR response. We then add the GSR scores on all one hundred tests and divide each individual score by this total. The effect of this operation of ipsatization is, first, to remove or "partial out" differences in general GSR reactivity, and this is the main aim; also, however, the operation reduces everyone's mean score on the total set of interests to the same figure. This is, strictly, *semi-ipsative* scoring, for it brings all people to the same mean interest score but leaves them with different standard deviation. Full ipsative scoring brings all people both to the same mean and the same standard deviation on the total set of interests.

Ipsative scoring is logically feasible whenever we have a series of tests that differ in the stimulus situations but use the same type of response. Thus, just as normative scores are derived from a distribution either over people or occasions, so ipsative scores are a form of standardization over a series, or a population, of stimulus situations. Ipsative scoring is a form of standardization within the individual, as normative scoring is standardization within the group. However, it is not the only possible form of standardization within the individual: We can also speak of *performative* or *temporal standardization* when the same test is used on many occasions and is standardized for one person in terms of these various occasions.

After treating scores ipsatively we can again treat them normatively, by a double standardization. Thus interest in sports may be at the 70th percentile in Brown's interests, ipsatively, and this may place his sports interest at, say, the 55th percentile in a final ipsative-normative scoring, indicating that in relation to other people the 70th percentile position for sports is hardly higher than average.

There are a number of special properties of ipsatively standardized scores of which the user should take account. For example:

1. No mean difference will be discoverable between one group or person and another on *total* interest scores in the ipsative form.

2. If Group A is higher than Group B on one subset of interest variables, it is bound to be lower on the complementary set.

3. The average correlation between n interests that have been measured ipsatively and intercorrelated must be $\dfrac{-1}{n-1}$.

4. Significant correlations between *particular* interests and general personality and ability traits may arise, but no significant correlation of such variates with *total* interest can show up.

Although ipsatization of the kind we have described has been useful in practice, the solipsistic assumption on which it is based is probably not realistic except as an approximation or simplifying assumption. A possible way of retaining the advantage of the procedure without being tied to the restrictive assumption will be tried out in the future standardization of motivation batteries. The proposed method follows. One first finds the relative proportions of variance in the total battery traceable, respectively, to motivation and device factors. If these variances are a and b, then the aim is to ipsatize b (device variance) but not a. Each person's score on a particular interest, I_j, is therefore multiplied by $\dfrac{a}{a + b}$ to give the best estimate of his device-free score. This still allows individuals to differ on their *total* interest scores.

Finally, a brief note is necessary on the standardization of tests when several equivalent forms, such as Forms A, B, C, and D of the 16 PF, are available. There is no need at all for equivalent forms to produce an equal mean and range of raw scores, but the standard scores obtained from each form should be equivalent. This does not mean that a particular individual or group of individuals who average a standard score X on Form A should be expected to reach score X on Form B. So long as two forms do not correlate perfectly, as will always be the case in practice, there will be regression to the mean from one test form to the other equivalent form. Consequently, if the person scores X, which is much above average, on A, the value of X' on B will be a bit lower than X, and vice versa if X had been below average. Similarly, the variance of the scores on $(A + B)$ as a single total test will not be the simple sum of the variances of A and B, but can be found from the well-known Equation 7.10 below.

7.10 $$\sigma^2_{A+B} = \sigma^2_A + \sigma^2_B + 2r\sigma_A\sigma_B$$

Anyone's standard score on the total test $(A + B)$ will be the mean of his standard scores on A and on B, but it cannot be obtained (as is sometimes absentmindedly done) by halving his total raw score and looking up the standard score from A or B tables alone.

Section 7 The Numerical Expression of a Standardized Score

As every student of psychological testing knows, there are two main ways in which to convert raw scores to standard numerical values through a reference population, as follows:

1. By rank orders, such as percentiles, which transform the raw scores to the percentile mark they would occupy in the general population.

2. By converting the raw scores to standard scores, which are expressed as standard deviation units above or below the mean of the population.

Two other possible methods exist in theory:

3. Where a psychological measure is expressed in equal units, and is correlated with another such measure, a standard score on the first variable can be transformed to a corresponding score on the second.

4. Where psychological qualities are related to physical or economic units, a form of standardization is possible in terms of the latter. For example, an intelligence measure could be standardized (if mean salaries and intelligence levels of occupations were monotonically related) against earning levels, or a measure of cyclothymia could be similarly standardized in terms of the number of acquaintances possessed. However, methods 3 and 4 are at present theoretical, and would always tend to be esoteric, so only 1 and 2 are considered further.

Percentile ranks have the disadvantage, as described in every statistical textbook, that where further computation is required they cannot be treated as equal-interval units, though they are useful in giving an immediate idea of a person's relative position.

Standard scores may be of two kinds, based either: (a) on the standard deviation, which we may call simply *standard scores*; or (b) upon values derived from the assumption that the standard scores are really normally distributed, which we may call *normalized standard scores*. In (b), we first obtain percentiles and then assign to each raw score the standard score that would go with the percentile rank for that raw score in a normal distribution. Unequal intervals between raw scores will then correspond to equal intervals between standard scores.

We have already discussed the rather shaky assumption that the normalizing of scores ensures equal units of measurement. Apart from this assumption, a standard score will have no particular claim to be an equal-interval score. Consequently, its use in adding, averaging, and other computations has only a comparatively limited advantage over the use of percentiles. Psychologists are habituated in this situation to accepting the lesser of two evils. The ideal procedure would be to convert raw scores to equal-interval scores and then to convert the latter to standard scores, but no one has yet discovered a convincing way of doing this.

Besides these theoretical difficulties, there is the minor practical disadvantage that simple standard scores are rather inconvenient. They are therefore commonly converted to T-scores, stanines, or similar derivatives. Although stanines have been widely used, mainly because they suited the purpose of American military psychologists in the last World War, the present senior author has argued that what he has called stens are preferable. Both are based on standard scores, but stanines form a nine-point, and stens a ten-point, scale. The main advantage of the latter is that most countries are becoming more accustomed in applied work to the decimal system, so that a scaling that covers the range in ten points (each being divisible into ten decimal subunits if finer scoring is required) fits easily into habits of thought in the measurement field. Second, if each sten is made equal to half a standard deviation, the full range, down to a fraction of a per cent, is covered, whereas stanines on the same assumption leave 2 per cent of the normal distribution outside the range of their scale.

SUMMARY *of Chapter Seven*

1. The higher-order properties of tests, which we have called universality, efficiency, and utility, are in many ways more fundamental and more useful than the familiar concepts of validity and consistency from which they are derived.

Universality refers to the consistency of a test's validity coefficients against various criteria. *Efficiency* in the simplest sense is validity per minute of testing time. It can be more broadly conceived as validity per unit of time consumed in the whole testing process, including marking and analysis, and can also be extended to take cost into account. *Utility*—generalized validity —is perhaps the most fundamental property of a test. The idea of one unique validity for a test is highly misleading, as has already been implied in the definition of universality, for every test has many possible validities. Consequently, a new concept is required to express the range or breadth of a test's validities, and this we have termed "utility." Provisional formulas for the quantification of these new concepts have been described.

2. Although the properties of tests are conceptually independent, the relations between these properties, such as between homogeneity and reliability or between validity and homogeneity, are interesting and important. Thus reliability acts as a condition or limit of validity, as is indicated by the correction for attenuation; corrections also have been made for length of test, as in the Spearman-Brown and Cattell-Radcliffe formulas, and for range of sample, which affects both validity and consistency.

(In the Appendix, some new formulas are also presented [worked out by Cattell and Tsujioka], relating homogeneity and factor trueness, and homogeneity, test length, and validity. Whatever the length of the test, however, maximum homogeneity is incompatible with maximum validity.)

3. Methods of scaling and standardization are examined from a general and catholic viewpoint. The great majority of current treatments of scaling apply only to one type and model of test—the particulate and unstructured—

which is uncommon in the newly developing areas of measurement. For most personality traits, therefore, the scaling problem is better conceived as one of weighting subtests in a battery to obtain a factor score and then of scaling the numerical values thus obtained. There are three degrees of possible accuracy, in practical procedure, for weighting subtests to yield an estimate of score on the factor.

4. Rough approaches to equal-interval scaling, such as the assumption of a normal distribution, have long been available; a new approach with potential and theoretical advantages is described under the title of relational simplex scaling. A special and general theory of the relational simplex are outlined.

5. The standardization of psychological tests may involve: (a) a reference group on whom the tests are standardized; (b) the modification of standardization with respect to subclasses of age, culture, and so forth; (c) a particular unit of measurement in which the standard scores are expressed. Standardization could advantageously be done with stratified samples smaller than are usually supposed adequate, since sampling error is usually not large, compared with other sources of error, in norms that frequently shift with cultural change. Corrections to general test norms are often required for cultural subgroups, and such corrections are probably more conveniently made by the use of subtables than by raw-score regression corrections, but the multiplication of such tables entails clear decision as to the correct reference group needed.

6. Special problems arise in the standardization of tests of motivation, particularly in preventing unwanted "device" effects, such as general power of memory or GSR reactivity. One solution is to adopt the solipsistic assumption and to standardize these motivation batteries *ipsatively.* Ipsative scoring makes the individual the "reference population," standardizing within one person. *Ipsative, semi-ipsative,* and *temporal* (or *performative*) approaches are distinguished as modes of standardization within one person and their properties discussed. Ipsative scores can later be normalized.

7. Standard scores are generally preferable to percentile ranks in standardization. In practice, standard scores are usually changed into T-scores, stanines, stens, or some similar measure for the sake of convenience. Some advantages of stens over the other measures are described.

Chapter Eight

THE PLANNING AND DESIGN OF A RESEARCH INTO THE PREDICTION OF SCHOOL ACHIEVEMENT

Section 1   Some General Requirements of Research

So far we have discussed the theoretical background and psychological principles that we believe will be most relevant, in the long run, to educational guidance in schools and, in particular, to the prediction of achievement. We are now equipped to turn to an actual research into the sources of achievement that will illustrate some of these concepts and techniques. The basic problem is to extract from the complicated network of processes that we call education—and the even more complicated individuals for whom it is organized—some of the crucial facts and relationships that will have a general application.

We have already pointed out that achievement is a function of the environment and its characteristics—encouragement at home, healthy surroundings, effective teaching conditions—and of the individual characteristics of the particular child. We shall imagine the environmental characteristics as held constant for the time being and shall concentrate on individual differences among children. The prediction of what a particular child is likely to achieve will therefore be in terms of psychological, not of sociological, factors; and these factors will fall into the three main types already discussed, that is, factors of ability, personality, and motivation.

But there is a large practical gap between this theoretical formulation and the obtaining of the required measures in a scientifically meaningful and experimentally valid form. The first half of this chapter will deal with some of the means of bridging this gap.

On the one hand lies the Scylla of obsessional perfectionism. In this state, the researcher may spend so much time in developing a narrow scale of measurement, for example, and in applying it to a small and highly selected sample of people, that his results, when they are eventually published, are

145

of more interest as a "five-finger exercise" than as a contribution to psychological knowledge. At the other extreme is the Charybdis of vague theorizing and technical inadequacy. This attitude to research may produce even worse consequences, for perfectionism should at least provide accurate if narrow and even irrelevant results, whereas excessive vagueness in planning research, or lack of the most searching thought about what one is trying to do and whether it can be done with the instruments one is using, will clearly undermine the whole project at its foundations. Such lack of planning can never be remedied at a later stage by any degree of skill and effort in analysis.

Let us first discuss, then, the general principles that must apply to any worthwhile research in educational psychology, before dealing in more detail with their application to a particular problem. We are not referring here to the technical requirements of the various measuring instruments used, which have already been considered in Chapters 6 and 7. Let us assume that a selection of these is available that appears adequate to our needs and consider rather the wider planning of the survey or experiment. This should include an examination of the problems of human interaction, which are at least as important to the success of any such research as the selection or construction of the actual tests.

The one overriding principle that really subsumes a number of practical recommendations is that the results of the research should be capable of generalization, i.e., that they should be relatively invariant over a wide range of people and conditions. This is to some degree a counsel of perfection, and a whole chapter will later be devoted to showing how the principle must often be modified. But it remains the underlying principle for most of the practical methods and precautions that need to be adopted, and the sections below are, in an important sense, descriptions of means to attain this one aim. A brief discussion of the four following headings may help to make this clearer:

1. The problem of sampling
2. Replication or repetition of the experiment
3. Standardization of the conditions of test administration
4. Adequate methods of analysis

Section 2 **The Problem of Sampling**

The connection between the problem of choosing a sample of children to test and the principle of effective generalization of results is clear enough. No one would choose a class of mentally defective children to test, if his aim were to draw conclusions about the abilities of normal or gifted children. In some sense, therefore, the sample tested must be typical or representative of the wider group about which one hopes to generalize. A great deal of work has been done on the statistical theory of sampling procedures, and in recent years a number of excellent books have been published in which the application of this theory to actual situations has been described (e.g., Yates, 1960; Deming, 1955; Hansen, Hurwitz, and Madow, 1953). But although these go far to explain the requirements of the mathematical statistician to the psychologist or educationist, much further in fact than earlier and more abstract expositions, a basic difficulty still remains.

Statisticians insist that fully adequate generalization, in a statistical sense, from sample to population is only possible when random selection from a defined population has been practiced at some stage of the sampling procedure. Otherwise, the sample will be a "judgment" rather than a probability sample; and, strictly speaking, no inference at a known level of probability about the properties of the population will be possible.

Unfortunately, the educational researcher is very rarely in a position to follow this recommendation of probability samples. He may wish to generalize about all the seventh-grade children in Illinois or all the eight-year-old children in Scotland, but a random sample of these children (and statisticians interpret the word "random" rigorously) is usually impossible. The extent of the difficulty may be confirmed by a glance through the journals of educational research; it will be found that a very high proportion of the studies reported, far from being based on random or probability samples, have made use of the subjects most easily available.

There is no easy escape from this problem: The requirements of the sampling statisticians and the administrative arrangements within the scope of the individual teacher or educational psychologist who is planning a research tend to be almost diametrically opposed. Suppose that one wishes to select a sample of children to be representative, say, of the thirteen-year-old age group in a particular city. A simple random sample of suitable size will almost inevitably involve picking a child here and a child there from a large number of different schools, with the consequent maximum interference with a large number of separate timetables. A second and more serious disadvantage from the researcher's point of view is the very large amount of time, correspondence, telephoning, and general administration required before such a sample can be tested, not to mention the considerable difficulty in standardizing the conditions of testing on dozens of different occasions. In fact, simple random samples, although they remain the paradigm of sampling to the statistician, are so administratively inconvenient as to be virtually unknown in practical research in education.

The impracticability of simple random samples can, it is true, be somewhat reduced by certain modified procedures that still retain the principle of random selection at some stage. The chief of these modifications are (1) stratification, and (2) the sampling of entire groups rather than of individuals. This latter method is often known as cluster sampling. But even these modified techniques usually retain a great deal of the practical inconvenience that virtually rules out simple random samples. There is a strong case for using them when the *primary* purpose of the research is the establishment of statistical norms and confidence limits for a neatly defined population. In exploratory research, however, it is much more debatable whether the theoretical and statistical advantages outweigh the severe practical difficulties.

To sum up, the researcher in education must adopt the most suitable sampling plan for his particular research and must exercise insight and care to avoid obvious bias in choice of sample. Sometimes he may be able to incorporate the principle of random selection, but much more often this will not be possible. The teacher or researcher who wishes to study the relative advantages and disadvantages of the various methods more fully, without having to probe too deeply into the mathematical statistics, is referred to accounts by Moser (1958) and by Butcher (1966).

If the researcher decides, as the vast majority have, that random sampling is ruled out, a few partially reassuring facts remain in his favor. First, existing evidence suggests that nonrandom methods may produce adequate results, even though they suffer from the disadvantage that standard errors and similar statistics are not properly interpretable (Moser, 1958, p. 106).

Second, the problems of primary concern to the educational psychologist at the present stage differ from those that the expert sampling statistician has in mind. He will—at least if he is in sympathy with the general approach of this book—be less concerned with setting precise limits to the estimation of norms than with the charting of the general structure of ability and personality.

Section 3   Replication of the Experiment

Repetition or replication of research by different investigators on different samples also provides a powerful means of overcoming the sampling difficulty. Where different or conflicting results are obtained, it may not be easy to say whether these are due to genuine and systematic differences in the samples studied, or to incidental and arbitrary differences in the methods of research. Where agreement is obtained, however—and this is the main point—by different investigators, with presumably different sampling biases, the probability is very high that such agreement is not fortuitous, but represents a genuine advance in knowledge.

Another aspect of the replication of research deserves brief mention. Although a repetition by the same investigator or even by members of the same team will not carry the same weight as two independent researches, it may yield advantages in other ways. In the research to be described, it was possible to attempt to predict school achievement either for urban and rural children separately or for the combined group. To confine the analysis to the combined group would have produced some technical and statistical advantages, for the predictions would have had a smaller error because of the larger sample used. It was decided, however, to perform the analyses separately, because it seemed possible that the personality factors and interests of rural children might form a rather different pattern from those of children in towns and thus have a different bearing on their achievement.

This use of replication is the opposite, in a sense, to that previously described, because one is looking for differences rather than similarities in the results. If such differences appear, however, they will be more convincing if found by the same investigator under controlled conditions, whereas if they emerge from two separate researches, the chances that they have resulted from differences in testing method or other accidental bias would tend to be increased. Both these types of replication are obviously necessary to the advance of knowledge, and to a large extent they are complementary.

Section 4   **Standardization of Testing Conditions**

At the risk of laboring the obvious, it is worth reminding psychologists, teachers, and anyone else engaged in empirical research in education, of the importance of adequate standardization of conditions. Strict attention and careful preparation are needed. The timing of tests often provides an opportunity for things to go wrong; many a significant difference in the literature has arisen from a moment's absentmindedness or a sticking stopwatch. Another kind of difficulty can be equally dangerous. Usually, one or two children in each class, particularly where classes are not "streamed" or grouped by ability, have great difficulty in understanding even quite simple instructions, particularly when these are given by a stranger. Unless one is very careful and patient, one can easily be rushed, particularly with a tight schedule for a battery of tests, into starting the class off when the slower children are still comparatively bewildered. Small details, even such mundane and apparently minor preparations as ensuring an adequate supply of spare pencils, can easily introduce additional error into test results. A good illustration of the appearance of an extraneous and unwanted variable among statistical results can be vouched for by the authors, as follows.

In a factor analysis of responses to a number of pieces of recorded music, a rather puzzling factor appeared that was difficult to interpret and that linked an apparently random selection of responses. After a protracted investigation and the rejection of every other plausible possibility, it was at last clearly shown to be a factor of background noise, discriminating between the records on which the subjects heard music alone and those on which they also heard a certain amount of hiss and scratch.

A rather unobvious but important factor in the standardization of test conditions is the attitude of the teachers, and through them, of the children. This is often unobvious, one should say, to psychologists, but obvious to teachers. Testing may have been done in a particular school, for instance, in such a way that complaints were received from parents (even quite unjustified and unreasonable complaints), leaving a residue of suspicion among all but the most long-suffering or interested teachers, and this attitude may last for months, if not for years. Technical and statistical expertness in the planning of experimental research in education, while extremely desirable, are not, therefore, nearly sufficient to ensure valid and generalizable results. Less tangible and less easily assessed factors—such as the varying attitudes of the teaching staff, the day of the week (Monday is generally a bad day), the imminence of school examinations, ignorance of the hour at which the students expect a five-minute break, impatience with the slower-witted members of the class, carelessly mimeographed test booklets with blurred instructions; and the list of disturbing possibilities could be greatly extended—must all be taken into account and neutralized to the best of the psychologist's ability. Otherwise, he may introduce a great deal of extra error variance into what may already be a provisional and approximate study.

Section 5   Adequacy of the Analysis of Results

We have already tried to emphasize that the most subtle analysis may only make error more manifest if the groundwork of the research has not received sufficiently careful thought. But provided that this care and thought have been devoted, modern statistical and analytic techniques can sift out an astonishing amount of valid information. The development of these techniques and their application to psychology have advanced enormously during the last twenty or thirty years and are advancing even faster at the present moment.

The variety available is indeed almost bewildering, but this confusion may be lessened by imposing certain broad classifications on the methods most generally used in psychology. A preliminary distinction between univariate and multivariate methods of analysis delimits the field considerably. *Univariate methods,* as their name implies, are those which take one variable at a time, the scores on one test, for instance. They may be descriptive, so as to compress and clarify a mass of data in the way in which an average score of a class of children on a test gives the best picture that can be given by one figure or index of the general level of that class. Such methods may also involve statistical inference in terms of probability, as in tests of significance.

Multivariate analysis, on the other hand, deals with a whole set of variables simultaneously. Two kinds of multivariate analysis that are frequently featured in this book are factor analysis and multiple correlation. The reader will already be familiar with the aims and some of the historical development of factor-analytic methods from earlier chapters. A brief explanation of multiple correlation will be given in Chapter 9, in which results obtained by that technique will be reported.

In the past, multivariate methods of analysis have suffered from certain drawbacks when compared with the simpler univariate methods, with the result that they have probably not been used so widely in psychology as they might profitably have been. First, the sheer computational problems were formidable, but these have now been virtually overcome by the use of high-speed electronic computers, although even for these a multiple-correlation program involving more than about twenty variables is not always straightforward. Second, the technique of factor analysis (as distinct from component analysis) has always been looked upon with some suspicion by mathematicians, with the result that the main attacks on the many thorny problems that the method presents have generally been left to statistically minded psychologists. These problems are by no means all solved, even some of the most fundamental, but there are many signs that the opposing schools of thought are slowly tending to converge. An example of the conciliation of such opposing viewpoints can be seen in the argument between British and American factorists on oblique primary mental factors versus a second-order factor or factors of general intelligence, which was discussed in Chapters 2 and 3. There, we have already shown that the controversy can be resolved by a full analysis into factors at both the first and second order.

It will already have become clear to the reader that this book is concerned with the kind of problem to which multivariate methods are most appropriate. Univariate methods will always have their place, particularly in classical experimental psychology, though even here the increased use of multivariate methods may be confidently forecast during the next decade or two. But in the field of human abilities, personality, and motivation, an overwhelming case has been presented for adopting methods of analysis that can handle a large number of intricately entangled variables simultaneously and can reduce what William James described as "a blooming buzzing confusion" to a simpler and more easily interpretable structure.

Enough has been said here to give some idea of the difficulties of sorting the grain from the chaff in any actual problem, as well as to indicate the lines on which we believe this may best be attempted. The rest of this chapter will be concerned with the planning of an actual attempt to determine the degree to which school achievement can be predicted from measures of ability, personality, and motivation.

Section 6   **Planning a Particular Research into the Prediction of Achievement**

The project to be described had two main aims. First, it was designed to be a continuation of a long-term research carried out in the Laboratory of Personality and Group Analysis in the University of Illinois on the structure of interests and attitudes among children and adults, with the principal aim of defining the basic, replicable factors in this structure. This program was already far advanced in the case of adults (Cattell, 1957, Chapters 11–13), and a considerable volume of preparatory work had been carried out with children, in particular by Cattell and Sweney.

The second aim was concerned not only with structure, but also with prediction. It seems very likely that children's school achievement, even in the sense of measured performance on standardized achievement tests (and still more if the term is used in a broader sense), is connected with their patterns of personality factors and of interests and attitudes. The second aim of the research, therefore, was to determine whether such a connection could be scientifically demonstrated. School achievement has long been known to be partially predictable by tests of ability, and particularly by tests of "general intelligence," as described in Chapter 3. More recently, it has been shown that personality factors can also be used to predict achievement, although demonstrations that this predictive power is additional to the predictive power of abilities alone have been scarce. The possibility that prediction could be still further improved by taking attitudes and interests into account has not yet been comprehensively explored.

A great deal of literature has indeed been produced on the subject of children's attitudes. But the present research is a pioneering and exploratory one in several respects. The ways in which it may represent an advance on earlier attempts are as follows: First, the range of attitudes sampled was a wide one, including thirty-two representative areas, selected from a still larger number used in an earlier research by Cattell and Sweney and found to have high loadings on the main attitude factors in children. Second, each of these attitudes was measured by five different types of test device, which again were selected as the most efficient from a much wider range of possible tests. Third, each of these tests was a disguised, not a self-evaluative, method and was objective in the sense that the children could not easily suspect that it was a test of attitude. Thus, one was apparently a test of memory, another of general knowledge, and so forth. Fourth, the methods of analysis ensured that these measures were not "contaminated" by ability; if in fact the scores used had been partly scores of ability, the object of the research would have been defeated. But this danger was eliminated in two independent ways, in one analysis by the ipsatization of test scores (see Chapters 7 and 11), and in the second, by the rotation of the attitude factors so that the ability components were separated out into separate factors. Fifth, the measures from which it was planned to predict achievement were factor scores or scores from tests developed by factor analysis; this applied equally to measures of ability, personality, and attitude. Sixth, and this is perhaps the main value of the research, it appears to be the first serious attempt to combine in one survey and to analyze together on an adequate scale the data from the three modalities, i.e., abilities, personality factors, and attitudes. These data, including a number of very large correlation and factor matrices, have been presented in more detail than is possible in this book by Cattell, Butcher, *et al.* (1961).

We planned to include both urban and rural children in the testing program, in order to investigate possible differences in psychological structure and in the pattern of prediction. It seemed quite possible that the patterns of personality and of interests and the pattern of factors most predictive of achievement might differ for city and country children. Accordingly, it was necessary to find suitable schools in both types of district, but to ensure at the same time that these were similar in certain respects. Thus the comparison of the prediction of achievement in terms of results on standardized achievement tests, which was one type of analysis planned, necessitated finding at least one school in a large city and another in a country district that used the same type of test as part of their annual curriculum. It was also desirable that the schools to be tested should not be too distant from the Laboratory of Personality and Group Analysis, in view of the long and concentrated test sessions that were envisaged. On the other hand, it was desirable that they should not be too close at hand, because the schools in the near vicinity of a university with large and enterprising departments of psychology and education tend to be overtested! These considerations illustrate rather nicely the kind of difficulty that typically occurs in reconciling the theoretical recommendations of sampling statisticians with actual existing circumstances, as discussed in Section 2 of this chapter.

After some preliminary consultation and planning with the respective superintendents of the school systems, it was decided to test the entire seventh grades in Benjamin Franklin Junior High School, Springfield, Illinois, and in East Lawn School, Paxton, Illinois. The numbers of students were about 160 and 130, respectively. Springfield is the state capital of Illinois, and the school in question was chosen on the advice of the school superintendent and the testing office of the local school system as containing a good cross section of all socioeconomic groups. Paxton is about 100 miles northeast of Springfield and is a small country town typical in many ways of the area. A high proportion of the students at East Lawn School are brought in by school bus from farms and small communities in the surrounding countryside.

The two school systems differ in that Benjamin Franklin is a self-contained junior high school containing sixth- to eighth-grade students, but the seventh-grade students at Paxton are still attached to the elementary school. This difference, however, is a general one between the school systems in large cities and in predominantly rural areas, so that any difference it might produce in the test results is a difference that should be included in a comparison of this kind.

Testing took place in two sessions at each school during December 1959 and January 1960. The total testing time at each school was a little over five hours. There were approximately equal numbers of boys and girls in each sample, and the mean age of the children was 12.7. The mean IQ of both groups (Thurstone PMA scholastic aptitude score) fell between 100 and 110.

Section **7**   **Description of the Tests and Other Psychological Measures Used**

The tests and other measures used fell into four main groups: (1) measures of ability; (2) measures of personality; (3) measures of motivation, i.e., of interest and attitude; (4) measures and ratings of achievement. These four groups will now be described in more detail, with particular emphasis on the tests of interest and attitude. The last-named played a prominent part in the experiment, because one of the two main aims, as already described, was to obtain information about the *structure* of children's attitudes. They also provided an interesting addition to the prediction aspect of the study, because many researches have already been reported that predict achievement from measures of ability, a few that also include standardized personality measures, but virtually none that also take account of factored attitude variables. For two reasons, the number of attitude measures in the research considerably outweighed the number of tests in each of the other categories; attitude measures were more novel and experimental, and less was known about the structure of children's interests than about the structure of abilities and personality.

Measures of Ability. The tests used to measure ability were the Thurstone Primary Mental Abilities test (intermediate form AH for ages 11–17) and the IPAT Culture Fair test of general intelligence (Scale 2, Form A). The Thurstone test consists of five subtests, designed to measure verbal-meaning, space, reasoning, number, and word-fluency abilities. The IPAT test consists of four subtests, designated "series," "classifications," "matrices," and "topology."

Measures of Personality. Personality measures were obtained from the IPAT High School Personality Questionnaire, Forms A and B. Each of these forms provides scores on fourteen primary personality factors, which correspond closely with the sixteen factors in Cattell's 16 PF test for adults. Four of the adult factors, however, have not been clearly established in children or adolescents of high-school age, but two other factors that cannot be certainly replicated in adult groups have been found repeatedly in children. These basic factors have already been described in Chapter 4; for a fuller account, the reader is referred to Cattell, 1957, Chapter 6, and to the manual of the test.

Measures of Motivation: Interest or Attitude. The terms "attitude" and "interest" are not easy to define precisely, and in general psychological usage they show considerable overlap. There has sometimes been a tendency to equate "interests" with vocational interests, but this is largely a historical accident with no particular logical justification. The measures to be described are certainly concerned with children's interests, but not in the narrow sense of vocational guidance only; they are equally concerned with attitudes, defined in Cattell's dynamic calculus (see Chapter 5) as "interests in various courses of action." For the time being, the two words will be used to some degree interchangeably or as representing two aspects of the same measures. The theory of motivation that underlies the whole series of interlocking researches, of which the one reported here forms a small part, has already been sketched out in Chapter 5.

Thirty-two attitudes were selected from sixty used in an unpublished research by Cattell and Sweney. The original sixty were carefully assembled to give a fairly complete coverage of the area of children's motivation; selection of thirty-two from the sixty available was made on the basis of their factor loadings in this earlier study. In general, the two attitudes with the highest loadings on each of the erg and sentiment factors that emerged in the Cattell and Sweney research were selected for inclusion in the present investigation.

The attitudes chosen are described in Table XIII. Note, however, that the description of each attitude does *not* represent any actual statement presented to the respondents, but expresses the conceptualization and guiding principle adopted by the test constructors.

The thirty-two attitudes listed in the table were all assessed by five disguised tests, representing five separate psychological principles. These were constructed after the trying out of a very large number of other possible devices (Cattell, 1957) as the most satisfactory and valid types of test to represent the five principal motivational components (Cattell, 1957; pp. 453–464). A brief description of these motivational components has already been given in Chapter 5; it will be remembered that these are factors that emerge when one attitude is measured by a number of different tests and the results are correlated and factor-analyzed. The erg and sentiment factors, on the other hand, are found by factor-analyzing a broad range of attitudes measured, generally speaking, on one kind of test device.

TABLE **XIII**

The 32 Attitudes Measured by Each of the 5 Attitude Tests in the Illinois Survey

1. I like to eat well so that I shall grow healthy and strong.
2. I like to see a handsome face and figure in the mirror.
3. I want to be the kind of person everyone likes to have around.
4. I want to have a good reputation for ideals and honesty.
8. I want always to show self-control.
10b. I want to show my father how awesome and admirable I think he is.
11. I want to have Mother there if something goes wrong.
16. I want my brothers and sisters to behave and mind me.
17. I want to be safe at home when the weather is bad.
25. I want to make things and draw pictures related to our school subjects.
26a. I want to read about the world.
29. I want my pictures to be beautiful and pleasant to look at.
31. I want my teacher to like me.
32. I want to spend more time with my friends.
33. I want to get even with other kids who have caused me trouble.
34. I want to spend more time with my girl or boy friend.
35. I want to go to parties where couples are invited.
36. I want the United States to protect small countries from Russia.
37. I want the United States to beat its enemies.
38. I want to worship God and obey him.
39. I want to pray for God's protection and mercy.
40. I want my team to win.
41. I want to go to games with my friends.
42. I want to have a pet to take care of.
44. I want to save money in a bank.
48a. I want to see more science-fiction movies and television programs.
48b. I want to have plenty of games, books, and other things.
50. I want to have nice clothes so that people will like the way I look.
51. I want to dress well in order to impress the opposite sex.
55. I want to have more holidays in order to rest and take it easy.
59. I want to be polite to adults.
60. I want to take things apart to see what makes them work.

It will be seen, therefore, that there is a cross-classification of test devices and attitudes, yielding a total of 160 interest scores for each person, since each of thirty-two attitudes is measured by five different types of test.

We have spoken of the five *principal* motivational components as being represented by the five types of tests, because seven such components have in fact been found in some other researches. Ideally, it would have been most satisfactory to have seven types of test, in order to represent all the motivational components so far identified, but the "eta" component was omitted as being less adequately substantiated than the rest, and the "delta" component proved difficult to represent satisfactorily by a group test. The five motivational components that were used are shown in Table XIV, together with the corresponding psychological principles and the tests used to represent them.

TABLE **XIV**

NAME OF TEST	Psychological Principle	Motivational Component and Interpretation
How Much and How Many	Autistic thinking	Conscious id
Information	Relation of information to interest	Ego
Paired Words	Word association	Superego
Memory	Selective memory	Repressed complexes
What Do You Think?	Decision speed	Impulsivity

The principle behind the How Much and How Many test was as follows. It was hypothesized, and the hypothesis had already been well confirmed by previous research, that degree of interest in a particular area can be effectively measured by the degree of autistic or "wishful" thinking displayed by the respondent. The items in this test were therefore constructed on a multiple-choice basis, each item having five possible responses, representing varying degrees of autism or "wishful" thinking. The children were asked to guess the answers to questions they found difficult. For example, "How many people prefer comedy programs to Westerns? 10%, 20%, 40%, 60%, 80%?"

The Information test was in some ways similar, being also a multiple-choice test, but the principle upon which it was based was that interest in a particular subject area of information almost inevitably results in possession of more information about the area. Thus a child who was particularly interested in science-fiction movies and television programs would normally be expected to be better informed about them. Respondents were asked not to guess. The following is an example of an item in this test: "The smallest of the following instruments is (a) the viola, (b) the violin, (c) the cello, (d) the bass violin."

In the Paired Words test, as its name implies, pairs of words were presented as alternative responses to a cue word. Each word in the pair represented a different interest area. The construction of this test involved some ingenuity in selecting cue words and pairs of possible responses such that (1) with very few exceptions, no two interests were paired together more than once, in order to avoid spurious negative correlation between interests; (2) each response word in the pair should represent an association of apparently equal plausibility; (3) each interest should be represented by an equal number of possible responses. For example,

Scissors	Paper	Moon	Romance
	Haircut		Rocket

The Memory test was designed to exploit the selective or differential effect of interests on power of memorizing. On each alternative page of the test, the children were required to memorize a list of ten words, each chosen as representative of a particular interest. Twenty seconds were allowed for this task. On the next page, they were asked to pick out, within a time limit of forty seconds, the ten words that they had memorized from a group of twenty-five words in all.

The What Do You Think? test was a test of decision speed. On each page of the test booklet, a group of questions representing a particular interest was assembled. These were all easy questions, to which the answer was planned to be sufficiently agreed upon and obvious not to involve much thought. At the end of each page, the time taken was recorded. The actual answers to each item were not scored, only the time taken forming the basis for a measure of decision speed in each interest area.

The thirty-two interests measured, which were the same in each of the five tests, were chosen as representative of the factors found in the Cattell and Sweney study already mentioned. It was necessary, however, to select the interests for the present research before rotation to simple structure in the earlier study had been quite completed. Thus the present research, even in the part that is concerned with the structure of children's interests, is not intended as a replication of the earlier work, but rather as an extension and development of it.

Measures and Ratings of Achievement. To measure achievement, scores on standardized achievement tests were obtained from the school records, and ratings of the children by their class teachers were also gathered. The standardized achievement test administered annually at each school was the Stanford, and the form given in April 1959 was the intermediate version, Form K.

The teachers were asked to rate the children on seven different scales, which covered such qualities as leadership, behavior record, achievement in sports, and so on. Examples of these scales are given in Chapter 9, Section 3.

Other Measures. In addition to the four main classes of test described above, of which the first three were thought of as predictors, and the last as criterion, a number of other auxiliary variables were included in the test program. In general, these were thought of as possible additional predictors, but as tangential to the main theoretical aim of the research.

These extra variables included a number obtained from a "student quiz," in which the students were asked about the amount of time they spent watching television and reading, their position in the family (eldest child, only child), and so forth. They also included a sociometric-type test, which was given by the class teachers, and which provided four types of score, consisting of the number of times accepted or rejected *by* other children, and number of acceptances or rejections *of* other children.

SUMMARY *of Chapter Eight*

1. The obvious but difficult requirement of all research in educational psychology, as in other areas, is that its findings should be generalizable beyond the specific circumstances of the experiment or survey.

2. Factors affecting this generalizability can usefully be summarized under four heads: (a) problems of sampling; (b) conditions and circumstances of test administration; (c) the repetition of crucial researches, preferably by independent research workers; (d) methods of analyzing data.

3. The sampling problem is a difficult one in educational research because theoretical requirements and administrative and practical possibilities are generally opposed. Random or probability sampling is theoretically desirable, but often virtually impossible, and has only been employed in a tiny minority of published studies. Where it is not practicable, careful, intelligent choice of samples and detailed reporting are essential.

4. Research using psychological tests has not always been satisfactory with regard to standardization of procedure. Test administration and results may be significantly affected by, e.g., the time of day, day of the week, degree of empathy between tester and subjects, the imminence of examinations, and similar circumstances.

5. An outline description is given of the plan of the Illinois survey described in Chapters 9–11 and of the main tests and other vehicles employed.

Chapter Nine

THE PREDICTION OF SCHOOL ACHIEVEMENT FROM MEASURES OF ABILITY AND THE STRUCTURE OF ABILITIES IN HIGH SCHOOL STUDENTS

Section 1   Principles of Multiple Prediction

The reader will already be familiar with the coefficient of correlation, which is an index showing the extent to which two variables, such as sets of scores on two tests, "go together," and the extent to which one can be predicted from the other. An extension of this statistic to multivariate data has already been mentioned in the last chapter. It is known as the coefficient of multiple correlation (R), and is an index of how far a whole series of variables (e.g., tests) will serve to predict another variable (the criterion).

In other words, if one has, say, three different tests of ability, and one wishes to discover the *combined* power of these to predict a measure of achievement, the appropriate statistic is R. Unlike the ordinary or "zero-order" coefficient of correlation, the coefficient of multiple correlation can never be negative, but ranges between 0, showing no prediction, and $+1$, showing perfect prediction. In fact, it operates by forming a weighted composite of the predicting variables, i.e., of the three ability tests in the example just mentioned. Thus, the best combination of the three ability tests, if one calls them A, B, and C, might be $2A + B - 0.5C$. The method of multiple correlation finds this maximally predictive combination and expresses the relation between this composite and the criterion. There is some danger of this method "capitalizing" on chance, in the sense that the particular weighting of the predictions may be peculiar to the sample of people, and it is well known that the weights require a large sample to attain a reasonable degree of reliability. This is an unfortunate characteristic of the method, and wherever appropriate we provide the calculated weights for more than one sample, so that the reader may himself assess the degree of stability.

Sometimes a set of tests will all correlate fairly highly with the criterion, yet the coefficient of multiple correlation will be very little higher than the correlation of the "best" or most predictive test. This means that the remaining tests are overlapping with the "best" test and, although quite highly predictive in themselves, are not adding much additional predictive power. In other words, the size of R depends on two main factors: (1) the general size of the correlations between tests and criterion; and (2) the pattern of intercorrelations between the tests. The interaction of these two factors is by no means simple, but the general aim of psychometrists is usually to find a battery of tests that have low intercorrelations, but that all correlate to a substantial degree with the criterion. The chief exception to this rule is that a test may sometimes function as a "suppressor" variable, which means that although it has negligible correlation with the criterion it still increases the coefficient of multiple correlation by "suppressing" or counteracting unwanted variance in one or more of the other predictors. Suppressor variables of this kind are very desirable in theory, but much less common in practice, because a great deal of technical knowledge, psychological insight, and plain luck is needed in order to include a particular test in a battery with any high expectation that it will function as a suppressor.

In the present chapter, we are dealing with the prediction of various measures of achievement from six measures of ability, consisting of five Primary Mental Abilities (PMA) subtests and the IPAT Culture Fair test. These measures of ability have moderately high intercorrelations, as can be seen from Tables XV and XVI, and therefore involve more overlap and redundancy than is ideally required among the predictors, according to the principles we have just outlined.

TABLE **XV**

Intercorrelations between ability measures (urban sample)

	2	3	4	5	6
1. PMA (V)	.36	.50	.51	.47	.44
2. PMA (S)		.27	.21	.22	.44
3. PMA (R)			.52	.39	.40
4. PMA (N)				.50	.22
5. PMA (W)					.31
6. Culture Fair					

With the addition of personality measures, however, as described in Chapter 10, we shall have the advantage of new dimensions that hardly correlate with the measures of ability and bring us nearer the desired theoretical position of virtually independent predictors.

Section 2   **The Consistency of the Measures of Ability**

In a factor analysis of the measures of the ability (to be reported later in this chapter) it was necessary to obtain part-scores on four of the five PMA subtests and intercorrelate them, because two variables are required to establish the presence of each factor. The nature of the subtest measuring Factor W, however, made it impossible to obtain split-half part-scores. Part of the object of the analysis was to find the loading of the Culture Fair test on the five PMA factors, so this test was not dichotomized.

Although split-half consistency coefficients obtained for the PMA factors have often been quoted, it may be of interest to report those obtained in the Illinois survey, for which see Table XVII.

TABLE **XVI**

Intercorrelations between ability measures (rural sample)

	2	3	4	5	6
1. PMA (V)	.31	.42	.32	.50	.39
2. PMA (S)		.25	.29	.23	.40
3. PMA (R)			.39	.37	.41
4. PMA (N)				.33	.30
5. PMA (W)					.30
6. Culture Fair					

TABLE **XVII**

Split-half consistency (homogeniety) coefficients of PMA

	Urban sample	*Rural sample*
V	.82	.89
S	.76	.82
R	.76	.78
N	.80	.74

Section 3 **Prediction of the Main Criteria**

It will be remembered from the preceding chapter that two main samples of children are involved in the Illinois survey (a third will be discussed in connection with the factor analysis of interests), these being predominantly urban (at Benjamin Franklin Junior High School, Springfield, Illinois) and rural (East Lawn School, Paxton, Illinois) respectively.

The main ability measures obtained were scores on the Primary Mental Abilities test and the IPAT Culture Fair test. The principal criterion of achievement was total score on the Stanford Achievement test, and the prediction of subsidiary criteria, i.e., Stanford subtests, was also examined. The idea of school achievement, however, was also interpreted more broadly, as including not only academic or scholastic performance but also such facets of all-around development as personal adjustment, social adjustment, and achievement in sports. Class teachers in each school made ratings on seven such variables, some guidance in interpretation being provided in the form of a semigraphical rating scale. Examples of these rating scales are reproduced in Table XVIII.

In Tables XIX and XX are shown, for the urban and rural samples respectively, the correlations between six predictors, consisting of the five Thurstone PMA factors and the IPAT Culture Fair test, and eight criteria.

TABLE **XVIII**

Teachers' rating scales

Please mark the scale below at the point which seems to describe the student's degree of interest in games and sports most accurately. Then mark the remaining scales in the same way to describe his (her) other interests and characteristics. Try to use the whole range of the scales, and not just the center segments.

1. *Interest in games and sports*

| Hardly any interest at all | Definitely less interested than the average student | Somewhat less interested than the average student | Just about average interest | Somewhat more interested than the average student | Definitely more interested than the average student | Exceptionally interested |

2. *Achievement in games and sports*

| Exceptionally poor achievement | Definitely lower than average | Somewhat lower than average | Just about average achievement | Somewhat higher than average | Definitely higher than average | Exceptionally good achievement |

3. *Social Adjustment*

| Doesn't get along at all well with other students | Definitely doesn't get along as well as most | Doesn't get along particularly well | Just about average in getting along with other students | Gets along pretty well with other students | Definitely gets along better than most | Gets along exceptionally well with others |

4. *Leadership*

| No signs of leadership ability | Definitely low on leadership | Somewhat below average | Average leadership ability | Somewhat above average | Definitely high on leadership | Outstanding as a leader |

The "ordinary" or zero-order correlations of each predictor against each criterion are in the columns headed *r*, with the multiple correlation from all six

TABLE XIX

Prediction of criteria from measures of ability: urban sample

PRIMARY MENTAL ABILITIES	TOTAL SCORE ON STANFORD ACHIEVEMENT TEST		Personal adjustment		Interest in school subjects		TEACHERS' RATINGS ON Behavior record		Leadership		Social adjustment		Achievement in sports		Interest in sports	
	r	β	r	β	r	β	r	β	r	β	r	β	r	β	r	β
V	.65	.40	.35	.11	.53	.26	.11	−.01	.54	.32	.38	.20	.30	.06	.25	.05
S	.36	.05	.29	.13	.37	.14	.13	.11	.38	.16	.29	.16	.15	−.02	.13	.00
R	.45	.03	.35	.15	.48	.19	.21	.21	.42	.15	.32	.11	.30	.10	.25	.09
N	.44	.13	.29	.05	.40	.07	.10	−.03	.31	−.07	.32	.12	.27	.06	.21	−.01
W	.40	.03	.31	.11	.39	.08	.10	.04	.40	.16	.26	.03	.34	.20	.34	.26
Culture Fair	.54	.29	.30	.09	.40	.10	.05	−.08	.42	.11	.23	.00	.29	.15	.22	.09
Multiple Correlation	.72		.45		.62		.23		.62		.45		.41		.37	

TABLE **XX**

Prediction of criteria from measures of ability: rural sample

| PRIMARY MENTAL ABILITIES | TOTAL SCORE ON STANFORD ACHIEVEMENT TEST | | Personal adjustment | | TEACHERS' RATINGS ON | | | | | | | | | | | |
| | | | | | Interest in school subjects | | Behavior record | | Leader-ship | | Social adjust-ment | | Achieve-ment in sports | | Interest in sports | |
	r	β	r	β	r	β	r	β	r	β	r	β	r	β	r	β
V	.63	.48	.27	.08	.56	.34	.39	.31	.39	.14	.36	.19	.26	.11	.32	.16
S	.31	.11	.20	.11	.24	-.01	.07	-.09	.19	.00	.15	-.03	.10	-.02	.11	-.07
R	.42	.13	.36	.29	.49	.21	.37	.23	.49	.35	.40	.27	.31	.23	.30	.12
N	.34	.07	.13	-.09	.45	.21	.26	.11	.23	-.04	.20	-.01	.11	-.08	.22	.05
W	.44	.10	.29	.15	.45	.12	.18	-.09	.37	.15	.28	.06	.22	.08	.27	.09
Culture Fair	.33	-.01	.19	-.02	.36	.04	.24	.05	.34	.11	.31	.12	.23	.10	.31	.18
Multiple Correlation	.67		.42		.67		.47		.56		.47		.36		.41	

predictors at the bottom of each such column. The columns headed β give the corresponding "beta weights" or optimal weightings for each test when expressed in standard scores.

Inspection of the tables will show the following points:

1. The Thurstone verbal-meaning (V) factor gives the highest correlations against most of the criteria of school achievement. This is true for both urban and rural samples.

2. For most of the measures of school achievement, the remaining abilities add rather little to the prediction provided by the V factor, although in the urban sample the Culture Fair test adds substantial predictive power against the main criterion.

3. There is considerable variation between the predictability of the various achievement measures. The Stanford Achievement test is the most predictable. The teachers' rating of the students' behavior record is, on the average, the least predictable.

4. The general pattern of correlations shows no striking differences between Table XIX and Table XX, i.e., between the urban and rural samples, although the beta weights, as usual, show low stability.

5. In particular, the order of predictability is quite similar between the two samples. In other words, for both urban and rural children, the Stanford Achievement test is predicted best, the rating on "interest in school subjects" next best, and so on.

6. After the V factor, the reasoning (R) factor appears to give the best predictions. Thus, in the rural sample, it provides the highest correlations with ratings on personal adjustment and leadership.

7. Almost all the correlations are significant, in the sense that a statistical test suggests they are very unlikely to have arisen by chance.

8. Comparatively few of the betas are statistically significant, roughly speaking those over .13. This is an approximation, since each separate beta weight has a different standard error and strictly requires a separate test of significance.

What do these results mean? A brief discussion will help to interpret them.

1 and 2. It is by no means surprising that the V factor should provide the best prediction of school achievement as measured by a standardized achievement test. The subtest of the Primary Mental Abilities test from which scores on this factor are derived requires the respondent to select a word from several alternatives, which is the same or similar in meaning to a given word.

EXAMPLE *(with correct answer underlined)*

SAFE   A. <u>Secure</u>   B. Loyal   C. Passive   D. Young

Because a command of language and understanding of English are basic to any measures of scholastic attainment, it would be expected that a well-constructed test of this kind should be highly predictive.

We should perhaps explain that a comparison of the predictive power of the V factor alone with that of all tests combined is better made by comparing not the actual coefficients, but the squared coefficients, which represent the actual proportions of the variation in achievement accounted for.

Thus, for example, the correlation of .65 between verbal ability and Stanford Achievement means not that 65 per cent, but about 42 per cent of the variation in achievement is accounted for by verbal ability. Similarly, the corresponding figure for all ability tests combined is $100 \times .72^2 = 51.8\%$. Thus the gain is rather more than would appear from a comparison of the coefficients (.65 and .72), amounting, in fact, to an increase of almost one-quarter.

The size of the correlation between verbal-meaning ability and achievement as measured by the Stanford test is closely comparable with results in other researches reported in the test manual and summarized in Chapter 3. The same is true also for the other PMA factors.

One might not expect that verbal ability would loom so large in relation to teachers' ratings, and this result may not mean quite what its face value would suggest. It is well known that when teachers (or other people) are asked to rate students (or friends) on a range of psychological qualities, as in the present experiment, one of the most common phenomena is the so-called halo-effect. This implies that most people, in their judgment of others, are unable to separate clearly their strong and weak points, but tend to be unduly influenced by an overall impression. If a student is dull and lazy, for example, a teacher may in spite of himself tend to "give a dog a bad name" and underrate his interest in sports or his social adjustment; similarly, the personal charm of another student may conceal certain defects. This difficulty is almost universal, whoever is rating, and is not of course confined to teachers' ratings of students.

In the present results, there is undoubtedly appreciable "halo effect," in spite of attempts to avoid it. The average intercorrelation between ratings is almost .50. This is certainly not all or even mainly because of "halo"; many independent studies, such as those of Terman, have shown that there is a positive correlation between almost all these psychological qualities, however they are measured, but one may suspect that it would not be so high as the corresponding figures obtained from these ratings. The intercorrelations of the eight criteria for both samples are given in Tables XXI and XXII.

On the other hand, there is certainly some evidence that the ratings are not entirely invalidated by this difficulty. For example, the markedly lower figures for the prediction of behavior record from abilities make good psychological sense. Or, to take another example, the teacher rating on interest in sports (but not that on achievement in sports) correlates more highly with the students' own account of time spent on outdoor sports than with any other external variable. Similarly, the teacher ratings on social adjustment and

TABLE **XXI**

Intercorrelations between eight criteria of school adjustment: urban sample

URBAN SAMPLE

	2	3	4	5	6	7	8
1. Total score on Stanford Achievement test	.41	.57	.07	.51	.32	.35	.25
2. Teacher's Rating (Personal adjustment)		.78	.53	.75	.74	.42	.32
3. TR (Interest in school subjects)			.44	.75	.65	.38	.30
4. TR (Behavior record)				.47	.59	.25	.16
5. TR (Leadership)					.74	.50	.45
6. TR (Social adjustment)						.42	.32
7. TR (Achievement in sports)							.77
8. TR (Interest in sports)							

TABLE **XXII**

Intercorrelations between eight criteria of school adjustment: rural sample

RURAL SAMPLE

	2	3	4	5	6	7	8
1. Total score on Stanford Achievement test	.37	.60	.36	.41	.34	.28	.31
2. Teacher's Rating (Personal adjustment)		.59	.42	.56	.53	.40	.32
3. TR (Interests in school subjects)			.65	.72	.61	.58	.62
4. TR (Behavior record)				.56	.61	.51	.53
5. TR (Leadership)					.76	.68	.65
6. TR (Social adjustment)						.74	.66
7. TR (Achievement in sports)							.89
8. TR (Interest in sports)							

leadership correlate reasonably highly with the pupils' own opinions of each other, as revealed in their responses to sociometric measures that were administered as a check. Nevertheless, here as in most similar researches, we must consider teachers' ratings of such traits as leadership and social adjustment to be heavily affected by goodness of class performance.

3, 4, and 5. The higher predictability of the Stanford Achievement test compared with the teachers' ratings follows naturally from what we have been saying. One would expect a test of this type both to be more dependent on the verbal-meaning factor, and to be more predictable from all measures than the relatively approximate teachers' ratings. This is not to say that the ratings are of less value—on the contrary, they provide valuable information in many areas where no very reliable objective tests exist.

The similarity of pattern between the urban and rural samples was expected. To analyze these separately was desirable, though, for the reasons discussed in Chapter 8. Although no great difference was expected in the results so far presented, we did think it very possible that the pattern of children's *interests* in town and country, and the relation of these interests to ability, personality, and achievement, might well show significant differences. This point will be discussed in more detail in Chapter 10.

Section 4   The Prediction of the Stanford Subtests

Total score on the Stanford Achievement test, which was our main criterion in the last section, is made up of six subtests, two of which test comprehension of written passages, two English-language skills, and two arithmetic skills. The correlations and multiple correlations of our six tests of abilities with each of these six achievement subtests is shown in Tables XXIII and XXIV.

Looking at Table XXIII first, which gives the results for the urban (Springfield) sample, we see that, as might be expected, the general pattern of correlations is somewhat similar for most of the subtests to the pattern

TABLE **XXIII**

Correlations and beta weights of ability measures against
six Stanford Achievement subtests as criteria: urban sample; N = 153

PRIMARY MENTAL ABILITIES	Paragraph meaning		Word meaning		Spelling		Language		Arithmetic reasoning		Arithmetic comprehension	
	r	β	r	β	r	β	r	β	r	β	r	β
V	.62	.42	.58	.49	.58	.30	.57	.28	.52	.16	.51	.06
S	.45	.15	.28	.01	.29	.03	.35	.07	.39	.09	.40	.12
R	.39	.01	.33	.02	.45	.06	.44	.05	.48	.13	.50	.10
N	.33	.04	.29	.00	.52	.23	.46	.17	.42	.16	.55	.33
W	.29	−.08	.26	−.06	.46	.13	.43	.10	.36	.00	.45	.08
Culture Fair	.58	.34	.44	.22	.40	.14	.48	.24	.59	.39	.56	.34
Multiple correlation	.72		.61		.67		.67		.70		.73	

TABLE **XXIV**

*Correlations and beta weights of ability measures against
six Stanford Achievement subtests as criteria: rural sample; N = 124*

PRIMARY MENTAL ABILITIES	Paragraph meaning		Word meaning		Spelling		Language		Arithmetic reasoning		Arithmetic comprehension	
	r	β	r	β	r	β	r	β	r	β	r	β
V	.58	.47	.62	.52	.57	.46	.52	.33	.52	.35	.42	.23
S	.27	.09	.22	.05	.10	−.10	.18	.00	.34	.13	.26	.05
R	.36	.12	.40	.17	.32	.05	.36	.13	.38	.09	.41	.16
N	.24	−.01	.26	.01	.35	.18	.23	−.01	.38	.15	.45	.27
W	.36	.05	.41	.09	.44	.17	.49	.28	.34	.01	.32	.03
Culture Fair	.32	.04	.25	−.08	.22	−.06	.25	−.01	.41	.13	.33	.05
Multiple correlation	.61		.65		.62		.59		.61		.57	

already discussed in connection with the main achievement measure, but with some interesting variations and contrasts between the subtests.

Considering first the two tests of comprehension in the first two columns of Table XXIII, the Thurstone V factor again plays the largest part in prediction, quite closely followed by the Culture Fair test. On the whole, the remaining four tests, that is to say Factors S, R, N, and W, play a fairly small role, rather smaller indeed than in predicting the total achievement score. The first criterion, i.e., the subtest called "paragraph meaning," is predictable to just the same degree as the total Stanford battery, with a multiple correlation of .72, which means that about 52 per cent of the variance in achievement is accounted for by the tests of abilities. Of this 52 per cent, the V factor provides 26 per cent, the Culture Fair 20 per cent, and the remaining four tests only 6 per cent together.

In the rest of the table, the predominance of the verbal factor as a predictor is still quite marked, but to a somewhat lesser degree. Looking at the last two columns, for instance, one can see that the beta weights of the IPAT Culture Fair test and of the PMA numerical factor are now the first and second highest. This is in line with expectation. The Culture Fair is a test of fluid *general* intelligence and should do relatively better than the test of verbal ability when the criterion is an arithmetical one. One would also expect it to predict success at arithmetic reasoning rather better than success at arithmetic computation, and this expectation is also fulfilled, although the obtained difference is a small and probably nonsignificant one. Similarly, of course, one would expect the N, or numerical, factor of the PMA test to become prominent as a predictor against an arithmetic criterion; in fact, however, it does not function so well as one might expect. Although it correlates highly with both the arithmetic criteria, the beta weights in both cases are lower than those of the Culture Fair test, negligibly lower for the criterion of arithmetic computation, but very substantially lower for the criterion of arithmetic reasoning. In the case of arithmetic reasoning, 49 per cent of achievement variance is predictable by the tests of abilities, of which 23 per cent is contributed by the Culture Fair, 8 per cent by the V factor, 7 per cent by the N factor, and 11 per cent by the three remaining tests.

The two criteria in the third and fourth columns, spelling and language, are intermediate in the respect we have been discussing, that is, the V factor plays a larger part in the prediction than it did in the prediction of the arithmetic criteria but a smaller part than in the prediction of the "comprehension" criteria in the first two columns. The N factor plays a surprisingly large part in predicting spelling and language achievement, larger than the Culture Fair for spelling but not for language. In all, 45 per cent of the language criterion variance is predictable by the battery of ability tests, of which 16 per cent is contributed by V, 11.5 per cent by the Culture Fair, and 17.5 per cent by the remaining four tests.

Turning to Table XXIV, we see first that the general pattern of prediction, including the average level of the multiple correlation coefficients, is noticeably lower for the rural sample. Why this should be so is not easy to say, although we shall see later that the same difference generally applies also to prediction from personality measures. Conceivably, it could be the result of less-standardized conditions of testing, because the children of Paxton were tested class by class, by three or four testers, whereas those at Springfield were all tested simultaneously in one large hall.

As with the urban sample, the V factor in general plays a predominant part in predicting all six achievement criteria; again as in the urban sample, the main exception to this is in the prediction of arithmetic computation. The R (reasoning) factor plays a rather larger part in prediction than with the urban sample, as does the W (fluency) factor, particularly in the prediction of language achievement. The N factor is relatively the same in both samples, except that the surprising predictive power against the language criterion on which we commented earlier in discussing the urban sample, is not repeated, which suggests perhaps that not too much importance should be attached to it. The Culture Fair test, for some reason, predicts much more poorly for the rural sample, its only fairly sizable contribution being to arithmetic reasoning, where it contributes 5 per cent out of 37 per cent predictable variance.

In interpreting the differential degree of prediction of the various subtests, it may help interpretation of the results to consider the degree of intercorrelation between the criteria. It is probably fair to say that if the criteria are themselves highly correlated, differences in the predictive pattern thereby become more significant. In general, as might be expected, the Stanford Achievement subtests are fairly highly correlated. The relevant correlation matrices are given in Tables XXV and XXVI.

Section 5 "Forward" and "Backward" Prediction

As explained in Chapter 8, much of the "prediction" with which we are concerned is not literally "prediction" in the sense that we are considering the administration of tests of ability with a view to foretelling performance or achievement years later. What we are largely concerned with is the *relationship* between abilities, personality factors, and motivation variables, on the one hand, and achievement, on the other, even though the relationship may be a simultaneous or even a "backward" one. Thus the Stanford Achievement test scores that we have described as some of our criteria were actually recorded a few months before the administration of the "predictive" tests.

However, for the rural sample, scores became available for a later administration of the Stanford Achievement test a few months *after* the main testing, when as part of the normal school program the appropriate Stanford

TABLE **XXV**

Intercorrelations between Stanford Achievement subtests: urban sample; N = 153

	2	3	4	5	6
1. Paragraph Meaning	.72	.64	.65	.68	.56
2. Word Meaning		.60	.60	.62	.46
3. Spelling			.71	.64	.61
4. Language				.70	.62
5. Arithmetic Reasoning					.70
6. Arithmetic Computation					

test for the seventh grade was given, all the criteria of this type previously described having been the sixth-grade versions.

A comparison of the "backward" and "forward" predictions of total achievement scores on the Stanford test is provided in Table XXVII.

It can be seen from Table XXVII that the multiple correlation in the "forward" prediction is considerably higher, perhaps because of the shorter interval of time (some four months, against eight months) between the administration of the ability measures and the achievement criteria. It is therefore possible that if the design of the survey and administrative circumstances

TABLE **XXVI**

Intercorrelations between Stanford Achievement subtests: rural sample; N = 124

	2	3	4	5	6
1. Paragraph Meaning	.78	.62	.67	.73	.65
2. Word Meaning		.67	.69	.70	.64
3. Spelling			.71	.57	.58
4. Language				.66	.64
5. Arithmetic Reasoning					.76
6. Arithmetic Computation					

had permitted a similar time relationship in the urban sample, the main computations would have shown a rather higher degree of prediction not only from ability measures but also from personality and motivation factors than will actually be reported.

TABLE **XXVII**

"Backward" and "forward" prediction of score on Stanford Achievement tests from ability measures: rural sample; N = 124

	"Backward" (Sixth-Grade)		"Forward" (Seventh-Grade)	
	r	β	r	β
V	.63	.48	.70	.49
S	.31	.11	.29	.02
R	.42	.13	.44	.07
N	.34	.07	.41	.12
W	.44	.10	.53	.18
Culture Fair	.33	−.01	.45	.13
Multiple Correlation	.67		.76	

Section 6 The Factorial Structure of Abilities

In Chapters 2 and 3, we discussed briefly the alternative methods of factoring data, distinguishing the Burt, Guilford and Vernon method of analysis into a general factor and bipolar group factors from the method of first searching for simple structure as pursued by Thurstone, Cattell, Eysenck, and other "functional" factor analysts. It was also pointed out that a synthesis of these two common viewpoints is possible through the approximation which the Spearman-Burt general factors makes to the second-order general factor in the Thurstone-Cattell analysis. We recommended a preliminary use of primary ability factors, plus the additional step of a second-order analysis to yield one or more general factors. It was suggested that the general factor or factors thus obtained possess the additional scientific advantage of being more determinate than the usual *g* factor, particularly if they are derived from the analysis of a battery containing adequate "hyperplane material," that is, tests and other measures outside the ability field, which will have very low loadings on the ability factors and thus define them more clearly by contrast.

An analysis of this kind was carried out on the Illinois data, with the urban and rural samples pooled in order to obtain more stable results. A short summary follows in this section, but for a fuller account, the reader is referred to Cattell (1963), and for a full reproduction of the correlation matrix to Cattell, Butcher, *et al.* (1961), while the theoretical background is given here in Chapter 2.

The variables analyzed, as shown in Table XXVIII, were (1) scores from Thurstone's Primary Mental Abilities test, as markers of primary abilities; (2) subtest scores from Cattell's Culture Fair Intelligence Test; and (3) personality factor scores obtained from the High School Personality Questionnaire (HSPQ), in order to provide the contrasting "hyperplane" material.

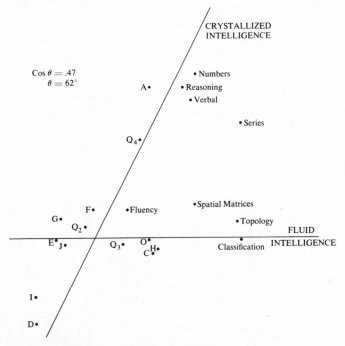

NOTE: All test points are peaced by oblique coordinates.

FIGURE **13.** *The empirical separation of fluid and crystallized intelligence*

TABLE XXVIII
The Second-Order Factor

The Factor Loadings (in Reference Vector Correlation Form)

	F_1 G_f	F_2 G_c	F_3 Extraversion	F_4 Anxiety	F_5 U.I. QIII	F_6 control	F_7 ?	F_8 ?
Thurstone's Verbal Primary	+.15	+.46	−.17	−.03	+.04	+.07	−.05	−.12
Thurstone's Spatial Primary	+.32	+.14	−.02	−.03	−.03	+.05	−.27	+.04
Thurstone's Reasoning Primary	+.08	+.50	+.08	+.02	−.02	+.02	+.38	−.14
Thurstone's Number Primary	+.05	+.59	−.04	+.05	−.07	−.05	−.10	+.03
Thurstone's Fluency Primary	+.07	+.09	+.52	−.18	+.12	+.26	+.13	−.07
IPAT Culture Fair Series Subtest	+.35	+.43	+.05	−.12	+.06	+.10	+.24	+.04
IPAT Culture Fair Classification Subtest	+.63	−.02	−.05	−.05	+.00	+.14	+.16	−.06
IPAT Culture Fair Matrices Subtest	+.50	+.10	−.23	+.04	−.01	−.08	−.25	+.42
IPAT Culture Fair Topology Subtest	+.51	+.09	+.16	+.12	+.03	−.03	−.14	−.00
IPAT HSPQ A Cyclothymia	−.04	+.52	+.31	−.23	+.05	+.11	+.20	+.03
IPAT HSPQ C Ego Strength	+.21	−.07	−.04	−.52	−.08	−.09	−.49	+.12
IPAT HSPQ D Excitability	−.04	−.44	−.44	−.09	+.09	+.04	+.14	−.27
IPAT HSPQ E Dominance	−.15	−.01	−.05	−.00	+.61	−.04	−.02	−.17
IPAT HSPQ F Surgency	−.05	+.09	+.39	−.07	+.06	−.40	−.20	−.09
IPAT HSPQ G Superego Strength	−.14	+.08	−.01	−.10	−.10	+.43	+.41	+.05
IPAT HSPQ H Parmia	+.21	−.04	+.55	−.17	+.00	+.13	+.03	−.03
IPAT HSPQ I Premsia	−.09	−.29	−.05	+.26	+.54	−.05	+.43	−.01
IPAT HSPQ J Coasthenia	−.10	−.04	+.01	+.39	−.12	+.45	+.01	+.16
IPAT HSPQ O Timidity	+.16	−.01	+.01	+.73	+.09	−.04	+.10	+.17
IPAT HSPQ Q_2 Self-Sufficient	−.06	+.05	−.37	−.05	−.43	−.04	−.04	+.05
IPAT HSPQ Q_3 Self-Sentiment Control	+.05	−.02	+.06	+.00	+.32	+.35	+.56	+.11
IPAT HSPQ Q_4 High Ergic Tension	−.04	+.37	+.03	+.45	−.00	−.37	−.14	+.05
% in ±.10 Hyperplane	.51	.60	.60	.51	.73	.55	.32	.60

TABLE **XXIX**

Third-Order Factors and Intercorrelations

Second-Order Factors	Third-Order Primary Factors			
	I	II	III	IV
Fluid Intelligence	+.69	+.02	−.07	+.00
Crystallized Intelligence	+.63	−.04	+.07	+.32
Extraversion-vs.-Invia (U.I. Q.I)	+.18	+.03	+.38	+.23
Anxiety-vs.-Adjustment (U.I. Q.II)	−.01	+.01	+.00	+.79
U.I. Q.III.	+.09	−.51	−.07	+.32
Control	+.01	+.99	−.03	−.05
F_7	+.06	+.03	−.74	+.04
F_8	+.02	−.69	+.08	−.06
% in ± .10 hyperplane				

Primary Factor Correlations at Third Order

	I	II	III	IV
I	+1.00	+0.38	+0.14	+0.25
II	+0.38	+1.00	+0.00	+0.10
III	+0.14	+0.00	+1.00	−0.16
IV	+0.25	+0.10	−0.16	+1.00

The results of this factor analysis are shown in Table XXVIII. It is noticeable, first, that *two* general ability factors were found, identifiable as fluid and crystallized general ability, as hypothesized according to the theory outlined in Chapter 2. Second, as illustrated in Figure 13, the fluid and crystallized ability factors are positively correlated, to the extent of about 0.47, as might be expected in children. One would expect that they would be positively correlated at *all* ages, but less so in adults than in children. Third, it is noticeable that the personality factors have some appreciable loadings on the second-order factor of crystallized ability, but smaller ones on that of fluid ability. This seems reasonable, as we should expect personality differences to influence the formation of crystallized general ability.

Here fluid and crystallized ability load a single third-order general factor, which is best interpreted as the "proto-fluid ability" factor. That is, it may represent the magnitude and nature of the fluid ability factor as it existed at the time during which the crystallized general ability was being formed. In this case, it would be, so to speak, the ancestor from which the present fluid ability factor is derived by lineal descent, and the crystallized general ability factor, by investment of time and interest. If this is correct, one would expect, at least in younger people all of the same age, that this third-order factor would load the fluid more than the crystallized ability (because more intervening contributors enter into the latter). Table XXIX shows this to hold, although not as strongly as would be expected.

One also notices that such tests as the Cattell matrices and topological tests (Figure 12) are highly loaded in the fluid general ability factor, but very little on the crystallized general ability, whereas such measures as the PMA verbal ability, numerical ability, and reasoning are loaded on both, but particularly on the crystallized general ability factor.

The results of this factor analysis, supporting the hypothesis of two general intellectual factors, strongly demand independent confirmation, and extensive researches by Horn (1966), Cattell (1967), and others have recently given thorough confirmation. Research workers, however, must use sufficiently sophisticated and sensitive methods of analysis to permit both factors to emerge, in any serious check on these findings.

SUMMARY *of Chapter Nine*

1. A survey is described in which two samples of junior-high-school students in Illinois (one urban, one rural) were tested with the Primary Mental Abilities battery, with Cattell's culture-fair test of intelligence, and with standardized tests of achievement. Other criteria of achievement included teachers' ratings on such qualities of leadership, behavior record, and social adjustment. Zero-order and multiple correlations were calculated between the tests of abilities and the criteria of achievement.

2. The single test that best predicted performance on the standardized achievement battery was the test of verbal ability in the PMA (.65 urban sample, .63 rural). The addition of other ability measures produced a multiple-correlation coefficient (R) of .72 (urban) and .67 (rural).

3. Prediction of the teachers' ratings of other aspects of achievement from ability measures was as follows: Urban sample—highest R's were .62 ("interest in school subjects" and "leadership"); lowest R was .23 ("behavior record"). Rural sample—highest R, .67 ("interest in school subjects"); lowest, .36 ("achievement in sports").

4. In addition to the prediction of total score on the Stanford Achievement test, the prediction of scores on subtests (e.g., "spelling," "arithmetic reasoning," etc.) was studied. In the urban sample, the "V" score of the PMA was the most effective predictor of subtests involving verbal and paragraph comprehension, and the same was true to a lesser extent in the prediction of the subtests "spelling" and "language." For the subtest "arithmetic reasoning," the IPAT Culture Fair measure was the most effective predictor; this was also true of "arithmetic comprehension," but here, the PMA "N score" predicted to almost as large a degree. In the rural sample, correlation coefficients, beta weights, and R's were again, in general, smaller, possibly on account of rather different conditions of testing.

5. Most of the "predictions" described were "backward predictions," giving the relation between measures of ability and scores on an achievement test taken some months *earlier*. In the rural sample, it was possible to compare these figures with those obtained by "forward prediction" of a comparable achievement test taken four months *after* the ability tests. The "forward prediction" figures were, in general, higher.

6. The ability measures (for both samples combined) were analyzed in such a way as to explore the hypothesis (already described in Chapter 2) that separate factors of *fluid* and *crystallized* general ability might be identifiable. To do this, it was necessary to include some personality measures in the analysis as "hyperplane stuff," or background material, against which the general ability factors would, so to speak, show up in contrast.

7. Two second-order general ability factors were indeed found and were identified as factors of fluid and crystallized general ability. They were positively correlated, as would be expected under this hypothesis, which predicts a higher correlation in children than in adults. In general, the PMA tests (in particular, N, R, and V) had high loadings on the factor interpreted as crystallized intelligence, whereas the IPAT Culture Fair subtests had higher loadings on the other factor (interpreted as fluid intelligence).

Chapter Ten

THE PREDICTION OF ACHIEVEMENT
FROM PERSONALITY FACTORS

Section 1 **Previous Studies of Personality and Achievement**

The relation of abilities to achievement, as found in the Illinois survey, and described in Chapters 8 and 9, corresponds fairly closely to the results of earlier research. In considering the predictive power of personality measures, and in particular of well-established and replicated personality factors, we are entering territory that has been much less thoroughly explored.

Vernon (1950, p. 37) writes:

> The psychologist's v, n, and other factors are usually based on tests which are fairly pure measures of the abilities at which they are aimed. Educational attainments, especially when measured by school or other examinations are naturally more complex, and we have already seen that a somewhat ill-defined factor of industriousness + interest, which Alexander calls X, plays a prominent part. . . . Although interesting attempts have been made to measure or assess personality factors relevant to scholastic success, it is doubtful whether they are practically applicable on a large scale. . . . At the moment, therefore, we know little about X, though further research would certainly be profitable. In particular, we would like to know how far it depends on (a) home background; (b) the "tone" of the pupil's school; (c) the stimulatingness of, or good teaching by, his teacher; (d) the pupil's interest; (e) his temperamental characteristics.

While fully in agreement with Vernon on the need for research on these general lines—the present book is in fact an attempt to answer the questions he raises—we must stress that "the somewhat ill-defined factor of industriousness + interest, which Alexander calls X," would appear to be a resultant of inadequate sampling of variables and the comparatively crude state of personality research before 1950, when these words were written. It is now possible to refine this concept of "industriousness + interest" into its basic components among the unitary factors of personality and motivation.

Alexander's work was published more than thirty years ago, but one must admit that relatively little progress in this field has been made by educators, whom Vernon here represents, in availing themselves of the basic advances in personality theory and measurement in the intervening period, particularly when one considers the volume of educational research produced. Thus it was possible to write even quite recently (Middleton and Guthrie, 1959) that "attempts to improve prediction by using non-intellective factors such as interest and personality traits have yielded quite discouraging results . . . The principal difficulty is probably the heterogeneity of the criterion, the antiquity of the personality measures used, and the nonsummative or nonlinear predictions." Although it is quite true that in the future it may be necessary to allow for nonlinear relations between measures of personality and interest and the achievement criteria, the present writers are also convinced that much progress yet remains to be made without such statistical subtleties. The discouraging results so far reported would seem to be accounted for more reasonably by the absence of a sufficiently far-reaching and systematic employment of factored personality and interest tests. The problem is undoubtedly a complex one, which requires more extensive and subtle methods of research than have been needed to show the value of tests of ability alone. But it is also of great practical, as well as theoretical, importance, and one can hardly carry on a conversation with an intelligent group of teachers or parents without hearing someone make the point that, in the past, psychological methods of selection and guidance have relied too exclusively on measures of intelligence and ability, and have signally failed to take into account many vital factors of personality and character structure.

There is now a fairly large and rapidly growing literature on the relation of personality factors to school achievement. Most studies have been concerned with the two broad second-order factors of anxiety and extraversion-introversion. Findings have conflicted, and the discrepancies can probably be assigned to some or all of the following causes:

1. Differences in national culture pattern, e.g., extraversion may be more of an asset in American primary schools than in British.

2. Different effects at different ages, e.g., it seems plausible, as suggested by Furneaux (1957), that introversion may be more of an asset at sixth-form and university level because of changed conditions of work.

3. Different definitions of the variables, and in particular a blurring of the distinction between anxiety and neuroticism. (A comparison, for instance, of anxiety scores based on the HSPQ and neuroticism scores based on the Maudsley personality inventory for children would be useful in this connection.)

4. Nonlinear relations between the variables, e.g., Cox's (1960) finding that a middling degree of anxiety favored schoolwork, and Grooms and Endler's (1960) that only with a high-anxiety group did a test of personality yield any improvement in the prediction of achievement.

5. Varying effects against different criteria, as in Lynn's (1957) finding that anxiety had a different effect, according to whether the criterion was schoolwork in English or in arithmetic.

6. Sex differences. Women have been found to have higher average scores than men on introversion in a number of studies (e.g., Anderson, 1960). It is also possible that the relation between introversion and school achievement shows a sex difference.

In view of these discrepancies, and of considerations of space, a systematic review of the literature will not be offered here. A useful survey of recent papers in this area is provided by Warburton (1962a; 1962b).

Section 2 **Personality Factors Measured in the Research**

The principles on which factored personality questionnaires were developed were described in Chapter 4, and some examples were given of the factors that they measure. The personality questionnaire used in the Illinois survey was the High School Personality Questionnaire (HSPQ), which measures essentially the same personality factors, though at the child level, as have been listed earlier (Chapter 4) for the adult 16 PF test. The questionnaire, when given in full, consists of two parallel forms, A and B, each of which requires forty to forty-five minutes of testing time. Both forms were administered to the urban and to the rural children in the Illinois experiment; this is always preferable if the full amount of testing time is available. Each form measures the same fourteen factors, and a more reliable score on each factor results from the larger number of items in the total questionnaire. These fourteen factors are described in Table XXX.

TABLE **XXX**

List of personality traits measured by the high school personality questionnaire

TRAIT DESIGNATION BY LETTER	*Technical title* *(popular title in parentheses)*	UNIVERSAL INDEX NUMBER
A	Sizothymia-versus-Affectothymia (Stiff, Aloof-versus-Warm, Sociable)	U.I. (L) 1
B	Mental Defect-versus-General Intelligence (Dull-versus-Bright)	U.I. (L) 2
C	Dissatisfied Emotional Instability, or General Neuroticism-versus-Ego Strength (Emotional, Immature, Unstable-versus-Mature, Calm)	U.I. (L) 3
D	Phlegmatic Temperament-versus-Excitability (Stodgy-versus-Unrestrained)	U.I. (L) 4

TRAIT DESIGNATION BY LETTER	*Technical title* *(popular title in parentheses)*	UNIVERSAL INDEX NUMBER
E	Submissiveness-versus-Dominance (Mild-versus-Aggressive)	U.I. (L) 5
F	Desurgency-versus-Surgency (Sober, Serious-versus-Enthusiastic, Happy-go-Lucky)	U.I. (L) 6
G	Lack of Rigid Internal Standards-versus- Superego Strength (Casual,Undependable- versus-Conscientious, Persistent)	U.I. (L) 7
H	Threctia-versus-Parmia (Shy, Sensitive- versus-Adventurous, "Thick-Skinned")	U.I. (L) 8
I	Harria-versus-Premsia (Tough, Realistic- versus-Aesthetically Sensitive)	U.I. (L) 9
J	Zeppia-versus-Asthenia (Dynamic Simplicity-versus- Neurasthenic Self-Critical Tendency)	U.I. (L) 10
O	Confident Adequacy-versus-Guilt Proneness (Confident-versus-Insecure)	U.I. (L) 15
Q_2	Group Dependency-versus-Self-Sufficiency (Group Dependent-versus-Individually Resourceful)	U.I. (Q) 17
Q_3	Poor Self-Sentiment Formation-versus-High Strength of Self-Sentiment (Uncontrolled, Lax-versus-Controlled, Showing Will Power)	U.I. (Q) 18
Q_4	Low Ergic Tension-versus-High Ergic Tension (Relaxed Composure-versus-Tense, Excitable)	U.I. (Q) 19

NOTE: Only two of these factors, D and J, are of little importance in adults. Four additional factors have been found in adults: L (Suspiciousness, Paranoia), M (Bohemianism, Hysterical Uncon-cern), N (Shrewdness), Q_1 (Radicalism-versus-Conservatism). For a fuller account, see Cattell (1957), Cattell and Warburton (1967), Nuttall and Cattell (1967).

Section **3**   **Scores of the Illinois Children on the Personality Factors**

Our main concern in this chapter is not with absolute level or norms, but with the *relation* between scores on personality factors and achievement measures. For completeness' sake, however, and to give some indication of how far the measurements of the Illinois students coincided with those of other groups, their scores are shown in Table XXXI, together with those provided as norms in the manual of the HSPQ.

It is not proposed to analyze these figures in detail, but two main points emerge from them. First, the Illinois students in general do not deviate very markedly from the samples from which the norms in the manual were derived. Second, if one compares the urban (Springfield) with the rural (Paxton) children, quite systematic differences appear in the area of anxiety versus general adjustment. An anxiety score can be derived from a weighted

TABLE **XXXI**

Mean scores of Illinois students on fourteen personality factors, compared with norms in HSPQ manual

FACTOR	Description	Illinois Samples urban	Illinois Samples rural	Handbook Norms A	Handbook Norms B
A	Affectothymia	11.1	11.6	10.8	10.4
B	Intelligence	14.1	13.7	13.6	12.8
C	Ego Strength	8.9	10.5	9.7	9.5
D	Excitability	9.6	9.3	9.4	9.6
E	Dominance	8.9	9.3	9.2	9.4
F	Surgency	9.8	10.0	9.9	9.9
G	Superego strength	12.5	12.1	12.0	12.2
H	Parmia	8.4	9.6	9.3	8.6
I	Premsia	10.1	10.0	10.7	11.4
J	Neurasthenia self-criticism	10.7	9.9	10.1	10.5
O	Guilt proneness	10.7	9.4	10.5	10.7
Q_2	Self-sufficiency	10.7	10.5	10.6	10.6
Q_3	Self-sentiment strength	10.2	10.6	11.0	11.2
Q_4	Ergic tension	9.3	8.7	9.1	9.4

composite of the following factors: D, Q_4, O, Q_3—, C—, H—, (see HSPQ Manual, p. 50). It can be seen from Table XXXI that on each of these six primary personality factors the urban children score in the "anxious" direction when compared with the rural children. Some of the differences between the average scores of the two groups are relatively small, but some, such as the difference in Ego Strength (C) and Parmia (H) are very marked and highly significant statistically. This seems to be in line with a fairly general belief that children are happier and more carefree when brought up in the country.

Thus Norman Douglas once wrote, "The boy of the streets, who sees nothing of flowers and living waters, is not a veritable boy at any time, since his youth is ended before it began," and again "All town bred persons, with the rarest exceptions, are incomplete. . . . They show a gap which, unlike other gaps (deficient learning or manners), can never be filled up in later years."

Observations of this kind and other suggestions about personality differences between town and country dwellers are common enough in literature and in general conversation, but have previously lacked scientific support. The present findings are certainly only provisional and depend only on one urban and one rural school, but they are at least suggestive, and the hypothesis suggested seems to be worth further investigation.

Section 4   **The Prediction of School Achievement from the Fourteen HSPQ Factors**

When one speaks of personality factors, it is a matter of definition and convenience whether or not one includes general intelligence as one of the factors. For most purposes, both descriptive and clinical, intelligence certainly needs to be included, but one of the aims of the present chapter is to assess the predictive power of personality measures *as distinct from* measures of intelligence. For this reason, the data have been analyzed in both ways, with general intelligence (Factor B) included in one analysis and omitted in the other. The present section will show the extent to which school achievement can be predicted by the complete HSPQ, including Factor B, and is of interest in showing the value of the questionnaire as a predictive instrument. Section 5 will be concerned with the extent to which the remaining personality measures (with intelligence left out) fulfill the same aim.

The correlations of the fourteen factors with various criteria of school achievement are shown below for the urban sample (the larger of the two groups tested). The last column of the table (Table XXXII) shows the multiple correlations obtained from all fourteen factors working together as predictors.

It can be seen from Table XXXII that Factor B (general intelligence) correlates more highly than any of the other factors with almost all the criteria of school achievement, the one exception being the teachers' rating on general behavior, which is more accurately predicted by two of the other factors.

This predominant influence of intelligence is not unexpected. What is quite surprising, though, is the very high efficiency of this one factor, comprising only one-fourteenth part of the test, or approximately six minutes' testing time, when one compares the corresponding correlations with achievement derived from quite long intelligence tests. Thus in Table XXXII, is can be seen that the correlation between Factor B and total score on the Stanford Achievement battery was + 0.62. Even when the two forms of the HSPQ were scored separately, so that each half-test of Factor B represented less than three minutes' testing time, the respective correlations with the Stanford Achievement score were + 0.50 and + 0.51. These are remarkably high when one recalls that, as shown in Table XIX, only one of the five Thurstone PMA factors yielded a correlation of over + 0.45, and that the multiple correlation produced by these five factors and the Culture Fair test was + 0.72.

In Chapters 6 and 7 we have argued the need for *standard* or *ideal* validity coefficients, which would be comparable owing to the removal of differences in test length, sample, etc. It certainly appears that Factor B of the HSPQ

TABLE XXXII

Prediction of school achievement from the HSPQ: urban children; N = 153 (table of correlations)

| ACHIEVEMENT MEASURES | | | | | | PERSONALITY FACTORS | | | | | | | | | MULTIPLE CORRE- |
TEACHER RATINGS	A	B	C	D	E	F	G	H	I	J	O	Q_2	Q_3	Q_4	LATIONS
Interest in sports	.15	.35	.08	−.10	−.18	.16	.14	−.09	.01	−.02	.05	.07	.01	.08	.49
Achievement in sports	.30	.39	.09	−.16	−.23	.05	.24	.01	.13	−.06	−.08	.11	.12	−.03	.51
Social adjustment	.21	.35	.09	−.07	−.27	.11	.24	.06	.04	−.06	−.14	.12	.13	.03	.48
Leadership	.21	.45	.10	−.19	−.23	.15	.28	.03	.02	−.04	−.16	.14	.14	.00	.56
Behavior	.13	.18	−.10	−.16	−.28	−.09	.18	.13	.23	.03	−.16	.15	.26	.06	.48
Interest in school subjects	.26	.53	.07	−.11	−.26	.07	.37	.01	.05	.08	−.16	.30	.19	−.03	.63
Personal adjustment	.20	.41	.11	−.09	−.21	.01	.31	.09	−.02	−.01	−.22	.29	.18	−.09	.52
STANFORD ACHIEVEMENT TEST															
Total score on Stanford battery	.17	.62	.02	−.09	−.22	.02	.34	−.01	.08	.06	−.04	.35	.18	−.02	.69
Paragraph meaning	.15	.57	.03	−.08	−.14	.05	.32	.08	−.05	.05	−.09	.35	.14	−.11	.64
Word meaning	.04	.58	−.02	−.05	−.08	−.01	.29	−.05	.02	.06	.03	.32	.13	−.05	.64
Spelling	.25	.53	−.03	−.06	−.30	.16	.33	−.02	.14	.09	.01	.18	.05	.06	.64
Language	.21	.53	.00	−.12	−.24	.02	.34	−.05	.13	.17	−.02	.22	.13	.06	.61
Arithmetic reasoning	.19	.54	.04	−.11	−.10	−.02	.31	.00	−.04	.01	−.03	.35	.12	−.05	.62
Arithmetic computation	.19	.46	−.08	.01	−.22	.01	.36	−.04	.00	.03	−.02	.26	.03	−.02	.58

NOTE: A correlation of .16 or higher is significant at the 5% level.

would have a very high standard validity of this kind. Conceivably, intelligence-test items are more valid when intermingled with other types of item, but further research would be needed to follow up this clue.

Some interesting conclusions emerge from a study of the correlations between the other factors and achievement in Table XXXII. Before considering the different patterns of prediction for the various criteria, one can see from inspection of the table that a few factors correlate quite widely with many or all the achievement measures, and other factors hardly correlate with any of them.

The factors which appear most to influence school achievement as a whole are, in approximately descending order of importance, G (Superego Strength), Q_2 (Self-Sufficiency), E— (Submissiveness), A (Affectothymia), Q_3 (Strength of Self-Sentiment), D— (Phlegmatic Temperament). The other factors are less generally relevant, though O, F, and I clearly play some part in predicting particular types of achievement.

This pattern makes gratifyingly good psychological sense, particularly with regard to G, Q_2, and E—, the three factors that exert most influence. One would certainly expect Superego Strength, with its consequences of conscientiousness and persistence, to have a marked positive effect on achievement, particularly in the sphere of schoolwork; and it can be seen that all the correlations between this factor and the various subtests of the Stanford battery are around + 0.30. Similarly, Self-Sufficiency or Resourcefulness is shown to be a considerable asset in most school subjects, although it is less predictive of the aspects of achievement that involve interaction with other students— reasonably enough, for the opposite pole of this factor is Group Dependency. The third main influence, E— or Submissiveness, again makes good psychological sense as a positive asset scholastically, and also in correlating more highly than any other factor with behavior record. There is one result here, however, that is hard to explain: the correlation of + 0.23 between Submissiveness and the teacher rating on leadership. One can only suppose that the rating has been unduly influenced by leadership in the rather narrow sense of excellence in scholastic study.

The consistent positive relation of A (Affectothymia) to the measures of achievement comes as more of a surprise. The other five of the six factors that we have shown to influence achievement in the present study were all expected to operate in approximately this way and to this degree on the evidence of some earlier research. Thus in the specification equation on page 48 of the HSPQ manual, all five are shown as operating in the direction we have described, and in general with about the same relative influences, although this equation was based principally on university students.

But there is a clear discrepancy in the case of Factor A, in that Sizothymia had previously been found to go with scholastic achievement. The pattern in Table XXXII, however, is so consistent that it can hardly be other than a genuine finding, and it suggests the interesting hypothesis that up to a certain age, or a certain educational level, affectothyme students achieve more, only to drop back later in relation to the more reserved and withdrawn sizothymes. There is also some support for this hypothesis in the work of Furneaux (1957) and Gorsuch (unpublished research). Furneaux advanced the theory that extraversion was an asset in schoolwork but later became a handicap at the university level, supporting this with test data, and suggested that this switchover was related to the conditions of work and degree of external discipline at the two stages. Gwynne Jones found extraversion to correlate positively with school achievement. Gorsuch's findings, on the other hand, obtained with American pupils in their last year or two in high school, confirmed the unexpected postive relation between Affectothymia and scholastic success reported in this chapter.

In this connection, though, we must stress that Factor A is only one component of the broad second-order factor of extraversion, and that the Illinois results lend little support to Furneaux's suggestion that extraversion *as a whole* is an asset in school performance and a disadvantage at the university level. The other main components of extraversion, i.e., Factors E, F, and H, *show no comparable switchover*, although comparison of Table XXXII and the specification equation in the HSPQ handbook suggest that there *may* be a slight tendency in the same direction in the case of F (Surgency), which is virtually unrelated to scholastic achievement at seventh-grade level, but appears to be negatively related at university level. This illustrates the weakness of using second-order in place of first-order factors in research.

The last two of the six personality factors that we have spoken of as exercising an influence on most or all aspects of achievement within the scope of the research are Q_3 (Self-Sentiment Strength) and D— (Phlegmatic Temperament, or Absence of Excitability). The former has less effect on scholastic performance than the factors already discussed but significantly affects some of the wider aspects of achievement as assessed by teachers—in particular, behavior and personal adjustment. Lack of excitability is related slightly but consistently to all measures of achievement, but particularly to leadership and achievement in sports.

Three more factors affect certain aspects of achievement. O— (Confident Adequacy, or lack of guilt) correlates significantly, or at the borderline of statistical significance, with all the teacher ratings except those concerned with sports, and with none of the scholastic achievement test measures. The highest correlation is with personal adjustment. The pattern of correlations suggests that this factor affects achievement mainly in the sense of getting along with other people in a social environment. The lack of relation to interest or achievement in sports is noteworthy and might perhaps suggest that guilt proneness and inhibitions are forgotten or temporarily in abeyance during intense physical activity.

Factor I (Premsia, or protected emotional sensitivity) is related significantly to only one criterion of achievement, but that is behavior record. This fits in well with the clinical picture of a protected, sensitive child.

Factor F (Surgency, Enthusiasm) is appreciably related only to interest in sports, leadership, and (oddly enough) spelling, but the correlations are barely significant.

So far our analysis has concentrated largely on the question of which *factors* are of greatest use in predicting various criteria of achievement, and we have extracted most of the information in Table XXXII that helps us to answer this question. But interesting as this question is theoretically and to the educational psychologist, the practicing teacher would be more inclined to put the question the other way round, and ask: "How can leadership (or behavior or achievement in arithmetic) best be predicted by a combination of factors?" To answer these questions we need to turn our attention to the *rows* of Table XXXII rather than to the *columns*.

Inspection of these rows will give us a general picture of the pattern we are seeking, and will tell us, for example, that "behavior record" is much less influenced by Factor B (Intelligence) and much more influenced by Factor Q_3 (Strength of Self-Sentiment) than are any of the scores on the Stanford Achievement tests. But in order to assess the respective contributions of the separate factors to the various measures of achievement, we need to explain a further statistical point.

If our factors were orthogonal and uncorrelated with each other, then separate correlations with a criterion of achievement (or simple functions of these correlations) would provide a good index of the extent to which each factor was contributing to the prediction in question. But the factors, being derived from rotation to simple structure, are not in fact completely uncorrelated. Their intercorrelations are shown in Table XXXIII.

Although these correlations, as indicated by their average value, are not, in general, very high, they are high enough to require attention in a multiple prediction. To find the true contribution of each factor, we need to assess its influence on the criterion when every other factor's influence is removed or "partialed out." This is exactly what we achieve with the technique of multiple correlation already described, but so far we have mainly confined our discussion to the total effect of all the factors together, i.e., to the "multiple R." But the technique also provides us with "beta weights," or standardized partial regression coefficients, and by multiplying each of these with the corresponding correlation between factor and criterion, we can obtain an estimate of the relative predictive powers of the separate factors against that particular criterion of achievement.

We then find that in most of the rows Factor B (General Intelligence) accounts for rather more than half of the predictable criterion variance, with the remaining predictable variance spread among two or three personality

TABLE **XXXIII**

Intercorrelations between fourteen personality factors: urban sample; N = 153

	A	B	C	D	E	F	G	H	I	J	O	Q_2	Q_3	Q_4
A														
B	.34													
C	.30	—.03												
D	—.41	—.06	—.38											
E	—.46	—.17	—.13	+.41										
F	.22	—.02	.17	.06	—.03									
G	.44	.24	.20	—.43	—.53	—.03								
H	.38	—.03	.45	—.43	—.26	.09	.23							
I	.15	—.02	—.45	—.08	—.23	—.19	.19	—.07						
J	—.02	.04	—.05	—.14	—.14	—.20	.26	.07	.13					
O	—.39	.02	—.56	.41	.26	—.19	—.25	—.54	.21	.05				
Q_2	.00	.26	.16	—.10	—.12	—.21	.28	.11	—.11	.23	—.15			
Q_3	.20	.06	.18	—.38	—.31	—.24	.42	.33	.23	.21	—.35	.26		
Q_4	—.28	—.02	—.56	.50	.16	—.05	—.17	—.46	.30	.00	.52	—.19	—.25	

factors. A notable exception, however, is the behavior record criterion, in which the predictable variance is spread rather evenly among at least half a dozen personality factors. Among the scholastic criteria, it is noticeable that of the 34 per cent predictable variance of the arithmetic computation test, more than 11 per cent, or one-third, is accounted for by the "Superego" or "Conscientiousness" factor, G, a higher proportion than with any other measure of achievement. This makes good psychological sense; it might well be supposed that work of this kind would owe more to conscientious effort than do, say, "language" or "arithmetic reasoning."

Section **5   Comparison of the Predictive Power of Ability and Personality Measures**

In this section, our primary aim is to determine whether the use of personality measurement in addition to measurements of abilities significantly improves the prediction of some or all the criteria of achievement. This is quite a severe test, since the starting point is the combined predictive effect of six ability measures, as described in Chapter 9. But it will also be of interest to reverse the question and consider whether the addition of abilities to personality measures gives a significant improvement. In view of the established position of ability testing and the comparative novelty of personality testing, any positive answer to the first question will be of considerable importance. On the other hand, most psychologists would confidently expect the addition of abilities to personality measures, which forms the basis for our second question, to give greatly improved prediction against almost any criterion of achievement.

Table XXXIV summarizes the data needed to answer our first question. In the first column are reproduced the multiple correlation coefficients derived from six ability measures, as in Tables XIX and XXIII. It can be seen that, for each of the fourteen criteria, abilities and personality measures together account for substantially more of the criterion variance than abilities alone. Rather more than half of the differences are statistically significant at the 5 per cent level or better. With regard to those differences that are not statistically significant, it should be borne in mind that in the test of significance, the more new variables that are brought in, other things being equal, the less likely is the difference to appear significant. In this instance, each test of significance involved the addition of fourteen new variables (the fourteen HSPQ factors), whereas for a particular criterion, as we have seen, the increase in predictive power was frequently concentrated in three or four of these personality factors. If for each criterion one compared not abilities alone and abilities plus fourteen personality factors, but abilities alone and abilities plus the three or four factors most predictive of that particular criterion, there is little doubt that one could obtain statistically significant improvement in almost every case.

TABLE **XXXIV**

Prediction of achievement from abilities alone and from abilities plus personality factors: multiple correlations; Springfield; N = 153

	R			PERCENTAGE VARIANCE	
	Abilities alone	Abilities + personality	Significance of difference	Abilities	Abilities + personality
Interest in sports	.37	.52	n.s.	13.7	27.0
Achievement in sports	.41	.54	n.s.	16.8	29.2
Social adjustment	.45	.53	n.s.	20.3	28.1
Leadership	.62	.69	.05	38.4	47.6
Behavior record	.23	.50	.01	5.3	25.0
Interest in school subjects	.62	.70	.05	38.4	49.0
Personal adjustment	.45	.56	n.s.	20.3	31.4
Total achievement (Stanford)	.72	.79	.01	51.8	62.4
Paragraph meaning	.72	.78	.05	51.8	60.8
Word meaning	.61	.73	.01	37.2	53.3
Spelling	.67	.73	n.s.	44.9	53.3
Language	.67	.72	n.s.	44.9	51.8
Arithmetic reasoning	.70	.75	n.s.	49.0	56.3
Arithmetic computation	.73	.77	n.s.	53.3	59.3

Looking at the question the other way round, it is instructive to see the extent to which the use of personality measures plus abilities improves prediction, compared with the use of personality measures alone. The nonstatistical reader may feel at first impression that the answer should be the same as to our first question, but this is not necessarily so. It would necessarily apply only if the personality measures were quite uncorrelated with the ability measures, whereas in practice there is always some degree of mutual influence.

The relevant data are summarized in Table XXXV. This table also contains for the main criteria of achievement details of the predictive power of the HSPQ and of the six generally most relevant factors, excluding Factor B. These six are A, D, E, G, Q_2, and Q_3, and are not, of course, necessarily the most predictive of any one criterion. However, the table provides a useful picture of how the amount of criterion variance accounted for gradually builds up as one includes more factors. The final two columns, which give the total predictive power of the personality and ability measures in combination are repeated for convenience from Table XXXIV.

Tests of significance of the difference in predictive power between the personality factors plus abilities showed, as expected, that the addition of abilities produced a significantly higher R in every case except one. The one criterion of achievement for which the ability measures failed to add significantly to the variance already predicted by personality factors was that of behavior record. The small size of the difference can be clearly seen in Table XXXV. These comparisons were made between the Rs derived from thirteen personality factors on the one hand and those derived from the entire HSPQ plus the ability measures on the other. If, however, the comparisons had been made between the entire HSPQ (including Factor B) and the entire

TABLE **XXXV**

Prediction of achievement from various combinations of personality factors, and from personality factors plus abilities: urban sample; N = 153

	Six personality factors		Thirteen personality factors		Entire HSPQ plus abilities	
	R	varce	R	varce	R	varce
Interest in sports	.22	4.8	.40	16.0	.52	27.0
Achievement in sports	.34	11.6	.40	16.0	.54	29.2
Social adjustment	.32	10.2	.38	14.4	.53	28.1
Leadership	.32	10.2	.42	17.6	.69	47.6
Behavior record	.35	12.3	.46	21.2	.50	25.0
Interest in school subjects	.46	21.2	.50	25.0	.70	49.0
Personal adjustment	.40	16.0	.43	18.5	.56	31.4
Total achievement (Stanford)	.36	13.0	.47	22.1	.79	62.4

TABLE **XXXVI**

Prediction of school achievement from HSPQ:
rural children; N = 124 (table of correlations)

ACHIEVEMENT MEASURES	PERSONALITY FACTORS														MULTIPLE CORRELATIONS
	A	B	C	D	E	F	G	H	I	J	O	Q_2	Q_3	Q_4	
Interest in sports	.08	.14	.09	.05	−.01	.08	.03	−.02	−.12	−.01	−.05	.19	.05	−.05	.34
Achievement in sports	.08	.11	.11	−.03	.02	.10	.03	.05	−.13	−.07	.02	.16	.07	−.07	.31
Social adjustment	.09	.20	.04	−.10	.02	.15	.06	.12	−.08	−.11	−.10	.07	.19	−.14	.36
Leadership	.15	.34	−.04	−.02	−.09	.01	.17	.07	−.03	−.08	−.07	.22	.24	−.09	.50
Behavior	.12	.26	−.04	−.18	−.14	.04	.16	−.01	.11	−.12	−.03	.00	.29	−.01	.47
Interest in school subjects	.18	.39	.00	−.13	−.15	−.04	.28	−.07	.02	.00	−.13	.09	.21	−.12	.52
Personal adjustment	.19	.27	.01	−.20	−.21	−.07	.19	−.06	.17	.05	.02	−.01	.25	−.12	.47
Total score on Stanford battery	.12	.51	.00	−.01	−.02	−.08	.18	.01	−.20	.02	−.11	.15	.10	−.02	.61
Paragraph meaning	.19	.25	.03	−.05	.00	−.09	.17	−.02	−.14	−.09	−.11	.19	.12	.02	.41
Word meaning	.13	.47	.13	−.05	.06	−.09	.21	.05	−.21	−.04	−.17	.19	.09	−.04	.59
Spelling	.09	.45	−.05	−.07	−.07	−.15	.23	.07	−.01	−.03	−.04	.10	.09	−.08	.56
Language	.11	.43	−.11	−.03	−.10	−.04	.14	−.03	−.12	−.01	−.09	−.01	.01	−.02	.55
Arithmetic reasoning	.11	.41	.03	−.07	.02	−.01	.10	.13	−.23	.06	−.17	.11	.10	−.09	.53
Arithmetic computation	.15	.32	.02	−.07	.00	−.03	.22	.08	−.11	.08	−.21	.13	.11	−.12	.46

HSPQ plus external ability measures, the addition of abilities would clearly have produced a smaller improvement in prediction, as can be seen by comparing Tables XXXII and XXXV. In other words, *the degree of prediction obtained from the HSPQ alone is not much smaller than that obtained from the HSPQ plus six external ability measures,* because the HSPQ contains a short intelligence scale.

Section 6   **Prediction of Achievement in the Rural Sample**

Results of testing the rural sample pointed in very much the same direction as those already reported in some detail for the urban sample, but a comparison of the data for the two samples shows first of all that the degree of prediction is lower for the rural children. Although the general pattern exhibited in Table XXXVI is quite similar to that in Table XXXII, the correlations, both those in the main body of the table and the coefficients of multiple correlation in the last column, tend to be quite markedly lower in the former. Why this should be is not easy to explain. It cannot, for instance, be accounted for in terms of the accuracy or reliability of the teachers' ratings of the two respective groups, because it applies also to the correlations with the Stanford Achievement test scores. Possibly the difference in prediction might be partly caused by some difference in rapport or testing efficiency of the kind that is not always easy to avoid, as described in Chapter 8. Certainly, testing conditions were more favorable at Springfield, where the students were tested in one large group by the same investigator, whereas at Paxton the testing was by classes and conducted by several testers of varied experience.

However this may be, the general pattern of correlations approximately reflects that already found with the urban sample. Factor B (General Intelligence) correlates most highly with most of the criteria, particularly the Stanford Achievement measures. It will be remembered that for the urban sample, the six factors other than B that yielded, in general, the highest correlations with the various achievement measures were G (Superego Strength), Q_2 (Self-Sufficiency), E— (Submissiveness), A (Affectothymia), Q_3 (Self-Sentiment Strength), and D— (Phlegmatic Temperament) in approximately that order. Table XXXVI shows that these factors tend to provide the higher correlations with achievement for the rural children also.

It is noticeable, however, that Q_3 is a rather better predictor in relation to the other factors than was true with the urban group, and also that I— (Harria or Tough Realism) comes into the picture more prominently, particularly as a predictor of the Stanford tests. The correlations are not very high (six out of seven between $+ 0.11$ and $+ 0.23$), but they are consistent in a way that was not true for the town students. There may perhaps be a reason for this in the different atmospheres of town and country schools, with the protected, emotionally sensitive child (I +) feeling more at home or receiving more encouragement in urban surroundings. It is the I + pole that correlates with behavior record, as was also true of the urban sample, but the consistent I— correlations with scholastic achievement appear only in the rural group.

The increase in prediction of achievement by the rural group when personality measures are added to measures of ability is shown in Table XXXVII. Appreciable gains in the amount of criterion variance predicted can be observed, although most in this rather smaller sample are below the level of statistical significance. When the two samples are pooled, however, giving a total number of 277 students, the gain in predictive power is statistically significant for each of the fourteen criteria.

Section 7   Evaluation of These Results

Although the effects reported are not spectacular, they are at least promising, particularly in view of the widespread and frequently quoted failure of most previous investigators to obtain significant improvements in prediction by the use of personality measures. In particular, it should be taken into account that the HSPQ with its fourteen factors, each represented by relatively few items, is designed as a general personality questionnaire, and not explicitly for the purpose of predicting school achievement. Thus in a statistical test of improved prediction, those factors that are not relevant to the particular aspect of achievement tend to lower the apparent statistical gain in predictive power.

As stated in the first section of Chapter 9, however, there is one serious drawback in the use of multiple correlation coefficients. These coefficients *maximize* the combined predictive effect of the independent variables by assigning to each a weighting that will result in as high as possible a value for the *R*. This, of course, is the object of the procedure, but, in a sense, it usually works too efficiently in taking advantage of a variation that is peculiar to the particular sample. Ideally, the weights should be tested again in another similar sample; it is then usually found that a different set of weights is required, and that the use of the original ones results in a much lower coefficient of multiple correlation. This procedure is known as cross-validation. It forms a stringent requirement, and studies in which a particular combination of weighted personality measures have been shown repeatedly to produce a high multiple correlation against any criterion of achievement are decidedly scarce.

Cross-validation of this kind was not attempted in the survey reported here, though two studies have appeared while we were in press which report very similar correlations of the HSPQ factors (Cattell, Sealy, and Sweney,

1966; IPAT, 1967). On the present samples, time and financial support did not allow the repetition of this work with further samples. Second, the main emphasis in this chapter has not been on the actual size of the multiple correlation coefficients (the prediction, for example, of behavior record with $R =$ 0.50 from 19 variables is far from spectacular), but principally on the significant increase that can be achieved by adding personality to ability variables. Convincing demonstrations of this kind are scarce in the copious literature on personality, because it is clearly fairly easy to demonstrate *some* predictive effect from almost any personality measure, but much harder to show that it produces any appreciable gain over that obtainable with well-standardized ability measures. A demonstration of this kind is, moreover, much less affected by the notorious inflation in multiple correlation coefficients, because, as here, it is based on the comparison of two multiple correlation coefficients obtained from the same sample, one involving ability measures only and the other involving ability and personality measures. The comparison is valid, for any such inflation will affect both coefficients, and there is no particular reason to suppose that it will affect one proportionately more than the other.

There is certainly a need, however, to replicate surveys of the kind described not only on similar samples, but in different kinds of school and in

TABLE **XXXVII**

Prediction of achievement from abilities alone and from abilities plus personality factors: multiple correlations; Paxton N = 124

	R			PERCENTAGE VARIANCE	
	Abilities alone	*Abilities + personality*	*Significance of differences*	*Abilities*	*Abilities + personality*
Interest in sports	.41	.52	n.s.	16.8	27.0
Achievement in sports	.36	.46	n.s.	13.0	21.2
Social adjustment	.47	.55	n.s.	22.1	30.3
Leadership	.56	.63	n.s.	31.4	39.7
Behavior record	.47	.58	n.s.	22.1	33.6
Interest in school subjects	.67	.70	n.s.	44.9	49.0
Personal adjustment	.42	.55	n.s.	17.6	30.3
Total achievement (Stanford)	.67	.74	.05	44.9	54.8
Paragraph meaning	.61	.67	n.s.	37.2	44.9
Word meaning	.65	.72	n.s.	42.3	51.8
Spelling	.62	.69	n.s.	38.4	47.6
Language	.59	.68	.05	34.8	46.2
Arithmetic reasoning	.61	.67	n.s.	37.2	44.9
Arithmetic computation	.57	.62	n.s.	32.5	38.4

other countries and cultures. It is possible that the extent to which measurable personality variables add any predictive power over and above ability measures varies according to environmental circumstances. It is also to be expected that the pattern of relevant factors should show some similar variation. Something rather similar has been found in attempts to repeat the studies on creativity of Getzels and Jackson (to be discussed in Chapter 14). Positive and negative results have been found in roughly equal proportion, and Torrance (1962), among others, has shown some systematic interaction with school atmosphere and teaching methods.

With respect to replication of our own findings, some confirmatory evidence of the general position that additional prediction of achievement can be obtained by the use of personality as well as of ability measures is described by Cattell, Sweney, and Sealy (1966). A comparison of the data reported in this chapter with some obtained in Britain has been made by Butcher, Ainsworth, and Nesbitt (1963), who found some tendency for the same factors, particularly G and Q_2, to be predictive of school achievement.

SUMMARY *of Chapter Ten*

1. It has proved much more difficult in the past to relate school achievement to personality measures than to measures of ability and intelligence, although it is widely believed that significant relations exist between personality and achievement. Shifting applied personality measurement to a new basis of meaningful source traits demonstrated by basic research in personalities and motivation over the last 15 years offers a fresh start for such predictions.

2. The HSPQ was administered to the samples of urban and rural junior-high-school students that have been described in earlier chapters. The aim was not only to see if various aspects of school achievement were predicted by scores on the personality factors, but also to see if these were predicted significantly more effectively by a combination of personality and ability measures than by ability measures alone.

3. Of the fourteen personality factors measured by the HSPQ, five or six proved to be systematically related to school achievement as assessed by the Stanford Achievement test. The strongest relation in both urban and rural samples was with Factor G (Superego Strength, or Conscientiousness). The second factor in terms of relationship to achievement was Q_2 (Self-Sufficiency, or Individual Resourcefulness).

4. In the prediction of success as measured by the Stanford Achievement test, intelligence was the most important single factor, supported principally

by two personality factors, as just summarized in item 3. But in the prediction of other aspects of achievement (e.g., leadership, sports) as rated by teachers, predictive power was more evenly spread among personality factors.

5. Several criteria were predicted significantly better by the addition of personality measures to a battery of ability measures. This was true of the larger, urban sample, and, to a lesser degree, of the rural sample. When the samples were pooled, the addition of personality measures significantly improved the prediction of every criterion.

6. An approximately similar pattern of prediction was found in both urban and rural samples. Correlations were generally lower, however, in the rural sample, possibly as a result of testing conditions.

7. There is some evidence, though provisional at present, that the relation of personality factors to school achievement is similar in American and British schools.

8. Since the organization of data for this chapter, several researches, completed but unpublished, have appeared with markedly consistent findings on personality factors predicting school achievement. There is constancy also across cultures as shown by the work of Butcher, Ainsworth, and Nesbitt (1963) and Cattell, Sealy, and Sweney (1966). Combining evidence with admittedly intuitive allowances from experience, to get the best possible achievement specification equation, from scores on $(A + B)$ forms of the HSPQ, hypothesizable from present evidence, one may summarize (rounding to nearest .05):

$$Ach = .15A + .50B + .10C - .10D - .15E + .10F + .25G + .10H$$
$$- .10I + .15J - .10O + .20Q_2 + .20Q_3 - .10Q_4$$

Depending on the correlations among the factors, in the sample, this gives a multiple R close to 0.7.

9. Several new researches are also coming to fruition with prediction at the college undergraduate student level, using the 16 PF. The best current estimate of the specification equation weights for American undergraduates is as follows:

$$Ach^* = - .10A + .35B + .15C + .05E - .20F + .10G - .10H + .20I$$
$$- .15L + .10M - .05N - .10O + .20Q_1 + .20Q_2 + .20Q_3 -$$
$$.10Q_4$$

(*Grade point average, here and elsewhere.)

The principal difference from the school level is the greater role of personality relative to ability which would be expected from the reduced range in intelligence. It is noticable also that the inviant factors—A, sizothymia, and F, desurgency—now behave oppositely from the school situation, as also do E and I, suggesting that invia and independence become favorable in the less guided situation. These results, on three groups of about a 100–200 each, will doubtless change as larger samples come in.

Results for second order factors and other 16 PF derivatives, at the college level, have been worked out by Meredith and others, summarizable as follows:

$$\text{Ach} = -.15\text{I} - .15\text{II} + .10\text{III} + .4\text{IV}$$

where I = Exvia; II, Anxiety; III, Cortertia; and IV, Independence, as defined by weights elsewhere (Cattell & Eber, 1967). With the IPAT Neuroticism Scale (the NSQ) achievement has correlated negatively, about −0.2.

Chapter Eleven

THE OBSERVED STRUCTURE OF
CHILDREN'S INTERESTS

Section 1 **Summary of Previous Findings**

A large quantity of existing literature is devoted to the study of interests in both children and adults, but comparatively few studies are both comprehensive and methodologically advanced. Most earlier work differs from that reported in the present chapter in one or more of the following respects:

1. It is concerned with specific interests in a fairly narrow area—these may be vocational, such as interest in nursing as a career (Jeffrey, 1951); or scholastic, such as studies of preferences for different school subjects (e.g., Shakespeare, 1936).

2. If more general and covering a wider area, the interests may be selected à priori or by empirical keying, as in the well-known inventory of Strong.

3. Earlier work makes use almost exclusively of direct, fakable questions, as opposed to disguised, objective test methods.

4. Few comprehensive studies make use of factor analysis; and of these, none, to the writers' knowledge, has been replicated as extensively as in the program of research on interests and motivation that has been proceeding for several years under the leadership of the senior author.

5. Few if any early studies have combined measures of ability and personality with a comprehensive set of interest measures in the same analysis.

By far the most widely used tests of interest are those of Kuder (1953) and of Strong (1949). Both are primarily vocational. The rationale, uses, and limitations are well summarized by Cronbach (1960, pp. 406–428). The former was based on a factor analysis of occupational interests and yields ten scores, in the following areas: Outdoor, Mechanical, Computational, Scientific, Persuasive, Artistic, Literary, Musical, Social Service, and Clerical. Strong's inventory, on the other hand, was originally constructed from an examination of the characteristics of successful practitioners in various jobs and professions and a concentration on the interests that were empirically found to distinguish between them. The Strong inventory has been developed with extensive work on large samples, and, given this approach, it is probably the most effective instrument for vocational guidance. Its worth was shown in the study by Kelly and Fiske (1951) on the prediction of success in clinical psychology, in which field a very large number of other tests and ratings gave markedly disappointing results.

The disadvantages of this kind of approach, however, are considerable. First, as already pointed out, the interest to the student of human motivation as a whole is limited, whether he be psychologist, teacher, or layman. Second, even within the field of vocational guidance, such questionnaires operate only at the rational, conscious level, to such an extent, indeed, that, as Cronbach points out, their use is largely limited to candidates for the professions or for highly skilled trades. Third, because the approach is blindly empirical and actuarial, it gives little psychological insight into why or how certain patterns of answers to questions predict success in a particular job; and this ignorance entails a dependence on particular, changeable social circumstances.

In addition to the Strong and Kuder measures of vocational interest, a number of recent tests of interests suitable for selection and prediction in a particular scholastic situation have been devised by, among others, Peel and his associates, and Wiseman, in Britain. Both Peel and Wiseman attempted to discriminate, by measuring interests, between children most likely to benefit from an academic, or from a technical, type of secondary education, respectively.

Peel (1959) used, among other devices, tests based on homonyms, i.e., on words with ambiguous meanings. For example, words such as "strut," "vice," "tender" could be given either a practical, technical meaning or a nonpractical one. A proportion of nonambiguous words was also included to obscure the purpose of the test. Peel's paper includes a theoretical section on the relation between ability, interest, and attainment, in which he makes the interesting suggestion that the best method of predicting attainment might be by a multiplicative formula of interest $\times$ ability, drawing an analogy with the well-known Hullian formula for habit-strength.

As already indicated, few of the reports in the psychological literature are based on a comprehensive sampling of relevant variables. Sandall (1960) writes that "with the possible exception of R. B. Cattell's Interest Test, there appear to be very few, if any, tests which have a classification arrived at by analysis of the whole field of interests." The work of Guilford and his associates (1954), however, covers a wide area; methodologically, it has many features in common with the approach recommended by the present writers. Besides its comprehensiveness, this study starts from careful hypotheses about structure and explores these by a sophisticated technique of factor analysis, replicated on two samples. In addition, Guilford is careful to state that he is interested primarily in motivation. "Although previous analyses have frequently shown factors interpretable along the lines of vocational categories, it is quite possible that a more thorough analysis would show that these can, in turn, be expressed as linear combinations of variables more obviously in the form of underlying motives. This possibility is comprehensively explored in this investigation." Finally, the inquiry used projective or semiprojective devices in many instances (although not, apparently, systematically), e.g., people were not asked, "Are you painstaking about work?" but, "Do you admire people who are painstaking about their work?"

Guilford found seventeen interest factors that appeared in the analyses of both samples, and a few more appearing in one or other sample. The two groups of subjects were composed of young United States airmen and Air Force officers, respectively. Several of these factors corresponded fairly closely to those we shall be reporting in this chapter from our own work, such as the mechanical, social-altruistic, amusement, and aggression-pugnacity factors, but there are also marked discrepancies.

The main reason for such discrepancies, most probably, lies in a rather different conception of the basic modalities. Thus, unlike most other researchers whose work we have touched on, Guilford and his associates would appear to have interpreted the field of interests and motivation *too* widely, and to have included variables that we should clearly allocate to the modalities of ability or of personality traits. For instance, variables 96–98 are described as "logical processes," "mathematical concepts," and "problem solving," and variables 32, 35, 38, 40, 74, and 80 are defined as "conformity," "dominance," "subservience," "autistic thinking," "carefulness," and "self-reliance." Furthermore, in spite of his concern with fundamental motivation, as distinct from superficial interest patterns, Guilford states that "for reasons that should be rather obvious, the so-called animal drives were not included." Consequently, it is not surprising that many of the factors (and particularly the ergs) found in the Illinois surveys did not emerge in the Guilford study.

Another very relevant and apparently comprehensive research into the structure of children's interests has been briefly reported by Sandall (1960). A wide variety of interests were first classified into twenty-eight main areas— artistic, athletic, collecting, dramatic, exploring, humanitarian, indoor games, etc.—and scores on each of these variables were derived by a forced-choice technique, apparently rather similar to the Paired Words test used in our own Illinois surveys.

From a factor analysis rotated to simple structure, the following main factors emerged, though with imperfect replication between boys and girls, whose results were analyzed separately:

A   Practical, rural interests
B   Sociable, display, dancing, etc.
C   Humanitarian, protective care for the aged and for younger children

D   Entertainment: diversions, indoor games
E   Athletic
F   Literate
G   Aesthetic
H   Scientific-mechanical

Although only a rather cursory account of Sandall's work has apparently been published to date, these results have suggestive similarities to the Illinois findings.

Section 2   **The Development of the IPAT Motivation Batteries**

As already described in Chapters 5 and 8, the writers take the position that for the measurement of interests in general, but most particularly where one is concerned with the deeper, less conscious, levels of motivation, direct, fakable questionnaires are unsuitable. Some details of the objective, disguised tests actually used have been given in Chapter 8. Here, we shall consider these in more detail, together with some of the technical considerations involved.

Before the Illinois series of researches into interest and motivation was launched, the whole range of possible projective and "indirect" methods of measuring motivation was surveyed by Cattell. Fifty-five new devices derived from basic motivation research, i.e., going beyond projective and "indirect" approaches, were invented, and, with older tests, constituted some 90 principles, each embodying a rather different psychological mechanism. They have been summarized, validated, and discussed (Cattell 1957, pp. 465–471). In a series of earlier studies, including those of Cattell, Maxwell, Light, and Unger (1949), Cattell and Miller (1952), Cattell and Wenig (1952), Cattell and Baggaley (1956), Cattell, Radcliffe, and Sweney (1963), Tapp (1957), and others, the more promising of these principles and devices were sifted out, then increasingly groomed and standardized for use with both adults and children. By 1960, the date of the surveys reported in detail in the present book, three well-developed tests of motivation were in existence: the Motivational Analysis Test (MAT) (Cattell, Horn, Radcliffe, and Sweney, 1964), the Vocational Interest Measure (VIM) (Sweney and Cattell, 1968), and the School Motivational Analysis Test (SMAT) (Cattell, Krug, and Sweney, 1968). The first two of these IPAT tests are for use with adults; the MAT being primarily oriented to clinical and guidance work, and the VIM to occupational and vocational psychology. The main concern here, however, will be with SMAT, designed for use with high-school and junior-high-school pupils.

In the earlier forms of SMAT, seven separate principles of motivation measurement were included, but these were reduced to five, and later to four, to economize testing time and make use of the methods found to be most efficient. Three groups of school pupils were tested in the Illinois survey: the two main groups at Springfield (urban) and Paxton (rural), and a subsidiary group at Monticello (rural). The main results already reported were based on the high schools at Springfield and Paxton, but advantage was taken of the availability of a further group at Monticello to repeat the structural analysis of interests for further confirmation and also to incorporate some modifications and improvements in the SMAT battery. For the testing at Monticello, the least satisfactory of the five tests of motivation was dropped, and the increased testing time made available was used to ensure a more thorough coverage of some interest areas. As a result of the analysis of the Monticello data, SMAT approached its final form, and its completion was largely the work of Sweney.

The reader will perhaps remember from Chapter 8 (see, in particular, Tables XIII and XIV) that we tested our main samples of children with respect to thirty-two interests, each being separately measured by five devices or types of test, as described in the last paragraph. We thus had 160 interest scores for each pupil, but before we turn to the analysis and interpretation of these scores, an important technical point needs some explanation. This is the question of ipsatization, already briefly considered in Chapter 8.

Let us consider first the Information test of interests, one of the five used. The principle on which this test is based is that an individual who is interested in a particular area will almost inevitably be better informed about the area. Thus someone who was interested in music, other things being equal, would be more likely to answer the following item correctly:

"The smallest of the following instruments is

(a) the viola; (b) the violin; (c) the cello; (d) the bass violin."

The reader may very reasonably, however, query the phrase "other things being equal" in the last sentence with a criticism of this type: "Other things never are equal. Surely many of the pupils will be well-informed *in general* and others will be ill-informed *in general*. The former will tend to come out higher in all interests on your test, simply because they are better informed, without necessarily being more interested. How are you going to separate out the 'interest' factor from the 'information' factor, when your test scores will presumably represent a mixture of both?"

This is a most important question arising from the use of objective tests of the type described. There are two main ways of dealing with the difficulty, both of which were used in the Illinois experiment. The first is the device of *ipsatization* of scores. In this method, each person's score on a particular interest is expressed as a deviation from his average score on all the interests measured (thirty-two in our experiment). Thus the effect of the instrument is neutralized, because the general level of the subject's information plays no part in the resulting scores, serving only as the base from which deviations are measured.

The reader who is familiar with the commoner concept of standard scores will see that the process of deriving ipsatized (or ipsative) scores is a kind of standardization, with the difference that in the ordinary table of test scores it is applied to each row (i.e., to each person's various scores) instead of to each column (i.e., to each test). Actually, the usual type of standardization of each test is also applied, and was in the current research; it is desirable to have a summated score for each person on each of the thirty-two interests—summated, that is, over the five types of test device. Thus one obtains a measure of each interest not based only on Information or on Memory or on one of the other tests, but an overall measure of each interest, which should be more reliable and trustworthy.

A fuller account and discussion of ipsative scoring is given in Cattell (1957, pp. 492–498). The mathematical aspects are explored by Clemans (1956). There is also a useful experimental study by Talbott (1960), who found, contrary to the belief of some psychometricians, that the predictive power of tests was not necessarily impaired by ipsatization.

This method of ipsatized scoring is the one we have used most commonly in the Illinois series of motivation researches. The alternative method is to factor the raw test scores and to concentrate the unwanted effect of each device into a separate "instrument factor." This alternative is, in a sense, more experimental, because, until recently, little was known about the characteristics of such factors, which in other situations are generally unwanted artifacts. A great deal of scope remains for further research in this area, but some light has been thrown on these instrument factors, and their varieties and subdivisions have been provisionally classified by Cattell (1961). The subject is a highly technical one, and our aim here is simply to clarify it sufficiently for the reader to understand the kind of evidence that exists about the structure of children's interests without plunging too far into the intricacies of test standardization and factor rotation.

The five tests used have already been listed in Chapter 8 and are summarized in Table XXXVIII.

These five tests were chosen as the best representatives available for five of the seven *motivational components* isolated in earlier factor studies of interests. These factors, unlike the sentiment and erg factors, which are found by analyzing a variety of interest measures by one type of test, are found from analyzing one interest area by a number of types of test. Cattell and Baggaley (1956) found five such motivational components in work with adults, which have also appeared in research on children, with two additions.

The first motivational component factor was identified as "conscious id," to use the psychoanalytic term, and is characterized by the general autistic "I want" quality. As shown in Table XXXVIII, the test chosen to represent this component was How Much and How Many?

TABLE **XXXVIII**

Types of test used to measure each of the thirty-two attitude areas in the Illinois survey

Name of test	Psychological principle	Motivational component and interpretation
How Much and How Many	Autistic thinking	Conscious id
Information	Relation of information to interest	Ego
Paired Words	Word association	Superego
Memory	Selective memory	Repressed complexes
What Do You Think?	Decision speed	Impulsivity

The second motivational component found in earlier research was labeled *beta* and interpreted as the ego component. This factor tends to be less distinct than some of the others and is related to sentiments rather than ergs, being strongest in realized, conscious, habituated interests. The Information test was chosen, because it is known to be reliably loaded on this factor.

The third component, *gamma,* is provisionally identified with superego mechanisms. The Paired Words test, shown in earlier research to represent this factor, was accordingly used.

The fourth component, *delta,* has so far only been found to load individual tests. Because the main experiment reported here called for group testing, no measure of this factor could be included in the battery.

The fifth component, *epsilon,* is represented by the Memory test. The principle here is of selective memory, and the retention of more material in one area than another is taken to indicate greater interest in that area. Taking into account a number of earlier researches, we are inclined to identify the epsilon factor as being related to and arising from repressed complexes. The evidence for this interpretation is summarized by Cattell, Radcliffe, and Sweney (1963), and this paper also contains extensive evidence on the interpretation and implications of the other motivational components.

The sixth component, *zeta,* was represented in the earlier SMAT battery by a test known as Opinions or What Do You Think? In this test, the speed of reaction to a set of easy questions was measured, and, as with the other tests, the *differential* speed in the various areas of interest was obtained by the process of ipsatization. The component, *zeta,* had previously been interpreted as a measure of "impulsivity" (Cattell, Sweney, and Radcliffe, 1960). This test, however, proved the least satisfactory of the five used in the earlier version of SMAT, which was given to the main samples, and was dropped both from the battery given at Monticello and from the final published version of SMAT.

Because these motivational components, obtained by the factor analysis of many different measures of one interest, are simple-structure factors and to some degree correlated, it is possible to carry the analysis a stage further and to derive second-order factors. These second-order motivational factors are of considerable theoretical interest and throw further light on the nature of the first-order components. Two such second-order factors were found, which seem clearly to group the motivational components into "integrated" and "unintegrated" (possibly "conscious" and "unconscious") categories. Of the five motivational components represented by tests in the earlier SMAT battery, two (*beta* and *gamma*) have been found to load on the "integrated" second-order factor, and the remaining three on the "unintegrated" factor. The dropping of the Opinions test from the later form of the battery left two tests representing "integrated" and two representing "unintegrated" components.

Section 3   **Previous Knowledge of Erg and Sentiment Factors**

In order not to satiate the reader with a mass of detail about a multiplicity of researches, we shall (1) present a brief overview of the common, replicated findings about the structure of ergs and sentiments in both adults and children before considering particular analyses in more detail individually, and (2) refer the reader to the systematic treatment of motivation and dynamic structure source traits in Chapter 5 above. The evidence about adults is fully reviewed in Cattell (1957); that about children is based on the extensive preliminary work of Radcliffe and Sweney, and on the samples of Illinois children at Springfield, Paxton, and Monticello.

In adults, seven ergs have been repeatedly isolated and can be considered well established. These are:

> Sex
> Gregariousness
> Parental protectiveness
> Exploration (curiosity)
> Escape (fear, need for security)
> Self-assertion
> Narcissism

Three others, apparently of lesser variance, have also been found. These are:

> Rest-seeking (liking for a quiet life)
> Appeal
> Constructiveness

Of these ten ergic factors found in studies with adults, nine have now also been found repeatedly in children, the only exception being that of Appeal. This erg is, as shown above, one of the three least important among adults, so far as can be seen at present. It is rather more surprising, perhaps, that it should not have been found in children, and possible reasons must include the relatively pioneering nature of research of this kind.

Section 4   The Structure of Children's Attitudes as Found in the Illinois Surveys

Meanwhile, however, let us consider the nine ergic factors that *have* clearly been shown to mediate children's attitudes, and the particular attitudes in which they are embodied. The factor loadings given below are based on both urban children (Springfield) and rural children (Monticello), analyzed separately to provide replication. In general, there are few discrepancies in pattern between the two groups. Where there are, these are pointed out. With these exceptions, the factor loadings shown are averaged from both analyses. The attitudes, as measured by different test devices and combinations of test devices, yielded varying loadings, and the figures below are based in general on the particular test that functioned most efficiently as a measure of the erg in question.

Sex	I want to spend more time with my girl or boy friend	.36
	I want to go to parties where couples are invited	.35
Gregariousness	I want to go to games with my friends	.36
	I want to spend more time with my friends	.28
Protectiveness	I want my younger brothers and sisters to behave and mind me	.33
	I want to have a pet to take care of	.24
Curiosity	I want to learn more about how the world works and science explains things	.29
	I want my pictures to be beautiful and pleasant to look at	.28
Fear	I don't want to see any ghosts or prowlers at night (Monticello only)	.34
	I don't want to be dangerously ill or badly hurt (Monticello only)	.25
	I want to have Mother there if something goes wrong (Springfield only)	.24
	I want my teacher to like me (Springfield only)	.16
Assertion (or pugnacity)	I want to get even with other kids who have caused me trouble	.32
	I want the United States to beat its enemies	.32

Narcissism	I want to dress well in order to impress the opposite sex	.35
	I want to see a handsome face and figure in the mirror	.33
	I want nice clothes, so people will like the way I look	.25
Rest-seeking	I want to have more holidays in order to rest and take it easy	.38
	I want to eat good food to grow strong	.29
Constructiveness	I want to make things and draw pictures related to school subjects	.33
	I want to take things apart to see what makes them work	.32
Submission	I want to be polite to adults	.25

It will be seen that the ergic factors in the above list correspond very closely—more closely than one might have expected—with those already known in adults. The failure of an Appeal erg to emerge is particularly interesting and throws valuable evidence on a point that had caused some dispute and uncertainty in finally determining the main feature of the adult structure. Briefly, two possible theoretical positions were tenable. The first was that what had been tentatively identified as an Appeal erg in adults was actually a manifestation of the Religion sentiment. Our opinion was already tending in that direction (Cattell, 1957, p. 523), on the grounds that appeal behavior among adults in our society has little scope for expression outside religion and near-religious activities. The other possibility was that an inadequate sampling of variables had not fully permitted the emergence of two separate factors.

As we shall see, a Religion sentiment was clearly found in both samples of children, and this finding, together with the absence of an Appeal erg in either, appears virtually to settle the issue, particularly because attitudes were included (e.g., awe and admiration for father, attitude to teacher, etc.) that might well have been found to load the hypothesized erg of appeal.

Besides the ten ergs we have already discussed, five others were hypothesized before beginning the whole program of research, as follows:

> Food-seeking
> Pugnacity
> Acquisitiveness
> Disgust
> Laughter

Attitudes were included in the researches with children, which, it was hoped, might mark the first three of these hypothesized factors, although none of the five had previously been firmly charted in the earlier research with adults. No factor interpretable as "hunger" or even as "greed" appeared, presumably because our civilization has progressed so far that few people (or at least few of our subjects) ever feel hunger pangs long enough for them to be a real motivating force. Consequently, there is insufficient variance in this respect for a factor to appear.

The case of Pugnacity is rather different. Here one might reasonably hope to find such a factor in children, whereas it might be less evident in adults through cultural pressure toward sublimation. At one point, the nonappearance of this factor among adults led to serious consideration of the idea that it might be in an entirely different category from all other ergs, perhaps as representing merely a measure of their frustration (cf. the well-known frustration-aggression hypothesis discussed by Dollard, among other psychologists). This idea was never more than provisionally and reluctantly entertained—common observation and consensus of psychological theory both point rather in the direction of an actual, measurable factor despite its reluctance to emerge in earlier studies.

We have already reported a factor in the Illinois children's data, which so far has been described as Assertion (Pugnacity) and aligned with the Assertion factor in adults. It is possible, however, that this factor is indeed one of Pugnacity, and this belief is strengthened by the existence of another factor, not yet described, which appeared in both analyses and which is probably identifiable as Assertion. Interpretation is further complicated by the fact that the test battery was slightly modified between the administrations at Springfield and Monticello, principally by being "thickened up" in just those areas where clearer definition and additional markers were required. Consequently, the Assertion factor (if the factor already reported is accepted as Pugnacity) is defined by different attitudes in the two analyses, as follows:

Assertion	I want my team to win (Springfield only)	.45
	I want to seek class office (Monticello only)	.41
	I want to read adventure comics (Monticello only)	.34
	I want the United States to protect small countries from Russia (Springfield only)	.31

This interpretation must therefore be taken as rather more provisional than those reported earlier, but the evidence is at least highly suggestive of separate ergic factors for assertion and pugnacity.

Finally, a factor of Acquisitiveness was found in both samples of children, this again being a hypothesized erg that had proved hard to isolate from adult attitudes, although one might have supposed the contrary. This was the least-well-defined ergic factor in the Springfield sample, so that the replication with the Monticello children proved particularly valuable in this respect.

Acquisitiveness   I want to save money in a bank   .35
I want nice clothes so that people will like the way
I look (Monticello only)   .32

This completes the list of ergic factors found in children in the Illinois surveys, but it is interesting to note at this stage, before considering sentiment factors, that the proportion of ergs to sentiments in the attitude structure is noticeably higher among children than among adults, with absolutely *more* ergs and fewer sentiments proving measurable among the former. This finding satisfies theoretical expectations: one would expect the basic "instinctual" structure to be clearly marked in children and, conversely, the structure of sentiments, which depends more on the gradual coalescing of interests and attitudes around institutions under social influences, to be more highly structured and more easily detectable among adults.

Seven main factors representing sentiments emerged quite early in the Illinois researches into adult motivation, as follows:

> Profession (Career)
> Sports and games
> Religion
> Mechanical*
> Self-Sentiment
> Superego*
> Patriotism*

The asterisks against three of these sentiments indicate that for different reasons they are somewhat less certainly established than the other four. In general, the structure of sentiments, although well established, is probably more susceptible to cultural variations and sampling differences than either the structure of ergs or of personality dimensions, for obvious reasons.

This variation will tend to produce greater differences between samples of adults in sentiment structure according to socioeconomic level, political and religious application, and so forth, than is found in ergic patterns. Similarly, we should expect to find greater differences between adults and children in the field of sentiments than in the more "instinctual" field of ergs.

However, to give the overall picture first, five of the seven sentiment factors found in adults appear also in the analysis of children's interests, although the identification in one or two cases is approximate and provisional. The main exception is the Profession or Career sentiment. Because the children in the Illinois surveys were in the thirteen-year-old age group, little material was included in the test batteries that would have allowed such a factor to appear, thus it is possible (but unlikely) that children's interest in their future career or profession is sufficiently structured at that age to permit assessment. The other partial exception is the Mechanical sentiment.

The loadings on these five sentiment factors, derived in the same way as those on the ergic factors already reported, were as follows:

Self-Sentiment	I want to have a good reputation for ideals and honesty	.38
	I want to be the kind of person everyone likes to have around	.31
Superego	I want always to show self-control	.28
	I want to show my father how awesome and admirable I think he is	.32
Play-Fantasy	I want to see more science-fiction movies and television programs	.36
	I want to have plenty of games, books, etc.	.35
Religious	I want to worship God and obey him	.36
	I want to pray for God's protection and mercy	.28
Patriotism	(Monticello only)	
	I want the United States to protect small countries from Russia	?

The attitudes on which these sentiments are loaded have not been so thoroughly explored as with adults (see Cattell, 1957, pp. 521 ff.), but enough evidence is available to show considerable similarity of pattern. Of the two adult sentiments that did not emerge, that of sentiment to Career or Profession has already been mentioned. The second exception, that of Mechanical sentiment, is only partial; even with adults, it was not at all clear whether this factor was indeed properly classified, or whether it should be thought of as an erg of Constructiveness. In reporting the results with children, we have chosen this latter alternative, because the attitudes loaded seemed to point rather in that direction.

Corresponding to some degree, but not entirely, to the adult sentiment concerned with games and sports is the children's sentiment that we have called Play-Fantasy, because this seems to describe best the nature of the attitudes on which it loaded in both samples. The difference here from the adult pattern is that, in a series of researches, children's attitudes concerned specifically with participation in and watching of outdoor sports have generally allied themselves with attitudes such as "I want to spend more time with my friends" and have thus produced a factor of Gregariousness rather than one of interest in sports as such.

To throw more light on this area, two further attitudes, rather similar to those loading on the Play-Fantasy factor, were added to the SMAT battery in the course of its development between the administrations at Springfield and Monticello, as follows:

"I want to hear and see Western and adventure stories on television"
"I want to see movies"
Analysis of the Monticello results produced, against expectation, an amuse-ment factor, defined by the two new variables, quite distinct from the Play-Fantasy factor.

Section 5   The Prediction of Achievement from Interests and Attitudes

It must be frankly admitted that in the Springfield and Paxton samples the raw test scores yielded generally very low and nonsignificant correlations with the criteria of achievement. The most consistent relation was with the measures of Submission, primarily represented by the attitude "I want to be polite to adults."

There are several possible reasons for this rather disappointing result. First, the motivation measures were, at that stage, experimental, compared with the tests of ability and personality. Second, it was clear from the detailed factor analysis of motivational measures, in which each attitude was meas-ured by five separate tests or instruments, that some of these were functioning better than others for particular attitudes. But for the purpose of correlation —because it was necessary to limit the number of variables to be analyzed, even by electric computer, to 110—it was necessary to have a general, overall measure of each interest or attitude. Third, because of the need to compress a very wide range of interest measures into a short testing time, reliabilities of individual measures were generally low, with consequent attenuation of correlations.

It was possible, however, in one of the later analyses, to estimate the cor-relation of the *factors* (as distinct from the individual measures) with the achievement *factor*. These estimates are shown in Table XXXIX.

In a more recent study than the main one reported in this book, Cattell, Sweney, and Sealy (1966) again compared the relative predictive powers against school achievement of tests in the three modalities. The criteria comprised both a standardized school-achievement test and an average of school grades. The version of SMAT used was further developed from that used in the studies already reported. Some of their findings are summarized in Table XL. Other evidence of the predictive potential of SMAT (with a sample of delinquent boys) is given by Pierson, *et al.* (1964). Later re-searches have shown an important gain from treating the U (unintegrated) and I (integrated) motivation scores from SMAT as conceptually and nu-merically distinct. They behave sufficiently differently to justify distinct weights in the specification equations.

Further studies are still required to substantiate the predictive power of these motivational tests, but from these results and unpublished results known to the senior author, the variance in school achievement falls approximately

TABLE **XXXIX**

Estimated relation of motivational factors to achievement factor

Motivational factors	Correlation with achievement factor
Constructiveness	+.36
Curiosity	−.20
Fear	−.24
Pugnacity	+.21
Gregariousness	+.17
Assertion	−.23
Religion	−.34
Submissiveness	+.50
Self-Sentiment	−.37
Superego	+.44
Narcissism	−.33
Sex	−.15
Acquisition	−.39
Protectiveness	+.21

TABLE **XL**

Multiple correlations between tests of personality, motivation, and ability and measures of school achievement (144 seventh- and eighth-grade pupils)

Test of personality, motivation, and ability	Number of predictor variables	CRITERIA	
		Standardized achievement test	Average of school grades
SMAT	15	.522 (.282)	.482 (.164)
HSPQ (less Factor B)	13	.520 (.329)	.597 (.462)
HSPQ + SMAT	28	.688 (.367)	.717 (.449)
HSPQ + SMAT + IQ	29	.854 (.734)	.813 (.650)

NOTE: The figures in parentheses are the multiple correlation coefficients corrected for shrinkage.

into four equal parts: 25 per cent predictable from tests of ability; 25 per cent each, from tests of personality and motivation; and the remaining 25 per cent accountable for jointly by the particular influence of the school and by random factors.

SUMMARY *of Chapter Eleven*

1. A brief survey of earlier work on interest and attitudes, particularly those of children and young people, shows that few studies do the

following: (a) cover the field at all comprehensively; (b) analyze inter-relations and structure by the use of factor analysis; (c) use disguised, unfakable tests; (d) relate interests to personality and abilities.

2. A program of basic motivation research has been carried out for some years under the general leadership of Cattell, which yields concepts fulfilling these conditions. The structure of adult motivation revealed by these methods is now fairly clear; that of children's motivation is becoming clear.

3. In the Illinois survey already described in Chapters 8–10, five *kinds* of disguised test were used for every attitude. Each of these was designed to represent one of the main motivational components discovered in earlier studies.

4. Thirty-two attitude areas were included in the survey. When scores were intercorrelated and factor-analyzed, some eleven or twelve ergic factors and four or five sentiment factors were obtained. The number of ergic factors in relation to sentiment factors is higher in this study than has usually been found with adults, and this finding has been paralleled in other studies with children and young people.

5. The relative predominance of ergic factors and absence of sentiments in children is in line with reasonable expectation and with psychological theory. Apart from one discrepancy, there is a remarkably close correspondence between the factors found in this study and those frequently replicated in studies of adults.

6. The following factors were identified: (a) *ergic factors:* Sex, Gregariousness, Protectiveness, Curiosity, Fear, Assertion, Narcissism, Rest-seeking, Constructiveness, Submission, Acquisitiveness; (b) *sentiment factors:* Self-Sentiment, Superego, Play-Fantasy, Religion.

7. In addition to the urban and rural samples of children described in earlier chapters, an additional rural sample of children at Monticello was included in this study of attitudes. Factor analysis of the data from Monticello revealed a similar pattern to that found in the main survey with the additional finding of a patriotism sentiment.

8. The prediction of achievement scores from raw scores on the individual attitude measures was disappointing, because the great majority of correlations were not statistically significant. When the correlation of dynamic structure factors, however, with an achievement factor (simple structure) was estimated, the relations were more definite; the highest relation was with the factor of submissiveness.

9. Further evidence has been coming in from more recent studies in the same general program of research, some of which suggests that motivation tests can add a substantial quota of predictive power in forecasting school achievement.

Chapter Twelve

THE ASSOCIATIONS OF ENVIRONMENTAL
FACTORS AND ACHIEVEMENT

Section 1 **The Effect of Cultural Differences on the Prediction
of Achievement**

In Chapters 9, 10, and 11 we have been concerned with the assessment
of individual differences in abilities, personality, and motivation and have
adopted an analysis in terms of traits and factors. All these individual differences depend in a complex manner on the joint influence of heredity and
environment, and for some of them we have mentioned what is known about
relative contributions. Generally speaking, however, our approach so far has
been as though these individual differences are present *within the child*, as
indeed they are.

But even the shortest survey of the factors affecting achievement would
be seriously one-sided without some consideration of environmental factors
as such. Sociologists, indeed, would often argue that these are of paramount
importance and that they largely dictate the individual differences that psychologists assess. This difference of emphasis arises from methodological differences in the disciplines, and few psychologists would completely agree with
the sociologists' view. But it has led to interesting and important findings,
which help to supplement a purely psychological analysis. A word of warn-
ing is necessary, however, about many of the findings described in this chapter.
Most of them are correlational, and the existence of correlation does not always indicate direct causal relation between the two variables, nor, even if
a causal relation exists, does it always show in what direction this operates.
Our account will be, inevitably, somewhat rough and ready, and it is easy to
slip into the habit of talking as though "a positive relation was found between
socioeconomic level and school attainment" is the same as "it was found
that a high socioeconomic level directly resulted in a high level of school
attainment." We suggest that the reader constantly bear in mind this dis-

tinction, particularly, perhaps, in interpreting the results of broad sociological surveys.

Statistical psychologists often appear to talk as if their ultimate aim was to obtain a multiple correlation of 1.0 between their measures and the criterion of achievement. That is, their ideal goal appears to account completely for the variance of achievement by means of psychological tests administered in school. But, obviously, any psychologist who announced that he had found a perfect correlation between his battery of psychological tests and some criterion of achievement would incur the immediate suspicion that he was a charlatan or had made a gross error in computation. For, technical considerations apart, this is an imperfect world, and no one would claim that the extent of an individual's achievement can ever be perfectly described by measures of his *intrinsic* qualities, however accurate and refined these measures become. As we are told in Ecclesiastes, "The race is not always to the swift, nor the battle to the strong. . . ."

This being so, what is the best multiple correlation likely to be obtained and repeated in practice when one tries to predict a measurable aspect of achievement from the most effective battery of tests? Would the psychologist settle for a correlation of, say, 0.8? As always in questions of this kind, there is no simple answer. First, the size of the correlation will be affected not only by the reliability of the tests, but also, as is widely known but frequently forgotten, by the reliability of the criterion. If the measure of achievement that is being predicted cannot be reliably assessed, the correlation will be correspondingly attenuated. Second, the degree of prediction will be affected by the interval of time between administration of the test or battery and assessment of the criterion measure. We have argued earlier in this book that the difference beween "simultaneous prediction" and prediction over an interval of time has sometimes been exaggerated. The two situations differ in degree and not in kind, but clearly, the longer the time interval, other things being equal, the greater will be the opportunity for both random and systematic changes to disturb and reduce the correlation. Third, the extent of prediction we can obtain will depend upon the kind of society and culture we are studying. It is obvious that we generally confine our attention to one society at a time, and that our possible prediction of achievement to the extent of a correlation of 0.8 will not apply to a mixed sample of children from, say, Sweden, Algeria, and Central Africa. In addition, within one culture or society, the "ceiling" of prediction, or best possible estimate of achievement from the intrinsic qualities of the individual, will be higher in a better-ordered society and lowest in one where the vicissitudes of ill health, unequal opportunity, turmoil, and injustice are most frequent.

Thus both technical and cultural reasons will establish the "ceiling" of achievement prediction, and the cultural reasons will be both intercultural and intracultural. The intercultural differences are obvious and enormous.

Even in our present age of rapid communications and increasing standardization, the contrasts between an Australian aboriginal or an African pygmy and a New Yorker are so marked as to need no emphasis or elaboration. Intracultural differences, on the other hand, have often been underestimated, until quite recently; and it has been one of the main functions of the relatively new discipline of sociology to throw light on them. Ever since Disraeli wrote of the rich and poor as "two nations," we have been dimly conscious of the different worlds inhabited by those with whom we rub shoulders in the street, but it is only in the last few decades that such differences have been studied systematically and conceptualized at all adequately.

It was indeed high time for an adequate range of techniques in social science to be developed. The pressure of economic change, the lightning development of technology, the emancipation of colonial nations, the universal growing appreciation of the practical value of education in achieving a satisfactory life have all been contributory sources of increased social and educational mobility. Nor is there any sign that these pressures toward mobility and change have passed their peak. In Britain, on the contrary, it has hardly been realized even now that full opportunities for the development of talent, regardless of social class, are no longer an idealistic or utopian aim, but a sheer economic and realistic necessity if the country's achievement and prestige are not to suffer a greater relative decline than has already occurred. The publication of the Robbins report (1963) on higher education is one sign that the problem is being taken seriously, but the situation is such that educational administrators will have to run hard even to stand still, in relation to the rate of progress in other Western countries. It is not yet clear whether the government, the educational administrators, the vice-chancellors of universities, and indeed educated public opinion, in Britain are sufficiently convinced of the need for a massive expansion in higher education. "More means worse" is a slick adage that is too commonly heard. It is fairly certain that the massive expansion is not too technically difficult, given the required level of motivation in influential circles. Whether this level of motivation has yet been reached is an open question.

Section 2   Cross-Cultural Research on Motivation for Achievement

This crucial question of motivation for achievement in a whole society is extraordinarily complex and extraordinarily interesting. Until quite recently, it has been a favorite topic for the armchair speculations of historians and a fertile source for the pointing of morals. Classical scholars of the old school delighted in the inexplicable and miraculous flowering of culture in Athens in the fifth century B.C. Moralists were very ready to predict the decline and fall of the Roman Empire (given the aid of hindsight) from its declining morals a few hundred years earlier. More recently, theories of climatic influence, of economic determination, and of racial superiority or inferiority have been involved. It is easy to poke fun at speculative and oversimplified explanations but a great deal harder to improve on them.

One of the most interesting attempts, to psychologists, at least, has been that of McClelland (1961), who ranges widely in time and space, seeking to account in psychological terms for the apparent vagaries of economic growth, stagnation, and decline. In 1950, the 7 per cent of the world's population living in North America enjoyed about 43 per cent of the world's wealth, while the 55 per cent of the population in Asia had only about 16 per cent. Such a difference can hardly be entirely accounted for in such terms as climate and natural resources. What then are the fundamental factors accounting for rapid economic growth and development? Many historians have virtually abandoned any search for broad generalizations, adopting the role of selective documenters relatively unaided or unhampered by theory. McClelland admits his rashness in rushing in where many learned professionals fear to tread, but nicely justifies himself with the argument that psychologists are so used to being told that they can never make generalizations about anything so complex and variable as human nature that they may be forgiven for assuming that history could hardly be more difficult to generalize about.

A more cogent reason for the psychologist to invade the territory of economic historians and sociologists is that, as McClelland (p. 11) points out:

> . . . economic theorists themselves seem to have always felt that sources of change in the economic system lay outside the system itself. Thus it was not really clear to them why technical inventions of practical importance should appear more frequently at one period in history than in another, or why, once having appeared in one country, they should spread more rapidly to country A than country B, and, as Meier and Baldwin [1957] put it, half humorously, "economic development is much too serious a topic to be left to economists."

McClelland's attempt to apply a psychological analysis in the explanation of economic growth centers around the concept of need for achievement and its different strength in different cultures. One of the main techniques employed to assess the strength of achievement motivation in a culture is to study the content of stories for children found in school textbooks for the second to fourth grades, and a plausible case is made that these represent a kind of "projective technique," in which the values of the culture are simply and vividly expressed. McClelland (p. 71) quotes Margaret Mead as saying that "a culture has to get its values across to its children in such simple terms that even a behavioral scientist can understand them." Thus when the content of the stories is rated by a panel to assess the extent to which it reflects a preoccupation with achievement, the expectation is that those cultures whose stories show a large extent of this preoccupation will also "in real life" be those that display an active interest in achievement and, in consequence, a vigorous economic growth. By and large, this is what Mc-Clelland actually found. He obtained measures of need for achievement by the "stories for children" method for some thirty countries, including some as advanced as the United States and Canada and some as undeveloped as Uruguay and Mexico, and including also some "Iron Curtain" countries. In most cases, measures were obtainable for the level of need for achievement in both 1925 and 1950. The main criterion of economic growth was, for various reasons we cannot summarize here, the increase in production of electricity measured in kilowatt-hours per head of population. When certain *ad hoc* corrections were applied to allow, for example, for effects of war damage and availability of waterpower, quite a good correlation was found between need for achievement, as expressed in children's books, and rate of economic growth. Interestingly enough, and as evidence for skeptics who might accept the relationship but have doubts about which variable was causally affecting the other, the achievement score appeared to be predictive of the economic growth several years ahead, whereas the converse was not found to be generally true.

How is the varying degree of need for achievement to be accounted for in terms of environmental circumstances and environmental differences between cultures? One may readily accept the two main points that emerge from this brief account of some of the work of McClelland and his associates, which are: (1) that many of the differences in economic progress and achievement between cultures can be accounted for satisfactorily in psychological rather than economic terms; and (2) that a relation can be found cross-culturally between general and economic progress, on the one hand, and, on the other, a generalized need for achievement that permeates the culture and can be assessed by psychological techniques. But it might be argued that we have only pushed the problem back one stage. Is the psychological need for achievement itself dependent upon and influenced by more fundamental causative factors, such as genetic differences, climatic conditions, or child-rearing practices?

McClelland attempts to answer this question in some detail, reviewing a considerable amount of scattered and sometimes contradictory evidence; and we can only briefly state his main conclusions. These are that the influence of genetic factors and of climate cannot be the exclusive or even the principal cause of differences in need for achievement, because the latter fluctuates too rapidly in single cultures. On the other hand, his review of the evidence tends to confirm the general thesis put forward by Huntington fifty years ago that there is a fairly high correspondence between temperate climatic conditions and the progress and achievement of cultures fortunate enough to enjoy such conditions. Favorable climatic conditions are therefore associated with general and economic progress but not fundamental to it.

A more fundamental factor appears to be the general pattern of child-rearing and socialization within a culture. We shall discuss this further under the heading of intracultural differences in environment, but McClelland's review of cross-cultural differences suggests the following conclusions. There is an optimal level of demand by the parents (and particularly by the mother) that the young child achieve a degree of self-reliant mastery. There is also an optimal, medium level for the mother's own need for achievement. If the child is pushed too hard or too early into an attempt at self-dependence, or if, on the other hand, he is overprotected, his need for achievement will be relatively low. The father's influence would appear to be less pervasive, but in a sense more crucial. Strong evidence was found cross-culturally that an authoritarian and restrictive approach by the father lowers the need for achievement.

Popular and suggestive though the above cross-cultural enquiries on "the achievement motive" have been they do not meet the sociologist's and anthropologist's need for a clear model of culture pattern, nor have they kept up with the advances in motivation measurement described in Chapter 5. The latter results show that even if the TAT scoring is fully reliable—which it is far from being—the validity against the totality of motivation component, i.e., the concept validity, is quite poor. The very concept of "*the* achievement motive" is fake, since, as Chapter 5 shows, the main attitudes and strivings which must be included in any reasonable semantic usage of "achievement" (and certainly those included by McClelland and his workers) actually spring from two quite distinct sources—the self assertive erg and the self sentiment —as well as two or more auxiliary sources—the super ego, and sometimes pugnacity. Thus there is no single scorable "need for achievement" but several distinct functional sources, which may stand at quite different levels in the same individual or community.

If the emphasis is on moral achievement and excellence then the super ego strength plays a prominent part. If we are dealing with school achievement then the level is significantly predictable both from the self sentiment and from the super ego strengths. Dominance, as Chapter 14 brings out, is actually negatively related to school achievement, though positively related to less docility-demanding situations than the school examination, e.g., research and business. In time the progress of "achievement" research to objective measurement devices, as in the MAT, and to respect for demonstrated functional unities in personality and culture, should clear up many obscurities and contradictions due to the methodological weaknesses of what has so far been published.

The cultural milieu is important not only in stimulating assertiveness and building economic, moral, or other achievement values into the self sentiment pattern, but also in determining changes in the specification equation, i.e., in the weights to be given to different source traits in predicting achievement. For example, where achievement motivation is uniformly high the correlation of performance with intelligence will tend to be higher than usual. The problem which has debarred anthropologists and psychologists from quantitative research progress in this area has been the absence of a precise model for culture patterns—one which works. Cattell (1955) has suggested the model of three "panels"—population dimensions, syntality dimensions, and internal structure dimensions—and, with the assistance of Breul and Hartmann (1952), has shown what these dimensions are for modern cultures. This model assumes that we first obtain the dimensions of syntality by correlating the behavior of groups *as* groups, e.g., their chosen constitutions, their alliances and involvements in war, their decisions on social organization, etc., and factoring. The same is then done for the population characters, with such traits of the average citizen as intelligence, size of family, years of education, amount spent on books, frequency of alcoholism, etc. From these two panels, laws may be sought relating the dimensions of syntality to those of the population, i.e., the behavior of the group to the behavior of the individual. Alone with the third panel, these dimensional measures enable us to quantify the culture pattern.

From the standpoint of achievement three of the twelve dimensions of national culture patterns found by Cattell and his coworkers are particularly relevant. They are:

(1) *Cultural Pressure,* which loads:
High cultural output (from mechanical patents to music)
Many Nobel prizes per million
High urbanization
High interaction with other countries
Frequency of involvement in wars
High complexity of social and governmental organization
High suicide rates

(2) *Affluence-Education-Intelligence*
High real standard of living
High level of expenditure on education
Freedom from preventable diseases
Low death and birth rates
High luxury and travel expenditure

(3) *Morale*
Low death rates from syphilis, typhoid fever, etc.
Low death rates from alcoholism

High percentage of eminent men eminent outside politics
(Science, charity, art)
Low gross birth rate
Fewer slum conditions
Fewer murders per 100,000
Absence of publicly licensed prostitution
Lower general crime rate

These researches indicate that there are independent dimensions, i.e., a given national culture can have any score on each, but they obviously bear in common on the role of achievement values in the culture, and particularly on actual creativity. What the field most needs at the moment is a research on a sufficient scale—say 100 countries—to yield dependable correlations between syntality dimensions, on the one hand, and population measures (including specification equations for school achievement on source traits), on the other.

A beginning has been made in obtaining and relating source trait measures across cultures by Butcher, Ainsworth, and Nesbitt (1963), Scheier (1961), Tsujioka and Cattell (1965), Andrade, de Alves, and Ford (in press), Cattell and Warburton (1961) and others. It has been shown, for example, that there are very significant differences, e.g., the higher scores of British and Australian children on dominance, of Japanese on introversion, of Italian, Polish, and especially Indian on anxiety. Cattell and Scheier (1961) have proposed that higher anxiety level in the population mean is a function of: (a) lower economic level in the syntality and (b) lower cultural integration in the syntality. It could also be a function of higher score on the cultural pressure dimension described above.

From the standpoint of creativity—invention, books written, musical compositions, Nobel prizes, scientific discoveries—the cultural pressure dimension shows correlations which make it easily the most important of culture pattern dimensions. Psychologically (Cattell, 1950) it has been hypothesized to represent the amount of long-circuiting which the culture demands for ergic satisfactions. As such it ties in with Freud's arguments in *Civilization and its Discontents,* emphasizing that conditions requiring sublimation are important for creativity.

Creativity is discussed more deeply in Chapter 15, but here we may note that within our culture some associations have been sought with such aspects of the milieu as age, school background, etc. For example, in a related area, that of creativity, Torrance (1963) and his associates, using nine verbal and nonverbal tests, found a generally increasing level of creativity in American children from the first to eleventh grades, but with fairly marked discontinuity. Setbacks or temporary regressions to a lower level of creativity appeared to occur at about ages five, nine, thirteen, and seventeen, which were ascribed mainly to pressures toward conformity from the children's peer groups. The same tests were given to children in five other cultures (Germany, Australia, India, Samoa, American Negroes), from grades one to six, with 1,000 children in each sample. Interesting cross-cultural differences were found and plausible explanations given in terms of varying environmental and peer-group pressures. Some practical conclusions were drawn bearing on the possible reduction of these cultural discontinuities.

Section 3 **Educational Achievement in Particular Racial and Regional Groups**

Turning to intracultural environmental differences and their effect on achievement, we find a great mass of empirical research, far more than on cross-cultural differences, and it will be possible to present a sketch of some of this work only in drastic summary.

First, we must distinguish between effects on measured intelligence and effects on achievement. The effects on achievement are universally admitted, and some effect on intelligence as usually measured is equally beyond dispute, but quite acrimonious arguments have been carried on about the extent of these effects. As we have pointed out at some length in earlier chapters, this argument can be made largely irrelevant by recognizing two forms of intelligence, fluid and crystallized, the first relatively unaffected by cultural influences, the second highly affected by them. But intelligence, as generally measured, is a mixture of the two and undoubtedly subject to environmental effects. It will therefore be necessary to include in our review some studies of the effects of environmental variation on measured intelligence as well as on achievement.

At first sight, racial differences in psychological functioning within one nation might not appear to be environmental, or not entirely so. But there is abundant evidence of their dependence on environmental factors and virtually none that racial differences exist, as such, whether in intelligence or capacity for achievement. The issue might appear fairly easy to settle, but in fact bristles with difficulties, and no crucial experiment would appear to be possible. Some of the methodological complications are well summarized by Anastasi (1958, Chapter 17). Numerous lines of evidence, however, indicate by inference that what were once thought to be real racial differences are in fact environmental ones. A considerable literature exists, in particular, on differences in measured intelligence between whites and Negroes in the United States. In general, the average score of white Americans has almost always found to be superior; and in the early days of mental testing, when quite striking differences on the Army Alpha test had come to light during the first World War, the belief in fundamental racial differences flourished. It was soon found, however, from the work of Klineberg in particular, that

Negroes in the North scored markedly higher on the average than those in the Southern states. Studies of this kind were criticized on the grounds that the gains in score might be due, not to the effects of an improved environment but to those of selective migration, with the more intelligent tending to migrate to the more favorable conditions. There is certainly evidence that a selective factor of this kind sometimes does apply to population movements. Gist and Clark (1938), for instance, showed that this applied to rural-urban migration in Kansas, and Franzblau (1935) showed that differences found between migrant groups into the United States of different nationalities do not necessarily reflect corresponding differences between their countries of origin. But the question remained open as to whether the superiority of Northern over Southern Negroes could be entirely or largely ascribed to this factor of selective migration. That it certainly could not be entirely so ascribed was shown by Lee (1951), who demonstrated fairly clearly, in a longitudinal study, that Negro intelligence scores increased regularly according to their duration of residence in the North. Nor was this due to increasing sophistication and familiarity with testing procedures, as was shown by the use of a control group. Of course, all traditional intelligence tests, as pointed out in Chapter 2, show rising norms as education lengthens and improves; and the question has still to be answered whether improved culture would show such shift on fluid intelligence measures.

Another approach to this problem of whether apparent Negro inferiority was genetic or environmental was to study and compare the performance of groups with varying degrees of Negro blood. According to the genetic hypothesis, one would expect a fairly steady increase in tested intelligence from pure Negro to pure white. Some writers have claimed to find such a trend, but Witty and Jenkins (1936), reviewing the evidence, concluded that the weight of experimental evidence was against any *marked* differences:

> The results of the most comprehensive, careful and recent studies indicate that there is a negative but insignificant relationship between mental test performance and Negroid characteristics. . . . Furthermore, one may conclude that the technique involving test score comparison is at present specious as a definitive single approach in racial studies.

It thus appears from the evidence quoted and from much that we have omitted that so-called racial differences in intelligence and capacity for achievement *could* be simply a special case of environmental intracultural differences, comparable with and overlapping with such other types as socioeconomic, rural-urban, and so forth. The issue is also complicated by differences in motivation between racial groups within one culture, which partly parallel the cross-cultural differences we have discussed in connection with McClelland's work. Differences between Jews and Italians in the United States with respect to attitudes and achievement motivation were reported by

Strodtbeck (1958). These were generally in line with expectation and popular stereotype in that the Jewish subjects were found to be more mobility-oriented, to have more favorable attitudes to higher education and to occupations of high prestige, to lay more stress on individual achievement, and to be more convinced that the world is amenable to rational mastery than the relatively fatalistic Italian Americans.

Further evidence of the effect of environmental association on intelligence as generally measured and on attainment is provided by the numerous studies in which rural children generally, and children in isolated communities and social groups in particular, have been shown to perform poorly when compared with urban groups. The pioneer study of Gordon (1923) on British canal-boat children is well known in this respect and was confirmed by the studies of Wheeler with East Tennessee mountain children. Wheeler (1942) found, for example, that in 1930 these children had an average IQ of about 80 on Dearborn and Illinois intelligence tests. A comparable sample tested ten years later showed a considerable increase, apparently because of the known improvement in the economic, social, and educational status of the area. In many of these studies, it has been found that children in isolated rural areas do particularly poorly in speeded tests. Smith (1948), describing children in the Outer Hebrides of Scotland, writes:

> A rigidly timed test does not seem to discriminate very well in the range of the intelligence scale. . . . There is little evidence of the modern tendency to race with time. It is rightly considered infinite and unlikely to interfere with the expected sequence of things; so in the normal course of events there is no need for undue haste. Probably if the children had grasped more fully the significance of the stop-watch in the experiment, the scores would have been more flattering to them.

Similarly, Moreton and Butcher (1963) found some indications that this attitude applies in lesser degree to rural children in less isolated areas. However, one must seriously consider, whenever significant differences of intelligence are found associated with differences of environment, that part of it is a real difference, i.e., a difference in fluid not just in crystallized intelligence due to migration of the more intelligent to better conditions. This is obvious in regard to social class, discussed below, and it has played an important part in rural-urban differentials. From the standpoint of biological scientists, moreover, we cannot overlook the possibility of real racial differences in intelligence. For example, the "brain drain" of selected high I.Q.'s from Britain to the United States, if not offset by equal migration at lower intelligence levels could, theoretically, affect the biological means of the two sub-races. Data showing that migrants from Britain to New Zealand average an I.Q. of 102 to 104 by British norms could (if not due to the "creep" of norms) point to a process of natural selection which would ultimately produce a biological difference of intelligence between the two populations. This is but one of several ways in which real difference of average intelligence could arise between races and racial combinations.

Section 4 **The Correlations of Economic Level and Social Class**

Of all environmental factors, however, that which has given rise to most concern, and rightly so, is the effect of socioeconomic level. This is, of course, closely related to some of the other factors already considered, as was illustrated in Wheeler's findings with Tennessee mountain children. But it is more pervasive and fundamental and has been the subject of heated controversy between those who feel that justice is already being done in our society in the provision of educational opportunity and those who feel that children in the lower socioeconomic classes are still being unjustly penalized and deprived of opportunities to fulfill their talents.

In Britain, a country with a more clearly stratified society and one with a more cautious and conservative attitude to educational change, the problem is more acute. An important research by Furneaux (1961) produced the following statement as the first of its conclusions: "The selection of students for admission to universities really begins when children are born, for a child's academic history is strongly influenced by the social class into which he is born." This does not mean, however, that social-class effects operate through bias on the part of selectors. The evidence is to the contrary. But, apparently because of less favorable conditions and attitudes at home, the standards achieved by the children of unskilled and semiskilled workers show a progressive relative deterioration throughout the secondary-school course. There is one exception. Once such children have entered on advanced work, these detrimental effects apparently cease to operate immediately before entrance to a university, if they get so far. Thus, if a male working-class child gets so far, he appears to have an equal chance. This is far from true for girls, as Furneaux points out. Because university places for women are relatively scarce, particularly at Oxford and Cambridge, an enormous reserve of untapped or partially unfulfilled feminine educational ability still exists in Britain.

Furneaux's findings have been supplemented by the work of Floud, Halsey, and Martin (1957), who deal mainly with the relation of social class to educational opportunity at age eleven, when children have been in the past and in many areas still are allocated to different types of English secondary school. They studied two contrasting areas in England (p. 139): "a traditionally prosperous district in the south of England . . . and an industrial county borough in the north which has had a chequered economic history and in which educational reform has had to face greater material difficulties." Their findings indicate, with some reservations, a very marked improvement in social equality of opportunity over about the last thirty years (p. 139): "If by 'ability' we mean 'measured intelligence' and by 'opportunity' access to grammar schools, then opportunity may be said to stand in close relationship with ability in both these areas to-day." But the picture is not entirely rosy, and some differences in educational opportunity between these types of area still remain. In the industrial area (p. 145), "there is still scope for attack on gross economic disabilities." In the more prosperous area (p. 145), "the influence of the home on children's educational progress is more subtle, and the problem of developing and utilizing their ability to the full is educational rather than social."

Another area of research that yields some, perhaps debatable, clues about environmental effects on achievement is the study of child-rearing and child socialization, and particularly the study of systematic differences between social classes. A useful survey of such work has been made by Bronfenbrenner (1958), who reviews research dating between 1932 and 1957 in the United States. He points out that there was a rather direct opposition of views on this topic between Davis and Havighurst (1948), on the one hand, who had found that middle-class parents "place their children under a stricter regimen, with more frustration of their impulses than do lower-class parents," and Maccoby and Gibbs (1954), who found by contrast that "the middle-class mothers were generally more permissive and less punitive toward their young children than were working-class mothers." After a careful examination of this, and other, evidence, Bronfenbrenner concludes that from about 1930 until the end of World War II, working-class mothers were uniformly more permissive than those of the middle class, including more breast feeding, more feeding on demand, later weaning, later toilet training, and so forth. Since World War II, however, this difference appears to have been reversed, with middle-class mothers more permissive in most of these respects; and there is evidence that much of this change is the result of the influence of books, pamphlets, physicians, and counselors.

However, this increased permissiveness on the part of middle-class mothers does not mean that in recent years they have come to expect less of their children or to exercise less "push" toward achievement. Throughout the studies reviewed, clear evidence points, as might be expected, to higher and more definite academic aspirations for their children among middle-class parents. It seems likely, therefore, that much of the frequently demonstrated correlation between achievement and socioeconomic level may be due to aspirations and pressures from the parents, though real differences of average intelligence and constitutional differences in personality factors have never been ruled out.

Section 5   **The Correlations of School, Neighborhood, Facilities,
and Atmosphere**

Bronfenbrenner's survey of a wide range of research, which we have just mentioned, indicated the importance of family attitudes, and particularly of parental aspirations, by showing a consistently more aspiring attitude to achievement in middle-class child-rearing. Fraser (1959) carried out a detailed survey of some 400 families in Aberdeen, Scotland, with the intention of relating family background to school attainment. Among her findings was that three of the factors most closely related to attainment of those investigated were parents' attitude to education and future employment, parents' income, and amount of space in the home. A very recent and detailed analysis of the effect of parents' attitudes on the achievement of primary school children is also contained in the report of the Plowden Committee on English primary education (February 1967). But, important as it is, family background is only one-half of the child's environment. In this section, we turn to the effect of school and neighborhood. Naturally, a considerable overlap exists between these two aspects of the environment—good homes and good schools will be commoner in "good" districts—but it is convenient to consider them separately, according to the main emphasis of the researches reviewed.

A recently-published and thorough British study by Wiseman and Warburton (Wiseman, 1964) deserves to be summarized in some detail, because it also incorporates comparisons with American findings. All fourteen-year-old children in the Manchester conurbation (with a population of about 1,400,000), except those in independent and direct-grant schools, were tested in reading comprehension, mechanical arithmetic, and verbal intelligence. In two subsurveys, limited to the cities of Manchester and Salford and involving about 14,000 and 2,000 children, respectively, school attainment was studied in relation to a wide variety of social factors, such as density of population, percentage of illegitimate births, incidence of mental deficiency, tuberculosis rate, and so forth. In the Salford study, the unit was the school; in the Manchester study, the ward, the smallest administrative unit for purposes of local government. Both these surveys took place in 1951, and the larger, Manchester, one was repeated on a stratified sample of schools in 1957.

Some of the results were as follows. Most of the expected correlations between social factors and attainment were found in all three surveys, and about to the expected extent. Thus fairly substantial relationships were found between the prevalence of backwardness in reading and arithmetic and such factors as the birthrate, the illegitimate birthrate, the tuberculosis rate, and the density of population. Many of the tables will repay careful study, but they cannot be summarized here. What was not expected, however, was that in each of these surveys the social factors correlated *more highly* with the measure of intelligence than with those of attainment. Although such findings are not unknown (e.g., Thorndike, 1951), they are, as the writers say, "in precise contradiction to theoretical expectations," and also in opposition to most other findings, such as that of Fraser already mentioned.

In an attempt to explain the discrepancy, Wiseman reviewed the literature and found that often reports of a higher correlation of social factors with ability than with attainment appeared to be limited to researches where the school or the neighborhood was the statistical unit, and that it never occurred where the individual child was the unit. He suggests, therefore, that the unexpected results depend on the greater amount of time and effort devoted by the teacher to the basic skills of reading and arithmetic in "poor" areas, and that if wider aspects of attainment were tested, the effect would disappear. Another possible explanation is the technical one that, if the intelligence measures were more reliable or internally consistent than those of attainment, the relations with the former may have been increased in comparison with those with the latter. A further report by one of Wiseman's students is promised, in which the unit is the individual child, and it will be interesting to see if the unexpected results are reversed.

It must be confessed, however, that educators and sociologists, because their "business" is environment, have not approached this question as broadmindedly as scientists should. It is not at all uncommon for sections such as the present to be headed "The *effects* of economic level, etc." rather than "The correlates or associations . . . ," thus begging the scientific question of whether higher native intelligence may not produce simultaneously the better achievement and the better level of real wealth. Certainly the "Education—affluence" factor in Cattell's analysis (1954) of culture pattern dimensions would fit such a theory, as would also the findings of Thorndike. In other words it is conceivable that differences of migration, of birth rate, etc., have led to slight regional differences of native mental capacity, even in a patchwork within one country, and that the intellectual acrobatics indicated above in trying to reconcile the correlations with the "theoretical expectations" could be greatly reduced if the theorists would back off and come to the problem with broader "sociological *plus* biological" theories. The present authors feel that no firm conclusions can be drawn here until a new generation of researchers apply culture-fair intelligence tests along with traditional tests, to sufficiently large samples, with simultaneous *dynamic* observations, i.e., on the relative intelligence of in and out migrants, etc.

In the Salford study, where the unit was the school rather than the neighborhood, it was found, as might be expected, that progressive methods of education, good social background, and good teaching conditions were significantly associated with school attainment. The degree of "progressiveness" in teaching methods was assessed by a rating, made by the local education authority, of the type of education provided in each school on a "formal-free" scale, ranging from the extremely formal, rigid, and orthodox to the most informal, free, and progressive. The relations of both size of class and size of school with attainment were less clear-cut than might have been expected, but there was some tendency for small classes and large schools to do better. There was a clearer trend in favor of good school buildings. Many of these findings have been duplicated in other researches, and we reproduce Warburton's table (Wiseman, 1964, p. 123), in which he compares his own results with those of Kemp (1955), who studied fifty London primary schools, and those of Mollenkopf's (1956) large-scale survey in the United States. The relation between "progressiveness" in school atmosphere and methods on the one hand, and on the other attainment and learning, is still a matter of debate, as is shown by the recent inconclusive findings of Pringle (1967).

Kemp's investigation, some of the results of which are summarized in condensed form in Table XLI, actually involved twenty-eight social variables and two criteria of attainment (in addition to the criterion of intelligence). These two criteria were composite, the first ("rote" in the table) comprising mechanical arithmetic, spelling, handwriting speed, and handwriting quality; the second ("comprehension" attainment) comprising arithmetical problems, silent reading, and general information. It is hard to find studies carried out at different times and in different countries in which the sampling procedures, social variables measured, and criteria of attainment are similar enough to justify direct and precise comparison, but the comparison of the three studies in Table XLI suggests some approximately similar relation between environmental circumstances and attainment in different cities and even different countries.

To conclude this chapter, Wiseman's account of the factors affecting educational attainment is worth quotation and illustration:

> The picture is not one of the pupil being surrounded by a multitude of forces, some favourable, some adverse—a picture that inevitably suggests that progress lies in the provision of adequate insulation from these forces—but rather that the pupil himself produces some of the forces and interacts with others. . . .
> It is essentially a *multivariate* problem and one which must be attacked by appropriate multivariate methods.

Factors suggested as influential are shown in Table XLII (Wiseman, 1964, p. 174), and it is pointed out that our knowledge of the interactions between some of these areas is still pretty scanty, largely because of the lack of interdisciplinary research.

TABLE XLI

Correlations between social and scholastic variables in Salford, London, and the United States

SOCIAL VARIABLE	SALFORD			LONDON					UNITED STATES		
	Mechanical Arithmetic (mean)	Reading Comprehension (mean)	Intelligence (mean)	Rote	Comprehension	Intelligence	Vocabulary	Sentences	English achievement	Mechanical arithmetic	Problem arithmetic
Socioeconomic status	+.18	+.20	+.34	+.47	+.56	+.52	+.31	+.27	+.20	+.20	+.17
Small-size class	+.13	+.08	+.16	.00	+.12	+.02	+.15	+.17	+.18	+.16	+.14
Large-size school	+.10	+.18	+.30	+.39	+.30	+.18	+.12	+.07	+.01	−.04	−.10
Good buildings	+.18	+.20	+.34	+.09	+.07	−.05					
Progressiveness	+.19	+.31	+.33	+.18	+.31	+.33					
Attendance	+.34	+.27	+.26				−.08	−.12	+.02	+.14	+.04

TABLE **XLII**

Some factors associated with educational attainment

I *Pupil*	II *Parent*	III *Teacher*	IV *School*	V *Home*	VI *Neighborhood*
1. Intelligence	5. Intelligence	9. Intelligence	15. Atmosphere	19. Atmosphere	23. Level of housing
2. Physical health	6. Temperament	10. Temperament	16. Status in the neighborhood	20. Cleanliness and order	24. Age of building
3. Temperament	7. Educational experience	11. Educational experience	17. Contacts with local industry	21. Type and severity of discipline	25. Economic level
4. Attitude towards school	8. Occupational experience	12. Training	18. Relations with youth clubs	22. Possession of books and papers	26. Occupational level
		13. Attitude towards children			27. Crime rate
		14. Attitude towards education and authority			28. Cultural provisions
					29. Moral climate

SUMMARY *of Chapter Twelve*

1. All prediction of achievement is affected by systematic intercultural and intracultural differences of environment as well as by individual differences in ability, personality, and motivation.

2. Prediction will be most effective in a society where vicissitudes and anomalies resulting from widespread ill health, extreme economic disparity, and inequality of opportunity are fewest.

3. There is significant relation of school achievement to socio-economic status of parents. The task of teasing out the causal connections is a complex one and has been obscured by all kinds of hasty inferences. Traditional intelligence tests are known to be subject to cultural influences, but the recent use of culture fair tests suggests that some small ($r = .2$) approx.) real differences of fluid intelligence across social classes may be involved in the achievement differences. The rest could be associated with: (a) class differences on personality factors, of which there is also evidence; (b) class differences in environmental opportunity; and (c) class differences in parental motivations,

ideals, and pressures. In Britain, and presumably *a fortiori* in the United States, the cruder manifestations of inequality of opportunity have greatly diminished. Insofar as they remain, they operate quite early, and more strongly at primary school than at university level. Studies such as Wiseman's suggest: (a) that neighborhood and school environment exercises an influence on achievement that overlaps with but is partly separable from home background; (b) that interschool and interarea comparisons require careful interpretation, because of the compensatory efforts of teachers in "poor" areas.

4. Evidence also indicates that the "progressive" or "traditional" atmosphere of a school exercises some influence on achievement, with "progressive" schools obtaining better results. But such evidence is at present rather tenuous, and some studies have produced inconclusive or negative results.

5. In regard to comparisons across national cultures and regional subcultures, it is well known that differences of up to a year or so in scholastic achievement level exist, e.g., as shown in the recent studies of Pidgeon in England and Thorndike in America. McClelland's studies on comparative achievement aspiration also suggest appreciable differences between countries, and that, in general, increase in motivation precedes economic advance, rather than the other way round. What is still lacking is research using a sophisticated model, such as may lead to more objective measures and more objective analysis of causal connections.

The work of Cattell, Breul, and Hartmann (1952) and of Rummel (1963) provides a means of scoring cultural pattern *syntality*, as such, and therefore, of relating it to mean levels of individuals in the population on personality source traits and achievement level. Three culture pattern dimensions isolated as independent functional unities, namely *cultural pressure, enlightened affluence* (or "affluence-education") and *morale* are related to achievement levels in the population. The first, which includes urbanization, complexity of living, suicide rate, and frequency of involvement in war, is especially correlated with creativity in the arts and sciences. The theory which Cattell has developed elsewhere, consistent with Freud's non-quantitative analysis, is that it represents degree of ergic sublimation demanded, and is simultaneously, therefore, correlated with creativity, frustration, and internally and externally directed aggression, as alternative, and frequently alternating, expressions.

6. Although cultural, environmental conditions must be given a large role in determining achievement, any but a narrow-minded approach must concede that scientific evidence indicates the probability, in individual and group, of innate differences also playing some role. Biological variation, natural selection, and migration may, as Ellsworth Huntington (1945) has reasoned, account for some of the correlations of intelligence test score, real standard of living, and school achievement, across regions. Research with culture-fair intelligence tests, surveys which include biological measures, more sensitive achievement tests, and more refined statistical methods can alone decide how much of these regional differences is due to either type of influence.

Chapter Thirteen[1]

THE PREDICTION OF ACHIEVEMENT
IN A WIDER CONTEXT

Section 1 Beyond the School: Achievement in Occupation, Family, and Society

A reminder of the constant tendency among psychometrists to substitute the criterion of performance in school examinations for performance in life, or in the occupations for which the school is only a preparation, has already been issued. Instances have been cited, notably in the occupation of scientific research, where the traits which make for success are very different from those which produce success in the qualifying examinations for such work. "Success in life" is therefore a new world with new facts to be learned about it.

One stresses "new facts," for the fundamental principles are the same, and the tests, such as the Culture Fair measures of fluid ability, the Sixteen Personality Factor measures, etc., have shown themselves equally capable of effective prediction here, when the criterion is firm. However, some new developments are necessary in the formulas, notably connected with the much greater age ranges to be encompassed and with the concept of "adjustment to an occupation" as a special form of success where the problem of the criterion looms larger than ever.

A good deal of attention will be given in this chapter to the problem of the criterion, and it will be evident that many failures in industrial selection and vocational guidance in the past have been as much due to unreliable and spurious criteria as to the poorly based personality and motivation measurement devices used. In school the criterion of "examination performance," though perhaps narrow, has at least become highly precise and psychometrically reliable.

Another respect in which life criterion prediction differs resides in the probably more complex dimensionality of the criterion and its great varia-

[1] This chapter has been written, along with the main authors, by three specialists in adult occupational psychology: Dr. Herbert W. Eber, Dr. William W. Ronan, Georgia Institute of Technology, and Dr. E. P. Prien, University of Akron.

bility from situation to situation. Parenthetically, this is yet another argument for "general purpose" tests, like the multidimensioned 16 PF, instead of "special purpose" tests made up by a particular psychologist for a particular situation. The weights in the general purpose test can be played by a psychometric artist to fit all changes in the situation. Among leading psychometrists, Horst (1942) has been one of the first to recognize that complex criteria are likely to be the rule in life success prediction and that the white rat in a maze and the student performing in an examination are poor models for leading us to the variety of predictors needed.

What most psychometrists recognize reluctantly, if at all, is that value judgments ultimately have to influence the criteria for life performances. Is the great general the one who wins more battles, or the one who is more magnanimous to the fallen? Is the good teacher the one who is most loved, or the one who teaches the most painfully necessary lessons? To ask an even more fundamental question was Newton, or Napoleon, or St. Francis most successful? Obviously, it is no solution to say that we want to include every aspect of the criterion: These different aspects must not only be included, but given appropriate weightings.

This problem arises in its moral-value aspects most clearly when one evaluates the performances of groups, and Cattell and Stice (1960) have attempted an initial answer to it. The problem cannot be pursued farther here, and the reader must be referred to an explicit treatment elsewhere (Cattell, 1961). The proposed solution lies along the lines of factor-analyzing the criterion dimensions and assigning weights to these obtained from combining the values that the population assigns to various specific performances. A similar method has been proposed by Cattell and Coulter (1966) for the pattern-similarity coefficient, as distinct from the linear equations assumed in the above.

An important distinction has been drawn between two kinds of criterion ("effectiveness" and "adjustment") by Cattell (1957) and by Cattell and Eber (1966). The first takes some criterion of *total effectiveness in the occupation* (a weighted derivative of many criterion dimensions) and attempts to estimate it (linearly or otherwise) from the test predictors. The second takes a group of people who seem "adjusted" to the job and its demands, by the evidence that they have stayed in it for years, and contrasts their personality (and other predictor) scores with those of the population at large. We already have evidence that these two approaches do not always yield the same result.

However, a means of translation between the two—admittedly with some rather strong assumptions—has been worked out by Cattell and Eber (1966) and below (page 260), which permits comparison of the different weights that would result from the "effectiveness" and the "adjustment" criteria.

One virtue of the adjustment approach, despite its not yielding so high a prediction of efficiency per se is that it implicitly takes into account the needs of other occupations in the total society. It aims at that best possible allocaion in the light of occupational criteria, on the one hand, and resources of personnel, on the other, which has been more explicitly handled by Hotelling (1936), Horst (1942), and others in terms of a definite linear model. However, the general problem of allocation of personnel resources in terms of the greatest good of society is beyond consideration at the present stage, for the economist would defeat the solution even if the psychologist provided it. We must be content with selection for the occupational or other (political, social) need specifically put before us.

As one gets to the problems of actual research to obtain formulas and constants in this field, the greatest practical difficulties arise from the broad age range mentioned above. Strong allowances for age changes, between twenty and sixty-five years of age, need to be made both in the criteria and in the personality ability measures. We are beginning to have a fair understanding of changes in ability with age (Jones and Conrad, 1933; Lorge, 1945; Horn and Cattell, 1966; Owens, 1966) and of personality (Cattell and Sealy, 1967), but the changes in the criterion are complex and baffling. For example, in many routine occupations, the popular view that seniority gives improved performance is now much in question. No one knows how much this is the result of changes in personality, ability, and the motivational situation (e.g., with increased security), and how much of the selection of the more effective for promotion to new and higher positions, which drains any stratum of industrial, military, etc., occupation of its above-average members.

The whole field of age-change effects is grossly underresearched, and for obvious reasons. Long-term evaluation requires a substantial interval of time between the gathering of the data and the evaluation of their predictive utility. Many social scientists do not have this time, or believe they do not have it; and despite conspicuous exceptions, such as Terman's monumental work, the most common prediction reported in the literature has been really postdiction, or at best the artificial statistical prediction that is possible through measurements and criteria obtained simultaneously. Unfortunately, those large-scale research programs that have attempted longitudinal study of human beings have rarely gathered the type of replicable psychometric data that would lead to the greatest gains in psychological theory.

To make matters even more complicated, it seems that most predictive studies have taken a much oversimplified view of the predictive situation. When one considers the complexities described by Horst, it seems incredibly naive to expect any single predictor to show a substantial relationship to total achievement. Actually, there exists in the literature a body of research showing that the prediction of achievement is possible at a high level of efficiency when some of the more important considerations in the predictor-achievement situation are taken into account. Three such considerations are:

(1) time as a condition that will allow predictor-achievement relationships to develop; (2) interpretations of validity coefficients in the light of predictor-performance reliabilities; and (3) attention to the dimensionality of achievement. Some of the material that follows attempts to illustrate the importance of these points by the use of selected studies; no attempt at an exhaustive review of the literature has been made.

Two other general points should be indicated before a detailed consideration is undertaken. One of these is that the longitudinal research studies of major consequence, for one reason or another, have tended to omit from the data those instruments resulting from the most modern psychometric developments that might have been of specific utility. Perhaps the reason is that longitudinal research tends to be done by clinically oriented psychologists, whose training and experience incline them toward the gathering of more impressionistic data. Unfortunately, however, the demonstration that a certain clinician can utilize such data for predictive purposes is only minimally helpful to the development of psychological science, because the measuring instrument in that case usually is as much the psychologist himself as the techniques he utilizes. The clinical skill and intuition of a Beck, a Klopfer, or a Schneidman, while quite impressive, nevertheless fails to constitute a replicable measuring instrument.

This point is represented by a variety of studies in the area of creativity. Although the fashion may be changing, creativity has been a highly popular area of research for several years, and research support has been substantial. Papers, monographs, and books have been published on the subject; and a reasonable measure of agreement has been displayed by various investigators, although each felt compelled to construct his own tests, to utilize his own definitions, and to develop his own, often ingenious, methods. Ten years have elapsed since the Cattell and Drevdahl (1955) comparisons of eminent researchers with eminent teachers and administrators and with the general population. The study was admittedly postdictive rather than predictive, but it certainly showed so clearly the relationship between measured personality characteristics and creative achievement that the findings might have been expected to become a take-off point for further work. Yet the work is barely mentioned, if mentioned at all, in many of the major studies since that time.

A second point concerns psychologists' apparent unreasonable disappointment in the order of validity that can be achieved and frequent abandonment of promising lines of research. A philosophical issue is at stake here, one that has been insufficiently discussed. In a discussion of vocational development, for example, Super (1957) describes the influence of family, of economic factors—such as business cycles, supply and demand, technological change, changes in taste and style, depletion of natural resources, public policy, and unionization—and of disability upon vocational patterns. Moreover, beyond these relatively definable influences, other patterns describable scientifically only as "chance occurrences" influence the development of vocational functioning. The point is that in a system where such a large number of factors influence the outcome, the desire for validity coefficients of +0.60 or +0.70 may represent quite unrealistic standards to be imposed upon himself by the industrial psychologist.

A recent study by Eber (1966) indicates a validity coefficient of +0.22 (corrected for shrinkage) in predicting the outcome of vocational rehabilitation programs for a client *who is not known*. It was demonstrated that the community in which the client lives and hopes to work and the counselor who deals with him have some influence upon eventual outcome, and so some prediction was possible even without knowledge of the client's identity. It is clear that a validity coefficient of +0.22, representing a prediction of slightly less than 5 per cent of the total variance, does not represent a high degree of validity; nevertheless, the standard error of that multiple correlation was +0.04, and the slight prediction that was possible clearly represented real prediction. The data involved had been gathered on an average of two and a half years prior to the predicted event, and 5 per cent of the variance is 5 per cent of the variance. More knowledge about the client raises the validity, but when one considers the various psychologically unpredictable events that influence a criterion of this sort, it seems that the psychologist should not be ashamed of small but significant prediction.

Section 2   Time and Achievement

The literature contains studies covering long time periods and showing high, sometimes amazingly high, predictor-achievement relationships. Conceptually, as historically, the issue begins with the utilization of simple IQ data.

Ball (1938), in a study of office workers, correlated scores on a relatively simple mental ability test with occupational level achieved after eighteen years. The correlation between the two was found to be +0.71; and although the finding has been questioned, there is apparently no contamination, and the reported figure may well be a fair estimate of the actual relationship. Obviously, this is much higher than coefficients usually found, and it is one of the earliest indications that short-time or "one-shot" studies are not reliable. Actually, the time variable is rarely reported in any study; often, one has no idea of what period is covered by performance data.

A much better known set of data, representing a substantial contribution in the area of general intelligence measurement, is the work of Terman and his associates (Terman, 1925; Cox, *et al.*, 1926; Burks, Jensen, and Terman, 1930; Terman and Oden, 1947, 1951, 1959). The facts of the study are well known to all psychologists and are discussed in some detail in elementary textbooks. The striking finding that the child of high general intelligence was, on the average, not handicapped or inferior in other respects contradicted the folklore regarding the natural occurrence of compensation. This group of gifted youngsters proved generally superior to the average person in most respects, tending to be of slightly better physique, healthier, more popular, less neurotic, more dominant, and generally on the favorable side of most dimensions. Few of these differences were large, but each can be considered fairly well established.

The picture needs some modification, particularly because the superiority of the gifted children was relatively slight in many areas. As might have been supposed, the greatest differences were in those aspects of behavior most closely related to intelligence, whereas those areas that make least demands upon conceptual thinking showed these intellectually superior children in a less dramatically favorable light. Moreover, it may certainly be true that the "compensation" theory is true of individual children, even though it was obviously not true of the gifted sample as a whole.

Another point that has perhaps been insufficiently discussed in the literature is that the instrument used initially to select the superior children was one whose scores are quite heavily influenced by socioeconomic advantages; hence it is difficult to say to what degree the obtained IQ's of 140 or above may have been in part a function of the excellent home background of these youngsters. To the degree that this was the case, one would certainly expect such youngsters to show superiority in most respects. The dramatic finding of Terman and his associates is tempered by the realization that nothing less could be expected. A comparable study utilizing less socioeconomically affected measuring techniques has not been conducted. Until such time as this is done, the Terman data remain primarily a promising hypothesis. An exciting, interesting, and quite reassuring hypothesis may be involved, but a hypothesis nevertheless.

Stead (1937), in a remarkably sophisticated study concerning department-store sales personnel, combined eight objective sales criteria into one achievement criterion. Year-by-year reliabilities were +0.83 to +0.98, suggesting that the total achievement criterion was at least a stable one. Multiple-correlation analysis with nine tests and some personal-history data yielded prediction of this achievement criterion at a level of +0.65; the significant predictors were five of the tests and some of the personal-history data.

Viteles (1929–1930), in a study of substation operations, has also shown the importance of time in allowing achievement to develop. In the study, nine selection tests were used, the scores combined into one. The criteria were classification, by superiors, into "best, average, and poorest groups," and a record of operating errors was kept for twenty-one months. Table XLIII shows the results; although neither validity nor reliability correlations as such are reported for the study, the direct relationships between predictors and the error criterion were obvious, because, it is presumed, the performance behavior was given an opportunity to develop.

TABLE **XLIII**

Group	N	Percentage of total errors	Average error/man	Average test score	Standard deviation
Best	17	6.3	0.24	81.4	13.6
Average	54	57.8	0.69	69.2	13.5
Poorest	13	35.9	1.77	53.5	15.6

RELIABILITY Comparison of operating errors of the three rated groups

Group	N	Percentage involved in error	Number of errors	Percentage of total errors	Average error/man
Best	17	23.5	4	6.3	0.24
Average	54	51.9	37	57.3	0.69
Poorest	13	76.9	23	35.7	1.77

Although it is rare to find time specifically utilized as a variable in determining predictor-achievement relationships, some studies do exist where this was done. Whitlock, *et al.* (1963) studied "unsafe behaviors" as related to the incidence of actual accidents on the job. The authors noted that the relationship between the two increased with time, and they stated the need to allow sufficient time for relationships to develop. Turner (1960) factor-analyzed data relating to performance of foremen in two different plants. The data consisted of objective measures, such as scrap, disciplinary actions, grievances, and so on, and of ratings by superiors. In terms of time, the author reported that "single monthly scores on criterion measures tend to have inadequate reliability across time. Averages of several monthly scores are needed to attain a satisfactory level of reliability." This statement was based upon reliabilities for one month of $+0.03$ to $+0.59$, whereas, over three and a half to five months, the reliabilities as estimated by the reported communalities ranged from $+0.14$ to $+0.92$. Many of the larger values were from rating indices, but even the objective measures had a median value of $+0.60$.

A study by Ronan (1964) has shown that batteries of predictors can be effective over long periods of time. The study correlated eight personnel history items, thirteen aptitudes, the Guilford-Zimmerman Temperament Survey or Guilford-Martin Personnel Inventory, and the Kuder Interest Inventory with four criteria of achievement. The criteria were four factor scores derived from a previous study and comprised: I, accidents; II, a training achievement index; III, a job-performance factor of rating, promotions, and disciplinary actions; and IV, a factor covering personality disorder, absence, shop rating, and grievances. The results are shown in Table XLIV.

TABLE **XLIV**

Correlations of predictors with factor scores

	N	M	SD	I	II	III	IV
PERSONAL HISTORY							
ITEMS							
Age hired	134	21.145	2.32	043	145	309*	040
Age apprenticed	134	23.606	3.99	−017	−053	067	−001
Place of residence	134	—	—	−217*	−183*	−121	−093
Broken home	134	—	—	142	081	−058	126
Relatives with							
company	134	—	—	061	−011	−167*	−013
Number of siblings	134	2.45	1.70	113	474*	178*	−066
Previous jobs (number)	134	1.66	1.14	141	−196*	−298*	048
Military rank	134	4.32	1.08	−096	−038	−098	008
APTITUDES							
Verbal meaning	116	32.09	6.18	072	−260*	−205*	020
Spatial	67	29.51	10.76	−081	−253*	−411*	022
Reasoning	67	16.37	2.16	−345*	−611*	063	010
Numerical	116	27.60	9.56	032	−362*	073	−023
Verbal fluency	64	41.98	11.13	−093	−131	−198	005
Total score	63	201.11	45.52	011	−353*	−417*	223
Perceptual speed	49	42.02	12.41	005	257	242	200
Spatial visualization	48	29.19	12.15	−011	−186	−174	322*
Assembly	52	278.08	40.37	−080	−041	363*	016
Disassembly	52	153.27	16.60	090	007	019	203
Mechanical com-							
prehension	132	42.09	7.72	−167*	−152	−359*	231*
Tools	47	43.09	2.86	−097	014	−339*	−185
Paper form board	74	47.03	6.98	−013	−030	−207	042
PERSONALITY							
G-Z G	67	18.99	5.09	212	−031	−024	165
R	67	19.10	4.16	−157	040	−112	158
A	67	16.39	5.08	068	−164	028	124
S	67	21.72	5.08	239*	−035	−005	011
E	67	20.73	4.40	173	−124	−015	−208
O	67	19.70	4.90	113	−294*	076	−095
F	67	16.67	3.97	143	087	075	−181
T	67	18.87	5.09	−022	035	207	−036
P	67	19.54	5.40	254*	−170	−308*	−159
M	67	21.06	2.68	069	−193	−063	−173
G-M O	57	57.86	8.66	125	079	−071	−110
AG	57	40.63	12.77	165	483*	390*	135
CO	57	66.72	14.53	−104	120	−055	−022
KUDER							
ME	128	69.99	22.74	039	178*	−027	079
CO	128	30.95	8.69	125	−049	082	−058
SC	128	46.69	15.42	−049	111	−169	104
PE	128	38.97	16.99	178*	281*	−107	052
AR	128	33.34	15.90	−057	260*	−086	087
LI	128	20.52	12.90	−018	024	−031	143
MU	128	12.27	8.28	−044	030	−151	179*
SS	128	45.24	18.37	197*	323*	279*	165
CL	128	37.61	11.44	−098	107	133	015

* Significant at 5 per cent level.

The study had as subjects skilled tradesmen in seventeen different trades, who, at the time of the study, had had a minimum of seven years' service. The conclusions, from the results shown in Table XLIV are that ". . . three independent dimensions of skilled craftsman performance are predictable over relatively extended time periods."

It is worth noting that an accident factor emerged that was predictable from general reasoning and mechanical comprehension, and, negatively, from sociability, personal relations, persuasiveness, and social-service measures. The relations found could not be corrected for what was felt to be a rather serious restriction of range.

The cited studies indicate that quite substantial predictor-achievement relationships can be found if enough time is allowed for such relationships to develop. Studies covering any substantial period of time are quite limited in number even though it is apparent that time is required for adequate evaluations. Such results as do exist lead to the opinion that the relatively low relationships that characterize many validity studies are of distinctly limited value. They may be quite misleading, in the sense that even psychologists are prone to decry the value of predictors rather than to assess the prediction situation properly. It is possible that adequate predictors do exist and that research conditions and emphasis have not allowed them to demonstrate their real worth.

It would seem necessary to plan studies with the intention of covering much longer time periods. The obstacles of sample attrition, record keeping, and the real danger of criterion contamination must be overcome if there is to be any real progress. Certainly, the studies cited do indicate that even relatively simple predictors can be quite effective over sufficiently long periods of time, even when the criteria are not too reliable. Equally certainly, there is a genuine paucity of research covering the longer time periods. The probable ultimate payoff makes it seem that research attention should turn from adding to the plethora of predictive instruments in the direction of designing more adequate studies of predictive power. Considerations of time would be a major component of such research design.

Section 3 Considerations of Criterion Reliabilities

Perhaps the best way to begin this section is to recall the now-classic study by Flanagan (1946). The study was done during World War II with Air Force pilot candidates. A random sample of 1,143 applicants was allowed to enter flight training regardless of scores on the battery of selection tests in use at the time. Of these, 878 failed to graduate as pilots, whereas 265 were so graduated. The criterion in use was the simple pass-fail used so widely in the World War II studies. This criterion, as estimated from several different studies, had a reliability of approximately $+0.50$. At graduation, the multiple correlation with this pass-fail criterion was determined and found to be +0.66, suggesting from a superficial point of view that less than one-half of the variance had been accounted for. However, if one takes into account the criterion reliability, the maximum possible correlation would be in the low +0.70's; Flanagan achieved, in fact, an extremely high relationship between predictors and a "hard" criterion. It might also be mentioned that another finding of the study was that 60 per cent of those candidates with "stanines" of 8 or 9 graduated successfully, whereas only 5 per cent of those with stanines of 1 or 2 were able to become pilots.

An even more dramatic demonstration of the issue of criterion reliability was that provided during the Second World War by the staff of the Office of Strategic Services (OSS Assessment Staff, 1948). The OSS was a wartime agency, set up by the President and Congress of the United States, to select and train agents to gather strategic information about the activities of the nation's enemies and to sift and analyze this information. The report referred to, entitled "Assessment of Men," deals in considerable detail with the selection procedures used both in the United States and abroad, and with their validation.

As the authors frankly admit, theirs was in many ways an almost impossible project from the point of view of scientific selection and validation. It is not unfair to summarize their report as saying, in effect—"This was a makeshift job, but we did as well as anyone could have done under the circumstances." Certainly, the difficulties were formidable. Not only were the types of assignment extremely multifarious and the conditions in which the selected agents would be working about as diverse as could be imagined, but the selection staff generally had little information about these various assignments and conditions (p. 11):

> It was many months before our conceptions of the different jobs were more than half accurate. We were given the briefest possible time in which to prepare. No one arranged a preliminary world tour for the staff so that the conditions at each base and the operators in progress could be observed at first hand. The information that came in from the theaters was scanty; and even if it had been ample and adapted to our purpose, there would have been too much to learn in the time available, too much to remember. Not until much later did some of us who visited installations in the field come to realize the magnitude of the discrepancy between even the better job descriptions—those received in the later months—and the various dispositions and skills that were actually required in the field.

Faced with this situation, the assessment staff was driven to employ a general set of criteria, which it took to be desirable qualities for almost all assignments, plus a number of specialized criteria for particular assignments. The general qualifications that were sought in all candidates were: (1) motivation for assignment; (2) energy and initiative; (3) effective intelligence;

(4) emotional stability; (5) social relations; (6) leadership; (7) security, i.e., ability to keep secrets.

These qualifications, and many others, were tested by a multitude of ingenious situational tests, varying somewhat from center to center. Many of these were of the "leaderless group type." Others were individual tests of initiative, and were sometimes made more difficult and frustrating by the assignment of "helpers," who were, in fact, disguised psychologists being deliberately dumb or uncooperative. A "stress interview" was designed primarily to test the candidates' capacity to tolerate severe emotional and intellectual strain. The strain was created by rapid and merciless cross-questioning under disagreeable conditions, with the aim of detecting flaws in a cover story that the candidate had been given only a few minutes to invent. It was markedly increased as follows (p. 136):

> After ten minutes of such grilling the examiner broke off the questioning abruptly with a dissatisfied air, saying, "We now have abundant evidence that you have not been telling the truth. That is all." Then the board of staff members whispered together for a few seconds as if arriving at a verdict. Finally the examiner asked solemnly, "Your name is Buck, isn't it?" When the candidate assented, the interrogator announced, "It is our decision, Buck, that you have failed this test." There were then about five seconds of silence while the candidate's reaction was observed. . . . Thereupon the candidate left to go to the Post-Stress Interview [which was based on the maxim that security breaks most frequently when a man is enjoying a moment of relaxation after a period of tension].

Unfortunately, validation of these and other less spectacular procedures was bedeviled with the same difficulties that have already been quoted. The dispersion and wastage in operational conditions made the process of follow-up even more difficult than that of job analysis.

In fact, the authors state frankly that "none of our statistical computations demonstrates that our system of assessment was of great value" (p. 423). In this they are perhaps a little overcautious; correlations between job ratings and staff appraisals were in some instances (when the coefficients were corrected for selection) as high as $+0.50$ on a group of eighty-three selected candidates. Most were much lower, however, and there can be little doubt that "although thousands of man-hours were spent in the evaluation process, the final verdict is a question-mark" (p. 392).

Perhaps no better description of the difficulties involved in any validation procedure could be obtained than that above. Granted that the difficulties were extreme, and that the industrial psychologist under normal circumstances does not encounter quite so spectacular a set of undefined conditions. Nevertheless, the critical problem was the poor reliability of the criteria to be predicted. If corrections could have been made for some of these, perhaps based upon similar data obtained in more well-structured situations, many of the statistical coefficients decried by the authors as of little value might have been demonstrated to be of considerably greater utility.

It is possible that psychologists have been fighting a shadow in decrying the low predictor-achievement correlations so commonly found in the literature. Two basic facts of measurement theory have been insufficiently considered: (1) unreliable criterion data are predictable only to a very limited extent; (2) if the sample is restricted, any coefficient used to describe the relationship with the criterion is attenuated. It is extremely rare in the literature to see reports regarding the reliability of the criterion used, and equally rare to see corrections for restrictions of range, even though both these problems are undoubtedly present to some degree in the great majority of studies.

On the question of performance reliability—criterion reliability in this context—a dearth of information exists, and that which does exist indicates that performance is *not* reliable. If such indication is true, it is possible that performance is being predicted to a much higher level than is generally believed.

There exists in the literature only one major effort to determine performance reliability, a series of studies by Rothe (1946a, 1946b, 1947, 1951), and Rothe and Nye (1958, 1959). The data were collected either by direct observation or from production records of the various organizations involved. In general, the studies show that job performance, with experienced personnel, tends to be highly erratic; a major conclusion of one study is that predictor measures are much more stable than the achievement measures they are used to predict. The two investigators measured performance in a great many different ways and obtained the same findings over diverse jobs, leading them to question seriously the reliability of performance. For example, in the first study, with butter wrappers, daily work curves were constructed for individual operators and for the group, and the values were correlated. The results are shown in Table XLV.

As can be seen from the distribution of individual correlations, and from the group intercorrelations, the conclusion that performance reliability is quite low seems well-founded.

In other studies, some of the major findings were a correlation of as high as +0.78 for week-to-week performance; ratios of highest and lowest average weekly performance as high as 7.20, with a median intraindividual ratio of 2.24; other frequency distributions of correlations between successive week outputs that approached normality; and a four-month to four-month productivity correlation of +0.71.

As the authors are at pains to point out, there is no valid evidence for the assumption that performance, even in these relatively simple occupations, is reliable. Indeed, from these data, one might seriously question the results of any study where criterion reliability is not reported. The authors explicitly

TABLE **XLV**

r of day-to-day work curves (same operators)		Group work curves intercorrelations by day of week			
r	N	T	W	T	M(3)
60-69	2	Monday (2) 22	34	31	08
50-59	1	Tuesday	26	53	−09
40-49	5	Wednesday		50	34
30-39	5	Thursday			−22
20-29	5				
10-19	8				
00-09	7				
−01-10	12				
−11-20	7				
−21-30	4				
−31-40	4				
−41-50	1				

concluded, in the 1958 study, "a second important result is the wide range of 'consistency coefficients' of output data, such that a researcher could be entirely misled by tests of statistical significance if he just happened to select a period of unusually high or low consistency." The results are enough to make any researcher quite uneasy as to how many times he has been so misled.

There seems little point here in detailing the specific studies that have reported such reliabilities—for two reasons. The first is that they appear to be highly specific to a given situation and the second, that they give the impression that some sort of single index of achievement can be derived.

Ghiselli (1956) has seriously questioned the concept of any single index of reliability and, in addition, (1960a, 1960b, 1963) has suggested that some of the classic concepts of psychometric theory are of questionable value in the measurement of achievement. In particular, he proposes the concept that unreliability of performance is a measurable individual difference and, as such, is to be investigated through studies of individuals rather than treated as a source of error variance.

In general, little is known about performance reliability and any related interpretations of achievement prediction. Because of this and because criterion reliabilities are so infrequently reported, the interpretation of correlations of predictors with achievement criteria is quite nebulous.

Related to reliability of performance is an aspect of achievement that seems largely taken for granted—judging by the lack of studies concerned with it—and that has a profound effect on performance reliability. Concretely, if it exists as presumed, the concept denies the utility of group indices of performance and demands the study of individual performance. This concept is that people perform in different ways to achieve the same end result.

Walker, *et al.* (1946) made a "preliminary investigation" of individual differences in landing an aircraft on a given spot. A series of four flights, take-offs, and precision landings was performed by five experienced flight instructors in a Piper J-3. Each pilot made two series of flights: (1) "without tricks," meaning a standardized flight where slipping, mushing, or such efforts to position the aircraft were not allowed—in other words, a standardized flying procedure; and (2) "with tricks," meaning that any procedure within the limits of safe flying (no added throttle) was allowed. Data were gathered using the Ohio State Flight Inventory, a vertical accelerometer to measure vertical acceleration resulting from ground contact, and photographic records of the instrument panel. Ten criteria of the actual landing were measured.

The study indicated that the performance of individual pilots was much more variable (F at $+0.05$) under the "without tricks" condition than under the "with tricks" condition. The implication of the study, which the authors conceded is limited because of the small N, is that pressure to perform in a standardized manner has the opposite effect; it makes performance of even experienced personnel *more* variable.

Cohen and Strauss (1946) made an extremely detailed (observation and motion pictures) study of the relatively simple task of sheet folding. They found a 1:3 ratio of time to complete the task and different methods of doing the same job; even when urged, some persons were unable to do a task in certain ways. They concluded, "From the point of view of the methods analyst, there are as many different methods of performance as there are operators."

There are very few studies in the area of "different ways of doing the job," even though it is virtually a cliché to make the statement. When this presumed fact is related to that of performance reliability, there is considerable doubt that any group index of performance reliability is meaningful.

The astute reader may have noted the absence of any mention of studies concerned with restriction of range to this point. If so, there is a quite good reason. To the knowledge of the authors, there is not a single study in the area of concern in this chapter, during the last ten years, that has reported correcting coefficients for any restriction. Nevertheless, such restriction must be frequent. For example, it is quite common in the industrial situation to establish minimum scores below which no applicant is considered for employment. Such a practice obviously attenuates any later test-achievement relationship, but if this is ever taken into account, it is not reported in the literature. Actually, restriction of range is very likely quite pervasive in most of the reported studies.

From the above, it is not too much of a strain to believe that the prediction of achievement may be less bleak than many psychologists would believe. If all the attenuating influences could be taken into account, possibly we are predicting achievement more effectively than is generally supposed. The brutal fact is, however, that we just do not know. Most predictive studies are inadequately reported and make attempts to interpret obtained relationship impossible. It is extremely rare to see any estimate of criterion reliability and virtually unheard of to correct predictor-criterion estimates for restriction of range.

In the absence of such information, most relationships can be interpreted as the minimum that exists, but even this is not really safe, because measurement might have been made in a period of "high achievement reliability." Without question, it can be concluded that there is little certainty as to just how adequate achievement prediction may be, and that the situation will continue until researchers begin to apply more sophisticated methods and concepts.

Section 4 The Dimensions of Achievement

It seems fatuous to say that, in order to predict achievement, it is necessary to know what is meant by the term. However, triteness is no contraindication of truth. The vast majority of published research has failed to attend to the criterion with the same degree of sophistication as has marked concern with the predictors. The literature contains hundreds of studies that have predicted some aspect of achievement, operationally defined, in widely diverse areas. For the most part, such operational definitions have consisted of a single achievement index. Probably, the most obvious example is the prediction of some sort of rating of job performance, progress under psychotherapy, child adjustment, or any possible area of human activity. The assumption has been that any achievement can be represented by some sort of number or descriptive phrase, and that the persons involved can be placed on a continuum with the prediction attempting to specify that place.

Another method of assessing achievement has been to select some single facet of the performance and to define this as the achievement. For example, the production rate of an industrial worker is taken as *the* criterion, and all other aspects are ignored. It is well known that prediction using such simple definitions of achievement has left something to be desired in published studies; there is no way of estimating how much other work has given negative results and has never been reported. It probably is not too far from the truth to infer that the correlation coefficients obtained in all studies, published and unpublished, would approximate a chance distribution with a mean of zero.

In spite of these disappointing results, psychologists continue to conduct studies using the single criterion approach with a zeal and dedication that appears to belie the effect of negative reinforcement. This is particularly surprising when one considers that this research is most often done by psychologists who, in their everyday professional functioning, emphasize repeatedly the complexities involved in even the simplest task. It is particularly amazing also when the implications of such complexity have been recognized for many years.

Kingsbury (1933), in his studies concerned with predicting executive achievement, made the statement:

> Some executives are successful because they are good planners, although not successful directors. Others are splendid at coordinating and directing, but their plans and programs are defective. Few executives are equally competent in both directions. Failure to recognize and provide, in both testing and rating, for this obvious distinction is, I believe, one major reason for unsatisfactory results of most attempts to study, rate, and test executives. Good tests of one kind of executive ability are not good tests of the other kind.

Despite this early recognition of various dimensions of achievement and, in particular, of differing levels of achievement among various individuals, it is only in recent years that any attempt has been made to isolate and define achievement dimensions. This situation holds true despite the emphasis that has been placed on isolating various aptitudes, traits, interests, and the multitudinous other individual differences that characterize people. It seems obvious that, if attention to the true dimensionality of predictors is rewarding, such attention to the dimensionality of the criterion would also be of use.

In summary, there has been tacit recognition for years that *the* criterion does not exist (Dunnette, 1963) and that performance is complex and multidimensional. If prediction is to be effective, the dimensions must be described, and the difficulty and complexity of the prediction situation recognized. Further, studies must be designed that will take such complexities into account. Some such studies have appeared in the past few years, and they point quite clearly in the direction that must be taken if achievement prediction is to be improved.

Kahneman and Ghiselli (1962) have presented a study with important implications for achievement prediction. With three diverse occupational groups—executives, office workers, and autobus repairmen—they trichotomized the groups on the basis of both criterion and test scores. Using a relationship statistic, "theta," the authors were able to show that ". . . in all three cases success and failure are due to quite different patterns of traits." As shown in three tables in the report, the specific validity coefficients become almost meaningless when viewed in the light of sorting predictor groups either by criterion or test scores. In the article, the authors question the routine use of the ordinary Pearsonian correlation coefficient to predict achievement. They say:

On the basis of the validity coefficients alone, one would be forced to conclude that the tests used with these workers at best have only very modest predictive power and, therefore, are of quite limited value in personnel selection. Yet the *theta* analysis clearly indicates that at certain ranges of scores the predictive power of some of the tests is excellent, with values of theta reaching magnitudes of predictive power equivalent to Pearsonian validity coefficients of the order of .70 to .80.

The study clearly indicates that achievement is differentially predicted at different levels of performance and that the relations of predictors and performance measures are not necessarily the commonly assumed linear and homoscedastic ones.

Thus the study clearly demonstrates the need for rethinking and for new approaches to the predictor-performance relationship. It demonstrates, too, how research results may be much more meaningful than first appearances might lead one to believe.

One of the pioneering studies in the attempt to reformulate the prediction paradigm was that of Rush (1953). This investigation was concerned with salesmen of office equipment. The study involved establishing acceptable criteria in terms of relevance, freedom from bias or contamination, and reliability. For selling, such criteria as per cent of quota achieved, average number of sales, and average monthly volume were all corrected by a base sales figure; in addition, grades in training programs and supervisory ratings on a nine-point scale were obtained. The predictors were personal-history data, aptitude tests, and a personality inventory. All data were intercorrelated, and from the matrix four factors were extracted. Using the predictor scores, Rush then predicted each factor using multiple correlation. Three of the factors were predictable at a significant level, whereas the fourth was not. One of the more interesting findings was that in the prediction of supervisory ratings, percent of sales quota achieved had a negative beta weight. Such ratings were best predicted by the personality inventory.

This study embodies many of the points previously discussed. For example, the range of performance reliabilities, estimated from the communalities, was from +0.24 (training grades) to +0.90 on a rating of potential value to the company. The communalities of the other objective variables were +0.57 for average number of sales, +.80 for percent of quota achieved, and +0.76 for average monthly volume. It might also be worth pointing out that the correlation between school grades and the three objective indices of performance were all low and negative.

This study could serve as a model, in that there are careful attempts to set up adequate achievement criteria and a wide selection of predictors, to determine the dimensions of achievement, and, finally, to relate various predictors to the separate dimensions in the achievement area. It was also suggested that the evaluation of performance can be quite crucial, because the study contains actual achievement in terms of objective indices negatively related to supervisory opinion. This same phenomenon was encountered by Ronan (1964), when two factor scores, as determined within a structure of four performance factors, were negatively correlated at a significant level. It is possible that, in the evaluation of performance, quality of performance on one dimension relating negatively to such quality in another might be a rather common occurrence. Only the most fragmentary evidence exists that this may be the case, but there is some evidence and it requires attention.

Morrison, *et al.* (1962) and Sprecher (1959) were both concerned with creativity in the work of technical personnel. The former used supervisory ratings of creativity and general performance and five-year patent disclosures as criteria. The correlations of actual patent disclosures with the two ratings were +0.18 and +0.14, indicating lack of agreement between rated and actual performance. Sprecher used simulated problem situations, patent disclosures, supervisory ratings, and peer ratings as measures of creativity. He says, "Little agreement between performance ratings and the more objective overall evaluations exists." In general, these studies indicate that there are dimensions of performance and evaluations of them, but, often, little or no agreement among the different evaluations.

A most comprehensive attack on the problems of the dimensionality of performance and its prediction has been conducted by the University of Utah group, as reported by Taylor, *et al.* (1964) and Richards, *et al.* (1965).

These investigators are involved in a long-term, extremely complex investition of physicians, both academic and practitioners. Because the findings for both studies are quite similar, only the former is discussed here.

Some eighty measures of physician performance were gathered by interviews, questionnaire listings in compendia, peer evaluations, medical college files, and a variety of other sources. The data were of such nature that some could be used as performance predictors (i.e., grades in medical school) or as achievement measures. All the data were intercorrelated and factor-analyzed, and for general practitioners in the sample, thirty performance factors emerged. In effect, it is possible to evaluate the achievement of these professional people on thirty different dimensions. Aside from this performance complexity, which the authors believe to be a conservative estimate of the total possibilities, one of the more interesting findings is that grades in pre-medical or medical school do not predict later achievement (recall the study by Rush described above). The fact that the specific training for two areas of achievement (sales and medical practice) shows no significant relationship to actual job achievement should encourage an attitude of humility both in educators who overvalue the influence of academic training and in psychologists who tend uncritically to accept training grades as a criterion.

A final point from the Utah studies made by the authors is that, with thirty performance dimensions to predict, only a very limited amount of the variance can be related to any one predictor. Indeed, they show that, in such a situation, "the maximum correlation that could be obtained between a predictor and each of the performance dimensions would be $\sqrt{.03}$ or .18."

The studies that have been presented are of relatively demanding activities and have indicated the complexity of the predictor-achievement relationship, in particular, the complexity of achievement. That these studies may be only scratching the surface is indicated by an analysis of one aspect of another complex activity, piloting an aircraft. Actual command of an aircraft is extremely complex, involving flight planning, crew supervision, communications, and other tasks over and above the actual flying itself. A study by Fleishman and Ornstein (1960) has concentrated on this latter aspect of the total achievement.

In this study, some sixty pilots were evaluated as correct or incorrect on twenty-four flying maneuvers. These were such things as a 90-degree climbing turn, gliding turn, power-on-stall, spin, and other exercises designed to show ability to maneuver an aircraft. Scores for the twenty-four maneuvers were intercorrelated, and six factors extracted from the matrix. These were named: I, Control Precision; II, Spatial Orientation; III, Multilateral Coordination; IV, Response Orientation; V, Rate Control; and VI, Kinesthetic Discrimination. Most of the maneuvers were factorially complex, some showing substantial loadings in three of the six factors and all in at least two factors. Here again is illustrated the complexity of performance and, in a limited aspect, of the achievement of a pilot in command of an aircraft. As the authors recognize, an even finer analysis of this rather limited aspect would be possible if our knowledge of psychomotor skills were more complete. Even so, if this quite limited aspect of a total achievement is so complex, it is difficult even to imagine the factorial composition of the entire achievement area.

A further example of a study in the prediction of achievement that did attend to the criteria with the thoroughness usually reserved for the test items also exemplifies the obvious, but often neglected, fact that psychometric data are not the only possible predictors.

Eber (1966) analyzed the records of 502 vocational rehabilitation clients in a single state, a stratified sample representing appropriately the cases handled by each counselor working in that state. The results indicated that life data of a rather simple type, the type of data often found in ordinary case files, can predict substantial blocks of the variance in outcome, even when the predictor data are gathered as much as two or three years prior to the criterion achievement. Factor analysis of sixty-one variables describing client status and achievement, including variables describing the client's vocational performance at case closure and at follow-up, yielded ten well-defined and meaningful factors. Two of these clearly were criterion outcome factors: one, the pattern of adequacy of outcome at case closure; and the other, the same adequacy at follow-up. The criterion factors represented two very general measures of vocational achievement, which loaded such items as salary, satisfaction with the job, promotion record, and independence from further rehabilitation services. Thus, in this study at least, the problem of which criterion to predict was found to be relatively easily solved, because two factors emerging organically from the data precisely matched the two end goals of the rehabilitation system. It is not known how often such resolution of the criterion problem may exist, but of course it will not be known until more effort along this line is made.

The extent of possible prediction in the above rehabilitation data was substantial. Possession of all the information about a client available at closure, for example, permitted the prediction of his vocational adequacy one year to a year and a half later with validity coefficients above $+ .60$, accounting therefore for more than a third of the variance. It is not inconceivable that there may be other fields of achievement in which similar analysis of the criteria would permit not only some reasonable definition as to what is to be predicted, but even some rather substantial predictive results.

In the last resort one must recognize that the criterion is not only multi-dimensional, but also that conflicting demands in a complex occupation may produce what Cattell has called *internal cancellation*. That is to say, any occupation breaks down into an appreciable number of sub-activities or critical activities, and there is every prospect, since occupations are not designed in some psychological heaven, that what the occupation demands for one sub-procedure will be different from, and sometimes incompatible with what is demanded by another. For example, creativity in research is strongly associated with introversion (Chapter 15), but acquaintance with obtaining research grants may be associated with extraversion. Or again, in a military general, there would probably be advantages from the imaginativeness which goes with high M factor (autia in the 16 PF), but this is also loaded in neurotic anxiety and might unfit the individual for stresses of encountering casualties.

In the factoring criteria, and the working of canonical correlations between criterion and personality factors discussed above, the statisticians concerned have paid all too little attention to the *meaning* of such factors. The meaning will depend on what variance is being factored. Mainly it has been that among: (1) men working in different sub-procedures factored together on variables common to all. In this case the factors represent to an appreciable extent the "shape of the environment," i.e., the different patterns of skills which men in different branches are required to acquire, or (2) men in exactly the same tasks. In this latter case the factors in the criteria should represent exactly the same personality and ability traits as in the tests! (Or if they do not, we should do something about the tests!) They will represent them through different kinds of measures and show different variances as factors, but in so far as they represent the same men "behaving" they must be essentially the same.

"Essentially" needs to be stressed, because in fact the differences of measures may make recognition difficult unless we correlate the factor scores. For example, the U.I. 22 factor, Cortertia, might be measured by reversible perspective and reaction time in the test situation, and by speed in radar recognition or tightening of nuts and bolts in the work criterion situation. Furthermore, we should expect different instrument factors (Cattell and Digman, 1964) in the two situations, and since instrument factors are rarely properly separated out in routine, applied factor analyses, some apparent failure of the essential *principle of test-criterion homology* is likely to be reported. Thirdly, it is of course very likely that there will not only be appreciable differences of variance contribution for the same factors in the two realms but that some factors, *representing skills learned on the job,* will be absolutely peculiar to the criterion factoring—until the test designer gets around to constructing new tests for that factor.

Even with regard for these technical realities, however, the fact remains that good occupational guidance and selection faces attenuation of its prospective power by the internal cancellation principle above. Let us suppose, for example, that a job consists only of two sub-procedures, which can be measured, as far as their most vital contribution to the occupational outcome is concerned, by the criteria c_1 and c_2. Suppose the specification equations, in terms of 16 PF factors (four only, for illustration), are as follows:

$$c_1 = .4A + .2B + .3C - .1E$$
$$c_2 = -.4A + .3B + .2C + .1E$$

If the total criterion performance $C = c_1 + c_2$ is to be predicted it is evident that we lose (by adding these) the predictive value in factor A, affectothymia, and factor E, dominance. One meaning of good business and industrial organization is the avoiding of job designs which require performances like c_1 and c_2 to be done by the same man. But such situations will always exist and that being the case, this realm of psychological practice will always face attenuations of its potential predictive power.

Section 5 The Predictive Utility of Various Types of Data

Having examined in some detail the criterion problems that have yet to be adequately resolved in a vast majority of the published work, a more optimistic look at the future, and at some aspects of the present and the recent past, may be warranted. Despite the severe criterion problems discussed, some results of substantial predictive utility have been achieved in a great many cases. Although the prediction of achievement has not yet achieved the scientific status now deemed possible, certain gross successes have been achieved, and a balanced picture requires some attention to these.

Some examples of gross success in the use of simple intelligence test data have been given above. To these might well be added a number of other studies, as well as some analysis of what is not shown by but can be inferred from the literature.

The chief advances possible in intelligence testing since 1960 are those arising from research confirmation of the concepts of fluid and crystallized general intelligence, and the provision of culture-fair tests, such as the IPAT Scales 1, 2 and 3 and the Raven Matrices, to measure the former with reliable distinction from what is measured (crystallized ability) in traditional intelligence tests. Indeed, it is in the occupational field that culture-fair tests have their greatest value, because (a) as individuals become more remote from the school situation the very concept of "crystallized general ability" becomes more erroneous. Variously culturally acquired abilities no longer generate so clear a general factor as at school, and individuals who have invested their skills in different occupation areas may be quite unfairly compared. (b) There are substantial age changes between 20 and 65, as discussed in Chapter 2, which make prediction of performance in a new setting more predictable from the culture-fair test design.

Regardless of whether culture-fair (fluid) or traditional (crystallized) intelligence measures are involved, the chief problem in the field today is the absence of adequate occupational guidance data from surveys of I.Q. means and sigmas in a sufficient range of occupations. It is remarkable that no researcher has in recent years devoted himself to a repetition of the first surveys made available some 30 years ago through the work of Cattell (1933), Fryer (1922), the Harrells (1963), and others. These are still our best guides, though Eber, Horn, Meredith, and other associates of Cattell in the work on Culture Fair Tests may be expected to obtain the new occupational norms needed for Fluid Intelligence test predictions, in the next few years. Meanwhile, a best estimate from crystallized ability means, as in Cattell's list of occupations, can be made by remembering that the standard deviation of I.Q. on present lists needs to be multiplied by 1.5 to give the I.Q. as calculated (classically) from Culture Fair tests.

Progressing beyond the field of simple intelligence measurement into the area of utilization of differential-aptitude predictors, some quite substantial successes have been reported. The failure of the specific-aptitude approach in certain essentially irrelevant situations has tended to attract wide publicity, whereas more meaningful and substantial results have, unfortunately, been inadequately reported.

It is not really surprising that a complete set of primary mental ability scores, or differential-aptitude test data of any kind, predict school achievement hardly better than a single IQ score. School performance is not, after all, the criterion that such instruments were designed to predict, and it is only the ready availability of captive student populations that perpetuates such marginally relevant research.

Unfortunately, the data obtained by the U.S. Employment Service with the General Aptitude Test Battery are not generally available. Technical criticisms of the tests have been frequent, and perhaps often deserved; validity data could probably have been reported more openly without jeopardizing the integrity of the tests; inordinate attention to speed in the measurement of test performance undoubtedly has reduced the differential aspects of the abilities measured; complexity of instructions and concentration upon the measurement of normally literate persons has undoubtedly resulted in the misclassification of socioeconomically deprived persons. Nevertheless, the developers of the instrument were able to demonstrate repeatedly that a set of scores on the GATB could be so classified that a certain cutting point would accept a high proportion of successful performers in a specific occupation and reject a correspondingly high proportion of those who later failed in that job. Moreover, it has been repeatedly shown in the development of these instruments that the ability patterns characteristic of various occupations are sufficiently different to permit differential prediction at a level in excess of chance. Again, the validities have not approached unity, but only the most naive misunderstanding of the situation would lead one to expect such performance. It seems obvious that the massive attempt to deal with the disruptive forces of a complex and changing society that was undertaken by the employment service has benefited from the predictive utility of the instruments developed.

In the realm of more available data, published information regarding the *differential* predictive validity of the Primary Mental Abilities, the Differential Aptitude Tests, the Employee Aptitude Survey, and similar instruments clearly supports the impression that, in the broader world of occupations, unlike in the narrower world of school, differential-aptitude measurement results in significant improvement in prediction as compared with the single IQ.

Beyond the matter of abilities lies the question of how the person will utilize them. Personality and motivation aspects of prediction have clearly been insufficiently explored, and this is particularly true when one is concerned with true prediction. Part of this is because replicable measurement of the relevant personality and motivation dimensions has not been possible until recent years, but again one feels that more has been possible than has been done. It is, of course, very easy, given a substantial data bank, to pull out of it all the test data describing persons in a certain occupational category, to compare the obtained mean profile with that of the normative group, and perhaps even to calculate highly sophisticated regression equations making these findings applicable to attempts at vocational prediction. Similarly, administration of a large number of items describing interests and attitudes to a sample of persons in a selected occupation, isolation of those items answered differently than by the general population, cross-validation upon a second sample, and publication of the residual items as a vocational interest scale constitutes a feasible technique within the limits of cross-sectional experiment.

Much more difficult and therefore less often performed is the task of gathering data upon a large sample of persons and waiting for the outcome. One hindrance in this area has been the fact that reasonable knowledge regarding the dimensionality of vocational performance has not been available, nor is it available at present. To state categorically that there must be such a thing as "clerical work," an entity different from other types of work, simply because there is a name for this type of performance seems to beg the question. It might seem that a proper classification of occupations into types, perhaps with prior investigation of the dimensionality in the occupational field, could be most helpful. The means for doing this objectively, by applying the pattern similarity coefficient r_p to adequate profiles of source trait measures has been worked out, with computer program, by Cattell and Coulter (1966). One of the co-authors of this chapter, Dr. H. W. Eber, has been requested, on several occasions, to asist in the development of validity data regarding the degree to which vocational predictions made by the staff of a rehabilitation center are confirmed in the client's later performance. Suppose for a moment that the staff predicted that the client could function well as a technician specializing in the repair of small electric motors, that the client insisted upon training himself as a watchmaker, and that he was successfully employed in this occupation for a number of years. Is this to be scored as valid prediction, as invalid prediction, or as some compromise between the two? If it is to be a compromise, how close is it to a "hit" as opposed to a "miss"? If a dimensional structure of occupations were first defined, it would then be possible to calculate the similarity between the job predicted and the one eventually obtained; present knowledge of the field does not permit such sophistication.

Despite the rather primitive state of affairs described above, some data do exist that suggest that the validity of occupational prediction can be enhanced by consideration of personality and motivation characteristics. A study by Heron (1952) utilized cognitive and personality measurements to attempt prediction of a productivity count and of "the extent to which a man is a source of concern to his supervisors." Factor analysis of the predictors yielded four factors: general mental ability, hysteric tendencies, emotional instability, and speed of approach to a task. The third factor, emotional instability, correlated -0.45 with the job-adjustment criterion, suggesting that good predictions with personality measures may be possible when the criterion is relevant. In this study, the phrase "source of concern to his supervisors" was probably quite meaningful to these supervisors and enabled them to make the needed discrimination in this context. However, if one attempted to use such personality data to predict achievement indices that are more dependent upon other types of traits, such as aptitudes, the chances of any sizable relationship would be considerably reduced. In any case, the Heron study would appear to indicate the need to define just exactly what aspects of achievement are related to, and can be predicted from, personality measures.

Beyond the question of multidimensionality of criterion achievement patterns, personality predictors face the additional problem that some findings may be specific more to a given achievement situation than to the achievement itself. Unfortunately, there is a genuine paucity of studies that stand on a surer footing, but a comparison of three might indicate that there is some stability to the results. The studies are by Heron (1954), Fleishman, *et al.* (1955), and Ronan (1963).

The first was a study of bus drivers, and six criteria were used to evaluate their performance. These were gross earnings, "shorts" on cash for tickets sold, number of periods of absence, disciplinary actions, times late for duty, and a rating on the degree to which the employee was a "source of concern" to his supervisor. The N comprised 147 drivers who had completed twenty-six weeks of training. The second study was of factory workers and covered an eleven-month period. There were quite extensive criteria and analyses, but three are of interest here—accidents, grievances, and proficiency ratings. The third study of skilled tradesmen covered a ten-year period and used eleven performance criteria. These included shop and school ratings and mathematics grades as apprentices, and, as journeymen, absenteeism, injuries, lost-time accidents, grievances, disciplinary actions, promotions, supervisory ratings, and diagnosed personality disorders. The factor analysis gave four performance factors. There were substantial correspondences between the intercorrelations of similar factors in the three studies, suggesting that some relatively gross criterion variables may be sufficiently general to describe a criterion dimension of major significance rather than something specific to a particular situation. Much work remains to be done, but the major point is that focus upon real dimensions, emerging organically from the data, may permit the utilization of personality data in much more sophisticated prediction than has been attempted heretofore.

The personality area, more than any other, has suffered from lack of agreement among scientists regarding which concepts should be measured, as well as even greater lack of agreement regarding the method of measurement. The philosophy of operationism and logical positivism, both so popular in American psychology during the 1950's, made the valid point that any concept must, in the final analysis, depend upon the operations performed in measuring it. An unfortunate by-product of this, however, was the denial that any concept might exist apart from a specific measurement; although this is analogous to saying that the concept of length, for example, has no validity of its own but only depends upon specific measuring techniques, that is precisely what was said. An unfortunate result was that many psychological investigators gave up all attempts to develop a common set of concepts by which communication could take place, each insisting that, for example, anxiety is what *I* mean when I perform such and such operations. Thus, voluminous literature is devoted to the relationship between anxiety and certain criterion performances, and even more voluminous literature is concerned with the relationship between various measures and techniques whose results have been labeled "anxiety."

Several proposals by personality theorists and practitioners to standardize the concepts have been made, perhaps the first being the brilliant attempt in clinical psychology represented by McKinley and Hathaway's compilation of the Minnesota Multiphasic Personality Inventory. These scientists were able, at least, to standardize the instrument sufficiently so that a vast body of data has accumulated, data that can be compared from place to place and from time to time, even though the scales derived from these data have reached such multiplicity that, at a recent time, over 260 different scales were reported as being scored from the pool of MMPI items.

Two notable attempts to bring standardization of concepts rather than of items into personality psychology have been those of Guilford and Zimmerman on the one hand and those of Cattell and his coworkers on the other. Neither of these theoretical systems, nor the test materials based upon them, have yet been utilized in applied psychology to the degree that their preeminent position in the field might be said to deserve. However, whereas Guilford's concentration upon the definition of human abilities has prevented his giving the leadership in the utilization of his personality concepts that might have encouraged their wider use, Cattell has maintained constant interest in the field for several decades. His interest and productivity have been reflected in a substantial body of work utilizing the tests that are available for predictive purposes.

The data tend to be of that type most easily obtained. Rarely have studies been conducted relating personality characteristics, however measured, to clearly defined criteria. Even more rarely have the predictive data actually been obtained before the performance whose achievement was to be predicted took place. Almost never has there been given to the analysis of the various critria the same careful attention that routinely is utilized in the analysis of test items. Because of these facts, much of the data that can now be reported are fragmentary and suggestive rather than detailed and definitive. Still, suggestive data are better than none at all.

The Handbook for the Sixteen Personality Factor Questionnaire (Cattell and Eber, 1967) contains profiles describing the personality test scores of large samples in over forty occupations. In many instances, the data have permitted the development of linear regression equations that give a different type of information. The measurement of 500 persons in a given occupation and the comparison of the mean scores with the means of the reference group does not really constitute true prediction of vocational achievement. In the first place, a variety of true achievement is represented within any occupational category, all the way from those individuals who are the true leaders in the occupation down to those who are discharged the day after testing because of their failure to meet job requirements. Besides, the people in any occupation, even those successfully employed, always represent a compromise between what the occupation might ideally need and what it can command in a competitive society. If a man has the makings of a great teacher or of a mediocre salesman, and he lives in a society that rewards mediocre salesmen much more than great teachers, then his scores are likely to be included in the salesman category rather than that of teachers, to the confusion of analysis in both.

Despite these problems, however, once the qustion is asked whether there may be some characteristic or set of characteristics that are helpful to success in a given occupation, then it is certainly reasonable to look for those characteristics among persons who are successful in that occupation. When such persons, on the average, exhibit known traits to a stronger degree than persons in general, the inference that these are of value seems essentially obvious. We would emphasize that this is not the place to end the testing of hypotheses but rather the place to begin. The published data from the 16 PF thus represent only a beginning, but it is a beginning in the personality area, and few other beginnings of a consistent sort can be reported. It has been shown that the profiles describing the mean scores of highly homogeneous occupational groups usually differ from those of the general population simultaneously on eight to twelve factors, each at an acceptable level of confidence. Thus the probability that the particular occupational group is really different from the population at large approaches certainty.

In connection with profile data representing various occupations, mention should be made of a method whereby a more rigorous regression model can be applied to profile data with results that have, to date, been insufficiently explored, but that probably warrant substantial further exploration.

Given the 16 PF profile representing means and standard deviations of factor scores for a specific occupational group, and with the available knowledge of the means and standard deviations of factor scores for the normative group, it becomes possible to translate each profile point into an estimate of the correlation between the criterion of membership in the occupational group and that factor score. Let x_o represent the mean score on a certain factor of the occupational group with σ_o as the corresponding standard deviation; let x_p represent the population mean on that factor, with σ_p the corresponding standard deviation. Further, let n_o and n_p represent the number of cases in the occupational group and in the normative sample respectively. Finally, let C represent an arbitrary cutting point, best chosen somewhere between x_o and x_p.

Making the assumption of normality of distribution, the proportion of cases in the normative group who lie above point C can be obtained by the formula

$$z = \frac{C - x_p}{\sigma_p}$$

where z is a deviate from the mean that can be looked up in a normal curve table and converted to proportions above and below that point. Similarly, proportions of the occupational group lying above and below point C can be calculated. The result is a two-by-two contingency table, representing the proportions of the normative group and of the occupational group, respectively above and below the same common score point. Such a fourfold table is easily converted into a correlation coefficient by tetrachoric or by serial methods. This leads to what may be called a "profile-derived specification equation" (Cattell and Eber, 1963).

Estimation of correlations between an occupational criterion and a 16 PF factor score in this manner is not a substitute for true determination of that correlation with a meaningful achievement criterion. However, the method represents a starting point and yields interesting hypotheses for further exploration. Once the vector of correlations between membership in an occupational group and sixteen different factor scores has been thus obtained, and the correlations between the predictors (factors) themselves are known, the regression model will yield a specification equation estimating effectiveness of a person with a particular set of factor scores in the given occupation. It should be emphasized that the correlations among the predictors required here are neither those that obtain in the normative population nor those that obtain in the occupational group, but rather those that obtain across the combined sample. When these correlations are used, and the assumption that the more easily obtained population correlations could be used is not made, the regression model permits also an estimate of the validity with which this "effectiveness" is being predicted.

Table XLVI contains a single example from the 16 PF literature, an example chosen to represent the fact that the regression equation does not always match the appearance of the profile. Whether or not this type of prediction will, in the long run, be more productive than more traditional methods cannot be said at this time. Nevertheless, the method holds promise and is presented for that reason.

It should be emphasized also that efforts to obtain true predictive validity studies with the newer, more sophisticated personality test instruments are under way, and the writers personally are aware of half a dozen or more such undertakings. The true predictive studies, however, take significant time, and only a relatively small amount of time has elapsed since the coming into general use of the more modern personality-measurement techniques. As is well known to most test authors, and perhaps to most psychologists, a sub-

TABLE **XLVI**

16 PF Characteristics of Salesmen; N = 284

FACTOR	A	B	C	E	F	G	H	I
Profile	6.5	5.1	5.4	5.8	5.9	6.2	5.7	4.3
Correlations	.31	−.12	−.03	.09	.12	.21	.06	−.37
Beta-weights*	.57	−.12	−.27	.18	−.03	.23	.18	−.42

FACTOR	L	M	N	O	Q_1	Q_2	Q_3	Q_4
Profile	5.3	4.6	5.9	5.2	4.8	5.1	5.8	5.4
Correlations	−.06	−.28	.12	−.09	−.22	−.13	.09	−.03
Beta-weights*	.01	−.46	.08	−.02	−.31	.13	.11	.06

* Estimate (in stens) $= 6.08 + \sum$ [each factor score $\times$ the corresponding beta-weight].

stantial interval of time usually elapses between the publication of a new instrument and its routine use in the field. When this time is added to that which must elapse before true predictive validity studies can be concluded, the present picture may be more encouraging than would appear on the surface. The reader is reminded again that evidence suggests that sufficient elapsed time may be a major influence in permitting relationships to develop and to become visible.

Turning finally to the area of motivation measurement, a highly promising new approach is available that may for the first time take this area out of the exclusive province of impressionistic data. This is the Motivation Analysis Test (Cattell, Horn, Sweney, and Radcliffe, 1964). In this area more than any other, the time elapsed since publication of the instrument has clearly been insufficient to permit the development of validity data either in a school situation or outside in the wider context. It is characteristic of the ease with which scholastic data are obtained that the test authors utilized such data for some of their initial reports of apparent validity. Still, the clinician or the researcher who has maintained for some years that it would be desirable to have precise measurements available in the motivation area may be somewhat taken aback to be provided with a set of forty-five scores describing a single individual. Although the scores all appear intuitively meaningful, and although intuitive clinical interpretation of these data is now possible, the issue is simply too complex to permit ready utilization of such data in controlled validity studies within a few months after test publication. Hopefully, a book of this type written ten years hence may report a more impressive state of affairs in the motivation area than now exists.

SUMMARY *of Chapter Thirteen*

1. Although the analysis and prediction of occupational and life success are the same in fundamental principles as for school performance, and the same general personality and ability measures are effective, they differ in requiring several special developments as follows.

2. There is probably a more complex dimensionality to the criteria, requiring still more explicit attention to including the greatest possible number of dimensions in the predictors, i.e., general-purpose rather than special-purpose tests, amenable to modification according to situation, are indicated.

3. In a complex criterion, weights have to be assigned to the various dimensions, and, in the last resort, this involves assignment of values. A general principle for this has been indicated.

4. A distinction has been drawn between the "effectiveness" and the "adjustment" (or "fitness") criteria in evaluating prospects of success in an occupation. A translation, given certain assumptions, is possible from one to the other, and there is then no complete coincidence of weights, because "adjustment" implicitly involves relations to opportunities in other occupations and does not confine itself to sheer efficiency as a criterion, even within the given occupation. Linear models exist for obtaining greatest correspondence with the criterion when allocating given resources of personality and ability to a given set of occupations, and the *profile-derived specification equation* is only an approximation to the latter.

5. A problem that assumes much larger proportions in occupational than in school success predictions arises from the need to predict over the whole life span and consequently from changes that characteristically occur with age in both personality and ability predictors and in the criteria of occupational success.

6. A relatively poor standard of prediction in much industrial, military, and vocational psychological practice in the past has been due partly to the above complications and partly to outdated techniques of personality and motivation measurement, but largely to inaptness and unreliability of the criterion. An extensive survey is given of research on the criterion problem.

7. In contemplating canonical correlation methods with multi-dimensional criteria one should reflect that, except for instrument factors, the factors in criteria behaviors should be expected to be the same source traits as appear in test behaviors. Power of prediction of occupational achievement is in practice reduced by *internal cancelation* of qualities demanded in various sub-procedures within the occupational activity.

Chapter Fourteen

ORIGINALITY AND CREATIVITY IN
SCHOOL AND SOCIETY

Section 1   **Creativity and Its Role in Society**

Educational psychologists have often been prone to interpret achievement too narrowly as the passing of examinations, the acquisition of skills, or as adjustment to the school and college situation. While paying lip service to originality and to the creative aspects of personality, they have, in fact, largely neglected the study of how these may be recognized and fostered. This is natural enough, perhaps, because these creative qualities are harder to assess than intelligence or attainment. The layman, however, has sometimes seen further than the teacher or the psychologist in his complaints that tests of ability and attainment, as developed in the last fifty years, have been missing something vital, and that often the child who has been assessed as most successful is not the one who is most original, most creative, or most productive in later life. But the difficulty of assessing creativity is not the only reason why the most creative, as distinct from the most intelligent, child has often lacked encouragement. There is some evidence that teachers prefer and rate more highly the child of high intelligence than the creative child. Getzels and Jackson (1962) compared a group of highly intelligent with a group of highly creative children. Despite a mean difference of 23 points in IQ and no ascertainable difference in motivation, the highly creative group reached the same level of achievement in school. But the creative group was not equally favored by teachers. As Getzels and Jackson put it:

> The data are quite clear-cut. The high IQ group stands out as being more desirable than the average student, the high creativity group does not. It is apparent that an adolescent's desirability as a student is not a function only of his academic achievement. Even though the scholastic performance is the same, the high IQ students are preferred over the average students by their teachers, the creativity students are not. This result is quite striking, for if anything, the

reverse should be true. Here is a student—the high IQ one—who is doing scholastically only what can be expected of him. Here is another student—the high creativity one—who is doing scholastically *better* than can be expected of him. Yet it is the former rather than the latter who is enjoyed more than the average student by his teachers!

Getzels and Jackson's research methods have not escaped criticism (de Mille and Merrifield, 1962), and many of their findings have not been easily repeatable, but their pioneer study was useful in drawing attention to a disquieting state of affairs that has often been suspected. For it appears to be almost a sociological law of education that what does not enter into pupil-evaluation reports eventually becomes more honored in the breach than in the observance. Admittedly, creativity is, in many respects, a vague term; but it describes a quality or complex of qualities whose importance can hardly be exaggerated, and it appears to be the best term for the wide spectrum of behavior involved. That spectrum includes scientific discovery, artistic production, musical composition, technological invention, political and social innovation, literary creation, and even religious leadership. It is generally agreed that cultural conditions and demands affect the adoption or rejection of innovations, but at least creative individuals have to be present and active to produce the innovations in the first place.

Writers on creativity have given much attention to major works of science, literature, and art, so that creativity has sometimes become synonymous with the possession of genius. Nevertheless, in one sense, creativity benefits society at all levels of capacity. In the first place, societies with flexibly minded citizens, who are able to develop creative and constructive solutions to problems of government, can expect to progress by peaceful evolution instead of staggering through revolutions. Second, let us not fall into the intellectual snobbery of denying the value present in creativity far below the level of masterpieces in art, music, or literature. The person who invents a new window fastener, composes a college fraternity song, arranges items in a store in a new way, or makes a pleasant design of the flower beds in his garden, is performing the kind of creative act that, repeated a million times, benefits society perhaps as much as do the greater inventions. In America, particularly, one cannot help being impressed by the increment in economic level and social happiness that arises from the inventiveness and mental adaptability of the bulk of the population.

A psychologist who is also a realist must make a reservation, however, that the increase of flexibility beyond a certain point may also bring disadvantages. In some situations, an intelligent person who knows what he is doing can advantageously question the rules, but a stupid person who does so can get into bottomless trouble. It is one of the difficulties of our reforming age that the intelligent person is seldom intelligent enough (some writings of Bertrand Russell are at fault in this respect) to realize that the world has also to be run for unintelligent people. In short, we may have to recognize, explicitly, that the teaching of flexibility has to be correlated with the intelligence level of the pupil. A more complete answer to this question requires more knowledge of the psychological ingredients in the area of flexibility and creativity, and one of the objects of this chapter is to examine such knowledge as we have.

Section 2 **Some Previous Research on Creativity**

We have already mentioned the deep gulf that has, in the past, separated the literary from the scientific approach to personality. Nowhere has this seemed wider or more difficult to bridge than when concerned with so apparently elusive and godlike a quality as artistic creativity. As Downey (1929) pointed out, it is unfortunate for the experimentalist that it is difficult (though not impossible) to summon the individual poet or artist to the laboratory for a really intensive examination. Occasionally, this has been done with a particularly amenable writer, for example, Émile Zola, but with rather dubious results.

More recently, something of the kind has been done by Anne Roe (1951a, 1951b, 1953), for eminent scientists, in an extensive series of careful studies. Although her measures of personality were principally projective techniques of debatable validity, such as the Rorschach and the Thematic Apperception Test (TAT), some interesting and useful conclusions emerged. Of particular interest, in view of the whole theme of this book, was the following conclusion (1953, p. 52):

> The range of test intelligence in the group is also of importance. All of the evidence confirms Cox's remark "high, but not the highest intelligence, combined with the greatest degree of persistence, will achieve greater eminence than the highest degree of intelligence with somewhat less persistence."

Interesting, and not unexpected, differences also emerged between the various types of scientist. Thus experimental physicists were relatively very high on spatial and very low on verbal tests, social scientists vice versa, with psychologists in between on both. It should be remembered, though, that these generalizations may apply only to the eminent and successful scientists who formed Roe's group and not necessarily to scientists in general. In terms of personality factors, Roe's firmest finding, and one on which she places emphasis, is the marked independence and self-sufficiency of these scientists. Of the group as a whole, she writes: "More of these men than not, as boys, pursued rather independent paths—playing with one or a few close friends, instead of a gang." Of the biologists, she adds: "They are a very stubborn lot and cannot be pushed around. They do not seem to need to feel dominant with respect to other persons, but they definitely are not subservient."

The statements of writers and artists themselves have also often been collected and studied, so that one has, so to speak, a distillation of the most typical insights into the creative process provided by those who have achieved most. Two useful collections of this kind are *Writers on Writing* (Allen, 1948) and *The Creative Process* (Ghiselin, 1955). The second, in particular, is of wide scope and contains such diverse and classic accounts of the mechanics of creation as that by Poincaré on "Mathematical Creation" and a famous letter by Mozart on his method of composition. A third useful source of this kind, though with rather less raw source-material and more interpretation, is provided by Harding (1940).

Evidence of this kind, of course, has been available for centuries and, in spite of its great psychological value, is essentially anecdotal rather than scientific. Its principal value, from the viewpoint of the scientific psychologist, is that it provides the most fertile and insightful source of hypotheses.

It is only fairly recently that a more direct psychometric attempt has been made to measure creativity. Guilford and his associates (e.g., Wilson, *et al.,* 1954) have proceeded first of all by factor analysis of possible measures, and then by the development of promising tests, to obtain direct scores on creativity. Guilford has found factors such as fluency of various types, and originality, all probably bearing some relation to creativity, but tending in our view, as do Guilford's factors in other areas, to be relatively specific and low-level factors. It seems at least plausible to suppose that if oblique simple-structure factors were extracted from Guilford's original measures, a more authentic factor of creativity might emerge as a second-order factor. We shall return to this and similar points in a later section. Be this as it may, many of the tests have proved useful in practice, as in the Getzels and Jackson research already referred to, where some were used in conjunction with parts of Cattell's Objective-Analytic Test Battery. Some evidence supports the view that Guilford's tests that load on his originality factor are, as one might suppose, more satisfactory in the identification of creative talent than those that load on, say, ideational fluency (Drevdahl, 1956; Piers, Daniels, and Quackenbush, 1960). Later in this chapter, we shall be dealing in much greater detail with the relation between creativity and primary personality factors, but worth noting at this point is the work of Barron (1955), who used some of Guilford's tests and some projective techniques. He found that more original or creative people tended to prefer complexity in their appreciation of works of art, to be more independent in their judgments, to be more self-assertive and dominant, and to reject suppression as a mechanism for the control of impulse.

An interesting, indeed classic, attempt to bridge the gulf between psychological theory and artistic and scientific creativity was made by Spearman (1930). Although Spearman's taste in the visual arts is, of course, different from the present fashion, his achievement was to account, at least partly, for the creation and appreciation of art in terms of his well-known noegenetic laws and principles. Such an approach proved valuable, not so much for giving a complete explanation, for inevitably it tended to underplay temperament and unconscious motivation, but because it refused to accept the creative process simply as an inexplicable miracle. As Spearman himself puts it:

> . . . one doctrine that has obtained much vogue is not so much an explanation as rather a refusal to explain. The power to create is simply accepted as an ultimate fact. . . . Now, in thus taking creativity to be itself the last word of explanation, there is nothing necessarily wrong. Some word must be the last, any way. But we are scarcely entitled to such a renunciation of all better understanding until we have at least made every feasible effort to obtain it.

Section 3   General Associations of Creativity and Pseudocreativity

The notion that there is some antithesis, not only in social terms but in the makeup of the individual himself, between routine efficiency and dependability, on the one hand, and creativity, on the other, is the very old one. It appears in Greek writings, as in the notion of "banausic" labor, and in our era in Dryden's much quoted comment on genius:

> Great wits are sure to madness near allied,
> And thin partitions do their bounds divide.[1]

Among writings by psychologists, since Galton and Havelock Ellis, the work of Hirsch and Kretschmer gives most support to the notion that a streak of pathological instability, of "warring heredity," or of unbalanced tension is essential to creativity. Among nonpsychologists the view is still more prevalent, as in Nietzsche's cry to the dull multitude: "Where is the madness with which you should be inoculated?"

What some regarded as the deathblow to this view was given by the results of Terman's scientifically impeccable *Genetic Studies of Genius* (already discussed at some length in Chapter 13). Here, he showed that the topmost one per cent, in intelligence, in our population, were significantly more physically fit, free of mental disorder, and so forth, than the general population. This outcome should surprise no one who is familiar with the convergent social and sexual selection of desirable personal traits, as analyzed, for example, by R. A. Fisher and by the present senior author. Unfortunately, what escapes many hypnotized by the term genius in the titles of Terman and others who naively labeled high intelligence "genius" is that these highly intelligent subjects did not turn out to be geniuses! Creativity is not simply high intelligence.

[1] John Dryden, *Absalom and Achitophel*, Part I.

Having little space for digression on this theme, we must handle it without qualifications for the finer issues. More statistically objective studies than Kretschmer's show that psychosis (or at least schizophrenia, which constitutes more than half of all psychoses) is actually less frequent among persons of high creativity, as are a variety of other mental disabilities. If we exclude anxiety neuroses, there is also no indication that geniuses are more neurotic. But there *are* indications that high creativity may be associated with unusual degrees of introversion and with certain kinds of high anxiety, as well as with flexibilities of imagination that are quite disabling in regard to high efficiency and freedom from oscillation in routine performances.

In addition, to reconcile the popular with the scientific view of creativity, one must bear in mind two facts. First, the popular mind recognizes normal people and deviants as two classes, failing to perceive that social deviants are themselves of two very different kinds—those ahead of their society, and those behind it. In any company of rebels and reformers can be found this unhappy mixture of those who want to destroy society because their psychological deficiences make the demands of *any* society a burden to them, and those whose intelligence and character are so much above the average that the existing society is not good enough for them. It is not surprising that, at a first glance, superiority and defect are confused in the picture of the deviant, just as in conversation, "original," unusual remarks consist of those that are witty and those that are gauche. Second, and on rather similar lines, we must recognize that the popular mind is apt to see high fluency as creativity; but to the psychologist, high fluency is perceived to arise either from a vitality of the unconscious or, by contrast, from defective powers of inhibition in the ego, and creativity so defined is therefore a mixed blessing.

Nor is it only nonpsychologists who fall into this trap. The idea of "brainstorming" involves a confusion of fluency and creativity, and its more reckless advocates must have drowned many a committee's proceedings in a sea of irrelevancies. Similarly, to overemphasize, as some psychologists are inclined to do, the fluent, impulsive, incontinent aspects of creativity is to miss half the point. In art, it is true, criteria of excellence are subjective, so that originality can logically be equated with deviation from the norm. But whereas of art and literature the poet can say:

> There are nine and sixty ways of constructing tribal lays,
> And every single one of them is right![2]

in science there are usually a hundred theories and only one that works—tolerably! In art there is a need to be realistic about the technical limitations and properties of the medium, and in science this need for the imagination to come to grips with reality has spread over the whole creative process. But what the scientist does when he personally buries so high a proportion of his

---

[2] Rudyard Kipling, "In the Neolithic Age."

intellectual children is, in principle, no different from, say, a golf champion, who makes only one combination of movements out of a very large possible number of them.

Spearman, in *The Creative Mind,* pointed out that new mental content appears by one of two processes, by *eduction* (of fundaments and relations) or by *reproduction.* The latter, by sheer relaxation of normal control, as in dreams, can produce chance combinations, such as a green elephant reading algebra, that are novel. The former is likely to produce something new by an unusual combination of relations and fundaments, as by asking what happens when the idea of a square root is applied to negative number, or by possessing such unusual mental capacity that one is able to educe a fundament where no one has been able to before, as in Wells's description of a time machine, or Newton's demonstration of how to weigh the earth. Lewis Carroll's *Alice in Wonderland* is a beautiful example of eduction and reproduction rioting together.

Section 4 The Relation of Cognitive Abilities to Creativity

Because the level of complexity at which a person can successfully educe relations and fundaments is probably the best definition of the general ability factor, *g,* it is not surprising that intelligence test scores always correlate substantially with ratings of creativity by skilled judges. Creativity is more than intelligence, as we have taken pains to show; but whatever other cognitive and temperamental qualities may operate, they cannot operate successfully if the individual does not have the intellectual capacity to evaluate correctly the new cognitive material that arises.

The correlations of intelligence with creativity, however assessed, are substantial, but not always so high as one might expect. In the Getzels and Jackson study, for example, the correlations between individual tests and IQ were usually around +0.30, and the intercorrelations between the five measures of creativity were all positive, ranging between +0.15 and +0.53. These intercorrelations were somewhat larger on the whole than the correlations with intelligence, so that some evidence was provided that the battery was assessing a unitary trait distinct from general intelligence. On the other hand, Burt (1962), Thorndike (1963), Marsh (1964), and Vernon (1964) have all reanalyzed or reinterpreted the data, maintaining that *g* is still the main operative factor, with Burt concluding that "indeed, the new tests for 'creativity' would form very satisfactory additions to any ordinary battery for testing the general factor of intelligence."

One should also point out that Getzels and Jackson's study was based on a highly untypical (too intelligent) group in a private school near Chicago. Repetitions of the experiment on unselected cross-sections of children have usually failed to confirm Getzels and Jackson's results (Edwards and Tyler, 1965; Hasan and Butcher, 1966). But even though measures of creativity and intelligence commonly correlate quite highly, much of the variance in creativity is still to be accounted for by other things. Some of these "other things" may still be in the realm of intellectual equipment. For example, an individual who has found a certain kind of eduction of relations to be more than normally useful in problems in a particular area may, consciously or unconsciously, develop habits of applying that technique. In many scientific problems, for instance, the understanding of something in a particular species is aided by a quick glance at corresponding structures in other species. Personal emotional problems are sometimes better tackled by sleeping on them before making a decision. Any good work on the research process or the history of scientific or artistic activities will contain numerous instances of habits and approaches to work that tend to be acquired by creative workers. We shall say a little more about these in Chapter 15, but because this book is more concerned with those contributions to creativity that are "given" and must be selected, rather than with what teaching can contribute to creativity, we shall not follow this much further. In any event, the general trend of research evidence makes it fairly clear that when we have a job requiring creativity, it proves more effective to pick out, than to try to train, a creative person. Some of this evidence does also suggest, however, that creativity in the normal range (particularly among children) may be harder to diagnose in an uncongenial atmosphere. Torrance has accounted for some of the discrepancies in the literature in this way, and the work of Wallach and Kogan (1965) suggests that creativity in young children may be easier to detect in informal, non-competitive situations.

By far the most systematic and experimentally advanced study of the *cognitive* factors in creativity are those found by Guilford and his associates, whom we have already briefly mentioned in Section 2 as pioneers in the systematic application of psychometric methods in this area. To understand Guilford's contribution to the theory of creativity (apart from the impetus given by his presidential address to the American Psychological Association in 1950), it is necessary to consider his schema or frame of reference a little more closely than in earlier sections. The main feature is a three-way classification of abilities, according to: (1) the type of mental operation performed, e.g., remembering, or making an evaluative judgment; (2) the material on which the various operations may be performed, e.g., single words, geometrical figures, or complex concepts; (3) the resultant form into which the data are processed in the course of the operations, e.g., into classes, systems, or relations. The complete model contains up to 120 cells resulting from this three-way classification, and each of these is hypothesized as representing a possibly distinct ability. Guilford and his associates claim to have isolated and to have developed tests for a considerable proportion of these numerous facets of ability.

One of the five kinds of mental operation distinguished by Guilford is of particular importance in the study of creativity. This is the kind called "divergent production," in which is included the performance of open-ended tasks, or the solution of problems that in general have no one unequivocally right answer. The distinction made here between "divergent" and "convergent" production" is similar to, but rather wider than, the distinction commonly drawn in the area of mathematical problem-solving between algorithms and heuristic procedures, where the former term describes an essentially mechanical method of solution, particularly suitable to be programmed on a computer, and the latter a kind of procedure more suited to problems for which there may not be an answer of the kind sought. Heuristic procedures will commonly involve hunches, shortcuts, "shots in the dark," and so on.

Confining ourselves, therefore, to the operation of divergent production in Guilford's model, we still have twenty-four cells in his table, representing four kinds of material by six kinds of product. One of the four kinds of material we can eliminate from the discussion at once. This is, roughly speaking, information about human behavior. Although the idea is interesting that particular abilities may be found concerned with awareness of human attitudes, thoughts, and so on, and although this area of "social intelligence" deserves further research, practically no research data are at present available. Very recently, however, Guilford and his associates have reported the beginnings of systematic research in this area (O'Sullivan, Guilford, and De-Mille, 1965). The remaining three kinds of material are described as figural, symbolic, and semantic. Creativity factors specific to each of these kinds of material and, within these, to particular kinds of product, have been found, but not for every cell of the cross-classification. They are thickest in the "semantic material" sector, whether because more intensive research has been devoted to creativity expressed in terms of meanings and ideas than, say, in terms of visual and auditory patterns (the "figural material" sector), or because the semantic factors are easier to isolate. Some, however, have also been found in the "symbolic material" sector. For example, the divergent production operation, when employed on symbolic material to produce units, results in the ability factor described as word fluency.

This brief account of Guilford's theoretical system should illustrate some of the advantages and disadvantages of his approach. First, this elaborate, hypothetical, three-dimensional grid helps to clarify thinking about the structure of abilities, but it would be surprising if the entire empirical factor structure proved to be quite so neat and logical. Second, the model has the advantage of integrating the study of abilities and the study of the cognitive aspects of creativity in one framework, and the creativity factors and their corresponding tests have a prima facie validity as tests of immediate creativity. This is also borne out by the stimulus they have given to research and by their widespread use by other investigators. Third, there is the disadvantage that even within their cognitive sphere, they appear to operate at rather too specific and narrow a level to have a great deal of practical predictive value. Hunt (1961, p. 301) puts this point strongly, probably too strongly, when he says "in no situations are these minute, splinter-like factors of predictive significance." But we should prefer, and this will come as no surprise to readers of earlier chapters, rotation to simple structure, combined with a second-order analysis to produce a factor or factors of general cognitive creativity. If such a general factor can be isolated, it seems more likely that in most populations it will be to some extent correlated with any other general cognitive factor (as has indeed recently been found by Cropley, 1966). As with other abilities, a double (i.e., first-order *and* second-order) analysis would combine the theoretical advantage of a rational criterion of rotation with the practical advantage of providing factors at two levels of generality. Just as it is sometimes more practicable and convenient to use a broad measure of general intelligence and sometimes desirable to break this down into primary mental abilities, one would certainly imagine that in the future the same, or analogous, requirements will be felt and met in the domain of creativity.

Finally, Guilford's model allows only for the cognitive, intellectual aspects of creativity and not for the temperamental and motivational, which are clearly of great importance. Long-term, as distinct from immediate, prediction should be assisted by a study of these personality correlates.

Section 5   The Roots of Creativity in Personality Studied Biographically

Although the modern study of creativity and personality rightly makes use of and largely depends upon experiment, clinical observation, psychological testing, statistical analysis, follow-up studies, and so forth, it would be foolish to neglect entirely the illuminating clues and suggestions provided by historical and biographical studies. Impressive pioneer studies of this kind, attempting to reassess outstanding men and women of the past in terms of modern psychological knowledge and concepts were made by Galton (1870), Havelock Ellis (1946), and Cox (1926), among others.

More recently, Cattell (1959) has surveyed the lives of a large number of eminent research scientists and has summarized his findings in terms of the primary personality factors described in Chapter 4 of this book. It is important to note that this summary of findings, which will be briefly reproduced in this section, although first made widely accessible in 1963, was arrived at some ten years earlier, before the empirical studies, such as those with Drevdahl, already cited, and was presented to the New York Academy of Sciences in 1954. It would have been a pity to study the biographies only after a knowledge of the psychometric results on eminent contemporaries.

As it is, however, the extent of concordance between the two approaches can be guaranteed not to be an artifact. The biographical survey, although the result of perhaps a thousand hours' reading, was in the nature of a first attempt to assess retrospectively the personalities of scientists of genius in terms of recently described personality factors. It was not on the scale of, say, Cox and Terman's monumental similar study in terms of intelligence. A larger and more detailed systematic and confirmatory research of this kind would still be well worthwhile, in spite of its formidable difficulties. We hope that a research team with a generous supply of energy and funds will undertake it.

To report the biographical findings factor by factor or man by man and to illustrate them with the wealth of fascinating and often amusing anecdotal support available would make this section disproportionately long. Here are some of the salient points.

First, in terms of broad, second-order factors, the typical research scientist of genius appears introverted and stable. The predominant, although obviously not universal, tendency to introversion observed particularly among physical scientists (e.g., Lord Cavendish, Dalton, Priestley, Lavoisier, Scheele, Avogadro, J. J. Thomson) is logically not surprising in view of the nature of fundamental research. Today, scientific research is increasingly a matter of teamwork, and the leader, or innovator, or inventor may appear to be highly dependent on effective cooperation and even on conventional social skills. But even in these conditions and in the field of technology and applied research, it has been frequently pointed out (e.g., Tuska, 1957) that the individual, fertile originator remains the crucial factor in scientific progress; and this applies even more strongly in theoretical fields, perhaps especially in mathematics (Hadamard, 1945). On the whole, therefore, one would expect that the ability, characteristic of introverts, to withdraw, to exclude the outside world in long periods of concentrated thought and speculation, would outweigh in creative scientists (and even more in creative artists) the superior ability of the extravert to communicate socially. This is indeed what was generally found.

On the other hand, to say that creative scientists appear from the biographical evidence to be introverted rather than extraverted is too simple a statement and needs some qualification. The very broad second-order concepts of introversion and extraversion are useful for a first approximation, but can conceal as much as they illuminate, and a description in terms of primary factors may be needed to make the picture clearer and more consistent. Certainly, this seems to be so for eminent scientists. The general tendency to introversion just mentioned does not apply to all the components, but seems to be largely concentrated in the A factor, of which a detailed description was given in Chapter 4. Our reference in this section to the apparently introverted nature of Lord Cavendish, Dalton, and others was mainly referable to a typical A— character, skeptical, withdrawn, unsociable, critical, precise. Cavendish's biographer, for instance, gives a vivid picture of his dislike of formal, pretentious social gatherings and describes one occasion when, required to meet eminent foreign scientists, he broke away and ran down the corridor "squeaking like a bat"! But if it appears to be generally true from the study of biographies that eminent scientists have been low on Factor A, the same is not true of another component of introversion-extraversion, Factor H. Here the strong impression is that they are, in general, well up at the positive end of the scale, with high "parasympathetic immunity," and displaying a characteristic resourcefulness, adaptability, and adventurousness (probably largely constitutional). On Factor F, however (Surgency-Desurgency), one gets the overwhelming impression that eminent scientists of the past have been low (desurgent), compared with the general population and with many particular professions and callings. One has only to think, for instance, of Pascal, William Hamilton, Newton, Boyle, Dalton, and Faraday to form the opinion that introspection, restraint, brooding, and solemnity of manner, all indicators of desurgency, have been highly characteristic.

These observations suggest a certain paradoxical structure within the general introversion second stratum factor, in that traits that generally tend to correlate positively in the general population may very well correlate negatively among creative scientists, and this may be the basis of Kretschmer's notion of "warring heredity," in that such people appear to have a constitutionally low susceptibility to inhibition, as would be shown by a low score on Factor H, while yet being highly inhibited, as would be shown by a low score on Factor F. Similarly, it may be noted that Abeim (*The Psychology of the Philosopher*) found a high degree of inhibition to be characteristic, though not so generally combined (as in scientists) with an essentially dominant personality.

So much for the apparently rather complex question of introversion. The general impression of stability among scientists requires less discussion. One must agree with Terman that, among scientists at least, the average level of ego strength and emotional stability is noticeably higher among creative geniuses than among the general population, though it is possibly lower than among men of comparable intelligence and education who go into administrative and similar positions. High anxiety and excitability appear common (e.g., Priestley, Darwin, Kepler), but full-blown neurosis quite rare.

To digress for a moment, it is probably in this respect that creative scientists and artists diverge most markedly. Among the latter, particularly perhaps in the nineteenth and twentieth centuries, neurotic, psychotic, and addictive tendencies are so frequent as hardly to need illustration. This applies least, perhaps, to composers, though from Beethoven to Ravel, Bartok, and Peter Warlock (Philip Heseltine) their lives have often been stormy or unhappy. The tendency among writers, from Flaubert, Ruskin, Nietzsche, and Strindberg in the nineteenth century to Proust, Eugene O'Neill, and Dylan Thomas in the twentieth is clearer, and possibly clearest of all among painters (Van Gogh, Utrillo, Modigliani). Many different explanations, temperamental, sociological, and economic, could be given for this greater susceptibility to nervous disorder among artistic than among scientific geniuses. In this sphere the "great wits to madness near allied" contention has most plausibility, but has little explanatory value. The topic is a fascinating one, and a gram or two of scientific research would be welcome in contrast to the mountains of romantic speculation that have been piled up.

Returning to the characteristics of creative scientists, one or two further features stood out from a wide reading of their biographies. They appeared to have the socially rather uncongenial and "undemocratic" attitudes, associated with dominance, E, and perhaps also with the L factor. We have already described somewhat similar findings by Roe and by Barron. This dominance, amounting to a belief that most people are rather stupid, seems to be the root of a rugged independence of mind, and a readiness to face endless difficulties and social discouragement, which are needed in any pursuit of a completely novel project. Last, these people have a quite exceptional degree of *intellectual* self-sufficiency. They depart freely from all the customary judgments of the world, yet are not appalled by their isolation. They appear, indeed, barely to notice that they are eccentric, and they expect as a natural right the freedom to be "odd" that they themselves would fairly grant to others, but that the average man is often quite unwilling to grant. In personality research, a dimension of this kind, labeled Q_2 in our series, has long been known. It is interesting to see that what it usually connotes—a rich supply of inner resources and interests—is typically present in the biographical evidence, too.

To cut short what really justifies a wide anecdotal illustration, we summarize the personality profile that appears to have distinguished the creative scientist from both the average man and the professional man successful in a routine occupation. It is a profile of schizothyme hardness, high intelligence, stability, dominance, desurgent taciturnity, and high self-sufficiency.

SUMMARY *of Chapter Fourteen*

1. Creativity, although not easily definable, is of great importance, both in the advance of civilization and in the smooth running of society. It may be manifested in a wide range of situations and at widely differing levels, from discovering the structure of an atom to laying out a garden.

2. The generality of the concept and the difficulties of assessment have

contributed to the relative neglect of creativity in the past, but they have not been the only reasons for this neglect. Some evidence indicates that teachers have often been too narrowly concerned with more conventional aspects of ability and have preferred relatively less creative children.

3. Various sources of information, including psychological surveys and the biographies of scientists and artists, suggest that both cognitive and temperamental components are important in the prediction of creativity.

4. On the cognitive side, the work of Guilford has provided a useful classification of kinds of ability that has a logical, as distinct from a purely empirical, basis, i.e., the classification does *not* correspond to that which would be made on the basis of simple structure primary abilities and the natural second stratum ordering which arises among them. But by analyzing abilities into factors that are at a more specific level than those of most other investigators, he has also thrown light on the particular aspects of ability that are most closely allied to creative thought, and which need to be factored in future objective analyses.

5. The personality correlates of creativity have been studied in two main ways: biographically, by the study of the lives of eminent scientists and artists; and empirically, by the administration and analysis of personality questionnaires and other tests. The two methods in general suggest similar findings.

6. Neither the biographical nor the empirical studies confirm the "great wits are sure to madness near allied" theory of an association between creativity and neurosis. It appears, on the contrary, that the temperamental stability of eminent scientists in particular is above average, though they may often be high in anxiety. For artists, the position is less clear and requires further research.

7. On the broad second-order factor of introversion-extraversion, it appears that creativity is on the whole more often allied to introversion. But this statement conceals differences between possible patterns of introversion. The main tendency, at least in eminent scientists, appears to be high sizothymia (Factor A—), as evidenced by skeptical, withdrawn, unsociable behavior.

8. The typical personality pattern found in eminent research scientists appears to be one also of high (but not necessarily exceptionally high) intelligence, dominance, desurgent taciturnity, and self-sufficiency.

Chapter Fifteen

THE PREDICTION, SELECTION, AND CULTIVATION OF CREATIVITY

Section 1   The General Problems in Fostering Creativity

From the general introduction in the previous chapter, we may conclude that four main tasks await those who would foster creativity:

1. Selecting persons who can safely be predicted to be highly creative
2. Educating thought processes to maximize creativity
3. Setting up special institutions to support creative work
4. Providing suitable working conditions and incentives in such institutions and elsewhere.

The prescribed area of this book is strictly the first of these. Yet because no facet can be well understood in isolation, and because selection cannot be accurately undertaken unless we know the conditions for which we are selecting, we shall begin this chapter with a discussion of institutions and conditions and later work back to the first two points.

From the Middle Ages until this generation, the university has been looked upon as the institution for cherishing and stimulating creative work in scientific and philosophical, and to some extent in literary and artistic, fields. For much of this time, the churches also played their part, with varying felicity, according to whether a Michelangelo or a Galileo was involved. Because of the conservatism or inadequate organization of such institutions, however, creative genius has always had to make its own way, alone and largely unsupported. Increasingly, however, since the foundation of the Royal Society in Britain and of the Academy in France in the seventeenth century, scientific, literary, and artistic societies have been offering some moral and even material support to highly creative individuals. But it is certain that these institutions have succeeded in giving opportunities for successful expression to only a fraction of the talented people available.

So much has been written about wasted talent, and so rapid has been the growth of universities in recent times, that it would be easy to assume complacently that the needs of creative ability will henceforth be well met. The chief reasons for doubting this are:

1. Human reactions to disturbing new ideas have changed very little.

2. The universities, though often explicitly founded for both "the advancement and the propagation of knowledge," have always been dominated by the second, i.e., the teaching function. The students are always there, and the ideas are not. Furthermore, the rapid increase in this generation in the endowment of universities and the consequent astonishing increase in the percentage of the population taught in them have brought a corresponding increase in attention to the teaching function.

The prosperity of our times is not primarily the result of better education, and still less of any great improvement in conducting business intelligently, but is largely the result of scientific discoveries by a few creative men. It is, therefore, a matter of simple self-interest to any community—quite apart from more lofty considerations—to plow back an appreciable proportion of this increased wealth into the support and encouragement of creative scientists.

To a gratifying degree in the United States, Germany, Russia, and Sweden, and to a recognizable degree in Australia, Britain, France, Italy, and other countries, a fraction of the community gain has been fed back to the goose that lays the golden eggs. Not all this fraction has been fed in the right way to the right geese. A great deal of money for research, both in Britain and America, goes to professors too harassed by heavy loads of teaching and administration to make the best use of it. Admittedly, some enterprising universities (neither Harvard and Yale nor Oxford and Cambridge excel in this respect) have set up research professors in their science departments and leading painters and composers in their art and music departments. But even these relatively few and apparently fortunate individuals are only too often isolated in the wrong sense in universities as they are currently organized. Relative freedom from administrative duties frequently means that the administrative machine pays little regard to their interests. Almost universally, too, they find it impossible to climb the university promotion ladder without veering abruptly between alternate spells of research and teaching. This situation has arisen from adherence to the rarely challenged shibboleth that the best teacher is also the best researcher and creative scholar. The time has come for an objective and unprejudiced examination of this bland formula. For whom and for what is this sedulously fostered type of intellectual amphibian "best"? Is it true that the best teacher from the standpoint of the undergraduate's needs (in large classes that every high-school graduate may attend) is also the most original scholar? If it is good for the teacher to be a researcher, is it also necessarily good for the researcher to be a teacher? These are questions that urgently require dispassionate reconsideration—

reconsideration unhampered by traditional preconceptions. There is no reason why they should not be answered by psychological and educational research.

Section 2 **For What Working Conditions Are We Selecting Creative Individuals?**

What then is the best environment for creative work? Certainly, the current academic environment has serious drawbacks. Teaching traffic may disturb and distract from research concentration, and, in particular, the simplified, dramatized presentations of undergraduate teaching may conflict with the subtlety and tolerance of ambiguity necessary in research. It may well be, therefore, that as far as research is concerned, the role of the university should be that of a proving ground, in which the good researcher and the good teacher can give demonstration of their respective talents. Between the ages of thirty and forty, the individual of proven flair in research should perhaps be directed to an institution shaped purely for research work. Such institutions, exemplified in the Rockefeller Institute, the Max Planck Institutes in Germany, and the various pure research centers formed by private enterprise, e.g., the Salk Institute and the Stanford Research Center, have sprung up rapidly, as experiments in a new form of organization, in the last fifty years.

Some appreciable light on the conditions required for creative work has been thrown by experimental investigation in the last few years. This has supported, as far as the main outlines are concerned, reports in the autobiographies of a series of creative men—Poincaré in mathematics; Kekulé in chemistry; Cannon, Carrel, and Pasteur in physiology; Rutherford in physics; and many a literary and artistic genius.

These men describe a period of immersion in the problem, in which they familiarize themselves with all the relevant facts (or, in the case of the artist, the moods and half-unconscious indications). At this stage, they deliberately avoid any premature solution and try to hold in balance a rich variety of alternative directions of solution. Of this stage, Kuhn (1963) well says "ability to support a tension that can occasionally become almost unbearable is one of the prize requisites for the very best sort of scientific research."

After this, a period of withdrawal from the problem ideally follows. This incubation period, however, must not be filled with any strenuous mental activity of a different kind. It is an intellectual gestation period, in which even vigorous discussion of the problem itself with others would be as inappropriate as acrobatics for a woman in late pregnancy. During this period energy is needed in the unconscious, to develop, to rearrange, to wipe out the errors of conscious logic and those "errors of the market place" and

common semantics described by Francis Bacon. From this period of con-
solidation and unconscious invention there will finally spring into conscious-
ness, if the creative process goes well, the inspirational solution. And as these
creative persons have recorded, it may come at the most untimely places—
as the behavior of his bath water brought the cry "Eureka!" from Archimedes.

Thus considering the teaching institution as a place of research, one per-
ceives how different the conditions for effective teaching and effective research may be. For undergraduate teaching, one must simplify, and draw a
picture in black and white; for research, one must watch for every faint clue
and listen attentively to a whole symphony of theories. There is the danger
that when an investigator has made a good, simplified point in class three
times, he will begin to believe it himself! And whereas the teacher does best
to keep to a timetable, the creative worker needs his incubation periods.
When overtaken by the birth pangs of a new concept, he must avoid a still-
birth, even though it means ignoring the committee meeting previously set at
that hour. Fortunately, the issue of whether the best mental makeup for
teacher and researcher is the same is not one to be bandied endlessly in
debate. It can be settled by research. And the evidence in the following
sections shows important personality differences.

If these views are valid, it follows that the university may most advantageously recognize two kinds of specialist in its ranks. Probably the retention
of the single teacher-researcher type is necessary up to a certain age. For as
we have suggested above, the university faculty may well play the role of a
nursery and proving ground to permit later emergence of the two specialized
types. Surveys suggest that not until thirty-five or forty years of age can the
candidates for each type be recognized with reasonable confidence, and it is
only then that one can decide with some reliability who has the bent for
sustained research creativity and who has the mellow gifts of a first-rate
teacher. Whether, at that point, it may be desirable to have special institutions
for the researchers is a matter to be settled by research on research (or
"zetetics" as Tyckociner has named it). Experience with the Max Planck
Institutes in Germany, the Royal Society Research Professorships in England, and the above-mentioned remarkable growth of basic research laboratories sustained by private enterprise in America, may well show that creativity reaches its most effective expression in institutions separate from teaching
institutions, planned to provide for research and creativity as a way of lfe.

Because most of our discussions so far has been devoted to creativity in
science, one should not assume that literary, artistic, musical, managerial,
ethical, and other kinds of creativity have not been kept in mind. Although
an Edison or a Marconi may pay his own way, it is largely true that basic
scientific and philosophical discoveries are not self-supporting, whereas literature and the arts may often be highly remunerative. This is one reason,

though clearly not the only one, why special institutes are more appropriate to scientific research. On the other hand, both the principles for selecting creative people and the working conditions and roles for which selection has to be carried out appear to be not so very different for the various areas of creativity.

In science, and in existing research institutions, surveys have been made of the conditions that people consider desirable. The needs of genius are not unique; they are largely echoed by anyone doing research work of any importance. As Taylor (1964), Knapp (1963), Thistlethwaite (1963), Chorness and Nottelmann (1957), and others indicate, individual freedom to follow the problem wherever it may lead is highly prized. So also is that freedom from interruption that we have seen to be essential to the incubation process. But in the existing institutional situations we see also some problems of organization and incentive not stated by the free-lance scientist.

One point of particular importance is the difficulty that the young researcher meets in obtaining close, apprentice-like contact with distinguished leaders, and this is a further reason for not inflicting on the latter a heavy load of administration and routine teaching. It may well be—as we discuss in Section 5 below—that little can really be done to "train" for creativity, but what little learning can occur must occur largely through this close association with successfully creative people in solving problems. Research of any importance and creative thought in general are not a matter of intellectual tricks and classroom-acquired procedures, but spiritual activities, tied to value systems and ways of life best acquired by living association. Creativity is perhaps best acquired by association with creativity. For whatever time the individual has to spare between completing examinations and launching his self-directed researches he may well be much better occupied in a research assistantship or associateship than in an unattached "fellowship." The procedures of prediction and selection that we recommend are thus aimed at finding an individual who, after his apprenticeship, can function effectively in an atmosphere of self-directing freedom, with minimal teaching or managerial duties.

Section 3 Defining the Creativity Criterion

From discussion in early chapters, the reader will realize that although various modes of estimating the criterion from tests exists, such as, for example, the adjustment model and the effectiveness calculation, the psychologist can get nowhere without a firm criterion to predict. Seldom has psychology been asked to undertake so ambitious a task as that of defining the creativity criterion. If getting a reliable criterion for "success as a bus driver" has its difficulties, it will be evident that obtaining a criterion score on "creativity" to check the predictive power of our tests is going to present formidable conceptual and practical problems.

For safety, one should perhaps first work with creativity separately and operationally defined in each specific field. However, the fact evidenced below that substantially the same personality factors predict creativity as defined in science and art strongly suggests that because the criteria themselves are so positively correlated we shall find them to contain a strong common factor, i.e., creativity may prove a very similar thing across many fields.

Up to this point, we have been content to define creativity in a general way. It has been the creativity of developing new concepts in scientific research and the originality to produce the experimental means to test them, or it has been invention, or artistic and literary production, or even originality at lower intellectual levels in how to farm a hillside or to solve some problems in a mailman's round. As we approach measurement, the criterion necessarily has to become more precise.

Originality in its simple logical sense of responding with something "new and different" or creativity in its root sense of "producing" are obviously not intended here. Both are far too broad and could characterize thousands of inept, bizarre, or simply false responses. As in biological mutations, so in cultural mutations, the great majority of innovations that could be made would be lethal mistakes. Some adaptation or usefulness is therefore implied in the use of "creativity" in the present concept. We shall define it as that which enables us to reach desired goals in a more effective way. (In the group context, this will include finding individual goals that have more group-survival value than existing individual values).

Obviously, a score of a performance simply for oddity of response will not meet this definition. Failure to realize the high percentage of wrong responses in random cerebration, and the lack of "depth" in uninhibited free associations, has been responsible, incidentally, for a gross overvaluation of "brainstorming" committee sessions. Sheer oddity of response, as Eysenck's research on inkblot responses and our own studies in objective personality tests have shown, is more characteristic of the neurotic, brain-damaged, and the pathological failure generally. It is this same failure to recognize the difference between the new response that is merely new and the new response that has peculiar adaptive value that partly accounts for the folklore belief that insanity and genius are closely allied. As Saunders reports (1963), "[attempts to predict creativity] by scoring the remote, uncommon response gave us nothing." When Disraeli referred to a political opponent as affected by "a constipation of ideas and a diarrhoea of words," he was making this important distinction. Although these points may seem obvious, they have sometimes been neglected by psychologists who overemphasize fluency as a constituent of creativity.

When we seek to apply the criterion of adaptiveness across all fields of cultural creativity, we at once encounter the unfortunate fact that it is far easier to apply in science, in mechanical invention, and in politics, than it is in literature, art, or music. A moon rocket works or it does not. Whether a painting on the wall of the Guggenheim Museum deserves to be there or not may be determined by which school of art is politically in the ascendant. At best, one can take a poll of the percentage of people who claim a spiritual experience from it. One may be convinced that there really is a sense in which a work of art reaches certain adaptive standards and thereby achieves a potent emotional message, but, as psychologists, we must admit that today we do not know how to evaluate this criterion and that our attempts to be objective are premature.

Present treatment of the criterion must therefore be confined to scientific creativity, and even here the difficulties are great. The human evaluation still intervenes to some extent. We may doubt that the most creative scientist is always the one who receives most acclaim from his fellows. For the kind of originality most liked is that which makes an impressive splash but is not fundamentally disturbing and "controversial." Shall we then score creativity by the number of scientific research articles published? Or score most highly the scientist who makes the largest number of inventions that prove patentable? It is easier to make fun of the crudity of such criteria than it is to find effective substitutes. Scholars who publish little or who regret the pressures of competitiveness, are apt to assert that there is an inverse relation between quantity and quality of publication. What evidence does exist, however, makes this claim doubtful, or at least not of universal application.

In this dilemma, one obvious and easy solution is to add all the scores—ratings by contemporary specialists on quality of output, amount of output, patents—and so to obtain a single total score. But here we encounter the difficulty, recently revealed by the work of Taylor, that many of these subcriteria may be quite uncorrelated.

Taylor's (1957) correlation and factor analysis shows at least eight sources of criterion evaluation with practically zero intercorrelation, as follows.

1. Originality and significance of reports as rated by experts (this also has loading in patent rate and effective suggestions within the laboratory)

2. Creativity as seen by head people in the same organization

3. Ratings of personal qualities of flexibility, independence, cooperativeness as made by immediate supervisors

4. Productivity rated in the laboratory by peers

5. Creativity counted by publications. This also loads consultantship activities and *un*cooperativeness as rated by supervisor

6. Awards, participation in conference papers, number of people supervised (with some negative relation to originality in the first source mentioned)

7. Quality of finish in organizational reports

8. Popularity and likeableness

The above analysis is based on 166 scientists at government basic research centers. As Taylor observes, the features that strikes one most is the poor agreement even between such sources of evaluation as supervisors and laboratory chiefs. Other less extensive data, e.g., our own and Harmon's (1963), suggest that Taylor's orthogonal analysis has removed a slight general positive relation among these sources, but that with this proviso his conclusions are probably typical. The theory of instrument factors (Cattell, 1961) should reconcile us to the expectation that different groups and situations of raters will throw in prejudiced observations from each special angle. Similarly, the theory of ipsative scoring (page 205) should make us realize that whenever there is a limiting total shared by all scores—in this case that there are only twenty-four hours in a day—the correlations of diverse performance will approach a negative value. In simple words, although a general potential excellence may exist in men, if more time spent on X involves less time spent on Y, the result will be that excellence in actual performance over a diversity of fields will not be general.

The often noted mutual interference of research and organizational activities and of social (conference activity and conference rewards) with publication contributions stands out clearly in such analyses of criteria. Because a value judgment—or at least a definition of creativity—is unavoidable, we would argue that the criterion we are seeking is best represented by No. 1 above—namely, ratings of originality and significance of work by high-level scientists, together with number of patents and so forth, when scorable—and by No. 5, i.e., the number of research articles good enough to be accepted by reputable journals. Indeed, the product of 1 and 5, of quality ("level") by quantity ("extent"), might make the best possible single index. Much of the rest is a farrago of local popularity, political activity in national societies, personality ratings that have no proven relation to creativity, and time spent in peer interaction.

In such a proposed criterion, however, one weakness remains—that inherent in the rating for significance of scientific work even by the most intelligent and highly qualified raters who are remote from the disturbing local effects. We cannot escape from using human judgment, but with sufficient ingenuity we may find ways of partialing systematic errors in human judgment out of the final evaluation. Probably the two greatest systematic sources of error are : (1) the evaluation of what belongs to the future by concepts that belong to the present and the past; (2) the overvaluation of what can be understood by the many at the expense of what can only be understood by the few.

Research needs to be conducted on evaluations of diverse scientific contributions at, say, ten-year intervals, in the hope that we can locate those elements in contemporary evaluations that characteristically agree better with the evaluations made ten years later. Similarly, we should aim to partial out the popularity effect by finding what discoveries decline in importance as we go from the ratings of the average professional group to those of the most eminent researchers—and then subtract something of this even from the latter evaluations, because they also will not be entirely free from the same error. Undoubtedly, the next few years will see improvements along these lines for Factor 1 in the above criterion pool. Meanwhile, we must treat many published studies of the relation of this or that to "creativity" with a wary eye regarding the criterion of creativity in the given study.

Section 4 Creativity Prediction by Psychological Tests Aimed at a "Creative Type"

It is necessary to bear in mind the distinction between *adjustment* and *effectiveness* calculations of fitness for a task. In the former, we ask what characteristics distinguish the person in the job from those in other jobs. In the latter, we obtain regression coefficients of personality, ability, and motivation factors upon a criterion of effectiveness or efficiency among those actually in the job. Both these criteria have been used in research on creativity. With a few exceptions, however, both have very often been studied with *ad hoc* scales and supposed measures of creative ability of unknown factor composition and meaning, so that psychological insight and generalization have been impaired. Among the exceptions are the studies of Drevdahl ("adjustment" criterion), Jones, Chambers, and Tollefson ("effectiveness" criterion).

The first study using primary personality factors (as described in Chapter 4) was carried out by Drevdahl (1956) with graduate students. His criterion was the creativity shown by these students in essays, research, and class discussion, as evaluated by professors familiar with them. He found statistically significant differences between students of high and low creativity on the 16 PF test in that the former were more schizothyme (A—), self-sufficient (Q_2), desurgent (F—), and radical (Q_1).

The more extensive study that was next made was concerned specifically with creativity in the scientific field. A careful search was made for 46 leading research physicists, 46 distinguished research biologists, and 52 productive researchers in psychology (all selected by committees in their particular fields, and all of whom completed both A and B forms of the 16 PF Questionnaire). A full account of this investigation is given elsewhere (Cattell and Drevdahl, 1955), but chief among the questions that can be asked are:

1. In what way does the personality profile of the creative scientists differ from that of the average man?

2. How does it differ from persons of equal intelligence and similar education whose eminence is in teaching or administration rather than research?

3. How is the profile of those talented in science different from that of innovators in radically different areas, as in art and literature?

The answer to the first question is shown in Figure 14, from which it will be seen at once that the personality profile is very different from that of the average man (indicated by the central dark band), no fewer than five factors deviating at a $P = 0.01$ significance or beyond.

FIGURE **14**

Mean 16 PF profile of eminent researchers (N = 144) in physics, biology, and psychology

Personality dimension label at lower pole	Mean stens	PLOTTED MEAN STEN SCORES 1 2 3 4 5 6 7 8 9 10	Personality dimension label at upper pole	
A— Sizothymia	3.36		Affectothymia	A+
B— Low intelligence	7.64		High intelligence	B+
C— Low ego strength	5.44		High ego strength	C+
E— Low dominance	6.62		High dominance	E+
F— Desurgency	3.15		Surgency	F+
G— Low group superego	4.10		High group superego	G+
H— Threctia	6.01		Parmia	H+
I— Harria	7.05		Premsia	I+
L— Low protension	5.36		High protension	L+
M— Praxernia	5.36		Autia	M+
N— Simplicity	5.50		Shrewdness	N+
O— Low guilt-proneness	4.38		High guilt-proneness	O+
Q1— Conservatism	7.00		Radicalism	Q1+
Q2— Low self-sufficiency	7.52		High self-sufficiency	Q2+
Q3— Low self-sentiment	6.44		High self-sentiment	Q3+
Q4— Low ergic tension	4.91		High ergic tension	Q4+

NOTE: A new "control" group for the general adult male population has become available since this profile was first published. The slight changes in norms do not affect the stated conclusions.

Moreover, the differences in every case support, through measures on contemporary research leaders, the kind and direction of deviation we had inferred from the biographical accounts of historically important researchers. Notably, the researcher is decidedly more sizothyme, more intelligent, more dominant, and more inhibited or desurgent. As we pass toward the bottom of the diagram, into dimensions we have not previously discussed, we notice other divided peaks and troughs indicating that researchers are also significantly more emotionally sensitive $(I+)$, more radical (Q_1+), and somewhat more given to controlling their behavior by an exacting self-concept. It is noteworthy that insofar as the conclusions from our different instruments can overlap, Anne Roe's results, already described in the previous chapter, and our own are in essential agreement.

As far as comparison with the general population is concerned, physicists, biologists, and psychologists are close together and form one family. However, if space permitted, we could study some interesting minor differences, e.g., the finding that the physicists are even more sizothyme than other researchers, and the psychologists (perhaps we should say with embarrassment!), more dominant and less desurgent.

In answer to our second question, it is clear that, when compared with the general population, eminent researchers have a good deal in common with those who have achieved an outstanding reputation for teaching and administration. For example, both are decidedly above the population average in ego strength, intelligence, dominance, and social obligation as shown in the self-sentiment. Nevertheless, it would be foolish to leave out of our calculations, or our selection formulas, whatever makes for high achievement *as such,* regardless of field. In separating the potential creative researcher from the equally able administrator and scholar, we must discern where to drive in the wedge. At the one-per-cent significance level, researchers are more sizothyme, less emotionally stable, more self-sufficient, more bohemian, and more radical than are successful administrators and teachers. Compared next with the general college population from which they come (using the general undergraduate population norms), researchers are again more sizothyme and more intelligent, more self-sufficient, more withdrawn, more paranoid and anxious, and more inhibited (F−).

When we consider second-order personality factors, the most striking fact is that the researcher is uniformly lower on all primary personality factors involved in the second-order *extraversion* factor. On the implications of this decided introversion of the researcher, we shall have more to say in a moment. But there is a relevant, detailed discussion by Broadbent (1958) of the application of information theory to brain action, in which one of his main propositions is that as long as you use a lot of the channels for input, you have too few free channels for scanning. That could explain a good deal here. The typical extravert conceivably has too many channels taking in information—or at least, alert to the external trivia of everyday life—and not enough for scanning accepted material. Or, to quote Wordsworth instead of information theory: "The world is too much with us." And if we paraphrase his next line: "Talking and visiting, we lay waste our powers."

Let us turn to the third question, namely, "To what extent are creative persons in one field like those in another, e.g., those in science like those in the arts?" (Or, in other words, "Is the creative personality a recognizable type despite differences in the area of operation?"). Here we again receive a definite answer.

In the first place, within science itself, we have evidence from the work of Jones (1964, 1966) on groups very different from the leading academic researchers here considered. With groups of chemists and chemical engineers in New England, 45 and 35 of whom were very carefully rated for their creativity and inventiveness in the work situation, he obtained correlations with personality factors as shown:

	C	E	G	H	O	Q_1	Q_2	Q_3	Q_4
Chemists	.27*	.64*	—.29	.48*	—.64*	.64*	.04	.43*	—.49*
Engineers	.38*	.28*	—.07	.27*	—.43*	.38*	.40*	.24*	—.29*

It is interesting to compare this also with the correlations obtained by Meredith for creativity on students ($N = 162$) as measured by the Maddi SPI:

A	B	C	E	F	G	H	I	L	M	N	O	Q_1	Q_2
—.04	.17*	.08	.27**	.06	—.25**	.11	.24**	—.03	.35**	.05	—.14	.17*	.19*

Q_3	Q_4
—.06	—.12

A commendably large sample for contrasting creative areas was investigated by Chambers (1964, 1966), who checked the relation to personality factors E, H, and Q_2 on 400 chemists and 340 psychologists, carefully evaluated for creativity. The general findings for E and Q_2 stood up on both samples, with *t* values ranging from 2 to 5. Unfortunately, the full range of source traits on the 16 PF was not included, but the importance of high dominance, E, and high self-sufficiency can be considered now thrice demonstrated.

Finally, we can look at the pooled results of the most substantial research (in numbers, criterion objectivity, and breadth of personality factors involved) yet accomplished in this area, combining the Drevdahl, Jones, Tollefson, and Chambers findings and comparing pure and applied researchers (Figure 15).

As more research on creativity is done, increasing the accuracy of determination of personality by using two or more forms of the 16 PF, and by extending measurement to include motivation factors in the MAT, it will become appropriate to concentrate on what test factor weights determine creativity in different fields. At present, we have to deal only with "indications" of differences, but the common pattern is strongly evident. The latter is not necessarily that of an accommodating and popular personality, and its qualities of independence and forthrightness would commonly evoke the criticism "tactless." As Lowell Kelly's results with medical men show, this pattern of personality tends to be subjected to group antipathy and derogation. Central in it is a dominant independence, E, some high inhibition (in F, not unlike that in the neurotic), low conformity (on G), high self-sufficiency (Q_2), high adventurousness (H), high radicalism (Q_1), and tough disregard for sentimentality (A—). (The high premsia, I, seems to be characteristic of certain groups, e.g., it is marked in Meredith's students, and in Drevdahl's artists, but absent, as a true *contributor* to the criterion, from Jones' chemists and engineers of mature years. (Possibly it is a necessary youthful "process variable.")

FIGURE 15

Profile of Basic and Applied (Industrial) Researchers*

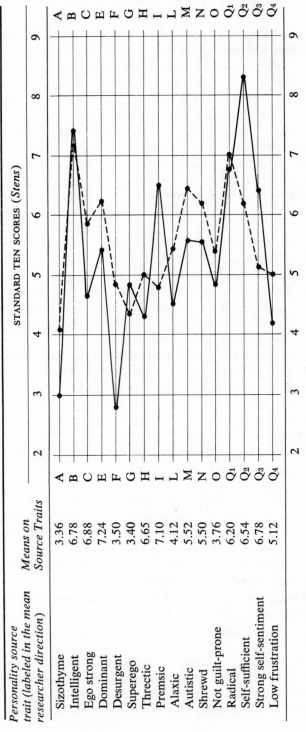

Personality source trait (labeled in the mean researcher direction)		Means on Source Traits
Sizothyme	A	3.36
Intelligent	B	6.78
Ego strong	C	6.88
Dominant	E	7.24
Desurgent	F	3.50
Superego	G	3.40
Threctic	H	6.65
Premsic	I	7.10
Alaxic	L	4.12
Autistic	M	5.52
Shrewd	N	5.50
Not guilt-prone	O	3.76
Radical	Q₁	6.20
Self-sufficient	Q₂	6.54
Strong self-sentiment	Q₃	6.78
Low frustration	Q₄	5.12

Academic creative researchers ————

Industrial, applied creative researchers ------

* This combines with suitable weighting results from the Cattell, Chambers, Drevdahl, Jones, and Tollefson researches referred to in the text.

An equally clear answer can now be given, through the work of Drevdahl, to the question of whether creativity in the arts depends on similar personalities or very different ones. A study of 153 writers of imaginative literature (Drevdahl and Cattell, 1958) shows a profile on the 16 PF that, by any pattern similarity coefficient (an index designed to express overall similarity between two profiles), would definitely be placed in the same family as the profiles for the creative scientists; and the same is true of artists, taken from persons listed in *Who's Who in American Art*. This similarity also holds, as Drevdahl (1956) has shown, for those who are graduate students in the field of liberal arts and who are selected as highly creative.

In setting up these experiments, we had actually expected some major differences between those talented in science and those creative in the arts. Doubtless, further search will reveal other dimensions, but even on these primary dimensions a few statistically significant differences can be found. For example, artists and literary men provide some contrast with scientists in being more bohemian (M factor), more emotionally sensitive (I factor), and at a higher ergic tension level (Q_4 factor) (Cross, Cattell, and Butcher, 1967). This may well be a more specific statement of that general tendency to greater instability and emotionality that Terman found in historical instances of men eminent in the arts, compared with those eminent in the sciences. However, the emotional "instability" or "immaturity" here is that of the high I factor rather than ego weakness (C—). That autism (M factor), the tendency to follow through one's inmost urges regardless of external demands, should distinguish artistic from scientific creativity is exactly what one would expect from an analysis of the essential differences between these types of creativity. The creativity of the scientist is always tempered by a host of brutally unsympathetic and inexorable facts, for his theory must always in some sense work out in practice. The higher ergic tension of the artist may sustain the conclusion that the artist is a more frustrated person, or that high anxiety is less inimical to artistic than to scientific production.

Although such differences of personality and motivation between artistic, scientific, and other areas of creativity can be found and will doubtless continue to be found in more refined studies, the really remarkable feature of these research findings, especially for our present concentrated survey, is the high degree of similarity and consistency of the personality picture across *all* areas. It would almost seem as if the differences between science, art, and literature are differences of particular skills and interests only, and that the fundamental characteristic of the creative, original person is a type of personality.

It is on this basis that we have argued above that the diversity of criterion factors found by Taylor is likely to converge on one general second-order creativity factor, loading particularly his primaries 1 and 7, for in all these diverse fields of performance there is evidently something substantially in common.

Section **5** **Creativity Prediction by Regression on a Criterion of Effectiveness Within a Research Group**

So far we have asked what distinguishes the *type* of the creative student, in terms of abilities and personality traits, from the average one, or from the equally intelligent but uncreative adult. But let us now turn to the alternative examination by a *weighting of attributes* calculation. The weakness of the adjustment criterion is that it merely defines who stays in the job, and that it indicates not only those who are good at that job but also inevitably to some extent those who have failed alternative jobs. For example, it used to be not uncommon to find among psychology students some who had wanted to follow a science but had failed the mathematics necessary for chemistry or physics. And we have all heard of academic men who became administrators because they failed to find a successful research trail.

It is conceivable, of course, that a person in research is a failed teacher, but there are reasons for believing that the selection that has produced the personality profile typical of research workers is not, in the main, a backfiring selection. It is a selection tending to concentrate in the field the people who are better at it. However, the defects in the "job adjustment" profile assumptions make it vital also to have data showing the relation of personality factors and actual research effectiveness. We need, in fact, data in terms of regression of personality measures upon a criterion of research productivity. Usually, we seek at first a linear regression equation, but it can progress to nonlinear prediction. What data we have so far are as precious as they are fragmentary. But at least these exploratory studies, e.g., by Jones and Cattell (1966), Tollefson (1961), and Chambers (1964) on predictors and by Taylor (1955, 1957) and his colleagues on the criteria, are highly encouraging.

Among the first studies of research efficiency or productivity measured on the job, one should note that of Van Zelst and Kerr (1954), who found, among other characteristics of productive researchers, a disbelief in egalitarian "committee-like" practices in research groups and a need for withdrawal and cogitation. This finding again appears reasonably in line with the personality characteristics we have already shown to be typical.

A first study to deal with well-known, replicable personality factors is that of Tollefson (1961), measuring fifty-three Ph.D. chemists in the research department of a nationally known oil company. Here the indicated correlations between primary factors on the 16 PF and rated magnitude of contribution to research were as in the following specification equation:

$$\text{Research Performance} = .25B + .46C + .32E - .46I + .33N + 45Q_1 + .29Q_2 - .35[1]$$

[1] This is a constant added so that when the individual's 16 PF scores are entered as stens the performance estimates will come out in stens. When the regressions are zero, the factor is not entered.

Here B is General Intelligence, C is Ego Strength, E is dominance, I is Emotional Sensitivity, N is Shrewdness, Q_1 is Radicalism, Q_2 is Self-Sufficiency. The criterion in this study was based partly on the number of papers produced and partly on their rated importance. This is reasonably in line with what would be expected from the differences between researchers and other academics listed in the preceding section, except for Source Trait I, Premsia-versus-Harria, which needs comment. Evidence is accumulating that the I source-trait dimension is related to early home background. It appears that 95 per cent of the variance arises from environmental determination and only 5 per cent from hereditary determination. So far as preliminary evidence can show, the increase of Premsia, i.e., of protected emotional sensitivity, has to do with overprotection and indulgence in childhood. Because this factor was found by Cattell and his associates to be negatively related to various kinds of achievement, and by Cattell and Stice (1960) to be related to "hindering" and "self-centeredness" in small group behavior, it is hard to interpret the rather high I found in academic researchers (not, be it noted, with industrial researchers) as advantageous. More likely, we are dealing here with an incidental and nonuseful characteristic of academic selection!

However, before any dependable conclusions can be drawn about the causes of differences of pattern between job adjustment profile and the criterion performance profile, it is necessary to study further groups; one can readily conceive that the specification equation quoted will apply to all kinds of research performance. The work of F. E. Jones has provided us with fairly substantial checks on the personality and ability regressions for industrial research creativity, and the planned continuation of his work to larger, cross-checking samples and the inclusion of motivation measures such as the MAT may yield still more complete predictive powers.

Working with an exploratory sample of 45 research chemists of mature years, in industry, he found that Ego Strength, C; Dominance, E; Parmia, H; Radicalism, Q_1; stronger Self-Sentiment, Q_3; and Low Ergic Tension, Q_4-, were significantly related to the rating criterion of creativity and, in fact, gave a multiple correlation of 0.8, even with intelligence omitted (actually, 63 per cent of the variance of the criterion was accounted for by these source traits in chemists, and 52 per cent in engineers). Later (Jones and Cattell, in preparation), with a mixed group of 88 researchers in the U.S. Rubber Co., and using a creativity criterion composed of 12 ratings (originality, self-reliance, etc.) by 25 observers (pooled) he obtained the relations shown in Table XLVII.

The reliabilities on both sides of the correlations in Table XLVII are sound, that of the criterion being $+0.88$ and that of the personality factors being about the same, due to the experimental thoroughness of using all three equivalent forms (A, B, and C) of the 16 PF at once. It is worthy of note

TABLE **XLVII**

Specification of creativity in industrial research chemists by personality and ability measures

PERSONALITY FACTORS	*Correlation with creativity*
Ego Strength (C factor)	+.25
Dominance (E factor)	+.36
Parmia (H factor)	+.24
Guilt-proneness (O factor)	−.31
Radicalism (Q_1 factor)	+.35
ABILITY FACTORS	
	(not available for whole group
Fluid General Intelligence	but approximate)
(Culture Fair Test)	+.30
Logical reasoning*	+.31
Mathematical reasoning	+.29
Ideational fluency*	+.33

* The first of these has been demonstrated as a primary ability by Thurstone, though the test used here is Guilford's. The second has been shown to be a distinct ability-temperament factor by Cattell and Winder (1952) and by Guilford and his associates (Guilford and Hoepfner, 1963).

that the above measures are the survivors—the highest correlating tests—out of no fewer than 53 tests tried by Jones, on the suggestion of one experiment or another that they would be predictors of creativity. Most—notably the personality scales—correspond to factors having only the usual slight correlations of oblique factors. But behind the personality factors there stand the general ability factors, though the correlations show that their predictive power arises appreciably from specific reasoning and ideational fluency.

It is not surprising that with this degree of independence of predictors, multiple correlations have been obtained by Jones with this battery as high as 0.95 for chemists and 0.83 for engineers, though in the group here cited and with correction for such bias as might enter a second sample, the R is 0.67. Trying the weighting formula on 10 new research chemists, Jones found that the "rank order of the [estimated] creativity scores divided the cases at the median exactly in accordance with the [performance] rating division."

Further work along the same lines has been done by Chambers (1964), who took 400 chemists and 340 psychologists and compared personality and biographical data for the top and bottom 50 per cent of each. This division may have confounded eminence with creativity, which should be taken into account when considering Table XLVIII. The personality factors distinguishing the more from the less creative were: A−, E, F, I, Q_1, and Q_2, the strongest emphases being on E and Q_2.

Section 6   The Broader Context of the Predictive Problem

If we may, for a first approximation, make a certain discount of differences, such as that in the I factor, found by the "adjustment" approach, we can use the Drevdahl and the Jones evidence (Figure 15) as the basis for a biserial correlation. Thus we can derive from Table XLIX rough estimates of weights for various personality factors, combining the above with the Tollefson, Jones, and Chambers regressions.

TABLE **XLVIII**

Overview of evidence on approximate relative weights of personality factors in predicting creativity

Research	PERSONALITY FACTORS															
---	A	B	C	E	F	G	H	I	L	M	N	O	Q1	Q2	Q3	Q4
*4 groups by Drevdahl and Cattell	−4	+5		+2	−2	+1	+1	+1					+3	+4	+1	−1
*1 group by Jones	−3	+5	+1	+2	−1									+1		
1 group by Tollefson		+3	+5	+3					−5			+3	+5	+3		
1 group by Jones			+3	+4		+3						−3	+4			
1 group by Chambers			+4									+4				

Suggested present best compromise of weights:

$$-.3 \quad +.5 \quad +.3 \quad +.3 \quad -.2 \qquad +.1 \qquad\qquad +.2 \qquad -.1 \quad +.4 \quad +.3$$

* These two researches are by the "adjustment" criterion; the rest by "effectiveness."

The consensus of these studies on the importance of B (General Intelligence), C (Ego Strength), E (Dominance), Q_1 (Radicalism), and Q_2 (Self-Sufficiency) is considerable. A number of *ad hoc* scales, such as Ghiselli's initiative scale, have also shown significant relations in single studies, but because the 16 PF is founded on the total personality sphere it is highly probable that these are substantially correlated with 16 PF scales and therefore included in its predictions. And because they do not correspond to frequently investigated personality structures, it is not easy to see what such specific scales are doing.

If the main emerging personality associations in the measurement approach are compared with the qualitative personality observations of the previous chapter, e.g., those of Roe, or with those of the systematic studies of Knapp, the agreement is obvious. Knapp (1963), for example, finds his creative researchers stating that they were solitary, felt more distant from parents and others, and recorded fewer group activities. They were more cautious and realistic (desurgent), aimed at more distant goals, and were more assertive (dominant) and authoritative, whereas the uncreative controls were more acquiescent and submissive. They are also more consistent in the rewards they sought (Q_3, Self-Sentiment) and had more well-differentiated value hierarchies.

Before asking about the dynamics of our formula, however, we should recognize that another source of prediction resides in the situational, biographical data, as found in the work of Knapp, Chambers, and Taylor. Some differences exist among these studies and, for example, those of Parnes and Meadow (1963), regarding the predictive value of grades. The latter, for example, found a triserial r of $+0.06$ between undergraduate grades and research merit; but Chambers found that in high school the creative scientists far more frequently had a straight A average. (The selection differences may well account for the predictive differences.) Chambers found creative scientists graduating from high school at a younger age, given to wider reading, and less interested in religion and community affairs. Knapp's extensive work shows very clearly that *scientific* creativity is apt to arise more often relative to creativity in art and music, in lower middle-class than in upper middle-class homes. It may be that art and music are easier, more immediately emotionally appealing expressions of intelligence for those in more protected or indulgent environments, such as tend to produce high I-factor scores. Knapp also shows that scientific creativity is higher in Protestant and Jewish than in Catholic religious backgrounds, and that in the Protestant family background it frequently occurs in the transition from a disciplined, restrictive religious ethos toward agnosticism.

The use of social and biographical material in prediction has practical limitations, such as: (1) much of it is difficult to obtain accurately; (2) it may overlap with the personality data already included; (3) it is more likely to lose its predictive value with change of locality and period. By contrast, what we see in the personality area suggests a dynamic relation that is likely to last. First, the curious inversion in the introversion factor, in which H tends to run in the extravert direction, suggests a constitutionally extravert person whose upbringing has made him inhibited (F—, desurgent) and skeptically hard-headed (A—, sizothyme). His inner life is more intense both by reason of the self-sufficiency of Q_2, which gives him confidence in his own reasoning, and because of high autia (M), which supplies a rich spring of ideation.

Probably, as research proceeds, we should give more attention to A— than is covered by the above reference to its role in introversion. Sizothymia-versus-Affectothymia (or Cyclothymia) is a dimension characterized by warm-heartedness, social dependence, and sentimentality at the affectothyme pole, and a cold realism, a dry precision, and an icy independence at the schizothyme extreme. The latter is responsible for some of the lack of social small talk and even downright tactlessness described in many biographies of creative men. But the warmth of the affectothyme is often unreliable in its promises and unreal in its handling of problems. There are certain resemblances between realism in war and in research. Of the former, it has been said that good intentions and "going through the motions" are not enough, because "there is no substitute for victory." And, similarly, the researcher has to be judged by whether he solves, discovers, and invents, not by his superficial carrying out of social shibboleths. It is the uncompromising, unexcusing realism of the sizothyme that makes his research genuine.

The role of radicalism is evidently to free the thinker from complacent attachments to things as they are, permitting instead ready emotional investments in the new and strange. Probably, ego strength is also functioning in the capacity needed to tolerate more readily the ambiguities and changes of beliefs constantly involved in scientific work—or indeed in creative work anywhere. That dominance should have so strong a role may seem strange, unless one reflects on the need for armor against that hostile criticism so frequently aimed at the "controversial" innovator. (Newton perhaps lacked enough of this—since the criticism of his theories of light made him "sometimes regret ever having published"—but Pasteur illustrates more clearly the strongly combative reaction to detractors.)

What we still lack in the psychological predictions is evidence on the relation of motivation (attitude), over and above personality, to creativity. The preliminary work of Jones, although using only "preference statement" tests of interest, found additional significant correlation with the criterion. And when factored and objective test measures, such as MAT (Cattell, Horn, Radcliffe, and Sweney, 1964) are added, it is surely likely that they will cut into the remaining criterion variance here, just as they did (see Table XL) into the school achievement criterion.

Finally, in any consideration of creativity we must not forget the overriding importance of general mental ability. If the correlations of intelligence and creativity fall low in certain groups, it is almost always because they have already been selected for intelligence. And if some discussions make much of the fact that creativity is not just intelligence, it is not because intelligence is unimportant. It is rather to direct attention away from mere academic achievement and to emphasize the decisive role of personality dimensions. Nevertheless, unless we are going to speak of creativity in matters of only individual social impact—the way in which I plant flowers in my garden, the way in which a child plays a game, the way in which a mother bakes a pie—the role of a high level of intelligence is paramount. That the ability to educe new relations and fundaments is a substantial part of major cultural creativity is amply illustrated in Spearman's *Creative Mind* (1930).

With that ability, a person of one personality will be creative, and another not. But without it, neither can be creative—in the cultural sense at least.

Section 7 Applications in Education

So far we have accumulated and checked evidence about creativity at the adult level. Although the general aim of this book is to reach conclusions that will help to improve selection, examination, and teaching practices at the high-school and university level, we would yet argue that our emphasis on adult development is correct, or at least consistent with the position stated in Chapter 1. There, we maintained that the process of education was by no means only an end in itself, but also a preparation for adult life. One difficulty, also, in repeating these investigations at the child level is that it is then very hard to evaluate the creativity criterion, as indeed is also true of lower intelligence levels in adults. Torrance, Barron, and Mackinnon have all plausibly suggested that up to a certain level (perhaps about IQ 120 for many purposes), intelligence and creativity are remarkably hard to distinguish; but that above this level, creative abilities attain a steadily increasing importance. Another difficulty is the lack of certainty that those who are more fluent and "creative" as children will be those who are fundamentally creative under the restrictions and demands of adult life.

A riddle and a dispute long in evidence among educators concern the discrepancy that exists between school examination-passers, on the one hand, and those who achieve outstanding success in later life or show great cultural creativity, on the other. It has even been said that whole classes, or whole races, are good at one and not at the others. Admittedly, the differences have been exaggerated, and if we examine good intelligence test measures, we can quite easily account for *positive* correlations among success in all three spheres. But, by and large, it is still true that the best school examination-passer becomes a scholar[2]—often an academic man—while the Darwins and Winston Churchills can point to a school career in which they were not always appreciated—to say the least.

This ancient problem, as we have tried to show, has begun to yield in a very encouraging way to knowledge obtained from ability, personality, and motivation tests. Although ideational fluency and special reasoning abilities play their part, the biggest difference between the creative and the uncreative person appears to lie in the realm of personality and to involve differences of

---

[2] Although there are certain *ad hoc* skills and kinds of low cunning and photographic memory specific to examination-passers, yet, on the whole and in the long run, there is probably only minor error in equating the good writer of scholarly examination papers and the scholar.

dynamics. As Drevdahl has pointed out, a substantial aspect of the personality difference consists of a need for nonconformity and a capacity to tolerate it. But it is not the nonconformity of the criminal or the neurotic "beatnik," although society may sometimes blindly class all three together as public nuisances.

In the classroom, high dominance does have some delinquent associations, for the high-E individual is rated as disobedient and "going his own way." But the other creative characteristics are those of withdrawal (A—), of desurgency (F—), of inner intensity (M), of bold, radical thinking (Q_1), of lack of regard for general opinion (Q_2), of lack of interest in social reputation and "politics," and perhaps a dash of the instability that goes with high drive and anxiety (Q_4). This profile is actually negatively correlated, by the pattern similarity coefficient, r_p, with the profile of the most *popular* student among peers, and, to some extent among teachers. The finding of Getzels and Jackson (1962) that creative children were relatively unpopular with their teachers, to which we referred in Chapter 14, and which may at first sight have seemed surprising, is thus largely explained. On the other hand, the creative character is by no means so associated with unpopularity as the delinquent or the neurotic. Possibly, in an environment more favorable to introversion and independence of mind than are most existing classroom atmospheres, the creative character would be about neutral with regard to popularity.

The question of the school's attitude to creativity, and whether school methods could be improved, takes us rather outside the theme of this book, and space will permit only a few brief points. First, it is realistic to recognize that a classroom can operate only if certain limits to individual action are drawn, but within those limits there is obviously need for less conformity— especially in thought if not in behavior—than we currently demand. Second, one suspects that the Greeks were right about banausic labor and that the creative child would benefit from escaping an excess of drill and from more scope for initiating his own tasks. In the social life of the school, perhaps more could be done to "make society safe for introverts." To make any society congenial to introverts means finding ways to run it without the necessity for a great deal of social interaction. It probably means achieving, among other things, such a high standard of internalized morality that neither the dictator nor the demagogue is necessary or possible. To come to a practical conclusion, these conditions of order and good internal inhibition will probably be attainable only in special classes selected for high ability. And although we have agreed that creativity is important at all levels, we should perhaps not feel too great a sense of failure if our reforms succeed only in retaining it where it is most needed, at the top.

As to the deliberate cultivation of creativity, there has already been much experiment but little outcome. The popular move has been "brainstorming"—encouraging in small groups the throwing away of inhibitions and the contribution of all ideas, however far-fetched. This will result in more ideas than in the usual atmosphere, and if a constant 10 per cent of ideas have promise it will result in more promising ideas. But it is the diametric opposite of what we know to be the condition of originality per individual, and it will obviously yield more superficial than deep ideas. For one condition of originality is inhibition of the easy, habitual response and the forcing, by an inner tension, of uncommon yet adaptive responses. The possibility that one can gain from separating the production and the evaluation of ideas has been experimented upon by Parnes and Meadow (1963), with results not yet too clear. Their work, however, indicates that a desire for conformity, an excessive faith in logic, perfectionism, and reliance on authority are common destroyers of creativity.

Section 8 "Training for Creativity"

A great array of evidence, not assignable to sources in a brief survey,[3] suggests that training for creativity is far more a personality than a cognitive matter, and that we are not going to offset by some "intensive training courses in creativity" what may be fundamentally wrong in our values and way of life. "Training for creativity" is about as hopeful as training to be intelligent, when intelligence is defined as "handling well a situation that you have had no previous training to meet." However, when we have selected by wise psychological testing the most creative individuals, they could probably be helped by educational direction toward:

1. Learning how to manage their necessary nonconformity without being delinquent. For example, for a child who grasps a principle at once it would be reasonable to do only ten out of forty examples set for homework and to show that he has independently read further afield by doing examples in more advanced or specialized principles.

2. Avoiding being dragged into race-track competitiveness—it has been justly said that "competition, like alcohol, though it begins by stimulating, ends by bringing all to the same dull level," i.e., it brings all into the same track or race channel, instead of favoring exploration. This requires a high degree of inner security, such as we recognize in the Q_2 (Self-Sufficiency) factor.

3. Learning to spend time alone, reading and thinking, despite the temptation to constant social life. Nowadays, this would include breaking the habit of sitting for hours passively before the television "idiot-box."

4. Developing certain almost purely cognitive techniques, notably: (a) a

---

[3] We refer to the range of study that includes both the recent experimental work and the biographic analyses of Kretschmer (1931), Havelock Ellis (1946), Hirsch (1963), and the present senior author (1963).

habit of intensive study and discussion of the elements in a problem, followed by arranging an undisturbed incubation period in which one's energies but not one's conscious thought are devoted to the problem; (b) declining to take too seriously the conventional verbal terms in which the problem is commonly debated. Compared with visual imagery and mathematical symbolism, words involve a mode of reasoning that ties one to public views. They are relatively more tied to the symbolism of popular thought, and make it difficult to move from a common coin of alleged "logic" to an uncommon mold; (c) keeping close to reality. Although much creative thought must be of the nature of dreaming, rather than (initially) explicit logic, and although it avoids social checking, it should not become subjective in the sense of avoiding reality. Many theorists merely substitute for the existing public theory a highly individual and subjective statement that is equally insensitive to reality and equally unoriginal in being precast in conventional verbal terms, e.g., it may be merely the exact opposite—a mirror image—of the current public theory. Creativity requires an objectivity, in the sense that the mind is withdrawn from conventional, social formulations but is by no means withdrawn as is the psychotic. On the contrary, it must be devoted to realism.

When all is done that education (in the schools) can do, it will still probably remain true that more can be contributed to increasing creativity in our society by selection than by education. For one thing, certain of the ability and personality factors now known to be important for creativity appear from nature-nurture research (Burks, 1928; Burt and Howard, 1956; Cattell, Blewett, and Beloff, 1955; Eysenck and Prell, 1951; Freeman, Holzinger, and Mitchell, 1928; Gottesman, 1963; Vandenberg, 1956) to have substantial hereditary components. This is true of Intelligence (B factor: 80 per cent), Dominance (E factor: possibly 60 per cent), Parmia (H factor: probably 70 per cent), Autism (M), and Self-Sufficiency (Q_2 factor: probably 50 per cent), though not, of course, of Desurgency (F), Ego Strength (C), Radicalism (Q_1), etc.

Although, as far as the social need for scientific creativity is concerned, it is true that vastly increased numbers are now supported in research, it is probable that a proper return on this support will be gained only if research is organized so that much of it is directed by the most outstanding research workers. The need to recognize and choose the best is here greater than in almost any other field. With the weaknesses in the criterion that we have discussed in already-published research, it would not be appropriate to offer a specification equation taken to two decimal places. Besides, the equation must be finally modified for the age, range of ability, etc., in the group concerned. But from the above contributions of Drevdahl, Jones, Tollefson, and others, we can propose centrally, in the school range:

$$\text{Creativity} = -.3A + .6B + .3C + .3E - .2F + .1G + .1H - .1I \\ + .2M - .1O + .4Q_1 + .3Q_2 - 3.85$$

The weights are so adjusted that with stens (standard scores) for A, B, etc., the creativity score will also come out in stens (the constant, -3.85, being added to bring the mean creativity score at the sten mean of 5.5).

Undoubtedly, as research proceeds, the ability contribution will need to be increased, as the work of Jones and Sprecher shows, by adding special ability measures (Thurstone's Reasoning Factor, the "ideational fluency" factor of Guilford and Cattell, and several of Guilford's other factors). Also, the proceeding work will add motivation factors. As to personality factors, although the above shows significant weights on only twelve of the sixteen in the 16 PF (or the fourteen in the High School Personality Questionnaire), it is probable that more exact work will show slight weights on the others. In any case, if the maximum prediction is required, it is best—and more convenient in testing and scoring—to use the whole 16 PF or HSPQ.

SUMMARY *of Chapter Fifteen*

1. Before selecting for creativity, we ought, as part of the criterion definition, to ask about the conditions under which the creativity is to be exercised. The assumption that the combined teacher-researcher—long the ideal of the academic world—is the most desirable product of education, for this purpose, is questioned. Teaching and research may require, in part, different skills and ways of life. Society is likely to see an increase of institutes devoted purely to research. Selection for creative work must take into account these conditions and also the conditions of "free-lance" creativity in art and literature.

2. In predicting creativity, the assessment of creative performance itself offers unusual difficulties. Originality cannot be equated with oddity. Psychopathology also results in oddity, and this is one reason for the folklore assertion of a kinship between genius and insanity. Actually, men of genius have a lower-than-average incidence of mental disorder, and the creative product has involved a process of objective adjustment. It is "odd" only because it has not been reached before.

3. Literary and artistic genius is known to have lesser emotional stability and freedom from pathology than has scientific genius. In other respects, however, the personality profiles found for leaders in art and science have a marked similarity, which suggests that selection for creativity can proceed along much the same lines in both.

4. The criterion is more easily examined in the scientific field, whereupon it is discovered that it contains several distinct instrument (source of evaluation) factors, such as the number of good research articles produced, evaluation by supervisors, popularity and esteem among laboratory associates, role in national science association politics, originality as rated by senior

research leaders and shown in patent inventions. Two of these seem essentially to exemplify creativity and may be positively correlated.

5. The relation of personality and ability measures to the creativity criterion shows that the psychologist possesses substantial predictive resources. Moreover, the meaning of the factors found agrees well with that emerging from the qualitative, biographical approach of the preceding chapter. Creative individuals are more "introverted" (actually, sizothyme, desurgent, self-sufficient), more dominant, radical, and autistic than persons of the same intelligence and education who have made a name in teaching or administration.

6. The relationships have been examined by both the "adjustment" and the "effectiveness" types of criteria. The former can proceed in practice with the pattern similarity coefficient, r_p, and the latter by the factor specification equation. A general specification equation is set out for use in schools, universities, and industry, but ultimately it will need to be tailored to particular groups.

7. Although a high level of creativity must depend on a high level of intelligence, because the final capacity to educe relations depends on fluid ability, and although special reasoning and ideational fluency measures contribute significantly to prediction, the selection in any professional group of the more creative persons depends decidedly more upon personality characteristics. Creativity in a one-hour examination-like situation may depend more on abilities, but creativity over years, in the life situation, is clearly more determined by personality as a way of life, and by motivation factors yet to be measured.

8. The cultivation of creativity may turn out to be the development of personality—nothing less. However, cognitive habits play some role, and minor increments may result from suitable "training." Four major ways are suggested for the cultivation of creativity. They may be so disruptive of ordinary classroom procedures as to be best reserved for selected individuals only, and at the upper mental-age levels.

9. Creativity in any individual varies with age and circumstance. By age, productivity is higher at an early period in relatively abstract studies such as mathematics and modern physics, and at a later age in biology, history, politics, etc., where large realms of fact and experience have to be absorbed (Lehman, 1953). However, any peak at an early age is partly an artifact (Dennis, 1958) and partly a failure to free outstandingly creative persons in later life from excessive organizational responsibilities. Creativity differences are far more the result of individual than of age differences. Even with the rapid increase of research support, it is as important as ever (some personality factors in creativity being relatively innate) to select for creativity, regardless of age, and to organize increased research resources around the selected individuals.

Chapter Sixteen

THE ORGANIZATION OF PRACTICAL
PSYCHOLOGICAL PROCEDURES FOR
PREDICTING ACHIEVEMENT,
CREATIVITY, AND ADJUSTMENT

Section **1**   **Integrating Technical, Social, and Moral Aspects of
Organized Psychological Services**

So far, our concern has been with research findings and basic principles. The findings described predictions from particular types of tests, and the principles have covered the psychometric properties of tests in general. Now, we must move to the issues that arise when test results are employed in a practical setting for selection, diagnosis, and prediction of achievement, creativity, and general adjustment. This consideration of practical organizational procedures and social controls will also require some extension of technical formulations, notably of validity and reliability, as introduced basically in Chapters 6 and 7. But its novel ground will reside largely in consideration of some wider social values and particulars of school organization.

If psychological measurement has made radical gains in depth of scientific understanding, in extension to personality and motivation, and in sheer validity, as the first part of this book has tried to show, then two tasks face the psychologist-educator who wishes to express these gains in actual school progress: (1) translating the above research findings into the most efficient and practical choice of tests and of organized testing procedures; (2) educating public opinion to understand sympathetically the methods and goals of testing, so that progressive changes may be efficiently introduced, along with control from a democratic framework of values.

Let us, in this opening section, deal with the broader problem, first, of social and moral aspects of testing, and then converge within that framework on the technical arrangements.

The great majority of people in civilized countries today—especially in the technically more advanced societies—have come to appreciate psychological tests. At the very least, most individuals take achievement and aptitude tests in school, in examination for military or civil service, or in a clinic. So long as people lived in small face-to-face communities, where everyone knew—or thought he knew—the general intelligence and personality traits of his neighbor, selection for positions might be made with some reliability by reputation, by interview, and so forth, without tests. But in a vast and mobile society, a more impersonal and efficient system of evaluating any man or child for any position has been needed. The weakness and bias of the interview, the essay, and countless other devices of the past have been exposed. Psychological testing has demonstrated superior technical powers and made it possible, at least, in the computer, to discount bias from race, creed, and origins.

Such a change has not occurred without discomforts and criticisms. Both education and psychological testing proceed to the accompaniment of public debate, often affected by unfortunate waves of fashion. To judge by books published,[1] criticism of psychological testing was at the crest of a wave around 1960. Better education, test construction, and understanding of purposes may help gradually to take some of the froth off these waves and narrow the issues to reasonable proportions. An airing of the issues in the *American Psychologist* of October 1965 may have brought the era of less responsible criticism to a close. Undoubtedly, mistakes have been made by psychological testers, with results that could be almost as tragic as those by surgeons or air pilots. But those who can count themselves severely misled or ill-advised are few, compared with those who have benefited. For example, the testing of draftees in the Second World War alone resulted in the provision of a university education for many thousands of individuals, whose talents would otherwise have been unrecognized and who would have wasted high ability in limited occupations.

Testing is aimed at benefiting both the individual and society. For example, in school it is good for the individual to be in the right class, but it is also good for the class—in terms of effective forward motion—to contain the right individuals, rather than struggle to encompass an incoherent range of ability and achievement. At present, this double aim, and the nature of the means to implement it, have seemingly been focused maturely by only a minority of teachers and a still smaller minority of parents. Meanwhile, the need to know what testing is doing, and why, becomes more urgent as psychological science increases its powers of analysis, prediction, and control. It becomes particularly important to crown the technical discussion in this book by integrating testing into broader social values, especially because we have been extending the discussion and practice of testing from the conventional area of abilities into new realms of personality and motivation measurement.

---

[1] The writings of Gross, Hoffman, and Young are among the more egregious, but there have also been many poorly informed magazine articles.

In the many hundreds of years (thousands if we include Sumerian and Chinese records) of examination in schools by ordinary attainment tests, different emphases have been placed at various times on the functions of testing. Examiners have been interested in selecting students, evaluating teachers, motivating students, protecting the public from unqualified practitioners, providing more accurate personal stocktaking of progress, and so on. These functions are multiplied again, in the present era, with the introduction of personality and motivation measurement. If one considers, for a moment, "personal stocktaking," or self-knowledge, as an objective, it is at once obvious that typically neither the student nor the ordinary subject-oriented teacher is qualified to make reliable use and analysis of technical test results. The widespread practice of denying knowledge of IQ scores to pupils and parents is based, in situations where this censorship is appropriate, on the assumption that the real implications of the IQ will be misunderstood. (Also, indefensible reasons are often given for denying this knowledge.) With modern, recondite personality and dynamic concepts, the possible dangers arising from knowledge of scores without technical understanding of their meaning are still greater. The sooner schools install fully qualified psychologists to discuss results with individuals—psychologists who will stand to the class teacher as a medical doctor does to the physical-education trainer of the athletics team—the more valuable and beneficial will be the results of technically good psychological testing.

The aspect of mental testing that is probably most in need of public discussion and understanding is that connected with the selection of limited sections of the population for special education. Here, one thinks mostly of the backward, the very advanced, those who are to be chosen to have additional years of education, and candidates for scholarships and special professional opportunities. With respect to all these, one should recognize that long before the professional psychologist appeared there were perpetual minor revolts against examination systems. Some were fully justified by the incompetence of the examinations. Space precludes examining the peculiar distortions of the health and advance of society that examinations can, in various ways, produce. Perhaps, when sheer falsity and unreliability of examinations are set aside, the outstanding remaining danger is that examination systems will select for better education the people who do well *in* school rather than those who do well *after* school.

But when wrong social values and aims, test inefficiency and unreliability, some unfairness to individuals of certain backgrounds, some biasing to fill the needs of small pedantic groups in higher education, and so on, have been set aside, objections and discontents will still boil over. At this point, the psychologist has to recognize "psychoanalytic" mechanisms, notably sheer rationalizations by individuals who either dislike the demands of reality, or who are repeatedly unsuccessful in tests. When, as in the recent British system (now, however, changing, for better or worse), the "eleven-plus" selection procedures permit only one child in five to enter "grammar schools" (which form a necessary first stage for entering most professions)—and thus virtually "fail" far more than they pass—it is not surprising that more people criticize than approve, and that episodic revolts appear in educational journals and newspapers. Nevertheless, mature people realize that at countless points in social promotion "many will be called and few will be chosen."

The use of personality tests and motivation-assessment devices encounters some extra resistances beyond those found with ability tests. A particular charge brought against them is that they invade personal privacy, a notion that, incidentally, also retarded acceptance of the practices of stripping for a physical examination or of being evaluated for income-tax contributions. But most pervasive and fundamental among the influences that obstruct psychological testing and a good public psychological service is that widespread, primordial conservatism and inertia that attempted to block the steam locomotive, that allowed millions to die of smallpox after Jenner's discovery of inoculation, or that, among "no-nonsense" skippers, permitted scurvy to kill ocean travelers for two centuries after the remedy had been demonstrated. Only time and education can reduce opposition from this source.

The psychological service provided in school is properly regarded as an extension, on the one hand, of the medical or psychiatric service provided privately and, on the other, of the teaching services already organized by the community in its schools. As such, it is necessarily limited in its technical reliability by the present state of the sciences of psychology and medicine. It is also limited in its human values and wisdom by the present status of our sociopolitical development. Dissatisfaction with the scientific limitations is as acute among discerning psychologists as it is among the general public. The good professional psychologist is not hypnotized by the finality of a number, such as an IQ (as happens sometimes with parents), and he is extremely careful not to take action on personality measures, e.g., scores on neuroticism scales and so forth, beyond the reliabilities of the instruments. Yet the very journalists and others who attack psychological testing on the pseudomoral claim that "no man is good enough to judge the personality of another" judge their employees readily enough in interviews, and judge the people they attack in editorials even more readily, often on far more dubious information than a psychologist would accept.

As to the necessary social and ethical values, let us not forget that everyone is being judged by someone every day. One hopes that these judgments are not attempts to pass a verdict on the fundamental worth of a human soul, but only to assess fitness for a special situation, e.g., entrance into a difficult profession or a scholarship for a special kind of school, or to provide help with a neurotic emotional problem. At least, it is explicitly this latter form of judgment with which the psychologist knows himself to be concerned. The social and ethical question is not whether we shall be judged—this is inevitable—but whether we shall be *reliably* judged. It has been abundantly proved by research that methods, such as the interview, that the practical man has so long depended upon, are far less reliable than the average good psychological test, even of twenty years ago. Surveys have also made it abundantly clear that individuals needing clinical treatment do not go to clinics soon enough. Without mass psychological-screening tests, such as can be incorporated as readily in school systems as periodic medical examinations, many individuals will head for neuroticism or delinquency who might, with earlier attention, have become happier people.

In a democratic community, psychological, medical, and educational services will in general be offered rather than dictated—except at that point where refusal to accept them imperils a man's neighbors. Certainly, in the psychological field, and at the present state of our knowledge, treatment is a matter only of advice, tentatively offered to the autonomous individual. So far as selection for higher education and for scholarships is concerned, the psychologist only selects; the ideals of the community direct what varieties of education shall be offered. The psychologist is only a servant. As a citizen, he can argue for rational and fair social goals, but, professionally, his task is to see that they are put into effect as reliably as possible. History shows that if a goal is absurd, the more efficient pursuit of it will more quickly reveal its absurdity. The equal treatment of unequals, or rather the provision of exactly the same educational goals for individuals of intrinsically different capacities and personalities, is such an absurd goal. A democratic respect for the potential of the individual and the maximum happiness and security of the community, alike, require equal *opportunity* and richly diverse *alternatives* in education for everyone.

Beyond these sources of obstruction to testing residing in pervasive emotional misunderstandings is the additional source of intellectual misunderstanding, namely, the inability of the untrained mind to think statistically. The psychologist makes an assertion about "the *average* child," and the layman thinks he is speaking of *every* child; or he says the IQ of a given child is 120 ± 5, and the layman takes it as an assertion that it is exactly 120. H. G. Wells has pointed out in a penetrating essay the difficulties in sociopolitical life arising from the inabilities of electorates to accept and understand truths in the form of probability statements, "maxima and minima," and so on. In psychology, perhaps half the troubles that arise with individual teachers and parents over test results spring simply from failures to understand the notion of a "standard error." When the day dawns, for which Galton hoped, on which some three or four simple statistical conceptions are universally taught in schools, we can expect more rational appreciation of what testing means, and, for that matter, also of what many important medical, social, economic, and political statements mean.

Section 2   **The Centralization of Psychological Testing Information and Services in the School System**

Assuredly, the educational psychologist, as a philosopher, should thus clarify the relation of technical educational and psychological goals to general social and ethical goals and seek to eliminate confusion in the waves of popular and journalistic attention to testing practice. Yet his main task is a technical one, and the realization of technical and social goals in the school system offers a great organizational and technical challenge. At what points, for example, should psychological services be provided, and by whom?

As to the first, the three main points of application in the school are those of educational evaluation, occupational guidance, and mental health:

1. The improvement of examinations (a) for directing into appropriate channels the exceptional child, i.e., both the bright and the retarded, and (b) for analyzing the achievement anomalies of any individual in difficulties.

2. The improvement of vocational guidance, at the end of ordinary schooling.

3. The provision of clinical "child-guidance services" for diagnosis, prophylaxis, and treatment for neurotic, difficult, disturbed, and delinquent children.

As to the second—the sources of these services—it happens historically that they grew up in different organizational settings, i.e., in the schools, in medical services, in public and private vocational-guidance centers, and so on. Nevertheless, we shall argue that both the logic of the situation and public economy point to the desirability of some centralization of services—whether by public or private enterprise—whereby records can be systematically stored and predictive, computational facilities maximally developed. At present, this ideal is largely an abstraction, for concretely we find that scholarship and ability examination work is confined largely to the schools, using intelligence and achievement tests; the clinical[2] work is often out of the

---

[2] The first recorded *psychological* (as distinct from psychiatric) clinic was set up by the psychologist Lightmer Witmer, at the University of Pennsylvania in 1896. Subsequent child-guidance, delinquency, and mental-health services in America developed more conservatively around medical services, whereas the schools developed their ability evaluations separately, and job-selection procedures developed yet more ability batteries and differing concepts.

Only very occasionally, as in Thorndike's development of vocational-guidance methods in schools, and certain developments of clinical methods in personnel work in industrial and military psychology, were the boundaries of clinics, school, and job surmounted. A conspicuous instance of integration occurred in 1930, when the City of Leicester, in Britain, under F. P. Armitage as director, initiated a school psychological service in which the psychologists centrally handled: (1) the referral of retarded children to special classes and schools; (2) the clinical treatment of neurotic and delinquent children; (3) the organization of vocational-guidance testing; and even (4) some examination of teaching methods in the light of psychology. It was certainly the first to

control of psychologists and proceeds with "patent," "special purpose" clinical tests like the Rorschach, in a subjective penumbra of psychoanalytic theory. Meanwhile, vocational guidance and selection has had virtually no theory and has proceeded in commerce and industry with endless special-purpose tests, merely mimicking the skills apparently required in various occupations. The bringing of these into a single psychological service has always had obvious technical, organizational, economic, and communicational advantages. Few have perceived that technical progress in testing would soon provide basic psychological measures simultaneously potent and meaningful for most applied fields. Much of the research reported above supports the technical possibility of understanding performance in all fields in terms of the same laws, concepts, and test measurements.

Because the *same* young person is involved in school examinations, in possible difficulties in home and school adjustment, and in the need to find a suitable and rewarding job, it is basically illogical to test him by different batteries in each setting. We need to know the organically interdependent personality and ability structures and motivational adjustments of that one person. The time has come for the psychologist to abandon rule-of-thumb immersion in the restricted test jargon and test practice peculiar to each area. Instead, he should rationally consider switching to the use of tests capable of revealing the intrinsic personality, ability, and motivation in the individual's life. Let us at the same time recognize that, insofar as certain particular criterion variables must be predicted with finer precision in some areas than others, the practitioner may need to put relatively strong emphasis on certain types of test. But this should not obscure the more fundamental principle that all criterion performance prediction involves the *total* person, and that the same *main* dimensions of personality and ability need to form the core in any effective design of test batteries.

Let us designate the well-chosen core of routinely used tests in any institution an *installation*. A farseeing psychologist, setting up such a testing plan, will in general install tests that at different ages measure the *same* important factors, in order to gain: (1) the value of meaningful growth and developmental comparisons; and (2) the maximum application of psychological laws centering on known functional unities. A child-guidance behavior problem, for example, can be far better understood if records of personality and motivation source-trait levels over the preceding years can be consulted. Measures from the age of four to adulthood on the same personality factors are available now in the Pre-School Personality Questionnaire (PSPQ), the Early School Personality Questionnaire (ESPQ), the Child Personality

---

set up a central temporary "hospital school," not for children of low intelligence, but for children of normal ability who were failing in achievement or were emotionally disturbed. This school provided intensive individual psychological attention and therapy until they had "caught up" and could be returned to their local schools.

Questionnaire (CPQ), and the High School Personality Questionnaire (HSPQ). Indeed, the possibility exists that with routine application of such measures an alert psychologist can foresee and forestall the trouble in a great number of cases.

If it is psychologically erroneous to vivisect the child into noninteracting cognitive and emotional compartments, it follows that it is wasteful and perverse to have him examined in school by a psychologist who knows only "mental tests," in the clinic or guidance situation by someone who examines only for "emotional adjustment," and so on. We should not accept unquestioned an organization of psychological services based on the premise that the measurement of achievement and intelligence is a task for the school psychological service, whereas the measurement of personality development and adjustment, to be done only for a few maladjusted cases, is the task of psychiatrists in a child-guidance clinic. The wisely educated and technically trained psychologist cannot accept the equally suspect premise that vocational guidance in the last school year can be effective when the necessary data from personality and motivation evidence is often secluded in the clinic.

Some degree of difference of test emphasis must naturally exist, but the school organization should reflect the basic unity of scientific psychology, by planning for a common set of developmental records and a basic comprehensiveness of psychological measurements. Over the age range from nursery school to high school, a vigilant and sensitive psychological eye should focus upon results from a theoretically well-chosen array of personality, ability, and motivation measurements, applied at regular intervals and systematically recorded.

Section 3   Personnel and Planning of School Psychological Testing Programs

One conclusion is usually reached by those who have observed, over the past decade, the school psychological systems of the United States, Britain, Germany, The Netherlands, Italy, Sweden, Japan, France, Australia, and other countries that have given some explicit attention to developing a practicable system. It is that the practices that have grown up so far have been too much determined by accidents in the scientific development of psychology, by "trade union" boundaries, expediencies of local government organization, and so on. For these reasons, they sometimes do not even begin to approach a rational, reasonably efficient, design. The whole organization of psychological services, as of the middle of this century, needs to be thought through afresh, in terms of the present potentialities of psychology. Throughout the child age range, it is surely reasonable to look to the school, public or private, as the central referent for problems of backwardness, scholarship selection, child-guidance work, delinquency control, and vocational guidance.

A central plan for gathering data on children by a regular psychological "check up"—a plan aimed to pick up with maximum efficiency what is relevant alike to mental health, the understanding of achievement, and wise vocational guidance—necessitates the provision of appropriate professional personnel. Any intelligent plan one makes for this provision may seem fanciful today. No country yet has an organization of trained personnel that will even dimly approach the needs of such a situation. Even in those Anglo-Saxon, Scandinavian, and West European countries that have started earliest and gone furthest, one still finds only a vague conception of the ranks and specialists needed. For example, most school psychologists in England have only a two-year diploma, or an M.A. or even a B.A. (rather than a Ph.D.) degree. As for available professional help, America has gone further than most in the idea of having a psychologist-guidance specialist in each large school; but even there one is apt to find, in less advanced states, that this guidance specialist may be a genial former football coach, now a little too plump to run around the field. His contact with children may be very good, but his understanding of intelligence, and especially, personality and motivation, tests may leave him at the mercy of every publisher's salesman. His lack of the barest, elementary statistical training means that his efficiency—even when supplied with good test instruments—is far below that possible with a properly qualified psychologist, e.g., in making class predictions and analyzing sources of difficulties. True, the training recommended for school counselors, in America, is a master's degree in counseling, which would be reasonably adequate; but, at a rough estimate, more schools lack than possess such qualified counselors.

The American Psychological Association, through its Psychological Test and Professional Ethics Committees, is at present in an embarrassingly unrealistic position on these issues. The qualifications that it requires for test users are probably possessed by only one in ten of those men and women who are professionally required, by their employers—the school systems, clinics, and industrial vocational specialists—to administer psychological tests. Even apart from this major dislocation between the assumptions of academic psychologists sitting on would-be-authoritative "committees on professional standards" and those in the hurly-burly of practice, there exist further misunderstandings on the part both of these academic committees and the "practical men" concerning what can and cannot be well done by various specialists. In particular, there is a failure to recognize the quite different levels and kinds of training required for: (1) giving a test; (2) scoring a test; (3) interpreting test results diagnostically, prognostically, and selectively; (4) engaging in therapy; and (5) talking to parents and children. The *administration* of even fairly complex tests does not positively *require* the presence of a highly qualified psychologist. Many teachers do an extremely good job of test administration, both in individual and group situations (except for the few in a rut who feel they must teach while they test!). Even a clerk, if she happens to have the right personality and has had hundreds of hours of experience of giving and timing one particular test, may do it better than a trained psychologist vaguely familiar with the administrative details of a hundred tests. As for test scoring, most modern and reliable tests can be objectively scored by clerical help and are nowadays increasingly scored by computers. Indeed, it is poor planning to use the expensive time of professional psychologists for scoring. Good tests are generally designed so that raw scores and transformed scores can be derived by routine procedures, which can readily be computerized or taught to a clerical staff.

When the stage of test interpretation and discussion is reached, clerical help can obviously have no role; but a teacher with the usual year of courses in psychology can go a long way *when operating in a properly provided framework of systematic advice provided by the fully trained psychologists in the school organization.* The present authors have seen operating, in America and Britain, systems in which the recognition of retarded children proceeds efficiently, from intelligence testing initially done by teachers—most likely to recognize children who may be considered retarded—through a final test check by the psychologist. Teachers also successfully carry out in various school systems the routine administrations of the CPQ and the HSPQ. Equally practicable is the classroom administration of such screening tests for clinical child-guidance work as the short Neuroticism Scale and the Anxiety Scale. The Motivation Analysis Test (MAT), for the purpose of vocational guidance, is, on the other hand, too complex in interpretation for immediate preliminary decision-making by teachers, but the sheer administration is something that a classroom teacher can perform, with brief guidance from the psychologist or sufficient preparation from reading the handbook. And whereas the full interpretation and use of all records from such tests ultimately requires the fully qualified psychologist, teachers can utilize the scores (1) at the descriptive level; (2) for simplified discussion of results in conservative terms with parents; and (3) for initial decisions regarding individual referral to a psychologist. The psychologically trained teacher or counselor, on the other hand, can also use them in final individual case analysis and statistical prediction.

In this connection, psychologists are just beginning to realize, as they recognize the utter economic impossibility of having enough high-level, statistically and psychologically trained Ph.D.'s or Doctors of Psychology to handle all cases effectively, that ways must be found in which to spread the influence of the trained specialists. The latter must be the insightful strategists on each case, diagnosing from test results, predicting by sophisticated computer methods, and directing the tactics of therapy. Their time is too valuable to use either in test administration and scoring, or in the prolonged interview and direct contact work of therapy and social work. Persons with a bachelor's or master's degree, less expensively trained than the Ph.D., but personally perhaps selected more than the latter for warmth and intuitive skill in contact work, can work in a team, with the leading psychologist, to implement the therapeutic and counseling *decisions* reached by his more complex methods.

Consequently, taking into account the progress of psychological testing and the laws of psychology, one foresees an organization in which each district has its nucleus of psychologists (trained to a doctoral level), working at an administrative psychological center. In a small city, or large town, of between 60,000 and 150,000 people, with about 10,000 to 20,000 children in schools, a staff of some five psychologists with the Ph.D. degree, variously specializing in clinical, vocational, and other areas, could, with a group of psychologist assistants at the master's, bachelor's, or diploma level, and with good liaisons with a guidance-specialist teacher located in each school, hope to handle the psychological needs tolerably.

To give truly adequate service to all children, normal and maladjusted, however, they will need to avail themselves of the very latest time-saving methods in group testing, automated scoring, and the use of computer help with prediction formulas. Needless to add, perhaps, their very batteries must avoid waste through testing with unfactored tests, such as have unnecessary overlap or which omit vital dimensions. Such an organization would simultaneously handle examinations, mental health, and vocational guidance, by: (1) a system of regularly spaced school psychological test surveys and records; (2) clinical treatment of delinquent, neurotic, and backward children, utilizing the regular records and home information; (3) placement of retardates; (4) advice on technical classification problems in ability groupings, etc., in the school generally; (5) use of teaching machines and other technical learning-theory developments; and (6) vocational guidance over the year or two before leaving school. The central psychological organization will achieve its best results only by a well-planned referral and communication system with individual schools and by good training liaisons with teachers of special classes and those who act as guidance psychologists or counselors. The tie of the central psychological organization with the counselor, well qualified with diploma or master's degree in counseling, is obviously particularly important.

Turning one's attention from children to young adults in the university or business apprenticeship, one must recognize that the issues and technical considerations that govern school achievement (in the broadest sense), in college, university, and industrial or business organizations are fundamentally the same as those in schools. Consequently, an appreciable parallelism in mode of organization is indicated. The counseling bureau of the typical American university already approaches, more closely than the school district organization, this ideal of a single center for the simultaneous handling of achievement and adjustment problems. It has available to it a variety of well-kept records from designated testing periods in the student's college life, although until recently these were confined to abilities. Nowadays, the use of normal personality and adjustment measures such as the 16 PF, the MAT, and the Anxiety Scale is becoming increasingly common. Some dependable means of keeping track of the psychological situation and development of every individual student thus becomes available, replacing the hitherto empty "personality-blind" practise of keeping only attainment and intelligence records.

Turning lastly to psychological services in industry and commerce, we have to recognize that, despite constant reiteration by personnel managers of the admittedly debatable view that "personality and native intelligence are more important in adult success than school attainment," the organization of testing to recognize these qualities has been quite poor—except in a few large firms. One can safely generalize—though the statement is certainly open to many exceptions—that the standards of psychological education necessary for wise choice and use of tests have been approached only in a few large industries. And, until quite recently, good technical psychological standards prevailed in the work of regrettably few "industrial management consultants," who engaged in much hocus-pocus with private, unresearched "test gadgets." It seems that effective psychological organization in a large firm commonly comes and goes with particular well-trained or inspired individuals. Furthermore, the potential advantages that industrial competition brings, in terms of enterprise (in the psychological field as in some others), are often more than lost through business secrecy about results, leading to inadequate samples and absence of exchange of principles.

Perhaps the coming decade will see fewer fads and more searching out by business firms of scientifically qualified management consultants to install effective systems of screening and promotion. Business is necessarily concerned with achievement in a far greater diversity of fields than in the standard scholastic area. This diversity has made it difficult to obtain well-standardized criteria of achievement and adequate cross-checking of validities. This, in turn, has perhaps largely accounted for the delay in providing the industrial psychologist with substantiated findings about the relation of criteria to basic ability and personality measures. (For example, Cattell's pioneer survey [1934] of intelligence levels in various occupations has been repeated only twice in thirty years.) As the recent surveys by Cattell and Scheier (1961) and Eber (1966) demonstrate, however, rapid progress is now being made in relating the 16 PF and the Anxiety and Neuroticism Scales to achievement in many jobs and professions.

This necessarily brief discussion of some needs in industrial psychology should not close without our pointing out the peculiarly intense concern of production and applied research organizations with that form of achievement that we have called "creativity." We have in Chapters 14 and 15 attempted to demonstrate that various forms of creativity are now fairly effectively predictable from patterns of personality.

Section 4   The Requirements in an Effective School Testing Program

Our contention above is that the conception of psychological testing as something that is applied only when a pupil gets into trouble—in becoming delinquent or neurotic or failing conspicuously in schoolwork—is a very short-sighted one. This truth is nowadays reasonably well recognized. Such "emergency" testing comes too late, is done under unfavorable emotional conditions, and tends to produce in the public an association of psychological testing with abnormality. Just as medicine has learned to substitute organized prophylaxis for hasty remedial treatment at the eleventh hour, so the school psychological service needs to be organized, with tests and record survey routines, to detect misclassification of pupils, ingrowing habits of underachievement, and crises of emotional maladjustment before they have acquired inveterate expressions.

This ideal of information-in-depth, available for every schoolchild at any moment, can be brought to actuality only by an explicit policy of: (1) comprehensive testing with a strategic choice of tests; (2) recording of results at well-chosen intervals over the typical school life; (3) choice and standardization of tests to ensure meaningful developmental comparisons throughout the age range; and (4) the organization of teachers and psychologists to ensure the fullest and most efficient use of the results in all fields—attainment, adjustment, and counseling.

Even with computer aids, it may not be economically possible to have such comprehensive testing and scoring done more than two or three times in each child's whole school life, and only then if, as discussed below, psychologists concentrate more on getting the greatest essential information with the fewest tests than they have hitherto done. The points at which testing will occur are bound to be dictated, first, by the ages at which reclassification occurs; because these differ locally, it is not easy to prescribe generally. Second, they are dictated by critical points in natural development, such as the onset of adolescence. As to the first, there are regional and cultural differences: Notably in Britain and Commonwealth countries, the three streams beginning at twelve (eleven-plus) years of age, and aiming roughly for semi-skilled, skilled, and management-professional occupational levels, have until recently remained effectively distinct, whereas in America the grouping by general ability levels is usually less final and less explicit.

No matter which degree of explicitness of adjustment of general ability to type of instruction is adopted, one needs to keep in mind that the school is not an end in itself but a gateway to life. Indeed, the point perhaps most often lost sight of in test selection is that an individual is normally not being selected to fit a school, but to fit those roles in later life for which that kind of school prepares. Teachers are, perhaps by the very keenness of their professional interest, the most inclined to forget that a school or university does not exist for its own sake, but for the later achievement in community service and cultural contribution of those who pass through the institution. Consequently, we need to beware of the constant tendency to select, for privileged schools and universities, those who will *do best in those schools and universities*. The real criterion is surely that involved in selecting for such special education those who will contribute most to society *after* such education. Researchers are much to blame for this emphasis, largely because they can get criterion data *in* the school much more easily than *later*.

The distinction may seem a subtle one, but it can be thrown into the limelight by the question, "Do we want in our selected centers of higher education merely facile and docile examination-passers or truly creative and characterful leaders?" The definition of achievement as academic achievement tends to make for the scholarly, but perhaps also vicious, circle whereby teachers train children to be teachers, with the academic or even pedantic standards of the teacher as the only definition of achievement. At the present moment, because of the lack of funds and research enterprise for those broader studies that are needed to examine predictive possibilities concerning the broader "after school" criteria, psychologists are now nearly always, if apologetically, compelled to adopt school achievement as the criterion of what their tests should predict. However, as we discovered in Chapters 13, 14, and 15, the conception of achievement can be made broader; and the psychologist, and the researcher who paves the way for his work, should surely begin now to aim at this broader conception whenever possible. One thing is almost certain: That as the psychologist comes to accept something beyond academic achievement as his target for prediction, ability tests will cease to predominate in educational psychological discussions, and tests that measure personality and motivation will assume more importance than they have had in the narrower, older practice. However, as our researches show, personality and motivation are more important even in scholastic achievement than teachers have generally been prepared to admit.[3]

---

[3] Some critics of psychological testing do not seem to realize that their criticisms attack the school system rather than the tests. For example, these critics are fond of pointing to individuals of high performance on intelligence tests who do little in later life, and conversely. But the *psychologist* himself is not unaware of the importance of personality and motivation gifts ignored in scholastic examinations. Much that has been accepted as criticism of the power of intelligence tests and school examinations *per se* is thus really a criticism that these, despite their demonstrable reliability, cover *only* a very narrow and "academic" aspect of the total personality expression. The psychologist

Insofar as one can generalize about the age points at which important classification takes place in various school systems, one recognizes that, for over a dozen national cultures, a major break is perceivable somewhere about eleven or twelve years of age. Here, at eleven-plus to be precise, the British, Australian, Dutch, French, and other systems finish the general primary education and sort pupils into three streams (Britain), four streams (Holland), and so on, that correspond roughly to preparations for unskilled and semi-skilled, skilled, clerical and managerial, and professional life. In this decade, and in some countries, it has been fashionable to focus criticism on this eleven-to-twelve-year-old classification point. While it is not within our scope to discuss this comprehensively, we may comment that: (1) the onset of adolescence (twelve-thirteen years) is a "natural point" and to forestall it by a year helps separate the internally determined adolescent stress point from the readjustment stress of an environmental change; (2) although some have criticized this as "too tender an age," the ever-deepening top hamper of culture requires that those who have to go far (the managerial-professional group) should start preparations early (deploring that he started to earn at the age when his grandfather had already started a family of four, Stephen Leacock, in *College Days,* heads a chapter "Life Ten Years too Late and Death on Time"); (3) most of the criticisms of stream classification at eleven would apply to any age—they are mainly veiled objections to recognizing individual differences as such.

In short, although better psychological methods of anticipating future performance are needed, and although later opportunities for corrective reclassification must be systematically introduced—to keep the decision made at eleven from becoming irrevocable—this age still remains a major decision point. In America too, in those school systems that have proceeded to classification within the high school, the eleven-fourteen region is also an important decision period. All in all, there seems little doubt that one psychological survey point should be staged in time for the eleven-to-twelve-year-old redistribution.

Granted this point, at what other developmental stages do we need comprehensive information? Clearly, because the earliest possible information is

---

should be the first to admit that ability tests ignore aspects of character and motivation that would be important *in predicting wider contributions in community life later.* But the teacher has hitherto attended little to possibilities of character and motivation measurement—although theoretically he agrees that the school should be concerned with developing character and motivation. The psychologist should be the first to recognize—and document—that in the last twenty years the assignment of scholarships to universities on the results of ability tests alone has tended to fill our universities with individuals more conspicuous for wit, or sometimes verbal intelligence (or, sometimes, capacity only to criticize!), than for enterprise, imagination, or drive. Assigning a proper testing weight to aspects of personality and motivation in selection procedures for higher education could pull us out of this slough.

needed in the school life, testing at the time of entry would be ideal. Admittedly, we meet quite definite technical difficulties here, in that the personality and ability structure has not been so well worked out at five and six as one would desire, and the reliability of tests is, at present, noticeably lower at this age. Further, again, perhaps we should avoid possible unreliability from placing the testing in a somewhat "disturbed" period—the first year in school. A suitable compromise might be to carry out the first systematic testing (apart from anything done at the preschool level, in some systems) at seven to eight years of age, i.e., Grades Two and Three in the American system. Moreover, this compromise is indicated because this is the earliest point at which some form of group testing can be carried out (though technical progress in psychology may alter this picture).

At this juncture in the development of psychological services, it seems realistic to conclude that only three points of major testing during the individual's school life will be generally acceptable, though annual testing will be the rule in achievement tests. Perhaps some personality and motivation testing (abilities change less) will soon be arranged biennially. In any case, in the interests of vocational guidance, the third major testing should come in time to help orientation during the last two years in school—particularly on the choice of whether or not to go to college, and on what occupations should be seriously considered. Perhaps we may thus settle on the following schema:

Major Points Indicated for
Comprehensive Routine Testing
(From the Standpoint Mainly of Classification and Guidance)

(1) First or second year in primary school, seven to eight years of age.
(2) Point of reclassification for secondary schools, ten to twelve years of age.
(3) Orientation to school leaving, sixteen to seventeen years of age.

Additionally, and later, for those who go to college or university:

(4) Counseling, mainly in the first, but also in the third or fourth (pregraduate) university years. This, in general, requires types and levels of tests distinct from those in (3).

However, if we consider also the perennial and constant clinical needs of the delinquent, neurotic, or maladjusted—a minority, but still a minority to which humanity dictates that we devote much attention—then these intervals are too uneven. Information on the genesis of psychological disorders is so valuable that the six-year gap between ten to twelve and sixteen to seventeen is too long, and a comprehensive record at the crucial point in adolescence represented by the year from thirteen to fourteen is indicated.

Furthermore, because, in classificatory terms, so much currently depends in many school systems on the examination at about eleven years of age, it would seem a matter of justice and scientific wisdom to base the decision on more than the single week of testing that, generally, is all that is set up. For all such short periods lack reliability and are liable to yield results upset by sickness or transient conditions. Technically, it would be better to include at least two separated testing periods, the first at ten years of age. That is, any selection—even if it were not at so "tender" an age—should be based at least on a *double* testing, the regression coefficients on the criterion being, of course, independently worked out for each. The three- or four-year interval to the next testing is appropriate (economically and organizationally—as is indicated by practice in many school medical examinations) and would manage to include the majority of children; those who drop out of school early are unlikely to do so before this period. A practicable solution to scholarship selection, provision for child-guidance clinic evidence, and preparation for vocational-guidance advice would therefore ideally be a minimum of four psychological examinations, spaced at three-year intervals through the school career, namely, at about seven years, about ten, about fourteen, and about sixteen to seventeen. Beyond these four points for the majority, a minority may be tested at four to five in nursery schools, and an additional minority will need the specialized testing installation in the university evaluation and counseling system.

Section 5   The Choice of Tests to Maximize Scientific Information

Granted purposes and school test-planning arrangements of the kind just discussed, what kinds of tests will have the long-term penetration, applicability, and optimal effectiveness required? Two testing ideals have been held up and exemplified in the earlier chapters:

1. Tests should cover not only ability-achievement measures of the kind hitherto so familiar in schools, but also two other areas—general personality dimensions and motivation-interest strengths.

2. The measures should not be on arbitrary, subjectively or traditionally chosen "scales," but on structural *factors,* found by basic research and integrated with the laws of scientific psychology. Around such realities, all kinds of scientific and criterion information can be dependably accumulated. As we have pointed out, this leads to what may be designated (to distinguish it from much current practice) *functional testing.* This definition implies such test usage as will facilitate the application of general psychological laws and understanding to prediction, over and above the use of any merely blind statistical prediction. That is, prediction will still be quantitative; but laws having to do, for example, with change of intelligence with age or physiological condition, or with the typical change of ego strength when a child

leaves home, or change of surgery when a second child arrives, can then augment prediction from the given measurement data, when placed in the hands of a truly qualified psychologist familiar with source trait concepts.

Let us recognize, however, that we stand today only at the beginning of this new movement in mental testing. On scientific grounds, structured measurement has every prospect of inaugurating new levels of understanding and prediction. We do not, at this moment, however, have more than a fraction of the necessary feedback of criterion information from the use of these new, structural tests whereby we might achieve the aims envisaged. Indeed, it should be recognized that the testing scheme proposed here is a fairly radical breakaway from what is most commonly being recommended for routine use. It will need an enterprising psychologist, the assured possessor of advanced technical skills, to inaugurate the proposed program in his local setting. He must conquer the difficulties commonly faced when introducing tests still labeled "experimental" into a routine setting, and when training personnel to understand tests to which they have not previously been accustomed. And although the new types of intelligence tests and the personality questionnaires have, as of 1966, been so widely tried out that they can be said to be well-groomed for use in almost any situation, the motivation-analysis measures and the objective (performance) personality measures are still experimental and may yet need modifications for maximum convenience. They stand open to development and improvement.

One feature of the shorter tests here is, as pointed out by Cronbach (1960), that their homogeneity "reliability" is not recorded as being as high as some readers are accustomed to find in publishers' handbooks. As Chapter 6 brings out, reliability: (1) is not so simple a concept as often supposed, and (2) can be raised to desired values in the present tests if users will take the requisite testing time. Some of the *reliabilities* of the many hundreds of tests advertised and sold before the days of structured tests are adequate. Indeed, they are often quoted as very high, but it is a poor exchange to accept a narrow test of high reliability that measures nothing of real importance for one of somewhat lower reliability that has appreciable validity and utility coefficients, by measuring a broad unitary personality dimension of widespread influence. Just how much reliability one can sacrifice for criterion validity and psychological lawfulness is a technical point we can discuss shortly. Meanwhile, for integrity with respect to the scientific position we have taken in the earlier chapters, we shall discuss in this final, applied chapter only those available tests that have met the basic research standards of correspondence with demonstrated unitary, factorial source traits.

When this requirement is rigorously applied—in terms of factors demonstrated as maximum simple-structure (oblique) dimensions, duly replicated as to pattern across cultures (Tsujioka and Cattell, 1966), or at least across social subcultures in our own country—it is surprising how many popularly used tests fall by the wayside. In the ability field, if these inadequate but very widely known tests are set aside, there still remains a sufficiency of extremely well-constructed tests aimed at "organic," source traits, notably Thurstone's Primary Mental Ability battery, and the corresponding ability batteries by Guilford, and others, capable of filling the practical gap. Again, at the adult level and for brief testing, Industrial Psychology, Inc., has a short battery of comprehensive Primary Aptitudes constructed on the same principles.

But in the realm of *personality* source-trait measurement, there appear to be only the Temperament Schedule by Thurstone, the IPAT Objective-Analytic (O-A) batteries for some eighteen personality factors, and the 16 PF test and its derivatives. (The Guilford-Zimmerman Temperament Survey is, of course, an orthogonally restricted choice [Gibbons and Cattell, 1966] of simple structure, whereas the Minnesota Multiphasic Personality Inventory is constructed for clinical patients, packed with "abnormal" items, and aimed at syndromes [clusters] instead of factors.)

The 16 PF and its derivatives—the HSPQ, the CPQ, the ESPQ, and the PSPQ, most recently completed—have the advantages of measuring essentially the same factors up and down the age range, and of being well standardized, cleared of difficult vocabulary, and designed directly to reduce the effects of most response sets, etc. They have certain shortcomings: partly those temporarily found in developments in an entirely new area, and partly those inherent in the questionnaire medium of measurement. For example, if teachers use only one of the equivalent forms, instead of all of them, as advocated by the designers, the reliability will not be above $+0.4$ to $+0.7$. This means that it is impossible at this stage of knowledge (indeed, it is achieved by no existing test) to measure a broad personality factor in so few as ten to fifteen items with a reliability higher than that stated. Even so traditional a device as an intelligence test, if reduced to ten items, achieves no higher reliability. The proper resort of the skilled psychologist here is always to use at least *two* equivalent forms, and, if possible, all four equivalent forms—A, B, C, and D—as now available for the 16 PF. The provided breakdown into forms—each one taking a little less than an average class period—should properly be regarded as: (1) a convenience for administration; (2) a device to allow the subject a rest and a change of occupation in between; and (3) a means of spreading the personality evaluation over the period of at least a week, if possible, to avoid effects of temporary moods, etc. Their existence should not be considered an invitation to base so important a matter as personality evaluation, with predictions affecting some years ahead, upon any single-form, three-quarter-hour test. (The latter works out at scarcely more than two minutes per factor dimension, e.g., it would be the equivalent of two to three minutes for an intelligence test!)

Indispensable in the psychologist's testing in such new areas as personality is perspective and a proper sense of values in psychometrics. Faced with the above problem of time demand, some less-informed psychologists have sought to solve it by aiming at the traditional high reliability through spending *all* the available time on some *one* factor measurement. However, as Chapters 6 and 7 and the brief discussion of multiple prediction in Chapter 9 will remind one, *when a certain immutable sum total of time is available, it is generally far better* (for a wide variety of predictive accuracies) *to spend it on briefer, less reliable measures of several factors, e.g., intelligence, ego strength, schizothymia, premsia, than on a more reliable measure of a single factor.* For example, the multiple correlational prediction of achievement by the sixteen factors, measured on Form A only, in the specification equation on page 119 is $R = 0.65$. If the same time were spent on testing a single factor (assuming the correlation of the given factor with the criterion to be approximately the average of the factors in this equation, say, 0.2) the increase in length by sixteen times would raise its reliability from 0.60 to 0.96, and this would raise the correlation with the criterion (according to Guilford's formula [Guilford, 1965]) to only $r = +0.26$. (As against 0.8 if we consider each of the 0.2 valid trait scales to be orthogonal and all to be used.)

For the same reason, even though *objectively* measured interest and motivation tests are new and, except at the adult level, not yet matured in either validity or reliability, it still pays to use them rather than leave evidence from this area untouched. In this area, the choice is between using such comparatively "seasoned" but exclusively verbal tests as the Strong, the Kuder, or the Edwards, on the one hand, and such objective but new tests as the MAT and SMAT (School Motivation Analysis Test) on the other. Consistent with our argument that verbal statements of attitude may grossly misrepresent the real and unconscious motivation, and the true strength of interest (such as was once sought by the Thematic Apperception Test [TAT] and other low-validity projective tests) of the individual, we believe the evidence cited in Chapters 9 and 10 compels any open-minded psychologist to turn to the objective devices. (The reader should be reminded that the latter do *not* depend on projection alone, but include other defense dynamisms, information, physiological response, and learning devices.) Furthermore, the TAT, the Rorschach, and even the Edwards are not simple-structure, factor-derived tests, and, except in special forms, not truly conspective (objective) in their scoring.

It would be a long and invidious procedure to give reasons why many quite popular tests among the hundreds listed in Buros' *Mental Measurement Yearbook* are not among those surviving in the compact battery finally settled upon here. Though great labor and care has often gone into their production, and their names are revered in textbooks honoring tradition as such, the scientific, impartial (and irreverent!) application of the standards of functional testing justifies the unconventionality of our rejecting them.

The more recent reviews in Buros will be seen, by the perceptive reader, to offer support for such a decision. On the other hand, for the purposes of "special purpose tests" (Chapter 5), i.e., for one quite specific criterion prediction only, many of these retain a vital role, and are excellent instruments for that role. As we have indicated, however, we believe the future lies, for the rest, in well-organized, comprehensive test installations, with general purpose tests. Beyond these considerations in our test choices are certain judgments of tests that lie virtually in the realm of taste and hunch. For the tests we have positively supported here, there exists an already sufficiently clarified rationale in the objectives stated for *structural test design* and *functional testing*.

Although the greatest future in personality measurement in the end lies with objective tests, as in the adult and child O-A batteries (Cattell, 1955), our recommendation for most immediate practical purposes is to test personality by source-trait (simple-structure) questionnaires; for these require emphatically less testing time and administrative cost. They must be questionnaires aimed at the same factors, for ready developmental comparisons and analyses, through the ages of four to six years (the PSPQ), six to eight years (the ESPQ), eight to twelve years (the CPQ), twelve to seventeen years (the HSPQ), and seventeen through adult life (the 16 PF). Incidentally, a few factors, such as Excitability (D), are measured in this series at the child but not the adult level, and others, such as Radicalism-Conservatism (Q_1), at the adult but not the child level, because in each case the variance declines in the new range. But, otherwise, continuity of concepts and measurements, necessary for measuring learning and growth, is maintained throughout.

In clinical work, the use of objective personality tests, such as the adult and child O-A batteries, has advantages that have been indicated. Furthermore, as the series of studies by Rickels, Cattell, Yee, and others shows, they are already eminently practicable, at the adult level, though even there they are, as of 1966, not fully standardized (the percentiles rest on 300 to 1,000 cases). Consequently, for school-centered work, it is at present practicable in routine test installations—if one must have only standardized tests and ample criterion-evidence—to think mainly in terms of questionnaires.

In the motivation-measurement field, the choice of the ten factors (more would be voted impracticable) to be measured by the adult motivational analysis test (MAT) and the high-school motivational analysis test (SMAT) has had to be a judicious compromise between the needs of clinical and counseling work, on the one hand, and those of school-achievement analysis, on the other. As to the form and nature of the ergs and sentiments defined, there can be little doubt after so many basic research replications. (See Chapters 5 and 11). As to their predictive value in clinical work (Cattell and Pierson,

1967; and others) and school achievement (Cattell, Butcher, et al., 1961; Cattell, Sweney, and Sealy, 1966; and others), there is enough to show that the ten factors have a wide field of diagnostic relevance. Nevertheless, one must remember that the peculiar nature of interests is the degree of their individual specificity. Consequently, in the last resort, and especially in the clinical and counseling field, the enterprising psychologist may well build onto the published test (using the same objective devices) measures of quite specific attitude-interests that are important for a particular purpose in the particular school system.

Compared with these new tests of personality and motivation, supported by positive research results where formerly there was nothing, our arguments for novelty in an old field, namely, in intelligence tests, will encounter more resistance from conservative psychologists. The arguments and experimental evidence for there being really two general ability factors have been presented in detail in Chapters 2 and 9. It is true that the crystallized general ability factor, because it already contains much of the criterion—namely, scholastic attainment—within itself, will, *for the moment*, give a higher correlation with next year's school attainment than will a culture-fair test. But on theoretical grounds, one would not expect such traditional tests as the Wechsler, the WAIS, the Stanford Binet, etc., to give so accurate a prediction as a combination of a culture-fair test *and* a last year's attainment test. For the traditional crystallized ability test has mixed these two ingredients in arbitrary proportions, to which explicit weights cannot be given as accurately as when they are freely separable.

What is more important is that such a conglomerate as the attainment-cum-intelligence test cannot *analyze* the *causes of backwardness* (or attainment-ability differentials) so well in the individual case, because an individual of low attainment but high natural intelligence will simply appear on a traditional intelligence test as of average intelligence. If one wants to find out how much of present performance is due to general mental capacity and how much to the fortunes of schooling and home background, then a culture-fair intelligence test, i.e., a measure of g_f, is definitely needed. And if one is looking to prediction ten years hence, as one should be doing in most scholarship selection, then the traditional intelligence test, with its hodge-podge of ability and earlier home and school advantages, is a less fair instrument.

For the reassurance of the conservative, and to put the matter to the test in the local situation by a kind of "action research," it might be advantageous to run for a while in many school systems a familiar test of the traditional type alongside the new Culture Fair scales. The "traditional type" will vary much in different countries. In Britain it may be a Moray House test, a Cattell Scale I, II, or III (Harrap); and in the United States, a WAIS, a Wechsler Bellevue, a Stanford Binet, and so on. Of the culture-fair tests, the IPAT CF Scales I, II, and III are at present the only ones standardized across several countries. These cover the age ranges four to eight, eight to fourteen, and fourteen through superior adult, with two equivalent forms at each age.

This section has given a general rationale of choice in relation to available test series. Section 7 below will look more closely at the actual proposed testing sequences and time conditions, etc., for these batteries. In the present section, we have aimed to bring out the general values governing any choice of final installation and to indicate that our evaluation in principle goes beyond indices of reliability, homogeneity, and validity, to consider the ultimate efficiency and utility indices developed in Chapters 7 and 8.

Section 6 Some Considerations of Practical Effectiveness with Derived Scores and Computer Aids

As the psychometrist, familiar with some of the general notions and statistical concepts employed in Chapters 6 and 7 will realize, this book cannot hope to broaden its purpose into consideration of all the principles of psychometrics as such. Nor can it present detailed statements regarding specific decisions or predictions to be made from the tests in the installation; such detail is to be found in the actual test handbooks, and in such guides to practical test use as those of Anastasi (1954), Cattell and Pierson (1967), Cronbach (1960) and others.

The general practice has, nevertheless, been sufficiently indicated above: to combine all predictors—cognitive, personality, and dynamic—in a single specification equation for each given criterion. This specification will normally assume oblique factors and linear relations, though by the use of the grid (Cattell and Eber, 1968) or a demonstrated formula, nonlinear predictions can of course be used. However, beyond this primary statement, we must leave such problems as correction for attenuation, determining the variance of weighted composites, finding weights necessary for maximally separating groups (e.g., successful and unsuccessful students) by discriminant functions, etc., or discovering natural groupings of individuals on the profiles from the above batteries by r_p (the profile-similarity coefficient) for appropriate textbooks.

Nevertheless, one or two matters of psychometric statistics most relevant to testing installations deserve comment. First, the teacher should recognize that the goodness of a prediction is better indicated by the square of a correlation coefficient than by the size of the coefficient itself. Every correlation (regression) coefficient when used to estimate a criterion from a test has a corresponding "error of estimate." A convenient way of recognizing this is by talking of the index of forecasting efficiency, E, as follows:

16.1 $$E = 1 - \sqrt{1 - r^2}$$

This index (multiplied by 100) expresses the percentage reduction achieved in the standard error of estimate by using the given predicting test, i.e., the

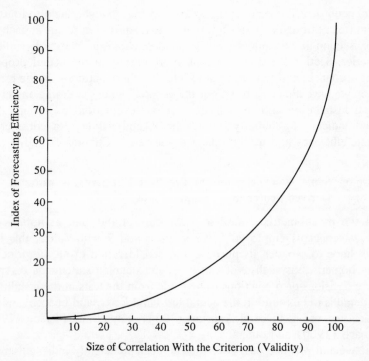

FIGURE **16.** *The relation of the criterion correlation size to forecasting efficiency*

reduction compared with having no prediction. Figure 16 shows this graphically.

It holds regardless of whether the correlation is a single one, or a multiple correlation such as we obtain from using the specification equation. The size of the multiple correlation is, of course, obtained from multiplying the weight of each factor in the specification equation by its correlation with the criterion, summing, and taking the square root, as in Equation 16.2.

16.2 $$R = \sqrt{r_1 w_1 + r_2 w_2 + \cdots + r_k w_k}$$

Another matter that comes up centrally in applied work of this kind is relating the reliability of the test as such (reliability as the *dependability coefficient*, page 113, not as the *homogeneity coefficient*) to the reliability to be expected in a single individual's score. Since reliability can be defined as in formula 16.3:

16.3 $$r_r = \frac{\text{True Variance}}{\text{Total Variance}}$$

then $\sqrt{1 - r_r}$ tells us how large the error of any single measurement is likely to be as a fraction of the total standard error. For example, if the sigma of the IQ is 16 points (as in most traditional tests), then an intelligence test of reliability $+0.75$ would allow a standard error of 8 points to any single score, i.e., there is a 50–50 chance of the correct value lying within $\pm.675 \times 8$ of the given score.

In connection with standard deviations, it may be helpful to remind the reader that most of the measurement results discussed in this book, for the 16 PF, HSPQ, CPQ, MAT, etc., are in *sten* (standardized 10-point) scores. The reason for using stens rather than simple standard scores or stanines or T-scores is their greater utility, and their convenience for persons accustomed to think in a decimal system (Cattell, 1957). The mean sten is exactly 5.5. This means that scores of 5 or 6 cover the central, "average" range and that we begin to talk of deviant scores only for 4's and 7's or beyond. One sten covers half a standard deviation. A distinction must be kept in mind between the ordinary sten, as just defined, and the *normalized stens,* or n-stens, in which the stens are fixed by appropriate percentile cuts on the raw score distribution, so as to make the resulting sten scores exactly normal. The handbooks for the 16 PF, HSPQ, MAT, etc., will commonly offer both kinds of stens or provide the data for calculating that which is not given in finished tables. For most research purposes, as distinct from routine work with individuals, greater precision is obtained from working with raw scores.

Another feature of scoring, as such, to be noted in this installation is that with the culture fair tests the standard deviation of the classical IQ, i.e., mental over actual age, $\times$ 100, is almost exactly 50 per cent greater than for traditional intelligence tests, namely, it is 24 points of IQ instead of 16. This greater range seems to be one of the characteristics of fluid as contrasted to crystallized general ability (see Chapter 2 and Cattell, 1963) and represents a sense in which the crystallized IQ is "wrong," i.e., systematically biased, as a result of the tendency of class teaching to make the bright mark time and to put pressure on the dull. Nevertheless, because many tables— and habits of evaluating what is a "high" or "low" IQ—are now based on the familiar standard deviation of 16, it has been arranged to have tables for the Culture Fair Intelligence Tests that will enable one to work out IQ both in the classical (sigma = 24) and in the "standard IQ" (sigma = 16) to which all intelligence tests can be artificially brought.

Because most of these issues will be familiar to readers of this book, it suffices merely to summarize such points briefly in Figure 17.

The assignment of sten scores of IQ's from any standardization tables requires a choice of reference population before looking up the equivalent of the raw score. For some purposes, we may wish to know standard scores of a boy relative to boys and a girl relative to girls, but in others, e.g., in scholarship competition where sex is irrelevant, we may simply want the standard score, in intelligence or a personality trait, *in relation to the total population.* Incidentally, it should be noted that because most personal-

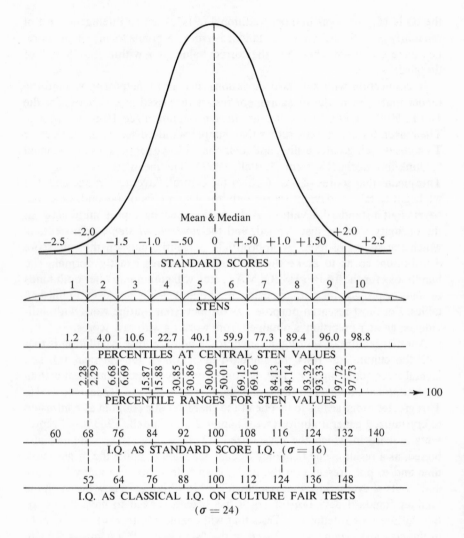

FIGURE **17.** *Some types of standard score*

ity traits are subject to regular age trends, just as intelligence is, though at different rates and in different directions, the conversion to standard scores of the test results we have been discussing requires reference also to age norms.

A more fundamental issue that arises constantly in the construction and scoring of factored, source-trait tests concerns the choice between using first-order and second-order factors. First-order factors are typically slightly correlated, and from factoring these correlations one can obtain broader second-order factors (also correlated), which may be regarded as broader "organizers" among the former. For example, in the 16 PF test—or in the rating factors that correspond thereto—two major second-order factors appear, known as *anxiety* (loading C—, Ego Weakness; O, Guilt-Proneness; Q_4, Ergic Tension; etc.) and *exvia-vs.-invia* (corresponding to the core of the popular concept "extraversion-versus-introversion" and loading F, Surgency; H, Parmia; Q_2—, Low Self-Sufficiency; etc.).

The possibility will now arise, as argued, for example, by Eysenck (1964), that it would be more economical to measure only on such second-order scales. Among IPAT tests this is easily done, incidentally, in either of two ways: (1) one can derive second-order scores from the 16 PF, HSPQ, etc., primary scores themselves, as described below; or (2) one can simply use the IPAT special scales (forty items for anxiety, and forty for exvia) briefly and directly to measure the second-order factors. However, one should decide which to use in terms of the real pros and cons for any shifting of predictive weight from first to second orders. In the ability field, where general intelligence is important, and in relatively restricted areas where there is gain from including the primary abilities, the single second-order fluid or crystallized general ability measure may be preferable. Indeed, both McNemar and Vernon have recently argued that testing *primary abilities* is less predictively valuable than keeping to "general intelligence." This may or may not be advisable; certainly, in the personality and motivation field, the balance of advantages generally favors basing predictive measures on first-order, *primary* factors. But let us look briefly at both fields.

In abilities, if and when there is advantage in going beyond the Culture Fair general fluid ability measure—the most economical predictor—it is largely in vocational guidance. In preparing special occupational advice, predictive power may be strengthened by using six to a dozen primary ability-factor measures, as in the Thurstone PMA, the Guilford Primary Ability battery, the Basic Aptitude Measures of Industrial Psychology, Inc., or French's Primary Ability Kit. It seems that both McNemar and Vernon have belittled the magnitude of the gain in criterion estimates from using primary abilities, because they have been preoccupied with narrowly scholastic criteria. Nevertheless, our recommended installation uses a general ability (Culture Fair) test, indicating that, in relation to available time, we consider that a nice judgment would use the second-order rather than primaries here.

On the other hand, in both the primary personality factors, twelve to sixteen in number (in the CPQ, HSPQ, and 16 PF), and in the motivation realm, where ten factors are available, there is comparative certainty that quite important predictive powers would be lost by dealing only with three or four broader, second-order factors. Actually, the question of primary versus secondary is not one of opinion, for it is always possible (in principle) to calculate how much prediction in any given field one loses by using, say, a single extraversion-introversion scale instead of the six distinct factors that are involved in exvia-vs.-invia. For example, in the chapters on creativity, we have shown that the creative person is, in terms of the extraversion-introversion second-order factor, a person who might well tend to score in the middle of the scale. Some of the factors in that pattern are effective for creativity in the introvert direction and others in the extravert direction. To be precise, the constitutional factor of Parmia-Threctia (H) favors creativity. That is, the person high in Parmia, who is, so to speak, *constitutionally extra-vert,* has advantages. But, at the same time, the qualities of inhibition and suppression ("Keeping up the inner steam pressure"), measured by Desurgency, which is an important factor in introversion, also favor creativity. Similarly, in the motivation area, a measurement on a dozen primary motivation factors tells us far more, and predicts far more, than would two or three measures on two or three rather generalized second-order factors. For, in general, we must remember that *perhaps only a half of the variance of the primary factors in any field is accounted for by the second-order factors.*

Part of the argument for the economy of using one second-order factor in the field of abilities stems from the simple quantitative fact that (in this particular cognitive field) these primary abilities happen to be quite highly correlated. Some evidence suggests, however, that this correlation is large only in *children,* and that among adults the second-order contribution is smaller. Moreover, in the ability field, as distinct from personality, *only two* major second-order factors exist. Consequently, in view of the above correlations in children, it is a practicable economy to let these do duty for the ten or more primary ability scores. Thus our conclusion is that in regard to the choice in abilities much may be said on both sides, and that the "primary-versus-secondary" decision is probably best made in the light of the needs of the particular testing program, the nature of the criterion, and, particularly, the age of the subject. Certainly, for university students (with smaller *g* range), and indeed, adults generally, the primary abilities are important; but for children we would tend to favor a single general-ability measurement, and thus an IQ. This practical decision we would justify, again, by the need to present a battery of maximum condensation. The present proliferation of ability measures should be cut down for practical reasons. At this stage in

Norms

16 P F TEST PROFILE

Date of scoring _____

LOW SCORE DESCRIPTION	Factor	RAW SCORE Form A	RAW SCORE Form B	Total A+B	Stand-ard Score	STANDARD TEN SCORE (IN STENS) 1	2	3	4	5	6	7	8	9	10	HIGH SCORE DESCRIPTION
RESERVED (Sizothymia)	A									· A ·				·		OUTGOING (Cyclothymia)
LESS INTELLIGENT (Low "g")	B							·	·	· B ·		·	·		MORE INTELLIGENT (High "g")
EMOTIONAL (Low ego strength)	C							·	·	· C ·	·	·	·		STABLE (High ego strength)
HUMBLE (Submissiveness)	E						·	·	·	· E ·	·	·	·		ASSERTIVE (Dominance)
SOBER (Desurgency)	F						·	·	·	· F ·	·	·	·		HAPPY-GO-LUCKY (Surgency)
EXPEDIENT (Low superego)	G						·	·	·	· G ·	·	·	·		CONSCIENTIOUS (High superego)
SHY (Threctia)	H						·	·	·	· H ·	·	·	·		VENTURESOME (Parmia)
TOUGH-MINDED (Harria)	I						·	·	·	· I ·	·	·	·		TENDER-MINDED (Premsia)
TRUSTING (Alaxia)	L						·	·	·	· L ·	·	·	·		SUSPICIOUS (Protension)
PRACTICAL (Praxernia)	M						·	·	·	· M ·	-	·	·		IMAGINATIVE (Autia)
FORTHRIGHT (Artlessness)	N						·	·	·	· N ·	·	·	·		SHREWD (Shrewdness)
PLACID (Assurance)	O						·	·	·	· O ·	·	·	·		APPREHENSIVE (Guilt proneness)
CONSERVATIVE (Conservatism)	Q₁						·	·	·	· Q₁ ·	·	·	·		EXPERIMENTING (Radicalism)
GROUP-TIED (Group adherence)	Q₂						·	·	·	· Q₂ ·	·	·	·		SELF-SUFFICIENT (Self-sufficiency)
CASUAL (Low integration)	Q₃						·	·	·	· Q₃ ·	·	·	·		CONTROLLED (High self-concept)
RELAXED (Low ergic tension)	Q₄						·	·	·	· Q₄ ·	·	·	·		TENSE (Ergic Tension)

A sten of: 1 2 3 4 5 6 7 8 9 10 is obtained
by about: 2.3% 4.4% 9.2% 15.0% 19.1% 19.1% 15.0% 9.2% 4.4% 2.3% of adults

	STANDARD SCORE A	B	A+B	SECOND-ORDER FACTORS AND DERIVATIVE PREDICTIONS (IN STENS) AVERAGE RANGE 1	2	3	4	5	6	7	8	9	10	
LOW ANXIETY													·	HIGH ANXIETY
INTROVERSION (Invia)				·	·	·	·	·	·	·	·	·	·	EXTRAVERSION (Exvia)
RESPONSIVE EMOTIONALITY				·	·	·	·	·	·	·	·	·	·	TOUGH POISE
DEPENDENCE				·	·	·	·	·	·	·	·	·	·	INDEPENDENCE
LOW NEUROTICISM				·	·	·	·	·	·	·	·	:	·	HIGH NEUROTICISM
LOW LEADERSHIP POTENTIAL				·	·	·	·	·	·	·	·	·	·	HIGH LEADERSHIP POTENTIAL
LESS CREATIVE PERSONALITY				·	·	·	·	·	·	·	·	·	·	CREATIVE PERSONALITY

FIGURE **18.** *Typical profile record sheet for primaries and secondaries* the development of psychological testing, most school systems will not be prepared to give as much time for personality, motivation, and ability *together* as a psychologist would consider desirable. However, where more time can be given, we would suggest that the basic testing program that we describe below should be augmented by the addition of the Thurstone PMA battery. For the basic program, as suggested at present, yields only a score on a single general second-order culture-fair ability factor of fluid general intelligence. The addition of the PMA would simultaneously provide, without extra testing, a measure of the second-order *crystallized* general ability factor (as a total of the Thurstone primaries) and measures of the separate primaries.

To satisfy the requirements both of those who prefer first- and those who prefer second-order factors, all IPAT scales have now been issued in a form that permits scoring for *both,* simultaneously, from the subject's results on the one score sheet. This requires that the primary scores first be worked out in stens, and that weighted composites of these stens, according to values given in the handbook, be computed for the second-order factors. Such computation of second orders can be done extremely quickly and accurately by electronic computers nowadays. Figure 18 shows the sheet used by IPAT and National Computer Systems, which combines automatic-scanning scoring of the penciled or inked answer sheet and goes right through with this to the first-order scores, the second-order scores, and various other derived scores—all in stens. As the reader will have noticed earlier, in the setting up of personality profiles, there is always available: (a) the list of technical terms for factors—as known to the psychologist; and (b) a list of popular terms—more understandable by parents and employers. The latter are less accurate and therefore more open to false impressions, but many users seem to want to have them available—at least until they become familiar with the technical terms. A more complete view of the role of the computer in scoring, writing descriptive reports, and decision-making is given in Section 8 below.

Section 7   **Proposed Testing Installation Plan for School Systems**

Section 4, above, pointed out that an ideal installation for the general purposes (achievement analysis, prediction, classification, clinical work, and vocational guidance) of most school systems would set up five occasions of comprehensive testing, as follows:

1. *Early School,* i.e., *at age seven,* immediately after the child has settled down to school work.

2. *Elementary Graduation,* i.e., *at age ten to twelve,* in the last year of the general elementary education and as a preliminary to reclassification for type of secondary education.

3. *Early Adolescent Check,* i.e., *at age fourteen,* a midsecondary evaluation, in the first year of senior high school in the United States.

4. *High-School Graduation,* i.e., *at seventeen to eighteen,* with vocational guidance as a major aim.

5. *College and Occupational Guidance,* i.e., *at about twenty to twenty-one,* in the mid-undergraduate years, for those who go to the university, military organizations, and industry, for general evaluation of adjustment to university or occupation and guidance on postgraduate goals or further occupational promotion.

As knowledge increases concerning the factor pattern of abilities and personality in children four to six years old, and more reliable and valid measures are developed, the four-year-old level should become increasingly a comprehensive initial testing point. For no other age is so important as this in relation to all future development. At this point, of course, the installation would be entirely concerned with individual testing.

The above may seem an ambitious installation plan, and it will indeed scarcely prove economically possible for all school systems until psychologists abandon the present frequent duplication of measures, strip down to essential factors, make central test record data simultaneously available to different services (clinic, counseling, scholarship, etc.), and make every effort to substitute for individual testing a set of effective group-testing procedures. The plan will become feasible, and indeed should prove the most economical way of fulfilling the aims of a comprehensive psychological service, primarily through the use of factored tests to assess the main dimensions of ability, personality, and motivation, with only one or two class periods for each. Naturally, even the best-chosen battery of factor tests cannot cover truly minor factors. For a truly universal service, it would be most practicable to aim at present at about a dozen dimensions in *each* of the three domains (ability, personality, and motivation), keeping to these same twelve unitary traits (with minor additions and deletions) through the whole developmental range. This could be tactically augmented according to the needs of the individual case.

With the test batteries and installation conditions here proposed:

All measures will be obtained by *group testing* carried out in the classroom, except for some *supplementary* individual testing at the Early School (six-to-seven-year) level.

The testing time will be divided into two parallel sessions, each of about three hours' duration (with rest intervals), spaced one or two weeks apart, in order to reduce error from temporary psychological states, i.e., "a poor day." The two sessions will be equivalent in pattern (because equivalent forms of the tests exist).

The scoring can be largely automatic or clerical and will end in profiles of standard scores, separately set out for ability, personality, and dynamic (motivational) factors, which, together with achievement scores, will fit conveniently on a single IBM record card. However, the profiles can also be drawn for visual inspection on the profile sheets provided with these tests.

The actual tests, times, etc., recommended for each of the five age-period installations are as follows:

I. The Early School Examination at 7 (6–8) years

ABILITY: *Culture Fair Intelligence Test, Scale 1 (CF 1).* Time: 22 mins. actual testing (35 mins. with instructions). Forms A and B (Equivalent forms, each 22 mins. Form B available in 1966).

This test has the following parts:

Test 1. Substitution	3 mins.
Test 2. Classification	2 mins.
Test 3. Mazes	2½ mins.
Test 4. Selecting named objects	2½ mins.
Test 5. Following directions	4 mins.
Test 6. Wrong pictures	2½ mins.
Test 7. Riddles	3½ mins.
Test 8. Similarities	2 mins.

Total raw score possible: 96 points.

This test was originally constructed by rejecting from the Binet the tests found to be of lower g saturation, while augmenting those of highest general ability validity (Cattell and Bristol, 1933). It is available from IPAT[4] in the U.S., NFER[5] and Harrap and Co. in Britain, and ACER[6] in Australia. The results can be divided according to two principles: (1) into a truly culture-fair, fluid general ability measure from adding only subtests 1, 3, 5, and 8, and a crystallized general ability measure from subtests 2, 4, 6, and 7; (2) into a wholly group administrable test, with subtests 1, 3, 4, 6, 7, and 8, and the complete test when the individual tests 3 and 5 are added.

PERSONALITY: *The Early School Personality Questionnaire* (ESPQ). Time: 30–50 mins.

This measures twelve personality factors and has two forms, A and B. Each form is divided into two parts (A_1, A_2 for A and B_1, B_2 for B), to allow for a rest pause or for the administration of the two parts in different class periods. It covers factors A, B, C, D, E, F, G, H, I, J, N, O, and Q_4. Note that this includes a second intelligence measure, B, which is *not* culture-fair, but "traditional" (crystallized general ability), and untimed, i.e., a "power" test. Obtainable from IPAT, NFER, ACER, etc.

[4] Institute for Personality and Ability Testing, 1602 Coronado Dr., Champaign, Illinois 61820.

[5] National Foundation for Educational Research, The Mere, Upton Park, Slough, Bucks., has Form A; Harrap and Co. have Form B.

[6] Australian Council for Educational Research, Frederick St., Hawthorne E2, Victoria.

MOTIVATION: There is at present no motivational analysis test adapted to this age level. There is, however, the Cattell-Meredith form of the O-A (Objective-Analytic) Personality Factor Battery, requiring 2 hours for the objective (nonquestionnaire) measurement of personality factors, about half being group administrable. At present this exists in experimental form, with brief but not extensive norms.

ADMINISTRATIVE PARTICULARS. The battery requires about 1 to 1½ hours and is best given in two parts over two or three days. Scoring can be entirely clerical; results are in IQ and stave scores. An equivalent battery, Form B of both tests, can be used to extend the testing period to increase reliability. It is strongly recommended, in view of the brevity of the tests covering thirteen dimensions, that both A and B forms be administered, a week or two apart, in the two sessions defined above.

II. The Elementary Graduation Examination at 11 (10–12) years
ABILITY: 1. *General: The Culture Fair, Scale 2* (CF 2). Forms A and B. Time: 25 mins. (50 mins. with instructions).

This group test has four subtests per form and yields a single IQ measure of general fluid ability. Obtainable from IPAT, NFER, ACER, etc.

2. *Special: The Thurstone Primary Mental Ability Test* (PMA). Time: 26 mins. (40–50 mins. with instructions).

This supplements the CF test by giving scores on primary abilities, plus a "crystallized" general ability measure from adding the primary scores.

PERSONALITY: *The Child Personality Questionnaire* (CPQ) Time: 35 mins.

This measures fourteen personality factors: A, B, C, D, E, F, G, H, I, J, N, O, Q_3, and Q_4; and provides equivalent A and B forms. Obtainable from IPAT, ACER, etc.

MOTIVATION: *The School Motivation Test* (SMAT) by Sweney, Sealy, and Cattell. Time: 40 mins.

Can be used with twelve-year-olds, but with eleven-year-olds only when the educational level is distinctly good. For description, see next examination below. A motivation measure for the nine-to-eleven range is under construction.

ADMINISTRATIVE PARTICULARS. The whole battery requires, with time for instructions, etc., about 3 hours and is group administrable throughout. It is best spread over a couple of days. Scoring can be entirely clerical or machine, but clerical is actually shorter on the multifactor scoring.

An equivalent B form exists for all tests; and it is strongly recommended, especially because of the decisions that commonly hinge on testing at this age, that both the battery and its equivalent form be administered, preferably two or three weeks apart.

III. The Early Adolescent Check Examination at 14 (13–15) years
ABILITY: 1. *General: The Culture Fair, Scale 2* (CF 2). Forms A and B.
Time: 25 mins. actual testing; 50 mins. in all.

This is the same test described in II. It has four subtests: series, classification, matrices, and topology; and A and B forms. Its degree of difficulty is appropriate for both the eleven-year (Examination Stage II) and the fourteen-year (Examination Stage III) levels.

2. *Special: The Thurstone Primary Mental Ability Test.* Time: 26 mins. actual testing time; 40–50 mins. in all. See Examination II above.

This adds to the special ability measures a crystallized general ability measure.

PERSONALITY: *The High School Personality Questionnaire* (HSPQ). Time: 35 mins. plus.

This measures fourteen personality factors: A, B, C, D, E, F, G, H, I, J, O, Q_2, Q_3, and Q_4; and provides equivalent A and B forms. Note that B gives a supplementary and informationally different intelligence score, namely, a crystallized ability under "power" conditions.

MOTIVATION: *The School Motivation Analysis Test* (SMAT). Time (one form): 50 mins. plus.

This gives scores on ten dynamic structures—six ergs (drives), and four sentiments. The six ergs are: Assertion, Sensual Pleasures or Narcissism, Sex Drive, Gregariousness, Protectiveness, Curiosity and Pugnacity; the four sentiments are: Self-Sentiment, Superego, Religion, and Patriotism. These enter with various weights into achievements and the understanding of personality adjustment. It is available in an A and B form from IPAT, NFER, and ACER.

ADMINISTRATIVE PARTICULARS. The whole battery requires about 3 hours, or 160 mins. if one restricts coverage to the basic measures and omits the special abilities. Its administration is best spread over a couple of days. Scoring can be done entirely by clerical help or IBM.

Because A and B equivalents exist for all tests, the whole battery can be administered a second time in an equivalent B form. To iron out "state" differences, due to illness, temporary conditions, and so on, it is recommended that the two testings, with the equivalent forms, be spaced out at least a couple weeks apart.

IV. The High-School Pregraduation Examination at 17–18 years
ABILITY: 1. *General: The Culture Fair, Scale 3* (CF 3). Forms A and B.
Time: 25 mins. actual testing; 50 mins. in all.

At this age, it is necessary to make a deliberate choice between the use of Scale 2, running from ages eight through fourteen (and suitable for average adults), and Scale 3, which is designed to give maximum discrimination among college students—say over the top $\frac{1}{6}$ of the intelligence range. Consequently, where, as in Europe, about $\frac{1}{6}$ go to the selective (professional) secondary school, or in those states in the U.S. where less than two-thirds of the total population graduate from high school, Scale 3 is recommended; but elsewhere Scale 2 is quite difficult enough to give a good "spread" for most young adults. For adults in unskilled occupations, and in age ranges—say above thirty—where the scores run lower, Scale 2, indeed, gives a *better* spread for the group as a whole. Scale 2 has already been described, and Scale 3 is exactly parallel to it in construction. It has four subtests: series, classification, matrices, and topology—just as in Scale 2; and A and B equivalent forms. Obtainable from IPAT, NFER, ACER, etc.

2. *Special Addition: The Thurstone Primary Mental Abilities Test*. Adult Form.: 30 mins. approx.

At this age, the special abilities become more important, both in the statistical sense and in relation to the practical problems of vocational guidance, so this test should not be omitted. A briefer alternative to the PMA, the Factored Aptitude Series (Industrial Psychology, Inc., 515 Madison Ave., New York, New York 10022), has a greater applicability in industrial and vocational guidance as such, because it covers *more* special aptitudes. These include vocabulary ("office terms," etc.), number, perception, fluency, memory, spatial ability, dexterity, and other known primary factors. The parts can be separately administered and take 5 mins. each, thus roughly 40 mins. in all.

PERSONALITY: *The High School Personality Questionnaire* or the *Sixteen Personality Factor Questionnaire* (16 PF). Time: 40 mins. and 50 mins. plus, respectively, assuming only one form used on the first of the two sessions.

Here, as in ability testing, a choice has to be made, according to local conditions and age of testing, between two tests: the HSPQ and the 16 PF. The decision rests mainly on the maturity of the individuals concerned and the time available. The HSPQ questions are directed more to the content of thought and interest of the high-school student, whereas the 16 PF is broadened to the life of adults generally. The HSPQ has fourteen factors; the 16 PF has sixteen, and also already has more equivalent forms—A, B, C, and D—whereas the third and fourth forms of the HSPQ may not be available for a year or so. If a briefer testing program is envisaged, the HSPQ will be preferred. For a longer testing program, with greater emphasis on thorough vocational guidance as such, the 16 PF is better. (Note, however, that though the 16 PF Handbook is richer in occupational profiles, etc., the same regression and pattern-matching calculations have been shown to apply to HSPQ factor scores when data on both have been available for comparison.) Obtainable from IPAT, NFER, ACER, etc.

MOTIVATION: *The Motivation Analysis Test* (MAT). Time: 50 mins. plus.

At the sixteen-to-eighteen year level, again, a decision has to be made between the High School Motivation Analysis Test, SMAT, which is for ages twelve to seventeen, and the MAT, for eighteen-year-olds and all adult levels. In this case, the dynamic structure changes so rapidly over the adolescent period that by eighteen it is better to use MAT. This measures the strength of ten dynamic structures, five ergs or drives—Self-Sentiment, Super-ego, Career, Sweetheart, and Parental Home. Differentiations on these are known for high and low achievers, delinquents-non-delinquents, and various clinical case groups. It has a B form in preparation. Obtainable from IPAT, NFER, ACER, etc.

ADMINISTRATIVE PARTICULARS. The total time for the battery described is about 3 hours, and it will obviously need to be spread over three ordinary class periods, preferably spread over a couple of days. Scoring is objective in all tests and can therefore be done clerically or by IBM. Because of the importance for vocational guidance at this point, it would seem desirable to test with equivalent A and B batteries, on all tests, spaced well apart (about three weeks) and adding up to 6 hours of total testing.

V. The College or Early Occupational Guidance Examination

Some difference of emphasis will naturally exist between such an examination in its various settings—undergraduates, officer candidates, young executives in business—but the test level assumes some selection of intelligence from the general population; the test choice depends upon suitable adaptations and additions by the psychologist in charge.

ABILITY: 1. *General: The Culture Fair, Scale 3* (CF 3). Time: 25 mins. actual testing; 50 mins. in all. Forms A and B together.

The CF 3 is a test deliberately adjusted in difficulty to give maximum discrimination at the college-student level and among adults of superior intelligence level. Since fine and reliable discrimination at this level has now become so important, e.g., in advising whether to terminate with a bachelor's degree or go further, in selecting creative scientists, etc., we would advise that *both* test forms be used, even in the first of the two sessions.

It may also be considered desirable to supplement this measure of fluid ability with a longer and more direct crystallized general ability measure than that which is available as a "secondary" from the PMA. Certainly, if crystallized ability is to be measured, it needs something more than the analogies instrument so often used at the college level. The latter is obviously restricted to one particular narrow subtest form and is heavily biased by V factor from a specialized vocabulary. The Cattell-Scale III, published by Harrap and Co., Holborn, London W.C. 2, is a wider crystallized general ability measure, with six subtests, and takes about 40 mins. for Form A (or

Form B). This test is the only test on which adult occupational norms have been set in Britain; it is used both in Britain and America in selecting superior adult intelligence level in the Mensa societies.

    2. *Special: The Primary Aptitude* (see above; Time: 30 mins. approx.) or the *Factored Aptitude Tests,* of Industrial Psychology, Inc. (see above; Time: about 40 mins.).

PERSONALITY: *The Sixteen Personality Factor Questionnaire* (see above; Time: about 35 mins. plus for A form).

This test is especially apt for the college-student population. In the setting where personality begins to have a larger role in achievement, and adjustment problems are *more* numerous, it is recommended that two forms be given (e.g., A and B, A and C, or B and D), even in the one battery. Furthermore, in the interests of clinical screening for college counseling activities, it is desirable to calculate, as shown in the handbook, the score on the second-order anxiety factor, and the weighted composite for degree of neuroticism.

MOTIVATION: *The Motivation Analysis Test.* Time: 40 mins.

This has been described above, under Examination IV. Again, as with the 16 PF, the clinical use of the results is an aspect of greater importance here, for, in a university of, say, no more than 10,000 students, there will normally be several hundreds whose needs should be recognized and met by psychotherapy or more limited guidance.

ADMINISTRATIVE PARTICULARS. The total time for the above battery is about 40 mins. Scoring is entirely objective and can be automated.

In some universities that have already started a testing installation essentially on the above lines, the battery has been administered *at the beginning of the freshman year.* Obviously, if good counseling use is to be made of the psychological examination, especially in relation to the large dropout almost universally occurring in the first year, the testing had better occur early in the freshman year. Nevertheless, if administratively possible, it would be better to avoid the very beginning of the first semester, so that one can evaluate the developed and relatively matured adjustment after due contact with college life. This suggests that two testing periods, one in the first semester and one in the semester before graduation would be better than the overeconomical single testing during college life so far envisaged. Because an equivalent battery can be built from the A and B forms of most constituents, it would also be possible to have the reliability of double length at the first testing, and to repeat both batteries at the second testing three years later.

The adaptations of this fifth, "early adult life" test installation to the somewhat different needs of selection of junior executives or officer candidates will be evident. In the intelligence field, a useful compromise consists in giving CF Scale 2, Forms A and B, on the first occasion and CF Scale 3, Forms A and B, on the second, thus achieving maximum discrimination across the wider range. Finally, in all fields, such as scholarship selection and occupational promotion, where motivational distortion or even plain faking can arise, much can be said (despite the availability of a motivational distortion scale on the 16 PF) for shifting to the objective personality batteries. (The ability and motivation panels are already objective.) The O-A (Objective-Analytic) Personality Factor Battery has recently been adapted by Hundleby (1967) to permit administration for only as many factors as may be desired, instead of the eighteen of the original full battery. It remains to be seen from actual use how practicable this makes the substitution of objective for questionnaire personality tests in school practice.

Section 8   The Processes of Decision in Evaluation and Counseling

An argument has been advanced in this chapter—and implicitly, earlier—that (1) actual test administration and scoring, and (2) the putting into effect, in classroom practice and counseling by personal contact, of decisions made by the psychologist, can be more economically and even more effectively carried out by persons less qualified than the professional psychologist. This assumes, however, that the classroom teacher, the B.A. or diplomate in psychology, or the person with a master's degree in counseling, works in close organization with the trained psychologist of doctorate and post-doctorate status. It also supposes that the last-mentioned is capable of using the most sophisticated combination of mathematical and psychological laws.

It is difficult in the space of one section—which confines one to remarks only on the total field—to comment effectively on the psychological decision process, because it is always to some extent local. However, as has already been pointed out (page 238), in general, a psychological diagnosis or prediction can formally take one of two models. In what may be called the *adjustment* or typing model, one finds the type profile of, say, the adjusted members of an occupation, and asks how well the profile of a given client fits this characteristic profile. If it fits well, one may conclude that the client will in some sense be adjusted to living that kind of life—because others with his profile have done so. Such a verdict of adjustment, however, is not necessarily a guarantee of how efficient he will be in it. In the second approach, therefore—the *fitness* or *efficiency* method—one obtains a measurable criterion of excellence of performance in the occupation and, by correlating this with the main ability and personality factors, obtains a linear specification or regression equation for predicting excellence. These two main approaches have certain possible special forms and modifications, and if the fitness equation is allowed to go nonlinear, they become very similar. But, for simplicity, let us say that we have the alternatives of: (1) calculating the similarity of the person's profile with the criterion (job or clinical classification); or (2) computing from a factor specification equation to get a criterion of efficiency estimate, as the formal basis of use of personality records in diagnosis, prognosis, vocational guidance, or any other decision in applied psychology.

Now, the human mind, even without explicit calculation, is also compelled to make judgments that must formally proceed along one of these two lines. But it goes without saying that decision must rest on calculation and cannot be left to "impression." When dealing with only two or three cases, the counselor may be excused for employing these old-fashioned "look and judge" methods, but whenever resources make use of a computer appropriate and easy, it is a potent ally. One can show that a judgment of the degree of pattern similarity of two profiles, when made by eye, is less accurate than when calculated. Similarly, the attempt to allow in the mind's eye for the different functional weights to be assigned to a number of factors that produce a certain outcome can yield anything from a rough to a wildly inaccurate judgment.

Quite apart from the accuracy of calculation, one well-known respect in which the computer and the human mind differ sharply is in the sheer number of factors that each can hold in view. Most psychologists today are familiar with Meehl's demonstration (1954) that intuitive predictions get little better as one continues to supply information to the clinician beyond five or six "bits." That is, the clinician's *personal* judgment gets no better, but if he uses the computer, it continues to wring better prediction out of the extra determining factors down to the last drop of relevance. Wherever the prediction or diagnosis is multivariate, the calculation from computer records does better than the unaided human mind. And there are extremely few applied problems that are not, fundamentally, multivariate in character.

At this point, some human critic, temperamentally averse to praising transistors above flesh and blood, will object that the computer may be a good mathematician but a very poor psychologist. He should be warned that his brickbat could easily become a boomerang. For, as has been argued elsewhere in this book, the formulation of this issue as one of actuarial versus clinical prediction, or statistics versus psychological intuition, has actually started us off on a misleading antithesis. A deeper analysis reveals that we are dealing with a two-dimensional difference, not a bipolar antithesis. The real alternatives are, on the one hand, mathematico-statistical calculation versus intuitive methods of judgment, and on the other, the use of psychological laws and principles versus purely actuarial, statistical probability laws without scientific understanding. In other words, the first of these—the use of mathematical calculation—should not be confused with the second—a restriction of principles to merely actuarial predictions. And we should also recognize that known psychological, mathematically expressed laws can be employed *either* in computer calculations *or* in intuitive evaluations in our heads. The false antithesis of "mathematically-skilled-psychological-ignorance" versus "psychologically-well-informed-intuitive-inaccuracy" arose partly because of a historical accident; the last generation's psychometrists were often not very deeply interested in *psychological* laws. They shoveled all kinds of tests or items into a hopper and were satisfied so long as they obtained some respectable immediate multiple correlation. About the psychological nature of what they shoveled in, they could not have cared less. They were primarily accountants and statisticians, out for some "good figures."

For the sake of perspective on the real value of psychometry, Cattell has elsewhere (1964b) drawn a distinction between this *itemetrics*, which consists of playing with test items as "atoms" of mental measurement, and *functional psychometrics* (or structuralism), in which one is interested in finding the natural structures and processes operating in human dynamics, and in addressing one's measurement techniques *only* to such meaningful entities. Psychometrists whose vocational profile is close to that of accountants have wondered why one feels the need thus to separate and define this other branch as *functional psychometrics*. But the well-rounded practitioner will agree that the psychologist who uses a computer, but is over-concerned with item statistics, advances psychology no more, on the one hand, than does the nonmetric intuitive and literary clinician (who has no use for computers) on the other. Each misses the important principle—which is to work with well-proven, research-based, functional laws of human behavior, explicitly stated and tried out in quantitative predictions.

Surely, it is important for the advance of psychometrics to approach the computer with measures concerned with the discovery of scientific psychological laws, upon which lawful extrapolations can be made to operate. The wisdom of the psychologist should be able to go into the computer along with his figures. This should be done both in the interests of greater effectiveness and of furthering explicit testing of the principles on which our science rests. For if the practitioner can scientifically formulate the psychological laws, upon which his intuition alone has formerly been working, the computer will do a better job than *he* can in their application, just as it does with the more restricted statistical prediction. Analogously, a physicist may know the basic laws of physics and all the weight and energy properties of a particular rocket very well, but without a computer he has no hope of landing the rocket on Venus.

There may be some reluctance to follow this advice. What we have called our psychological wisdom, i.e., the psychological laws and equations regarding personality and personality change, is perhaps not very impressive at the present time—at least when it is stripped of verbiage! But one can see that personality is beginning to put on muscles, partly from the scientific feedback from use in applied psychology of structural psychometric concepts (for example, from the use of defined factorial source traits instead of a hodgepodge of patent-medicine test devices), and partly from using functional specification equations. Chapter 11, for instance, shows that by adding a dozen personality factor measures to an economical set of primary ability measures, we can approximately *double* the accuracy of prediction of school achievement in relation to that obtainable from ability measures alone. And it has also been shown that by using measures of interest and motivation, as with the MAT, we can get a further increase. Our hypothesis, in fact, is that as these measures increase in precision and reliability we may expect to predict 25% of the criterion from abilities, 25% from personality, and 25% from motivation.

Nevertheless, the ultimate gain from thus knowing what classes of traits we are covering, by working in structural terms, and not factorially duplicating or missing any important area, is perhaps small compared with the advantage of dealing with entities, such as ego strength, surgency, the sex erg, and the self-sentiment, *about which personality theory can—and does— develop generalizations and laws.* For this means that we can project our predictions beyond immediate actuarial, blindly empirical calculation, by using equations intelligently modified by psychological laws, for changes of the stimulus situation, the age of the subjects, or even internal physiological changes that we may be informed will intervene in the given case. For example, a psychometrist may have an actuarial, immediate set of correlations for estimating the individual school performance in high school of a child living at home, at age sixteen. But he needs meaningful measures if he is to introduce psychological principles into the computer to extrapolate to age eighteen, when that person will, say, be living away from home, exposed to new peer-group pressures, and working under greater stress in the examinations themselves.

The computer thus has a deeper significance to the modern psychologist than as an aid to scoring and recording as such. It offers itself as a means of applying psychological laws *and* as a storage system for the accumulated wisdom of practice. The isolated practitioner should increasingly turn to it to refer to cases like that which he faces at the given moment to see "what happened later," and so on. If this seems impracticably futuristic, we must point out that there are already enough examples of successful response by individual practitioners to show that intelligent use of the computer, even with our present limited psychological know-how, can solve many a problem. For example, the descriptions of practice given by Eber, Swenson, Fowler (1964) and others already show that something very different from the traditional pedestrian rate of handling cases can now be achieved. Psychologists have been able diagnostically to handle roughly three times as many cases per year as typical practitioners now do. In the face of such pioneer demonstrations, it is unlikely that schools and child-guidance clinics will long remain satisfied with traditional methods. Such a transformation to electronic computer aids, despite the vigorous denials of the conservative practitioner, is likely to increase the number of cases handled, and produce *a gain in individual effectiveness* in guidance and treatment, when compared with the results of present intuitive methods.

Other uses of computer services now made available for users of the tests described are: (1) automation, by tape and headphones, of administrative instruction and the timing of tests; and (2) the translation of a profile of scores on the 16 PF, etc., into a complete verbal report on the case. The advantages of the second lie in both precision and speed. The psychologist who writes out his tenth case paper for the day (if indeed he gets that far) becomes a tired groper after new words. Partly through fatigue and partly to avoid monotony (to himself), he may begin to use adjectives and phrases that are no longer correct or accurate. If one follows the way in which Eber (1963) sensitively attached graded adjectives and verbs to different factor scores and combinations of factor scores, this danger disappears. Each case can be given a highly individual description, diagnosis, and prognosis, but the computer will always translate from score combinations to words in a known and dependable fashion (1963). As Eber pointed out, an unexpected bonus resides in the speed of computer printout, at least ten times faster than the average typist, providing a further economy. His fast turnover of diagnostic casework gives pragmatic proof of the effectiveness of this well-designed team of man and machine.

However, the provision of exact, compact, numerical and verbal descriptive records is only the first of the uses of computers in psychological practice. For, naturally, our measurements are not just for *preservation,* but for effective immediate *use,* too. This need to make psychological decisions from measurements need not, however, cut short our honeymoon with automation, but should extend into a long and fruitful marriage.

Like any practical change in human affairs, this is certain to cause repercussions in social, professional, and economic organization. Broadly, the advantages of computer handling arise from the peculiarly multivariate nature of applied psychology. It deals not only with many variables, but with many people and many occasions.

Perhaps a vision may be permitted of a well-organized future, in which every state psychological association has its own Telstar, beaming back to each consulting room numerical answers, and immediate advice on various decisions, based on stored psychological knowledge. A variety of complex alternatives will thereby be pointed out (as fast as Eber's present descriptive accounts) in immediate response to the test scores telephoned to it. The applied psychologists of the future may then look back with sympathy, perhaps not entirely unmingled with contempt, on his clumsy colleague of these cruder times.

Incidentally, greater resources of this kind would make more practicable the principle of *depth psychometry* (Cattell, 1967), which proposes that to factor—*source-trait*—measures we also add *surface-trait* (Cattell, 1946, 1957) measures. For example, if the MMPI and the 16 PF could both, through machine economy, be administered and scored for each adolescent in a child-guidance clinic, the relation between the surface-trait (correlation cluster) scores on the one hand and the source-trait (factor) scores on the other would give additional information. A given score on a syndrome (surface trait) such as the MMPI is designed to measure represents a symptom severity that can be reached or generated in a variety of ways—in terms of contributing source traits. For example, an obsessional neurotic score of such and such a numerical value on the MMPI may be derived from diverse degrees of contribution by Ego Weakness (C— factor), Ergic Tension (Q_4), Submissiveness (E—), etc., on the 16 PF. This principle of *depth psychometry*—of getting both the surface trait (or composite criterion) score *and* the underlying source-trait score—applies equally to school problems—underachievement, and so forth.

In the majority of the above applications of analytical testing, the psychologist will probably finish by applying the specification equation (rather than r_p in the "adjustment" method). The alert statistician should note, now that we have reached this point, that, because the factors of ability, personality, and motivation are in general somewhat mutually correlated, *the weights assigned to them in the specification equation will not be the same as their correlations with the criterion*. If he knows these latter correlations (V_{fs} below) *and* the correlations among the factors (R, below), then, in matrix terms, the calculation of the weights (W, below) becomes:

16.4 $$W = R^{-1} V_{fs}$$

An example of such weights for two important second-order factors and three criteria is given in the 16 PF Handbook (Cattell and Eber, 1967) as follows:

Anxiety Score = $3.74 - .18C - .17H + .19L + .30O - .20Q_3 + .38Q_4$
(In stens)

Exvia (Extra- = $1.26 + .17A + .33E + .41F + .48H - .16Q_2$
version)
(In stens)

Neuroticism = $6.33 - .08B - .30C - .19E - .44F - .11G + .12H + $
(In stens) $.25I + .30O - .10Q_1 + .40Q_4$

Creativity = $.50 - .37A + .37B + .18E - .37F + .18H + .37I + $
     $.18M - .18N + .18Q_1 + .37Q_2$

Leadership = $1.30 + .13B + .13C + .06E + .26F + .26G + .26H$
     $- .13I - .13M + .06N - .26O + .26Q_3 - .13Q_4$

Such weights are provided for a great variety of decision-making—in education, delinquency, occupational performance, and other criteria—in the handbooks for the Culture Fair Intelligence Tests, the 16 PF, HSPQ, and other personality questionnaires, and motivation tests in the installations above, and need not be pursued, except in general terms, here. However, because weights always vary with samples, additional accuracy may be gained from recalculating R and V_{fs} for the actual sample that the psychologist is using, and then recalculating W.

Possessing the weights, the psychologist will do well to calculate the multiple correlation ($\sqrt{w_{1c}r_{1c} + w_{2c}r_{2c} \ldots + w_{kc}r_{kc}}$, where w_{kc} is the weight and r_{kc} the correlation of the kth factor with the criterion, c). From this, he may get the standard error of estimate of the criterion ($\sqrt{1 - R^2}$) and thus know how far his estimate for a given individual is likely to be "off."

However, as repeatedly stressed above, the gain of functional testing is not, in the last resort, an actuarial one (a high predictivity for a given testing time) but one of individual psychological *understanding*. And here the psychologist looks not only at the estimate, e.g., of expected achievement, but at the personality and ability factors evidently most important in contributing to it in the given individual.

SUMMARY *of Chapter Sixteen*

1. Very substantial advances could be made in both education and industry in terms of better selection for special fields and for promotions; in the understanding of the individual's problems in relation to achievement; and in the recognition of needs for counseling and psychotherapy, if regular psychological testing installations at strategic periods were arranged as part of the system.

2. The obstacles to be overcome in initiating such improvements are: (a) technical, in translating research knowledge into economical and efficient group-testing procedures; (b) social, in dissolving irrational objections to new testing ideas, and in bringing enlightenment where misunderstandings now occur about the role, the nature, and the social aims of psychological testing; and (c) organizational, in centering the main psychological guidance of the growing child in some single testing and recording school system. This requires a central psychological service, simultaneously covering scholarship selection, diagnosis and treatment of backwardness, vocational guidance, and child-guidance clinics in a single intercommunicating system. Therein a symbiotic variety of psychological specialists would use common test records and a common communication and referral network, with highly trained

professional psychologists in charge, and a psychologist-teacher or counselor in each school to assist and implement decisions.

3. From a technical point of view, a testing installation has to be comprehensive of all aspects of the individual, while avoiding the widespread practice of achieving such comprehensiveness merely by a time-consuming and impractical accumulation of "special purpose" or ad hoc tests. The solution lies rather in structural testing, aimed at tapping the major ability, personality, and motivation dimensions known to the psychologist in general personality theory. More specifically, the functional use of structured tests requires: (a) proven factorial functional unities, about a dozen of which will cover each of the three main modalities—ability, personality, and motivation-interest; (b) using these same basic individual-difference measures for educational, clinical, and occupational guidance, and thus accumulating a really adequate set of specification equations for criteria; and (c) employing the psychological as well as the statistical laws that the advance of personality psychology is now building up around these concepts.

4. A record system is needed, whereby, whenever an individual case comes up for consideration, it will be possible to refer to his testing results, preserved developmentally over a number of years. This will bring added reliability of evaluation—for example, through having several intelligence measures rather than one—and added knowledge about past developmental trends.

5. For the developmental knowledge to be maximally useful, it must be in terms of concepts and patterns that have stability of identity and meaning over time. These are best achieved by the use of measures of the same set of basic unitary traits over a long period of time, a condition provided by, for example, the personality test series of the Early School, the Child, the High School, and the Sixteen Personality Factor Questionnaires, as well as by the School Motivation Analysis Test and the Motivation Analysis Test.

6. The statistical and psychological use of the results involves: (a) discovery of the regression coefficients on various success criteria; and (b) pattern-similarity calculations with the profiles to measure adjustment to the profiles of various occupations and clinical groups. No account is given of these procedures here because they belong to statistics and guidance courses; they are, however, illustrated in the earlier chapters of this volume. The major design for efficient use of such results has been described elsewhere (Cattell, 1957, Chapter 16) as the two-file system. Therein one file is kept for all individuals, consisting essentially of profiles in the ability, personality, and motivational domains. Another file consists of the profiles or the regression weights, for success in various school subjects and occupations, or prognoses in clinical treatment, and so forth. The latter can be made adequate only by well-organized research relating the same basic personality and ability struc-

tures to all kinds of important criteria. The beginnings of occupational profiles and clinical profiles for guidance—some forty or fifty of them—are available for the personality factors in the test handbooks described and are gradually being accumulated for abilities and motivation measures in psychological literature.

7. The requirements for monitoring of healthy development might be economically met by some five main occasions of examination, at 7, 11, 14, 17, and 21 years (preceded by testing in the infant period, as tests improve). These points are chosen for their relevance both to school systems (points of change and reclassification) and to important periods of natural development (e.g., the adolescent period). Sufficiently valid tests for sufficiently defined structures do not exist for five-year-olds, except possibly for intelligence. And economy may dictate that only one substantial testing be given during the college period. Installations are described for the five occasions listed above.

8. At each of the examinations, listed as Early School, Elementary Graduation, Adolescent Check, High-School Graduation, and College Counseling, a battery needing 2½ to 3½ hours, and described in detail above, is required. It covers intelligence, special abilities, personality factors, and motivation factors. These are group administrable; objectively, automatically, or computer scorable; comparable for developmental-analysis purposes; related to basic psychological concepts; and available in equivalent forms to increase reliability of measurement by testing on two or more occasions. Some of these measures in the personality field, particularly the new objective motivation batteries, have not yet reached the reliability levels to which we are accustomed in ability and achievement tests; whereas others, such as the O-A (Objective-Analytic) Personality Batteries, are cumbersome and require special skills for their administration. Despite the relatively experimental stage at which some tests currently rest, the core tests offered above are already capable of substantially increasing the understanding and prediction of achievement and creativity beyond that attained with aptitude and achievement tests alone. The expansion of the suggested central group-test installation into individual testing, where needed, will be evident to the trained psychologist. However, if services are to be made more effectively and widely available without impossible expenditures, the psychologist needs now to develop insightful structural testing, to organize common records and communications, to use automation of test administration, and to obtain more complex test derivatives through computers.

9. The reader is reminded of standard psychometric procedures in decision-making: the calculation of specification equation weights, multiple correlations, and errors of estimation of criteria. Although the handbooks provide weights for many criteria—educational, clinical, and occupational—there are advantages in recalculating these locally for new populations and

samples. Probability is the touchstone for all psychometric decisions. An aim beyond the classificatory, therapeutic, or adjustment decision is that of gaining insight into the individual's way of achieving or adjusting, and where the method of *psychometric depth analysis* has particular relevance.

10. It is pointed out that the computer has a deeper meaning for future psychological practice than merely one of machine scoring, or the writing out of case studies, or the calculating of derivative specification and second-order scores, important though these are. It can also store experience from practice and encode psychological laws, applying them in complex ways, beyond the span of the individual psychologist's capacity, and thus enable him to project to other times and situations from present measurement data.

TABLE OF REFERENCES

ALEXANDER, W. P. (1935). "Intelligence, Concrete and Abstract," *British Journal of Psychology Monograph Supplement*, No. 19.

ALLEN, WALTER. (1948). *Writers on Writing*. London: Phoenix House.

ANASTASI, ANNE. (1954). *Psychological Testing*. New York: Macmillan.

———. (1958). *Differential Psychology*. 3rd ed. New York: Macmillan.

ANDERSON, A. W. (1960). "Personality Traits of Western Australian University Entrants," *Australian Journal of Psychology, 12*, 4–9.

ANDRADE, E. M., DE ALVES, D. G., and FORD, J. L. *A Comparison of North American and Brazilian College Students' Personality Profiles on the 16 PF Questionnaire*. (On press.)

ARBOUS, A. G. (1955). *Selection for Industrial Leadership*. London: Oxford University Press.

BAKER, R., CATTELL, R. B., and COAN, R. C. (1968) *The Early School Personality Questionnaire (ESPQ)*. Champaign, Ill.: IPAT.

BALL, R. S. (1938). "The Predictability of Occupational Level from Intelligence," *Journal of Consulting Psychology, 2*, 184–186.

BARNES, P. J. (1955). "Prediction of Achievement of Grades 1 Through 4 from Otis Quick-Scoring Mental Ability Tests," *Educational and Psychological Measurement, 15*, 493–494.

BARRON, FRANK.(1955). "The Disposition Toward Originality," *Journal of Abnormal and Social Psychology, 51*, 478–485.

BENNETT, G. K., SEASHORE, H. G., and WESMAN, A. (1952). "Aptitude Testing. Does it 'Prove Out' in Counseling Practice?" *Occupations, 30*, 584–593.

BROADBENT, D. E. (1958). *Perception and Communication*. London: Pergamon.

BRONFENBRENNER, U. (1958). "Socialization and Social Class Through Time and Space," in E. E. Maccoby, T. M. Newcomb, and E. L. Hartley (eds.), *Readings in Social Psychology*, 3rd ed. New York: Henry Holt Company. Pp. 400–424.

BURKS, B. S. (1928). "The Relative Influence of Nature and Nurture Upon Mental Development," in *Twenty-seventh Yearbook of the National Society for the Study of Education*. Chicago: University of Chicago Press; (1940), Bloomington, Ill.: Public School Publishing Company. Pp. 219–316.

———, JENSEN, D. W., and TERMAN, L. M. (1930). *Genetic Studies of Genius*. Vol. 3, *The Promise of Youth*. Stanford: Stanford University Press.

BUROS, O. K. (1965). *The Sixth Mental Measurements Yearbook*. Highland Park, N.J.: The Gryphon Press.

BURT, SIR CYRIL.(1955). "The Evidence for the Concept of Intelligence," *British Journal of Educational Psychology, 25*, 158–177.

———. (1962). "Critical Notice of *Creativity and Intelligence* by Getzels and Jackson," *British Journal of Educational Psychology, 32*, 292–298.

————, and HOWARD, M. (1956). "The Multifactorial Theory of Inheritance," *British Journal of Statistical Psychology, 9,* 95–129.

BUTCHER, H. J. (1966). *Sampling in Educational Research.* Manchester: Manchester University Press.

————, AINSWORTH, M. D., and NESBITT, J. E. (1963). "Personality Factors and School Achievement. A Comparison of British and American Children," *British Journal of Educational Psychology, 33,* 276–285.

CATTELL, R. B. (1933). *The Cattell Intelligence Tests.* Scales 1, 2, and 3. London: Harrap.

————. (1934). "Occupational Norms of Intelligence and the Standardization of an Adult Intelligence Test," *British Journal of Psychology, 25,* 1–28.

————. (1935). "The Measurement of Interest," *Character and Personality, 4,* 147–169.

————. (1940). "A Culture-Free Intelligence Test," *Journal of Educational Psychology, 31,* 161–179.

————. (1943). "The Measurement of Adult Intelligence," *Psychological Bulletin, 40,* 153–193.

————. (1947). "The Ergic Theory of Attitude and Sentiment Measurement," *Educational and Psychological Measurement, 7,* 221–246.

————. (1949). "The Dimensions of Culture Patterns by Factorization of National Characters," *Journal of Abnormal Social Psychology, 44,* 443–469.

————. (1950). "The Discovery of Ergic Structure in Man in Terms of Common Attitudes," *Journal of Abnormal and Social Psychology, 45,* 598–618.

————. (1952a). *Factor Analysis.* New York: Harper.

————. (1952b) "The Three Basic Factor-Analytic Designs—Their Interrelations and Derivatives," *Psychological Bulletin, 49,* 499–520.

————. (1955). "A Note on Dr. Sloan's Evidence Regarding the Value of Culture-Free Intelligence Tests," *American Journal of Mental Deficiency, 59,* 504–506.

————. (1956). "Validation and Intensification of the Sixteen Personality Factor Questionnaire," *Journal of Clinical Psychology, 12,* 205–214.

————. (1957). *Personality and Motivation Structure and Measurement.* New York: Harcourt, Brace & World.

————. (1959). "The Personality and Motivation of the Researcher from Measurements of Contemporaries and from Biography," in *The 1959 University of Utah Research Conference on the Identification of Creative Scientific Talent,* C. W. Taylor (ed.). Salt Lake City: University of Utah Press. Pp. 77–93.

————. (1961). "Theory of Situational, Instrument, Second Order, and Refraction Factors in Personality Structure Research," *Psychological Bulletin, 58,* 160–174.

————. (1962). "The Relational Simplex Theory of Equal Interval and Absolute Scaling," *Acta Psychologica, 20,* 139–158.

————. (1963). "Theory of Fluid and Crystallized Intelligence: A Critical Experiment," *Journal of Educational Psychology, 54,* 1–22.

————. (1964a). *Personality and Social Psychology: Collected Papers.* San Diego: R. R. Knapp and Co.

————. (1964b). "Beyond Validity and Reliability: Some Further Concepts and Coefficients for Evaluating Tests," *Journal of Experimental Education, 33* (2), 133–143.

————.(1965a). *The Scientific Analysis of Personality.* London: Penguin Books.

————. (1965b). "The Configurative Method for Surer Identification of Personality Dimensions, Notably in Child Study," *Psychological Reprints, 16,* 269–270.

————.(1965c). "Some Deeper Significances of the Computer for the Practicing Psychologist," *Personnel and Guidance Journal,* Oct., 160–166.

————.(1966a). "The Trait View Theory of Perturbations in Ratings and Self Ratings (L. and Q. Data): Its Application to Obtaining Pure Trait Scores in Questionnaires." *Advanced Publication No. 2. Laboratory of Personality and Group Analysis.* Urbana: University of Illinois Press.

————, (ed.). (1966b). *Handbook of Multivariate Experimental Psychology.* Chicago: Rand McNally.

————, and BAGGALEY, A. R. (1956). "The Objective Measurement of Attitude Motivation: Development and Evaluation of Principles and Devices," *Journal of Personality, 24,* 401–423.

————, ————.(1958). "A Confirmation of Ergic and Engram Structures in Attitudes Objectively Measured," *Australian Journal of Psychology, 10,* 287–313.

————, BLEWETT, D. B., and BELOFF, J. R. (1955). "The Inheritance of Personality. A Multiple Variance Analysis Determination of Approximate Nature-Nurture Ratios for Primary Personality Factors in Q-Data," *American Journal of Human Genetics, 7,* 122–146.

————, BREUL, H., and HARTMAN, H. P. (1952). "An Attempt at More Refined Definition of the Cultural Dimensions of Syntality in Modern Nations," *American Sociological Review, 17,* 408–421.

————, and BRISTOL, H. (1933). "Intelligence Tests for Mental Ages of Four to Eight Years," *British Journal of Educational Psychology, 3,* 142–169.

————, BUTCHER, H. J., CONNOR, D., SWENEY, A. B., and TSUJIOKA, B. (1961). "Prediction and Understanding of the Effect of Children's Interest upon School Performance," *Laboratory of Personality and Group Behavior Report.* Urbana: University of Illinois Press.

————, and CATTELL, A. K. S. (1960). *"The IPAT Culture Fair Intelligence Scales 1, 2 and 3."* Champaign, Ill.: IPAT.

————, and COAN, R. W. (1958). "Personality Dimensions in the Questionnaire Responses of Six and Seven-Year-Olds," *British Journal of Educational Psychology, 28,* 232–242.

————, and COULTER, M. A. (1966). "Principles of Behavioral Taxonomy and the Mathematical Basis of the Taxonomè Computer Program." *British Journal of Mathematical Statistical Psychology, 19,* 237–270.

————, DAY, M., and MEELAND, T. (1956). "Occupational Profiles on the 16 Personality Factor Questionnaire," *Occupational Psychology, 30,* 10–19.

————, and DICKMAN, K. (1962). "A Dynamic Model of Physical Influences Demonstrating the Necessity of Oblique Simple Structure," *Psychological Bulletin, 59,* 289–400.

————, and DREVDAHL, J. E. (1955). "A Comparison of the Personality Profile (16 PF) of Eminent Researchers with that of Eminent Teachers and Administrators, and of the General Population," *British Journal of Psychology, 46,* 248–261.

———, and EBER, HERBERT W. (1968). *Handbook for the Sixteen Personality Factor Questionnaire.* Champaign, Ill.: IPAT.

———, and GREENE, R. (1961). "Rationale of Norms on an Adult Personality Test—the 16 PF—for American Women," *Journal of Educational Research, 54,* 285–290.

———, and HORN, J. (1963). "An Integrating Study of the Factor Structure of Adult Attitude-Interests," *Genetic Psychology Monograph, 67,* 89–149.

———, ———, and BUTCHER, H. J. (1962). "The Dynamic Structure of Attitudes in Adults: A Description of Some Established Factors and of Their Measurement by the Motivational Analysis Test," *British Journal of Psychology, 53,* 57–69.

———, KRUG, S. E., and SWENEY, A. B. (1968). *The MAT and the Handbook for the School Motivation Analysis Test.* Champaign, Ill.: IPAT.

———, ———, SWENEY, A. B., and RADCLIFFE, J. A. (1964) *The MAT and the Handbook for Motivation Analysis Test.* Champaign, Ill.: IPAT.

———, MAXWELL, E. F., LIGHT, B. H., and UNGER, M. P. (1949). "The Objective Measurement of Attitudes," *British Journal of Psychology, 40,* 81–90.

———, and MILLER, A. (1952). "A Confirmation of the Ergic and Self-Sentiment Patterns among Dynamic Traits (Attitude Variables) by R-Technique," *British Journal of Psychology, 43,* 280–294.

———, and NESSELROADE, J. R. (1965). "Untersuchung der-interkulturen Konstanz des Persönlickkeitsfaktoren in 16 P. F. Test." *Psychologische Beitraege, 8,* 502–515.

———, NUTTALL, R., and CATTELL, M. D. L. (1968). *The High School Personality Questionnaire (HSPQ).* Champaign, Ill.: IPAT.

———, and RADCLIFFE, J. A. (1962). "Reliabilities and Validities of Simple and Extended Weighted and Buffered Unifactor Scales," *British Journal of Statistical Psychology, 15,* 113–128.

———, ———, and SWENEY, A. B. (1963). "The Nature and Measurement of Components of Motivation," *Genetic Psychology Monograph, 68,* 49–211.

———, and SCHEIER, I. H. (1961). *The Meaning and Measurement of Neuroticism and Anxiety.* New York: Ronald Press.

———, and STICE, G. F. (1960). *The Dimensions of Groups and Their Relations to the Behavior of Members.* Champaign, Ill.: IPAT.

———, SWENEY, A. B., and RADCLIFFE, J. A. (1960). "The Objective Measurement of Motivation Structure in Children," *Journal of Clinical Psychology, 16,* 227–232.

———, ———, and SEALY, A. P. (1966). "An Appraisal of Personality and Motivation Factors in the Prediction of School Achievement," *British Journal of Educational Psychology, 36,* 280–295.

———, and TINER, L. G. (1949). "The Varieties of Structural Rigidity," *Journal of Personality, 17,* 321–341.

———, and TSUJIOKA, B. (1964). "The Importance of Factor-Trueness and

Validity, Versus Homogeneity and Orthogonality, in Test Scales," *Educational and Psychological Measurement, 24,* 3–30.

————, and WARBURTON, F. W. (1961). "A Cross-Cultural Comparison of Patterns of Extraversion and Anxiety," *British Journal of Psychology, 52,* 3–16.

————, ————.(1967). *Principles of Objective Personality Testing and a Compendium of Tests.* Urbana: University of Illinois Press.

————, and WENIG, P. W. (1952). "Dynamic and Cognitive Factors Controlling Misperception," *Journal of Abnormal and Social Psychology, 47,* 797–809.

————, and WINDER, A. E. (1952). "Structural Rigidity in Relation to Learning Theory and Clinical Psychology," *Psychological Review, 59,* 23–39.

CHAMBERS, J. A. (1964). "Relating Personality and Biographical Factors to Scientific Creativity," *Psychological Monograph, 78,* 584.

————. (1966). "Selecting the Potentially Creative Scientist." Unpublished Paper, Psychology Department, University of Southern Florida.

CHAUNCEY, HENRY. (1952). *The Selective Service College Qualifications Test.* Princeton: Educational Test Service.

CHORNESS, M. H., and NOTTELMANN, D. H. (1957). "The Prediction of Creativity Among Air Force Civilian Employees," *Research Bulletin,* AFPTRC-TN-57-36. Lackland Air Force Base, Texas: Air Force Personnel and Training Research Center.

CLEMANS, W. V. (1956). "An Analytical and Empirical Examination of Some Properties of Ipsative Measurement." Unpublished doctoral dissertation, University of Washington.

COAN, R., and CATTELL, R. B. (1959). "The Development of the Early School Personality Questionnaire," *Journal of Experimental Education, 28,* 143–152.

COHEN, L., and STRAUSS, L. (1946). "Time Study and the Fundamental Nature of Manual Skill," *Journal of Consulting Psychology, 10,* 146–153.

COOMBS, C. H. (1953). "Theory and Methods of Social Measurement," in *Research Methods in the Behavioral Sciences,* L. Festinger and D. Katz (eds.). New York: Dryden Press.

COX, CATHERINE M. (1926). *Genetic Studies of Genius.* Vol. 2, *The Early Mental Traits of Three Hundred Geniuses.* Stanford: Stanford University Press.

COX, F. N. (1960). "Correlates of General and Test Anxiety in Children," *Australian Journal of Psychology, 12,* 169–177.

CRONBACH, LEE J. (1951). "Coefficient Alpha and the Internal Structure of Tests," *Psychometrika, 16,* 297–334.

————.(1960). *Essentials of Psychological Testing.* 2nd ed. New York: Harper.

————, and GLESER, GOLDINE C. (1957). *Psychological Tests and Personnel Decisions.* Urbana: University of Illinois Press.

————, RAJARATNAM, N., and GLESER, GOLDINE C. (1963). "Theory of Generalizability: A Liberalization of Reliability Theory," *British Journal of Statistical Psychology, 16,* 137–164.

CROPLEY, A. J. (1966). "Creativity and Intelligence," *British Journal of Educational Psychology, 36,* 259–266.

CROSS, P., CATTELL, R. B., and BUTCHER, H. J. (1967). "The Personality Pattern of Creative Artists," *British Journal of Educational Psychology, 37,* 292–299.

DALE, R. R. (1954). *From School to University.* London: Routledge and Kegan Paul Ltd.

DAVIDSON, H. H. (1943). *Personality and Economic Background. A Study of Highly Intelligent Children.* New York: King's Crown Press.

DAVIS, ALLISON, and HAVIGHURST, R. J. (1948). "Social Class and Color Differences in Child Rearing," *American Sociological Review, 11,* 698–710.

DE MILLE, R., and MERRIFIELD, P. R. (1962). "Review of J. W. Getzels and P. W. Jackson, *Intelligence and Creativity,*" *Educational and Psychological Measurement, 22,* 803–808.

DEMING, W. E. (1955). *Some Theory of Sampling.* New York: Wiley.

DENNIS, WAYNE. (1958). "The Age Decrement in Outstanding Scientific Contributors: Fact or Artifact," *American Psychologist, 13,* 457–460.

DOWNEY, JUNE. (1929). *Creative Imagination.* London: Kegan Paul.

DREGER, R. M., and CATTELL, R. B. (1968). *The Pre-School Personality Questionnaire (PSPQ).* Champaign, Ill.: IPAT.

DREVDAHL, J. E. (1954). "An Exploratory Study of Creativity." Unpublished doctoral dissertation, University of Nebraska.

———. (1956). "Factors of Importance for Creativity," *Journal of Clinical Psychology, 12,* 21–26.

———, and CATTELL, R. B. (1958). "Personality and Creativity in Artists and Writers," *Journal of Clinical Psychology, 14,* 107–111.

DUNNETTE, M. D. (1963). "A Note on the Criterion," *Journal of Applied Psychology, 47,* 251–253.

DYER, H. S., and KING, R. G. (1955). *College Board Scores, Their Use and Interpretation. No. 2.* Princeton: College Entrance Examination Board.

EBER, HERBERT W. (1966). "Multivariate Analysis of a Vocational Rehabilitation System," *Multivariate Behavior Research,* Monograph 1.

———, SWENSON, W. M., FOWLER, R. D., and CATTELL, R. B. (1964). Symposium on Reporting of Personality Test Data. Division 5, APA Annual Meeting, Los Angeles, September 8. In preparation.

EDWARDS, M. P., and TYLER, L. E. (1965). "Intelligence, Creativity and Achievement in a Non-Selective Public Junior High School," *Journal of Educational Psychology, 56,* 96–99.

ELLIS, H. (1946). *A Study of British Genius.* New York: Houghton Mifflin.

EMMETT, W. G., and WILMUT, F. S. (1952). "The Prediction of School Certificate Performance in Specific Subjects," *British Journal of Educational Psychology, 22,* 52–62.

EYSENCK, H. J. (1950). "Criterion Analysis: An Application of the Hypothetico-Deductive Method to Factor Analysis," *Psychological Review, 57,* 38–65.

———. (1964). "An Improved Short Questionnaire for the Measurement of Extraversion and Neuroticism," *Life Sciences, 3,* 1103–1109.

———, and PRELL, D. B. (1951). "The Inheritance of Neuroticism: An Experimental Study," *Journal of Mental Science, 102,* 517–529.

FERGUSON, G. A. (1954). "On Learning and Human Ability," *Canadian Journal of Psychology, 8,* 95–112.

FINCH, F. H. (1946). "Enrollment Increases and Changes in the Mental Level," *Applied Psychology Monograph,* No. 10, 75.

———, and CARROLL, H. A. (1932). "Gifted Children as High School Leaders," *Journal of Genetic Psychology, 41,* 476–481.

FLANAGAN, J. C. (1946). "The Experimental Evaluation of a Selection Procedure," *Educational and Psychological Measurement, 6,* 445–446.

FLEISHMAN, EDWIN A., HARRIS, E. F., and BURTT, H. E. (1955). "Leadership and Supervision in Industry," *Bureau of Educational Research Monograph No. 33.* Columbus: The Ohio State University Press.

———, and ORNSTEIN, G. N. (1960). "An Analysis of Pilot Flying Performance in Terms of Component Abilities," *Journal of Applied Psychology, 44,* 146–155.

FLOUD, J. E., HALSEY, A. H., and MARTIN, F. M. (1957). *Social Class and Educational Opportunity.* London: Heinemann.

FRANZBLAU, ROSE N. (1935). "Race Differences Studied in Different Environments," *Archives of Psychology,* No. 177.

FRASER, ELIZABETH D. (1959). *Home Environment and the School.* London: London University Press.

FREEMAN, F. N., HOLZINGER, K. F., and MITCHELL, B. C. (1928). "The Influence of Environment on the Intelligence, Achievement, and Conduct of Foster Children," in *Twenty-seventh Yearbook of the National Society for the Study of Education.* Chicago: University of Chicago Press; (1940), Bloomington, Ill.: Public School Publishing Company. Chap. 9.

FRYER, D. (1922). "Occupational Intelligence Standards," *School and Society, 16,* 273–277.

FURNEAUX, W. D. (1957). "The Selection of University Students," *Report to the Imperial College of Science.* London.

———.(1961). *The Chosen Few: An Examination of Some Aspects of University Selection in Britain.* London: Oxford University Press.

GALTON, FRANCIS. (1870). *Hereditary Genius: An Inquiry into its Laws and Consequences.* New York: Appleton.

GARFORTH, F. J. DE LA P. (1945). "War Office Selection Boards," *Occupational Psychology, 19,* 97–108.

GARRETT, H. F. (1949). "A Review and Interpretation of Investigations of Factors Related to Scholastic Success in Colleges of Arts, Sciences and Teachers' Colleges." *Journal of Experimental Education, 18,* 91–138.

GETZELS, J. W., and JACKSON, P. W. (1962). *Creativity and Intelligence.* New York: Wiley.

GHISELIN, BREWSTER.(1955). *The Creative Process.* New York: Mentor Books.

GHISELLI, EDWIN E. (1956). "Dimensional Problems of Criteria," *Journal of Applied Psychology, 40,* 1–4.

———.(1960a). "The Prediction of Predictability," *Educational and Psychological Measurement, 20,* 3–8.

————.(1960b). "Differentiation of Tests in Terms of the Accuracy with which They Predict for a Given Individual," *Educational and Psychological Measurement, 20,* 675–684.

————.(1963). "Moderating Effects and Differential Reliability and Validity," *Journal of Applied Psychology, 47,* 81–86.

GIBBONS, B. D., and CATTELL, R. B. *Resolution of the 16 P.F. and the Guilford-Zimmerman Questionnaire into a Uniquely Determined Personality Structure.* (On press).

GIST, NOEL P., and CLARK, C. D. (1938). "Intelligence as a Selective Factor in Rural-Urban Migration," *American Journal of Sociology, 44,* 36–58.

GORDON, H. (1923). *Mental and Scholastic Tests among Retarded Children.* London: His Majesty's Stationery Office.

GORSUCH, R. (1960). Description of unpublished research, *IPAT Information Bulletin,* No. 4.

————, and CATTELL, R. B. (1965). "The Definition and Measurement of National Morale and Morality," *Journal of Social Psychology, 67,* 77–96.

GOTTESMAN, I. I. (1963). "Heritability of Personality: A Demonstration," *Psychological Monograph, 77,* 1–22.

GOULD, E. M., and McCOMISKY, J. G. (1958). "Attainment Level in Leaving Certificate and Academic Performance at University," *British Journal of Educational Psychology, 28,* 129–134.

GROOMS, R. R., and ENDLER, N. S. (1960). "The Effect of Anxiety on Academic Achievement," *Journal of Educational Psychology, 51,* 229–304.

GUILFORD, JOY PAUL.(1950). "Creativity," *American Psychologist, 5,* 444–454.

————.(1957). "Creative Abilities in the Arts," *Psychological Review, 64,* 110–118.

————.(1965). *Fundamental Statistics in Psychology and Education.* 4th ed. New York: McGraw-Hill.

————, CHRISTENSEN, P. R., BOND, N. A., and SUTTON, M. A. (1954). "A Factor Analysis of Human Interests," *Psychology Monograph, No. 375,* 68, No. 4.

————, and HOEPFNER, R. (1963). "Current Summary of Structure-of-Intellect Factors and Suggested Tests," *Reports from the Psychology Laboratory, University of Southern California,* No. 30. Los Angeles: University of Southern California.

————.(1966). "Structure of Intellect Factors and Their Tests." *Reports from the Psychology Laboratory, University of Southern California,* No. 36. Los Angeles: University of Southern California.

GULLIKSEN, H. (1950). *Theory of Mental Tests.* New York: Wiley.

GUTTMAN, L. (1950). "The Basis for Scalogram Analysis," in *Measurement and Prediction,* S. A. Stouffer (ed.). Princeton: Princeton University Press.

HADAMARD, JACQUES.(1945). *The Psychology of Invention in the Mathematical Field.* Princeton: Princeton University Press.

HANSEN, M. H., HURWITZ, W. N., and MADOW, W. G. (1953). *Sample Survey Methods and Theory.* New York: Wiley.

HARDING, R. E. M. (1940). *An Anatomy of Inspiration.* Cambridge: Heffer.

HARMON, L. R. (1963). "The Development of a Criterion of Scientific Competence," in *Scientific Creativity: Its Recognition and Development,* F. Barron and C. W. Taylor (eds.). New York: Wiley.

HARRELL, T. W., and HARRELL, M. S. (1945). "Army General Classification Test Scores for Civilian Occupations," *Educational Psychology Measurement,* 5, 229–239.

HASAN, P., and BUTCHER, H. J. (1966). "Creativity and Intelligence. A Partial Replication with Scottish Children of Getzels and Jackson's Study," *British Journal of Psychology, 57,* 129–135.

HAYES, K. J. (1962). "Genes, Drives and Intellect," *Psychological Reports, 10,* 299–342.

HEBB, D. O. (1949). *The Organization of Behavior.* New York: Wiley.

HERON, ALEXANDER.(1952). "A Psychological Study of Occupational Adjustment," *Journal of Applied Psychology, 36,* 385–387.

————.(1954). "Satisfaction and Satisfactoriness. Complementary Aspects of Occupational Adjustment," *Occupational Psychology, 28,* 140–153.

HILDRETH, G. H. (1938). "Characteristics of Young Gifted Children," *Journal of Genetic Psychology, 53,* 287–311.

HIMMELWEIT, HILDE T. (1949). "Student Selection. An Experimental Investigation." Unpublished report, London School of Economics.

HIRSCH, J. (1963). "Behavior Genetics, Individually Understood," *Science, 142,* 1436–1442.

HOLLINGWORTH, L. S. (1930). "The Child of Very Superior Intelligence as a Special Problem in Social Adjustment," *Mental Hygiene, 15,* 3–16.

HORN, J. F., and CATTELL, R. B. (1965). "Vehicles, Ipsatization and the Multiple Method Measurement of Motivation," *Canadian Journal of Psychology, 19,* 265–279.

————, and ————.(1966a). "Age Differences in Primary Mental Ability Factors," *Journal of Gerontology, 21,* 210–220.

————, and ————.(1966b). "Refinement and Test of the Theory of Fluid and Crystallised General Intelligence," *Journal of Educational Psychology, 57,* 253–270.

HORST, P., (ed.). (1942). *The Prediction of Personal Adjustment.* New York: Social Service Research Council.

HOTELLING, H. (1936). "Relations between Two Sets of Variates," *Biometrika 28,* 321–377.

HUMPHREYS, L. G. (1962). "The Organization of Human Abilities," *American Psychologist, 17,* 475–482.

HUNDLEBY, J. D., and CATTELL, R. B. (1967). *The IPAT Adult O-A Personality Test Battery (AOA).* Champaign, Ill.: IPAT.

————, PAWLIK, K., and CATTELL, R. B. (1965). *Personality Factors in Objective Test Devices.* San Diego: R. R. Knapp.

HUNT, JOSEPH McV. (1961). *Intelligence and Experience.* New York: Ronald Press.

HUNTINGTON, E. (1945). *Mainsprings of Civilization.* New York: Wiley.

JEFFREY, A. J. W. (1951). "The Effect of a Recruitment Film on the Attitude of School Leavers to Nursing as a Career." Unpublished master's thesis, University of Manchester.

JONES, F. E. (1964). "Predictor Variables for Creativity in Industrial Science," *Journal of Applied Psychology, 48,* 134–136.

―――― (1967). *Prediction of High-Level Creativity in Industrial Scientific Work.* Private circular from Renssalaer Polytechnic Institute, Troy, New Jersey.

――――, and CATTELL, R. B. (1965). *Weighting of the 16 P.F. Questionnaire Factors in Predicting Industrial Creativity.* Private circular.

JONES, H. E., and CONRAD, H. S. (1933). "The Growth and Decline of Intelligence: A Study of a Homogeneous Group," *Genetic Psychology Monograph, 13,* 223–298.

KAHNEMAN, D., and GHISELLI, EDWIN E. (1962). "Validity and Nonlinear Heteroscedastic Models," *Personnel Psychology, 15,* 1–11.

KELLY, E. L., and FISKE, D. (1951). *The Prediction of Performance in Clinical Psychology.* Ann Arbor: University of Michigan Press.

KEMP, L. C. D. (1955). "Environmental and Other Characteristics Determining Attainments in Primary Schools," *British Journal of Educational Psychology, 25,* 67–77.

KINGSBURY, F. A. (1933). "Psychological Tests for Executives," *Personnel, 9,* 121–133.

KNAPP, R. H. (1963). "Demographic Cultural and Personality Attributes of Scientists," in *Scientific Creativity: Its Recognition and Development,* F. Barron and C. W. Taylor (eds.). New York: Wiley.

KRETSCHMER, E. (1931). *The Psychology of Men of Genius.* London: Kegan Paul.

KUDER, G. F. (1953). *Kuder Preference Record.* Rev. ed. Chicago: Science Research Associates.

――――, and RICHARDSON, M. W. (1937). "The Theory of the Estimation of Test Reliability," *Psychometrika, 2,* 151–160.

KUHN, T. S. (1963). "The Essential Tension: Tradition and Innovation in Scientific Research," in *Scientific Creativity: Its Recognition and Development,* F. Barron and C. W. Taylor (eds.). New York: Wiley.

LEE, E. S. (1951). "Negro Intelligence and Selective Migration: A Philadelphia Test of Klineberg Hypotheses," *American Sociological Review, 16,* 227–233.

LEHMAN, HARVEY C. (1953). *Age and Achievement.* Princeton: Princeton University Press.

LIKERT, R. (1932). "A Technique for the Measurement of Attitudes," *Archives of Psychology,* No. 140.

LINE, W. (1931). "The Growth of Visual Perception in Children," *British Journal of Psychology Monograph Supplement,* No. 15.

LOEVINGER, JANE.(1948). "The Technic of Homogeneous Tests Compared with some Aspects of 'Scale Analysis' and Factor Analysis," *Psychological Bulletin, 45,* 507–529.

LORD, F. M. (1953). "The Relation of Test Score to the Ability Underlying the Test," *Educational and Psychological Measurement, 13,* 517–549.

———.(1956). "The Measurement of Growth," *Educational and Psychological Measurement, 16,* 421–437.

LORGE, L. (1945). "Schooling Makes a Difference." *Teachers College Record, 46,* 483–492.

LUNZER, E. A. (1960). *Recent Studies in Britain Based on the Work of Jean Piaget.* London: National Foundation of Educational Research.

LYNN, R. (1957). "Temperamental Characteristics Related to Disparity of Attainment in Reading and Arithmetic," *British Journal of Educational Psychology, 27,* 62–68.

MCCLELLAND, DAVID C. (1961). *The Achieving Society.* Princeton: D. Van Nostrand Company, Inc.

MACCOBY, ELEANOR E., and GIBBS, P. K. (1954). "Methods of Child Rearing in Two Social Classes," in *Readings in Child Development,* W. E. Martin and C. B. Standler (eds.). New York: Harcourt Brace.

MACDOUGALL, WILLIAM. (1945). *The Energies of Men.* 6th ed. London: Methuen & Company, Ltd.

MACKINNON, D. W. (1962). "The Nature and Nurture of Creative Talent," *American Psychologist, 17,* 484–495.

MADDOX, H. (1957). "Nature-Nurture Balance Sheets," *British Journal of Educational Psychology, 27,* 166–175.

MARSH, R. W. (1964). "A Statistical Re-Analysis of Getzels and Jackson's Data," *British Journal of Educational Psychology, 34,* 91–93.

MEAD, MARGARET. (1963). *Groups, Leadership and Men,* H. Guetzkow (ed.). New York: Russell and Russell.

MEEHL, PAUL E. (1954). *Clinical versus Statistical Prediction. A Theoretical Analysis and a Review of the Evidence.* Minneapolis: University of Minnesota Press.

MEIER, G. M., and BALDWIN, R. E. (1957). *Economic Development.* New York: Wiley.

MICHAEL, W. B. (1960). "Aptitudes," in *Encyclopaedia of Educational Research,* C. W. Harris (ed.). New York: Macmillan. Pp. 59–62.

MIDDLETON, G., and GUTHRIE, G. M. (1959). "Personality Syndromes and Academic Achievement," *Journal of Educational Psychology, 60,* 66–69.

MOLLENKOPF, W. G. (1956). "A Study of Secondary School Characteristics Determining Attainment in Primary Schools," *Educational Test Service Research Bulletin, 56,* No. 6.

MORETON, C. A., and BUTCHER, H. J. (1963). "Are Rural Children Handicapped by the Use of Speeded Tests in Selection Procedures?" *British Journal of Educational Psychology, 33,* 22–30.

MORRIS, B. S. (1949). "Officer Selection in the British Army," *Occupational Psychology, 23,* 219–234.

MORRISON, R. F., OWENS, W. A., GLENNON, J. R., and ALBRIGHT, L. E. (1962). "Factored Life History Antecedents of Industrial Research Performance," *Journal of Applied Psychology, 46,* 281–284.

MOSER, C. A. (1958). *Survey Methods in Social Investigation.* London: Heinemann.

NESSELROADE, J. R., and CATTELL, R. B. (1967). *The IPAT High School O-A Battery (HSOA)*. Champaign, Ill.: IPAT.

NEWLAND, E. (1963). "The Assessment of Exceptional Children," in *Psychology of Exceptional Children and Youth*, W. M. Crookshank (ed.). New York: Prentice-Hall.

NEWMAN, H. H., FREEMAN, F. N., and HOLZINGER, K. J. (1937). *Twins: A Study of Heredity and Environment*. Chicago: Chicago University Press.

NUNNALLY, J. C. (1959). *Tests and Measurements*. New York: McGraw-Hill.

OLIVER, R. A. C. (1955). *An Experimental Examination in General Studies*. Manchester: Joint Matriculation Board.

————, and BUTCHER, H. J. (1962). "Teachers' Attitudes to Education. The Structure of Educational Attitudes," *British Journal of Social and Clinical Psychology, 1*, 56–69.

O.S.S. ASSESSMENT STAFF. (1948). *Assessment of Men*. New York: Rinehart.

O'SULLIVAN, M., GUILFORD, J. P., and DE MILLE, R. (1965). "Measurement of Social Intelligence," *Reports from the Psychology Laboratory, University of Southern California*, No. 34. Los Angeles: University of Southern California.

OWENS, W. A. (1966). "Age and Mental Abilities: A Second Adult Follow-up," *Journal of Educational Psychology, 57*, 311–325.

PARNES, SIDNEY J., and MEADOW, A. (1963). "Development of Individual Creative Talent," in *Scientific Creativity: Its Recognition and Development*, F. Barron and C. W. Taylor (eds.). New York: Wiley.

PEEL, E. A. (1959). "The Measurement of Interests by Verbal Methods," *British Journal of Statistical Psychology, 12*, 105–117.

————, and RUTTER, D. (1951). "The Predictive Value of the Entrance Examination as Judged by the School Certificate Examination," *British Journal of Educational Psychology, 21*, 30–35.

PETCH, J. A. (1961). *G.C.E. and Degree, Part I*. Manchester: Joint Matriculation Board.

PIERS, E. V., DANIELS, J. M., and QUACKENBUSH, J. F. (1960). "The Identification of Creativity in Adolescents," *Journal of Educational Psychology, 51*, 346–351.

PIERSON, G. R., BARTON, V., and HAY, G. (1964). "S.M.A.T. Motivation Factors as Predictors of Academic Achievement of Delinquent Boys," *Journal of Psychology, 57*, 243–249.

PORTER, R., CATTELL, R. B., and SCHAIE, W. (1967). *The Child Personality Questionnaire (CPQ)*. Champaign, Ill.: IPAT.

RICHARDS, J. M., TAYLOR, C. W., PRICE, P. B., and JACOBSEN, T. J. (1965). "An Investigation of the Criterion Problem for One Group of Medical Specialists," *Journal of Applied Psychology, 49*, 79–90.

ROBBINS, G. D. (1963). *British Government Report on Higher Education* (Committee chaired by Lord Robbins). London: Her Majesty's Stationery Office.

ROE, ANNE. (1951a). "A Psychological Study of Eminent Biologists," *Psychological Monograph, 64*, No. 14.

————. (1951b). "A Psychological Study of Eminent Physical Scientists," *Genetic Psychology Monograph, 43*, 121–239.

————.(1953). "A Psychological Study of Eminent Psychologists and Anthropologists, and a Comparison with Biological and Physical Scientists," *Psychological Monograph, 67*, No. 2.

RONAN, W. W. (1963). "A Factor Analysis of Eleven Job Performance Measures," *Personnel Psychology, 16*, 255–267.

————.(1964). "Evaluation of Skilled Trades Performance Predictors," *Educational and Psychological Measurement, 24*, 601–608.

ROTHE, H. F. (1946a). "Output Rates Among Butter Wrappers: I. Work Curves and Their Stability," *Journal of Applied Psychology, 30*, 199–211.

————.(1946b). "Output Rates among Butter Wrappers: II. Frequency Distributions and an Hypothesis Regarding the 'Restriction of Output,' " *Journal of Applied Psychology, 30*, 320–328.

————.(1947). "Output Rates Among Machine Operators: I. Distributions and Their Reliability," *Journal of Applied Psychology, 31*, 484–489.

————.(1951). "Output Rates Among Chocolate Dippers," *Journal of Applied Psychology, 35*, 94–97.

————, and NYE, C. T. (1958). "Output Rates Among Coil Winders," *Journal of Applied Psychology, 42*, 182–186.

————, and ————. (1959). "Output Rates Among Machine Operators: II. Consistency Related to Methods of Pay," *Journal of Applied Psychology, 43*, 417–420.

RUMMEL, R. J. (1963). "Dimensions of Conflict within and between Nations." *General Systems Yearbook of the Society for General Systems Research, 8*, 1–50.

————, SAWYER, J., GUETZKOW, H., and TANTER, R. (1966). *Dimensions of Nations.* (In preparation.)

RUSH, C. H., JR. (1953). "A Factorial Study of Sales Criteria," *Personnel Psychology, 6*, 9–24.

SANDALL, P. H. (1960). "Young Interests: Analysing Personality Traits," *Times* (London) *Educational Supplement,* July 29.

SANDERS, C. (1961). *Psychological and Educational Bases of Academic Performance.* Melbourne: Australian Council for Educational Research.

SAUNDERS, D. R. (1963). "Some Measures Related to Success and Placement in Basic Engineering Research and Development," in *Scientific Creativity: Its Recognition and Development,* F. Barron and C. W. Taylor (eds.). New York: Wiley.

SCHAIE, K. W. (1965). "A General Model for the Study of Developmental Problems," *Psychological Bulletin, 64*, 92–107.

SCHEIER, I. H., and CATTELL, R. B. (1962). *The IPAT Adult Anxiety Scale* (Verbal). Champaign, Ill.: IPAT.

SCHMIDT, L. G., and ROTHNEY, J. W. N. (1954). "The Relationship of Primary Abilities Scores and Occupational Choices," *Journal of Educational Research, 47*, 637–640.

SCHNEIDER, E. (1956). "The Relationship Between the Thurstone Primary

Mental Abilities and the Iowa Tests of Educational Development." Unpublished master's thesis, Reed College.

SEALY, A. P., and CATTELL, R. B. (1966). "Adolescent Personality Trends in Primary Factors Measured on the 16 P.F. and the HSPQ Questionnaires through Ages 11 to 23," *British Journal of Social and Clinical Psychology, 5,* 172–184.

SHAKESPEARE, J. J. (1936). "The Relative Popularity of School Subjects in Elementary Schools," *British Journal of Educational Psychology, 6,* 158.

SHINN, E. O. (1956). "Interest and Intelligence as Related to Achievement in Tenth Grade," *California Journal of Educational Research, 7,* 217–220.

SHRADER, R., and CATTELL, R. B. (1967). *The (High School) Youth Anxiety Scale.* Champaign, Ill.: IPAT.

SMITH, C. A. (1948). *Mental Testing of Hebridean Children in Gaelic and English.* London: University of London Press.

SPEARMAN, C. (1930). *Creative Mind.* New York: Cambridge.

SPRECHER, T. B. (1959). "A Study of Engineers' Criteria for Creativity," *Journal of Applied Psychology, 43,* 141–148.

STEAD, W. H. (1937). "The Department Store Salesperson," *Occupations, 15,* 513–515.

STEVENS, STANLEY S., (ed.). (1951). *Handbook of Experimental Psychology.* New York: Wiley.

STEWART, N. (1947). "AGCT Scores of Army Personnel Grouped by Occupations," *Occupations, 26,* 5–41.

STOUFFER, S. A. (1950). *The American Soldier. IV. Measurement and Prediction.* Princeton: Princeton University Press.

STRODTBECK, FRED L. (1958). "Family Interaction, Values and Achievement," in *Talent and Society,* D. C. McClelland (ed.). Princeton: D. Van Nostrand Company, Inc.

STRONG, EDWARD K., JR. (1949). *Vocational Interests of Men and Women.* Stanford: Stanford University Press.

SUPER, DONALD E. (1957). *The Psychology of Careers.* New York: Harper.

SUTHERLAND, M. B. (1948). "The Prediction of Success in the University Faculty of Arts by Means of Marks in the Northern Ireland School Certificate Examination." (Unpublished research report.)

SWENEY, A. B., and CATTELL, R. B. (1961). "Dynamic Factors in Twelve Year Old Children as Revealed in Measures of Integrated Motivation," *Journal of Clinical Psychology, 18,* 360–369.

————, ————. (1968). *The VIM and the Handbook for the Vocational Interest Measure.* Experimental Edition. A. B. Sweney, Texas Technical College, Lubbock, Texas.

————, RADCLIFFE, J. A., and CATTELL, R. B. (1960). "The Objective Measurement of Motivation Structure in Children," *Journal of Clinical Psychology, 16,* 227–232.

TALBOTT, R. (1960). "The Multiple Predictive Efficiency of Ipsative and Normative Personality Measures." Unpublished thesis, University of Washington.

TAPP, J. T. (1957). "An Examination of Hypotheses Concerning the Motivational Components of Attitude." Unpublished master's thesis, University of Illinois.

TAYLOR, C. W., (ed.). (1955). *The 1955 University of Utah Research Conference on the Identification of Creative Scientific Talent.* Salt Lake City: University of Utah Press.

——, (ed.). (1957). *The 1957 University of Utah Research Conference on the Identification of Creative Scientific Talent.* Salt Lake City: University of Utah Press.

——, (ed.). (1964). *Creativity: Progress and Potential.* New York: McGraw Hill.

——, PRICE, P. B., RICHARDS, J. M., and Jacobsen, J. L. (1964). "An Investigation of the Criterion Problem for a Medical School Faculty," *Journal of Applied Psychology, 48,* 294–301.

TERMAN, LEWIS M., (ed.). (1925). *Genetic Studies of Genius.* Vol. I, *Mental and Physical Traits of a Thousand Gifted Children.* Stanford: Stanford University Press.

——, and ODEN, M. H. (1947). *Genetic Studies of Genius.* Vol. IV, *The Gifted Child Grows Up.* Stanford: Stanford University Press.

——, ——. (1951). "The Stanford Studies of the Gifted," in *The Gifted Child,* D. C. Wetty (ed.). Boston: Heath.

——, ——. (1959). *Genetic Studies of Genius.* Vol. V, *The Gifted Group at Midlife.* Stanford: Stanford University Press.

THISTLETHWAITE, D. L. (1963). "The College Environment as a Determinant of Research Potentiality," in *Scientific Creativity: Its Recognition and Development,* F. Barron and C. W. Taylor (eds.). New York: Wiley.

THORNDIKE, ROBERT L. (1951). "Community Variables as Predictors of Intelligence and Academic Achievement," *Journal of Educational Psychology, 42,* 321–338.

——. (1963). "Some Methodological Issues in the Study of Creativity," *Procedures of the 1962 Invitational Conference on Testing Problems,* 40–54. Princeton: Educational Testing Service.

——, and HAGEN, E. (1955). *Measurement and Evaluation in Psychology and Education.* New York: Wiley.

THURSTONE, LOUIS L. (1938). *Primary Mental Abilities.* Chicago: Chicago University Press.

——. (1947). *Multiple-Factor Analysis.* Chicago: Chicago University Press.

——, and CHAVE, ERNEST J. (1929). The Measurement of Attitude. Chicago: Chicago University Press.

TOLLEFSON, D. (1961). "Response to Humor in Relation to Other Measures of Personality." Unpublished doctoral dissertation, University of Illinois.

TORGERSON, WARREN S. (1952). "Multidimensional Scaling: I. Theory and Method," *Psychometrika, 17,* 401–419.

TORRANCE, ELLIS P. (1962). *Guiding Creative Talent.* Englewood Cliffs, N.J.: Prentice-Hall.

——. (1963). *Education and the Creative Potential.* Minneapolis: University of Minnesota Press.

TSUJIOKA, B. (1966). "Models and Meanings for Type and Type Search in Psychology," in *Handbook of Multivariate Experimental Psychology,* R. B. Cattell (ed.). Chicago: Rand McNally.

———, and CATTELL, R. B. (1965). "Constancy and Difference in Personality Structure and Mean Profile, in the Questionnaire Medium from Applying the 16 P.F. Test in America and Japan," *British Journal of Social and Clinical Psychology, 4,* 287–297.

TURNER, W. W. (1960). "Dimensions of Foreman Performance: A Factor Analysis of Criterion Measures," *Journal of Applied Psychology, 44,* 216–223.

TUSKA, CLARENCE D. (1957). *Inventors and Inventions.* New York: McGraw Hill.

VANDENBERG, S. (1956). "The Hereditary Abilities Study," *Eugenics Quarterly, 3,* 94–99.

VAN ZELST, R. H., and KERR, W. A. (1954). "Personality Self-Assessment of Scientific and Technical Personnel," *Journal of Applied Psychology, 38,* 145–147.

VERNON, P. E. (1950). *The Structure of Human Abilities.* New York: Wiley.

——— (1953). *Personality Tests and Assessments.* London: Methuen & Company, Ltd.

———, (ed.). (1957). *Secondary School Selection.* London: Methuen & Company, Ltd.

——— (1960). *Intelligence and Attainment Tests.* London: University of London Press.

——— (1964). "Creativity and Intelligence," *Educational Research, 6,* 163–169.

———, and PARRY, J. B. (1949). *Personnel Selection in the British Forces.* London: University of London Press.

VITELES, MORRIS S. (1929–1930). "The Human Factor in Substation Operation," *Personnel Journal, 8,* 81–113.

WALKER, R. Y., BENNETT, S. V., and EWART, E. S. (1946). "A Study of Individual Differences Among Flight Instructors in Making Spot Landings," *CAA Division of Research, Report #56.* Civil Aeronautics Agency, Washington, D.C.

WALLACH, M. A., and KOGAN, N. (1965). *Modes of Thinking in Young Children.* New York: Holt, Rinehart and Winston.

WARBURTON, F. W. (1952). *The Selection of University Students.* Manchester: Manchester University Press.

———.(1958). "Review of *Social Class and Educational Opportunity,* by Floud, Halsey and Martin," *British Journal of Educational Psychology, 28,* 88–90.

———.(1961). "The Measurement of Personality. I," *Educational Research, 4,* 2–18.

———.(1962a). "The Measurement of Personality. II," *Educational Research, 4,* 115–132.

———.(1962b). "The Measurement of Personality. III," *Educational Research, 4,* 193–206.

WELLMAN, F. E. (1957). "Differential Prediction of High School Achievement

Using Single Score and Multiple Factor Tests of Mental Maturity," *Personnel and Guidance Journal, 35,* 512–517.

WHEELER, L. R. (1942). "A Comparative Study of the Intelligence of East Tennessee Mountain Children," *Journal of Educational Psychology, 33,* 321–334.

WHITLOCK, G. H., CLOUSE, R. J., and SPENCER, W. F. (1963). "Predicting Accident Proneness," *Personnel Psychology, 16,* 35–44.

WHYTE, WILLIAM H. (1956). *The Organization Man.* New York: Simon and Schuster.

WILLIAMS, J. R. (1959). "A Test of the Validity of P-Technique in the Measurement of Internal Conflict," *Journal of Personality, 27,* 418–437.

WILSON, N. A. B. (1948). "The Work of the Civil Service Selection Board," *Occupational Psychology, 22,* 204–212.

WILSON, R. C., GUILFORD, J. P., CHRISTENSEN, P. R., and LEWIS, D. J. (1954). "A Factor-Analytic Study of Creative-Thinking Abilities," *Psychometrika, 19,* 297–311.

WISEMAN, S. (1964). *Education and Environment.* Manchester: Manchester University Press.

WITTY, P. A., and JENKINS, M. D. (1936). "Intra-Race Testing and Negro Intelligence," *Journal of Psychology, 1,* 179–192.

WOLKING, W. D. (1955). "Predicting Academic Achievement with the Differential Aptitude and P.M.A. Tests," *Journal of Applied Psychology, 39,* 115–118.

YATES, FRANK. (1960). *Sampling Methods for Censuses and Surveys.* 3rd ed. London: Charles Griffin.

APPENDIX

New formulas developed by Cattell and Tsujioka, concerning the questions discussed in Chapter 7, are offered in the passages below.

In connection with the development of structured personality measurement, using suppressor action, Cattell and Tsujioka have recently developed a number of formulas not hitherto available. They are made to apply to the general case of oblique factors—because most important psychological traits *are* somewhat intercorrelated—and they cover such concepts as *factor-trueness* (the extent to which the scale achieves validity in the common factor space).

7.11
$$r_{ft} = \frac{\sum\limits_{j}^{n} B_{jw} r_{jw}}{\sqrt{\left(\sum\limits_{j}^{n} B_{jw} A_{jw}\right)\left(\sum\limits_{j}^{n} B_{jw} r_{jw}\right) + \sum\limits_{u}^{k}\left(\sum\limits_{j}^{n} B_{jw} A_{ju}\right)\left(\sum\limits_{j}^{n} B_{jw} r_{ju}\right)}}$$

Homogeneity on the wanted factor (as distinct from general homogeneity):

7.12
$$r_{tp} = 1 - \frac{\sum\limits_{j}^{n} A^2_{jw}}{\sum\limits_{j}^{n} h^2_{j}}$$

and the *Evaluation of buffering (suppressor) efficiency,* by the formula:

7.13
$$t = \frac{k \, r_{ft}}{\sqrt{1 - r_{ft}^2}}$$

This latter—in which t is the density of items and k the number of factors—assumes that one is presented in a given area of research and test construction with a certain density of available items. Formula 7.13 shows how successful the test constructor has been in achieving buffering (mutual suppression on unwanted factors) with the particular richness or poverty of available items in the given field. Parenthetically, it follows from the Cattell-Tsujioka formulas that when making scales and batteries for oblique factors, we should: (a) choose the best items by high correlations with the wanted factor as given in the factor structure; (b) balance for suppressor action according to size of loadings, as given in the factor pattern matrix.

The upshot of this analysis for the relation of validity to homogeneity, and

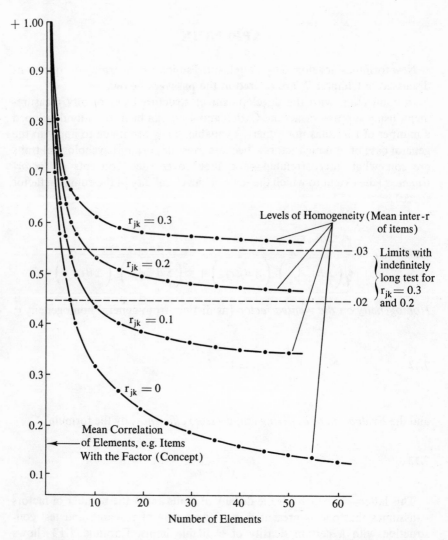

FIGURE **19.** *The relations of homogeneity, mean item validity, and number of elements in a completely valid scale*

to the number of scale elements and correlations among them, is expressed in Figure 19. It will be seen that for a given number of elements (items) in the scale the achieved validity is higher when the homogeneity (mean intercorrelation) is lower.

INDEX OF NAMES

Abeim, A., 278
Adler, Alfred, 53, 73
Ainsworth, M. D., 198, 199, 224, 355
Albright, L. E., 365
Alexander, W. P., 181, 182, 355
Allen, Walter, 270, 355
Allport, G. W., 53, 76
Anastasi, Anne, 34, 35, 225, 329, 355
Anderson, A. W., 183, 355
Arbous, A. G., 355
Archimedes, 284
Armitage, F. P., 312n.
Avogadro, Amedeo, 277

Bacon, Francis, 284
Baggaley, A. R., 80, 81, 204, 206, 357
Baker, R., 355
Baldwin, R. E., 220, 365
Ball, R. S., 241, 355
Barnes, P. J., 35, 355
Barron, Frank, 270, 279, 301, 355
Bartlett, F. C., 48
Bartók, Béla, 278
Barton, V., 366
Beck, S. J., 240
Beethoven, Ludwig van, 278
Beloff, J. R., 61, 64, 304, 357
Bennett, G. K., 36, 355
Bennett, S. V., 370
Binet, Alfred, 15
Bleuler, M., 53
Blewett, D. B., 64, 304, 357
Bond, N. A., 362
Boyle, Robert, 278
Breul, H., 223, 235, 357
Brigham, Carl, 46
Bristol, H., 338, 357
Broadbent, D. E., 291, 355
Bronfenbrenner, U., 229, 230, 355
Bryant, J., 59
Burks, B. S., 241, 304, 355
Buros, O. K., 121, 326, 327, 355
Burt, Sir Cyril, 5, 16, 17, 32, 54, 174, 273, 304, 355
Burtt, H. E., 361

Cannon, W. B., 283
Carrel, Alexis, 283
Carroll, H. A., 360
Carroll, Lewis, (Charles Dodgson), 273
Cattell, A. K. S., 357
Cattell, J. McK., 53
Cavendish, Henry, Lord, 277, 278
Chambers, J. A., 289, 292, 295, 297, 298, 299, 359
Chauncey, Henry, 47, 359
Chave, E. J., 130, 369
Chorness, M. H., 285, 359
Christensen, P. R., 362, 370
Churchill, Sir Winston, 48, 301
Clark, C. D., 226, 361
Clemans, W. V., 206, 359
Clouse, R. J., 370
Coan, R., 60, 61, 64, 355, 357, 359
Cohen, L., 250, 359
Connor, D., 357
Conrad, H. S., 239, 363
Coombs, C. H., 130, 359
Coulter, M. A., 238, 260, 357
Cox, C. M., 241, 269, 276, 277, 359
Cox, F. N., 182, 359
Cronbach, L. J., 91, 91n., 104, 201, 202, 324, 329, 359
Cropley, A. J., 276, 359
Cross, P., 294, 359
Cureton, E. E., 91

Dale, R. R., 48, 49, 359
Dalton, John, 277, 278
Damarin, F., 64
Daniels, J. M., 270, 366
Darwin, Charles, 278, 301
Davidson, H. H., 360
Davis, Allison, 25, 229, 360
Day, M., 357
Demaree, R. G., 131
De Mille, R., 268, 275, 360, 366
Deming, W. E., 147, 360
Dennis, Wayne, 306, 360
Dewey, John, 2
Dickman, K., 357

Digman, J., 131, 257
Disraeli, Benjamin, 219, 286
Dodgson, Charles. *See* Carroll, Lewis
Dollard, John, 211
Douglas, Norman, 185
Downey, June, 269, 360
Dreger, R. M., 360
Drevdahl, J. E., 240, 270, 276, 289, 292, 294, 298, 302, 304, 357, 360
Dryden, John, 271n.
Dunnette, M. D., 252, 360
Dyer, H. S., 46, 47, 360

Eber, H. W., 200, 238, 241, 255, 258, 260, 262, 264, 318, 347, 348, 349, 358, 360
Edison, Thomas, 284
Edwards, M. P., 274, 360
Eells, Kenneth, 25
El Koussy, A. A. H., 16
Ellis, Havelock, 271, 276, 303n., 360
Emmett, W. G., 43, 44, 360
Endler, N. S., 182, 362
Ewart, E. S., 370
Eysenck, H. J., 53, 55, 64, 94, 126, 174, 286, 304, 333, 360

Faraday, Michael, 278
Ferguson, G. A., 18, 360
Finch, F. H., 26, 360
Fisher, R. A., 95, 271
Fiske, D., 59, 202, 364
Fitzgerald, Edward, 5n.
Flanagan, J. C., 245, 246, 360
Flaubert, Gustave, 279
Fleishman, E. A., 255, 261, 361
Floud, J. E., 17, 228, 361
Ford, Henry, 97
Fowler, 347
Franzblau, R. N., 226, 361
Fraser, E. D., 230, 231, 361
Freeman, F. N., 17, 304, 361, 365
Freud, Sigmund, 53, 73, 83n., 85, 224, 235
Fryer, D., 258, 361
Furneaux, W. D., 45, 182, 189, 228, 361

Galilei, Galileo, 281
Galton, Sir Francis, 54, 271, 276, 311, 361
Garforth, F. J. de la P., 361
Garrett, H. F., 47, 361
Getzels, J. W., 198, 267, 268, 270, 273, 274, 302, 361
Ghiselin, Brewster, 270, 361
Ghiselli, E. E., 249, 252, 298, 361, 364
Gibb, C. A., 224
Gibbon, Edward, 97
Gibbons, B. D., 325, 361
Gibbs, P. K., 229, 365

Gist, N. P., 226, 361
Glennon, J. R., 365
Gleser, G. C., 91, 359
Gordon, H., 227, 362
Gorsuch, R., 189, 362
Gottesman, I. I., 304, 362
Gould, E. M., 48, 362
Greene, R., 137, 358
Grooms, R. R., 182, 362
Gross, A., 308n.
Gruen, W., 64
Guetzkow, H., 367
Guilford, J. P., 18, 33, 39, 40, 50, 54, 123, 174, 202, 203, 262, 270, 274, 275, 276, 280, 297n., 305, 325, 326, 362, 366, 370
Gulliksen, H., 130, 362
Guthrie, G. M., 182, 365
Guttman, L., 126, 130, 133, 362

Hadamard, Jacques, 277, 362
Hagen, E., 38, 369
Halsey, A. H., 17, 228, 361
Hamilton, Sir William, 278
Hansen, M. H., 147, 362
Harding, R. E. M., 270, 362
Harmon, L. R., 288, 362
Harrell, M. S., 258, 362
Harrell, T. W., 258, 362
Harris, E. F., 361
Hartmann, H. P., 223, 235, 357
Hasan, P., 274, 362
Hathaway, S. R., 262
Havighurst, R. J., 229, 360
Hay, G., 366
Hayes, K. J., 362
Hebb, D. O., 18, 362
Heron, Alexander, 260, 261, 363
Heseltine, Philip. *See* Warlock, Peter
Hildreth, G. H., 363
Himmelweit, H. T., 48, 363
Hirsch, J., 271, 303n., 363
Hoepfner, R., 40, 297n., 362
Hoffman, P., 308n.
Hollingworth, L. S., 363
Holmes, Sherlock, 95
Holzinger, K. J., 17, 304, 361, 365
Horn, J., 50, 81, 86, 136, 178, 204, 239, 258, 265, 300, 358, 363
Horst, P., 238, 239, 363
Hotelling, H., 239, 363
Howard, M., 17, 304, 355
Howarth, E., 61, 64
Humphreys, L. G., 33, 129, 363
Hundleby, J. D., 344, 363
Hunt, J. McV., 276, 363
Huntington, Ellsworth, 221, 235, 363
Hurwitz, W. N., 147, 362

Jackson P. W., 198, 267, 268, 270, 273, 274, 302, 361
Jacobsen, J. L., 366, 368
James, William, 57, 151
Jeffrey, A. J. W., 201, 363
Jenkins, M. D., 226, 371
Jenner, Edward, 310
Jensen, D. W., 241, 355
Jones, F. E., 289, 291, 292, 295, 296, 297, 298, 300, 304, 305, 363
Jones, Gwynne, 189
Jones, H. E., 26, 239, 363
Jung, C. G., 53, 60, 73

Kahneman, D., 252, 364
Kallman, F. J., 61
Kekulé, August, 283
Kelly, E. L., 59, 202, 292, 364
Kemp, L. C. D., 232, 364
Kepler, Johannes, 278
Kerr, W. A., 295, 370
Kilpatrick, William, 2
King, R. G., 46, 47, 360
Kingsbury, F. A., 252, 364
Kipling, Rudyard, 272n.
Klages, L., 53
Klineberg, O., 225
Klopfer, B., 240
Knapp, R. H., 285, 298, 299, 364
Koch, A., 59
Kogan, N., 274, 370
Kraepelin, Emil, 53
Kretschmer, E., 56, 60, 61, 271, 272, 278, 303n., 364
Kristy, N. F., 64
Krug, S., 86, 368
Kuder, G. F., 68, 91, 201, 364
Kuhn, T. S., 283, 364

Lavoisier, Antoine, 277
Leacock, Stephen, 321
Lee, E. S., 226, 364
Lehman, H. C., 306, 364
Lewis, D. J., 370
Light, B. H., 204, 358
Likert, R., 130, 364
Line, W., 364
Loevinger, Jane, 91, 364
Lord, F. M., 130, 364
Lorge, L., 26, 239, 364
Lunzer, E. A., 18, 364
Lynn, R., 183, 364

McArthur, C., 50
McClelland, D. C., 220, 221, 222, 226, 235, 364
Maccoby, E. E., 229, 365

McComisky, J. G., 48, 362
McDougall, William, 73, 80, 365
McKinley, J. C., 262
Mackinnon, D. W., 301, 365
McNemar, Quinn, 33, 333
Maddox, H., 17, 365
Madow, W. G., 147, 362
Marconi, Guglielmo, 284
Marsh, R. W., 273, 365
Martin, F. M., 17, 228, 361
Maxwell, E. F., 204, 358
Mead, Margaret, 220, 365
Meadow, A., 299, 303, 366
Meehl, P. E., 53, 345, 365
Meeland, T., 357
Meier, G. M., 220, 365
Meredith, G., 258, 292
Merrifield, P. R., 268, 360
Michael, W. B., 38, 365
Michelangelo, 281
Middleton, G., 182, 365
Miles, C. C., 26
Miller, A., 204, 358
Mitchell, B. C., 304, 361
Modigliani, Amedeo, 279
Mollenkopf, W. G., 232, 365
Moreton, C. A., 227, 365
Morris, B. S., 365
Morrison, R. F., 254, 365
Moser, C. A., 148, 365
Mozart, Wolfgang Amadeus, 270
Murphy, Gardner, 53
Murray, H. A., 73

Napoleon, 238
Nesbitt, J. E., 198, 199, 224, 355
Nesselroade, J. R., 358, 365
Newland, E., 18, 21, 365
Newman, H. H., 17, 365
Newton, Sir Isaac, 134, 238, 273, 278, 300
Nietzsche, Friedrich, 271, 279
Nottelmann, D. H., 285, 359
Nunnally, J. C., 36, 37, 365
Nuttall, R., 95, 184n., 358
Nye, C. T., 248, 367

Oden, M. H., 241, 369
Oliver, R. A. C., 48, 126, 365, 366
O'Neill, Eugene, 279
Ornstein, G. N., 255, 361
O'Sullivan, M., 275, 366
Owens, W. A., 239, 365, 366

Parnes, S. J., 299, 303, 366
Parry, J. B., 370
Pascal, Blaise, 278
Pasteur, Louis, 283, 300

Pawlik, K., 363
Peel, E. A., 43, 202, 366
Petch, J. A., 48, 366
Piaget, Jean, 18
Pichot, Pierre, 120
Pidgeon, D. A., 235
Piers, E. V., 270, 366
Pierson, G. R., 214, 327, 329, 366
Pintner, R., 23
Plowden, Lady Bridger, 230
Poincaré, Henri, 270, 283
Porter, R., 61, 366
Porteus, S. D., 23
Prell, D. B., 64, 304, 360
Price, P. B., 366, 368
Priestley, Joseph, 277, 278
Pringle, M. K., 232
Proust, Marcel, 279

Quackenbush, J. F., 270, 366

Radcliffe, J. A., 82, 85, 86, 204, 207, 208, 265, 300, 358, 368
Rajaratnam, N., 359
Ratner, S. C., 26
Ravel, Maurice, 278
Raven, J. C., 23
Rennes, 120
Richards, J. M., 254, 366, 368
Richardson, M. W., 364
Rickels, K., 327
Robbins, G. D., Lord, 219, 366
Rodd, 25
Roe, Anne, 269, 279, 290, 298, 366
Ronan, W. W., 243, 254, 261, 366
Rothe, H. F., 248, 366, 367
Rothney, J. W. N., 35, 367
Rummell, R. J., 235, 367
Rush, C. H., Jr., 253, 254, 367
Ruskin, John, 279
Russell, Bertrand, Earl, 268
Rutherford, Ernest, Lord, 283
Rutter, D., 43, 366

St. Francis, 238
Sandall, P. H., 202, 203, 204, 367
Sanders, C., 45, 367
Sarason, S. B., 23
Saunders, D. R., 57, 286, 367
Sawyer, J., 367
Schaie, K. W., 139, 366, 367
Scheele, K. W., 277
Scheier, I. H., 64, 224, 318, 358, 367
Schmidt, L. G., 35, 367
Schneider, E., 34, 367
Schneidman, M., 240
Sealy, A. P., 196, 198, 199, 214, 239, 328, 358, 367

Seashore, H. G., 36, 355
Shakespeare, J. J., 201, 367
Shakespeare, William, 1
Shaw, George Bernard, 48
Shinn, E. O., 34, 367
Shrader, R., 368
Smith, C. A., 227, 368
Smith, R., 131
Spearman, Charles, 15, 16, 17, 22, 32, 54, 63, 93, 174, 270, 271, 273, 300, 368
Spencer, W. F., 370
Sprecher, T. B., 254, 305, 368
Stead, W. H., 242, 368
Stevens, S. S., 130, 368
Stevenson, J. A. F., 63
Stewart, N., 368
Stice, G. F., 64, 238, 296, 358
Stouffer, S. A., 126, 133, 368
Strauss, L., 250, 359
Strindberg, August, 279
Strodtbeck, F. L., 227, 368
Strong, E. K., Jr., 68, 201, 368
Super, D. E., 240, 368
Sutherland, M. B., 48, 368
Sutton, M. A., 362
Sweney, A. B., 82, 85, 86, 152, 155, 158, 196, 198, 199, 204, 205, 207, 208, 214, 265, 300, 328, 357, 358, 368
Swenson, W., 347

Talbott, R., 206, 368
Tanter, R., 367
Tapp, J. T., 204, 368
Taylor, C. W., 254, 285, 287, 288, 294, 295, 299, 366, 368
Terman, L. M., 168, 239, 241, 242, 271, 277, 278, 294, 355, 369
Thistlethwaite, D. L., 285, 369
Thomas, Dylan, 279
Thomson, Godfrey, 5, 26, 32
Thomson, J. J., 277
Thorndike, R. L., 26, 38, 231, 235, 273, 312n., 369
Thouless, R. H., 29
Thurstone, L. L., 16, 19, 31, 33, 35, 36, 46, 130, 174, 175, 297n., 305, 325, 369
Tiner, L. G., 358
Tollefson, D., 289, 295, 298, 304, 369
Torgerson, W. S., 130, 369
Torrance, E. P., 198, 224, 274, 301, 369
Tsujioka, B., 94, 104, 120, 128, 129, 143, 224, 324, 357, 358, 369
Tuddenham, R. D., 26
Turner, W. W., 243, 369
Tuska, C. D., 277, 369
Tyckociner, J. T., 284
Tyler, L. E., 25, 274, 360

Unger, M. P., 204, 358
Utrillo, Maurice, 279

Vandenberg, S., 120, 304, 370
Van Gogh, Vincent, 279
Van Zelst, R. H., 295, 370
Vernon, P. E., 19, 32, 33, 40, 41, 43, 174,
    181, 273, 333, 370
Viteles, M. S., 242, 370

Walker, R. Y., 250, 370
Wallach, M. A., 274, 370
Warburton, F. W., 17, 47, 48, 63, 68, 103,
    183, 184n., 224, 230, 232, 358, 359, 370
Warlock, Peter, (Philip Heseltine), 278
Wellman, F. E., 35, 370
Wells, H. G., 97, 273, 311
Wenig, P. W., 204, 359
Wesman, A., 36, 355
Wheeler, L. R., 227, 228, 370
Wherry, R. J., 131

Whitlock, G. H., 243, 370
Whyte, W. H., 68, 370
Williams, J. R., 94, 370
Wilmut, F. S., 43, 44, 360
Wilson, N. A. B., 370
Wilson, R. C., 270, 370
Winder, A. E., 297n., 359
Wiseman, Stephen, 202, 230, 231, 232,
    235, 371
Witmer, Lightner, 312n.
Witty, P. A., 226, 371
Wolking, W. D., 34, 371
Wordsworth, William, 291
Wundt, W., 53

Yates, Frank, 147, 371
Yee, L., 327

Zimmerman, R. R., 262
Zola, Émile, 269

INDEX

Aberdeen, Scotland, 230
Ability, measurement of, 154, 191, 231, 337. *See also* Crystallized ability, Fluid ability, Primary abilities
Absolute scaling, 129, 131
Abstract reasoning (sub-scale of DAT), 36
ACE (American Council on Education's Psychological Examination), 46
Achievement: definition of, 251; measurement of, 158; motivation for, 219–225; prediction of, 8, 29, 145, 152, 153, 161, 162, 167, 182, 186, 187, 192, 193, 194, 195, 196, 198, 214, 217, 218, 249, 251, 252, 257. *See also* School achievement
Acquisitiveness, 210, 211, 212, 215
Administrative reliability, coefficient of, 111, 113
Administrator, personality of, 291
Affectothymia, 56, 58, 61, 185, 188, 195, 257, 278, 290, 299. *See also* Cyclothymia
Age-change, effects of, 239
Aiming (A), 38
Alexandrian conception of education, 2
American Psychological Association, 274, 315
Anxiety, 72, 182, 183, 272, 278, 316, 318, 333, 349
Appeal, 73, 78, 81, 208, 210
Artists, personality of, 278–279
Associational fluency, 40
Attitudes, 72, 73, 74, 76, 78, 80, 81, 84, 152, 153, 155, 212, 214, 275; children's, 152, 170, 209; factor analysis of, 75; measurement of, 154; subsidated chains of, 75, 76; unique, 76

Backwardness, causes of, 328
"Banausic" labor, 271, 302
Basic drives in man, 73, 78
BDRM (Basic Data Relation Matrix), 91–92, 99, 102, 104, 108, 115, 119
Benjamin Franklin Junior High School, 153, 163

Binet Test, 23, 26, 27, 120, 137, 328
Brain injury, 18, 20
"Brain-storming," 272, 302–303
Britain, opinions about education in, 2. *See also* Grammar school education in England, "Eleven-plus" selection in Britain
Buffered scales, 105
Bus drivers, performance of, 261

Child-centered education, 2
Child-guidance services, 312, 314, 316, 323
Child-rearing, 229, 230; and middle-class mothers, 229, 230; and working-class mothers, 229
Children's O. A. battery, 64, 327
Child socialization, 229
Clerical perception (Q), 38
Clinical observation, 9; approach to, 53
Clinician, attitude of, 9, 72, 240
Coefficient of test efficiency, 121
Coefficient of test equivalence, 105
Competitiveness, disadvantage of, 303
Computors, electronic, 317, 319, 346
Concept validity, 93
Concrete validity, 96
Consistency, concept of, 98. *See also* Test consistency
Conspection, coefficient of, 111, 113
Convergent thinking, 275
Correction for attenuation, 125, 133
Correlation coefficient, 14, 161, 252, 264
Council for Basic Education, 2
Counseling, 315, 317, 319, 322, 378, 334
Counseling bureau, 317
CPQ (Child Personality Questionnaire), 313–314, 316, 325, 327, 331, 339
Creativity, 3, 8, 40, 224, 240, 267, 268, 269, 270, 271, 272, 274, 275, 276, 281, 283, 284, 285, 286, 294, 296, 297, 298, 300, 301, 302, 303, 304, 319, 334, 349; adjustment criterion of, 289; cognitive factors in, 274; creative process, 270; difficulties of defining criteria for, 285;

Creativity—*continued*
effectiveness, criterion of, 289, 295; inclusiveness of, 268; and personality, 276; relation to intelligence, 273; in science, religions, correlates of 299; in science versus art, socio-economic correlates of, 270, 299; in science, eight criteria of, 287, 294

Criterion measures, unrepeatability of, 124; reliability, 245, 248, 285

Crystallized ability, 16, 18, 19, 21, 25, 27, 28, 45, 177, 178, 225, 258, 328, 331, 336

Cultural drift, 137, 139

Culture Fair Intelligence Tests (IPAT), 23, 25, 26, 27, 28, 29, 31, 113, 119, 120, 126, 135, 154, 164, 167, 170, 171, 172, 175, 176, 186, 237, 258, 297, 328, 331, 338, 339, 340, 350

Culture-fair intelligence tests, 20, 23, 29, 137, 231, 258

Curiosity, 73, 79, 80, 208, 209, 215

Cyclothymia, 56, 60, 80, 142, 176, 299; environmental determination of, 59, 61; hereditary determination of, 59, 61; occupational performance, 9, 59. *See also* Affectothymia

Daily work curves, 248, 249

DAT (Differential Aptitude Tests), 34, 36, 38, 259

Dependability coefficient, 110

"Depth" psychology, 9

Desurgency, 56, 61, 66, 67, 184, 278, 289, 290, 293, 299, 302, 304, 334

Difficulty factors, 131

Disgust, 210

Divergent thinking, 39, 275

Dominance, 56, 58, 59, 61, 176, 184, 185, 257, 279, 290, 291, 293, 296, 297, 298, 300, 302, 304

Durability, coefficient of, 120. *See also* Second-order properties of tests

Dynamic calculus, 84, 86, 87, 155

Dynamic lattice, 75, 76

Dynamic psychology, 71

Dynamic structure factors, 73

Dynamic traits, 72, 74

East Lawn School, 153, 163

Economy, 122

Educational guidance, 8

Effective decision-making per unit of time, 121

Efficiency. *See* Second-order properties of tests

Ego strength, 56, 61, 72, 138, 157, 176, 183, 185, 207, 278, 290, 291, 293, 296, 297, 298, 300, 304, 323, 326, 347. *See also* Superego strength

Elaboration, 40

"Eleven-plus" selection in Britain, 4, 41, 42, 43, 310

Employee Aptitude Survey, 259

Environment, 20, 25; effects of, 217, 221, 222, 225, 226, 227, 230, 232

Environmental differences, 17

Equal-interval scaling, 129, 131, 133, 134

Equal interval units, 131, 133

Erg, definition of, 73

Ergic goals, 75

Ergic tension, 56, 63, 67, 74, 78, 176, 184, 185, 290, 294, 296, 302, 333, 349

Ergs, 73, 74, 75, 76, 78, 79, 81, 83, 84, 86, 155, 203, 207, 208, 210, 212, 327

Escape, 73, 78, 79, 208

ESPQ (Early School Personality Questionnaire), 62, 313, 325, 327, 338

Examination, traditional purposes of, 6, 7

Excitability, 176

Executive achievement, prediction of, 191, 252

Exmodulators, 99, 102

Experimental physicists, psychological characteristics of, 269, 291

Exploration, 73, 80, 208

Exploratory drive, 79

Expressional fluency, 40

Extraversion, 66, 182, 189, 278, 291, 333, 349

Extremity-vector scaling, 131, 133

Factor analysis, 14, 27, 39, 54, 55, 75, 85, 126, 151, 153, 162, 174, 201, 202, 255. *See also* Objective personality tests, factor analyses of

Factor analysis of responses to recorded music, 149

Factor homogeneity, 105

Factor-homogeneous scale, 105, 106

Factor-pure scale, 106

Factors: group, 16; cooperative, 19

Factor-true scales, 105, 106, 108, 133, 134

Fear, 73, 76, 79, 208, 209, 215

Finger dexterity (F), 38

Flexibility, dangers of, 268

Flexibility of closure, 40

Fluency factor, 176

Fluid ability, 16, 18, 19, 23, 25, 27, 28, 29, 45, 177, 225, 237, 258, 331, 333

Food-seeking, 210

Foremen, performance of, 243

Form reception (P), 38

Functional psychometrics, 346
Functional testing, 323, 327
Function fluctuations, 108, 109, 110, 114

GATB (General Aptitude Test Battery) 38, 259
GCE (General Certificate of Education examination), 42, 47, 48
General ability, 13, 17, 19, 23, 27, 30, 231, 260, 273, 297, 300
General intelligence (G), 38
"Genius," 271
Grammar school education in England, 4, 41, 229, 310
Gregariousness, 73, 76, 78, 80, 87, 208, 209, 213, 215, 340
Guttman scales, 133

Halo-effect, 168
Heredity, 17, 20, 25; effects of, 217, 221, 226; warring, 271, 278
Homogeneity; *see* Test consistency
How Much and How Many test, 157, 206, 207
HSPQ (High School Personality Questionnaire), 15, 58, 61, 62, 67, 95, 120, 121, 123, 135, 138, 154, 176, 182, 183, 184, 186, 187, 188, 189, 192, 193, 194, 196, 215, 305, 314, 316, 325, 327, 331, 340, 350
Hunger, 73

Ideational fluency, 40, 297, 301, 305
Incubation period, 183, 184
Information test, 157, 205, 207
Information theory, 291
Inmodulators, 99, 102, 108
Intellectual self-sufficiency, characteristic of creative scientists, 279
Intelligence, general factor of, 15, 17, 19, 32, 56, 151, 175, 183, 185, 186, 190, 195, 290, 291, 296, 297, 298, 304, 326, 333
Interests, 72, 73, 84, 152, 155, 158, 182, 201, 203, 212, 214; children's, 203, 205, 206, 212; factors, 203; measurement of, 154, 202, 203, 204
Internal cancellation, 256
Interval scales, 130, 134
Introversion, 66, 182, 183, 272, 278, 299, 333; observed particularly among physical scientists, 277
Iowa Tests of Educational Development, 34
IPAT (Institute for Personality and Ability Testing) Tests, 15, 112, 138, 154, 162, 163, 164, 171, 204, 258, 325, 328, 333, 336

Ipsative scoring, 138, 139, 140, 141, 153, 205, 206, 207, 288
IQ, 19, 137, 215, 227, 259, 267, 301, 331; standard deviation of, 19, 29, 258, 331
Itemetrics, 90

Laboratory of Personality and Group Analysis, 63, 152, 153
Laughter, 210
L-data (or Life Record Data), 55, 65
Logical Positivism, 261
London, England, 233

Manchester, England, 230, 231
Manic-depressive psychoses, 139
Manual dexterity (M), 38
MAT (Motivational Analysis Test), 86, 204, 222, 265, 296, 300, 316, 318, 326, 327, 331, 342, 347
Max Planck Institutes, 283, 284
Mechanical Reasoning, 36
Memorizing ability, 16
Memory Test, 157, 158, 207
Mensa Society, 50
Mental Measurement Year Book, 326
MMPI (Minnesota Multiphasic Personality Inventory), 262, 325, 349
Monticello, Illinois, 205, 208, 209, 211, 213
Moray House test, 328
Motivation, 72, 202, 203, 219, 220; factors, 145; for the learning process, 81; measurement of, 69, 85, 114, 130, 139, 151, 155, 259, 265, 323, 334, 337, 339
Motivational components, 84, 85, 155, 157, 206, 207
Motor speed (T), 38
Multivariate analysis, 151

Narcissism, 73, 81
Need for achievement, 220, 221, 222
Neuroticism, 182, 183, 316, 349
NFER (National Foundation for Educational Research), 338
Nominal scales, 130, 134
Normal distribution, 131
Normalized standard scores, 142, 331
Non-Euclidean psychology, 94
N (number), 33, 38, 154, 171, 172, 176
Numerical ability, 14, 16, 36, 37, 178
Numerical aptitude (N), 38

O.A. (Objective-Analytic) battery, 64, 65, 135, 270, 327, 339; children's, 64, 327
Objective attitude measurement, 84
Objective personality tests, factor analyses of, 64, 65, 300, 327

Objective personality theory, 9, 262
Occupational level, prediction of, 239, 241, 245
O-data, 56, 65
Oddity, distinguished from creativity, 286
Office of Strategic Services (OSS), 246
Operationism, 261
Ordinal scales, 130, 134
Originality, 40
Otis quick-scoring mental ability test, 35
Overachievement, 68
Overdetermination of behavior, 77

Paired Words test, 157, 203, 207
Parmia, 56, 61, 66, 176, 184, 185, 278, 290, 296, 297, 304, 333 334
Paxton, Illinois, 153, 163, 184, 195, 197, 205, 208, 214
Percentiles, 142
Personality: development of, 8; measurement of, 9, 13, 69, 71, 90, 114, 126, 151, 159, 181, 191, 201, 259, 260, 261, 264, 265, 269, 310, 323, 337; a study of, 53, 54, 55; traits of, 13, 55, 69, 138, 182
Personality factors, 9, 21, 56, 57, 58, 67, 127, 139, 145, 152, 153, 177, 181, 182, 184, 186, 187, 190–191, 192, 193, 277, 291, 295, 297, 298, 304, 305, 334, 339, 350; heredity and environmental determinations of, 62, 64
Premsia, 56, 61, 176, 184, 185, 290, 293, 294, 296, 326
Primary abilities, 16, 19, 30, 32, 33, 34, 35, 36, 38, 39, 40, 86, 151, 162, 163, 164, 165, 166, 167, 168, 170, 171, 175, 178, 259, 325, 333, 336, 341
Primary Mental Abilities battery (PMA), 33, 34, 35, 36, 37, 154, 162, 175, 178, 259, 325, 333, 336, 339, 340, 341
Productive-thinking factors, 40
Protectiveness, 76, 209, 215; parental, 73, 80, 208
Proto-fluid ability factor, 177
PSPQ (Pre-School Personality Questionnaire), 62, 313, 325, 327
Physician performance, 254
Pilots, selection of, 245
Pilot skills, 250, 255
Power tests, 26, 36
Prediction, actuarial, contrasted with psychological, 9
Psychoanalysis, 9, 10, 54, 83, 83*n*., 313
Psychological services in industry and commerce, 318
Psychology students, as would-be physical scientists, 295

Psychologist: psychological characteristics of, 269; as servant of education, 7, 310, 311
Psychometric concepts, revisions of, 89
Psychometric parameters of tests, 89
Psychosomatic illnesses, 139
Pugnacity, 210, 211, 215, 222

Racial differences, 225, 226; in psychological functioning, 225
Ratio scales, 130, 134
Raven Matrices, 258
R (reasoning), 33, 37, 167, 172
Reasoning, 37, 154, 178, 305; abstract, 36; factor, 305; inductive, 16; mechanical, 36; verbal, 36
Recovery rate of neurotics, 53
Reference population, 136, 137
Relational simplex principle, 131, 133
Replication of research, 148
Researcher, personality of, 284
Research professors, distribution of, 282
Resistances to personality assessment, 310
Response, eccentricity of, 133
Restriction of range, 250
Robbins Committee, 49, 219
Rockefeller Institute, 283
Rorschach inkblot test, 63, 269, 313
Royal Society, 281, 284
Rural sample of high school students: correlations of abilities and achievements, 172; difference in personality factors, 184, 185; lower prediction for, 172, 195

Salesman success, prediction of, 253, 265
Salford, England, 233
Salk Institute, 283
Sampling, 146; probability samples, 147; random samples, 147, 148
Scaling: absolute, 129, 131; equal-interval, 129, 131; extremity-vector principle, 131; relational simplex theory, 133
SAT (Scholastic Aptitude Test), 46
Schizothymia, 56, 60, 71, 80, 279, 289, 291, 326; environmental determination of, 61; hereditary determination of, 61; occupational performance of, 59. *See also* Sizothymia
School achievement, 3, 7, 8, 13, 27, 28, 29, 33, 36, 39, 41, 42, 44, 66, 68, 149, 151, 152, 163, 167, 181, 182, 183, 186, 187, 188, 189, 196, 198, 214, 222, 225, 228, 229, 230, 231, 232, 234, 258, 267, 320, 327, 328, 347; distinguished from crystallized ability, 22

Scientists, personalities of creative, 277, 278, 279, 289

Second-order factor, 16, 270, 276, 291

Second-order properties of tests: durability, 119, 120, 126, (coefficient of, 120); efficiency, 119, 121, 143; universality, 119, 120, 126, 127, 143, (coefficient of, 120)

Selection for university, 43, 45, 48

Self-assertion, 73, 80, 208, 209, 211, 215, 222

Self-sufficiency, 188

Sentiment, 74, 78, 79, 81, 83, 84, 86, 155, 207, 208, 212, 213, 327; career, 81, 212, 213; hobby, 81; mechanical, 81, 82, 212, 213; patriotism, 212, 213; play-fantasy, 213; profession, 82; self-sentiment, 56, 81, 83, 184, 185, 188, 189, 190, 195, 212, 213, 215, 222, 290, 291, 296, 340, 347; structure, definition of, 74; superego, 212, 213; to sports and games, 83, 87, 212

Sex, 73, 76, 80, 208, 209, 215

Simple structure, 16, 73, 85, 106, 125, 179, 190, 276, 324, 327; invariance of, 32

Sixteen PF test, 56, 57, 58, 61, 63, 65, 67, 120, 121, 122, 135, 137, 138, 141, 155, 237, 238, 257, 262, 263, 265, 289, 290, 294, 296, 298, 305, 327, 331, 333, 341, 350; automated, 111; predictive value of, 57; translation of, 57

Sizothymia, 183, 188, 290, 293, 299, 302. *See also* Schizothymia

Skilled craftsmen, performance of, 245

SMAT (School Motivational Analysis Test), 86, 204, 207, 213, 214, 215, 326, 327, 339, 340

Social factors, 230, 231, 232, 233

Social scientists, psychological characteristics of, 269

Society for Research in Higher Education, 49

Socioeconomic level: effects of, 228, 242; social-class effect, 228

Solipistic theory of interests, 140

Spatial ability, 16, 33, 39, 154, 176

Spatial aptitude (S), 38

Spontaneous flexibility, 40

Springfield, Illinois, 153, 163, 184, 195, 205, 208, 209, 211, 213, 214

Stability coefficient, 110

Standardization of test conditions, 149, 150

Standard scores, 142, 206, 305, 331

Stanford Achievement test, 158, 163, 165, 166, 167, 168, 169, 170, 173, 174, 186, 187, 188, 190, 192, 193, 194, 195, 197

Stanford Research Center, 283

"Stress Interview," 247

Structural Test Design, 327

Submissiveness, 215

Superego strength, 58, 61, 66, 71, 72, 83, 139, 157, 176, 184, 185, 188, 191, 195, 207, 215, 222, 290, 293, 340. *See also* Ego strength

Surgency, 56, 61, 63, 66, 176, 184, 185, 189, 190, 278, 324, 333, 347

TAT (Thematic Apperception Test), 269, 326

T-data (objective test data), 56, 65

Teacher, personality of, 284

Teachers' ratings, 158, 164, 167, 168, 169, 187, 189, 195

Teachers' rating scales, 164; Achievement in games and sports, 164, 165, 166, 168, 169, 187, 192, 193, 194, 197; Behavior record, 165, 166, 167, 168, 169, 186, 187, 188, 189, 190, 191, 192, 193, 194, 196, 197; Interest in games and sports, 164, 165, 166, 168, 169, 187, 188, 190, 191, 192, 193, 194, 197; Interest in school subjects, 165, 166, 167, 169, 187, 192, 193, 194, 197; Leadership, 164, 165, 166, 169, 187, 190, 192, 193, 194, 197, 249; Personal adjustment, 165, 166, 169, 187, 189, 192, 193, 194, 197; Social adjustment, 164, 165, 166, 168, 169, 187, 192, 193, 194, 197

Teaching machines, 317

Test consistency, 91, 98, 101; coefficient of administrative reliability, 111, 113; coefficient of circumstance reliability, 112, 113; coefficient of conspection or conspect reliability coefficient, 111, 113; coefficient of dependability, 110, 113; coefficient of function constancy, 110, 113; coefficient of presophistication or practice immunity, 112, 113; coefficient of stability, 110; coefficient of transferability, 117, 120; homogeneity, 91, 98, 101, 102, 103, 104, 105, 107, 113, 115, 125, 129; index of transferability, 117, 120; reliability, 98, 101, 102, 103, 110, 113, 115, 125; transferability, 98, 101, 102, 103, 115, 116, 117, 119, 120. *See also* Second-order properties of tests

Testing installation plan for school systems, 336, 337, 338–343

Test reliability, 91, 92, 98, 108

Test sophistication, 29, 110, 112

Test standardization, 134, 135, 136, 138
Test validity, 92, 123, 125, 129; concurrent validity, 97; content validity, 92; degree of abstraction parameter, 92; degree of directness parameter, 95–96; degree of naturalness parameter, 95; face validity, 97; predictive validity, 97
Third-order general factor, 177
Transferability, 98, 101, 102, 103, 115, 116, 117, 119, 120
Topology, as culture-fair subtest, 25
Twins, psychological study of, 17

Underachievement, 68
Unifactor scales, 105
United States Department of Health, Education and Welfare, 1
Univariate analysis, 150, 151
Universality, coefficient of, 120. *See also* Second-order properties of tests
University: achievement at, 44; functions of, 282, 283

Urban sample of high school students: correlations of abilities and achievement, 171–172; difference in personality factors, 184, 185
Utility coefficient and index, 119, 122, 123, 143

Verbal ability, 14, 16, 38, 168, 178. *See also* V
V (verbal-meaning), 33, 37, 154, 167, 168, 170, 171, 172
VIM (Vocational Interest Measure), 204
Vocational guidance, 68, 155, 201, 202, 237, 312, 313, 317, 323, 341; rehabilitation, 255

WAIS, 120, 328
Weights in factor score estimation, 136
What Do You Think? test, 157, 158, 207
WISC, 26, 117, 120, 137, 328
W (word fluency), 33, 40, 154, 172, 275

"Zetetics," 284